# THE RISE AND FALL OF THE EAST

# THE RISE
# AND FALL
# OF THE EAST

How Exams, Autocracy, Stability, and
Technology Brought China Success, and
Why They Might Lead to Its Decline

## YASHENG HUANG

Yale

**UNIVERSITY PRESS**

New Haven and London

Published with assistance from the Mary Cady Tew Memorial Fund.

Yale University Press books may be purchased in quantity for
educational, business, or promotional use. For information,
please e-mail sales.press@yale.edu (U.S. office) or sales@yaleup.co.uk
(U.K. office).

Set in Janson Text with Janson Antiqua
type by Newgen North America, Inc.
Printed in the United States of America.

Library of Congress Control Number: 2022950978
ISBN 978-0-300-26636-8 (hardcover : alk. paper)

A catalogue record for this book is available from the British Library.

This paper meets the requirements of ANSI/NISO Z39.48-1992
(Permanence of Paper).

10 9 8 7 6 5 4 3 2 1

*Dedicated to the autocrats of the world.*
*They give us so much to write about.*

# Contents

PART V    THE FUTURE OF THE EAST MODEL

# Preface

FOR A FEW DAYS in November 2022, triggered by a deadly fire in Ürümqi, Xinjiang, hundreds or thousands of protestors in Shanghai, Beijing, and other cities took to the street and university campuses to demonstrate against the government's draconian zero-COVID controls. A few in the crowd shouted, and were echoed by others, "Step down, Xi Jinping," "Step down, the Communist Party." It was an incredibly brave act of defiance against a leader who had just consolidated power a month earlier at the Twentieth Party Congress. Some in the Western press quickly jumped on the narrative that this was potentially a game changer for the regime.

In some ways it was. Since 1989, protests in China have been scattered, localized, and issue-specific. For a protest that was nationwide in scale and had an explicit anti-regime tone, this was an extraordinary development. That said, the COVID protest is a protest, not—or not yet at the time of this writing—a movement. The size of the protests was at the most in the thousands compared with the millions who protested in 1989. Let's stack the size of the COVID protest against the grievance they were protesting against—effectively an incarceration of hundreds of millions of people in their homes and in field hospitals. The lockdowns led to suicides, miscarriages, fires, starvation, and many other horrifying abominations, and yet in a country of 1.4 billion people, just a few thousand came out to the street. The backlash is significant because it happened at all, not because of the size of its threat. To compare, at the time of China's COVID protests, millions of people in Iran demonstrated for weeks on end. Their grievance: the death of one woman in the hands of the country's morality police.

It was a COVID protest, not a COVID Spring, for a good reason—the Chinese state is incredibly strong. For many years, I struggled to come

ix

up with a coherent explanation for the power, reach, and discretion of the Chinese state. Certainly coercion and ideological indoctrination are at work, and probably a fair amount of societal consent as well. Also over the past four decades, the strong growth of the Chinese GDP and the alleviation of poverty have earned the Chinese state a healthy amount of "performative legitimacy." That has undoubtedly added some staying power to the CCP.

But there has to be more. Although the explanations above may be individually and situationally valid, they don't give us a wholistic explanatory framework. Performative legitimacy may explain the reform era, but how do we explain the Great Leap Forward and the Cultural Revolution? Didn't these catastrophes generate a nontrivial dose of "performative illegitimacy?" And we have not mentioned the longevity of imperial China.

My search for an explanation has been guided by two principles. One is parsimony. A variable is preferred over another one if it accommodates more of the questions or situations involved, or if it underscores those variables often proposed as causes. The other principle is proximity. That is, the closer the variable is to the explanatory vicinity of the empirical phenomenon under scrutiny, the better.

This is how I arrived at the first component of the EAST formulation: examination. If I am to name just one difference between China and other civilizations, I would say *Keju*, the civil service examination first implemented during the Sui dynasty, which was in power from 581 to 618. *Keju* is China's blessing but also its curse in more ways than one. I use this perspective to unlock and to make sense of the other three EAST components, autocracy, stability, and technology.

*Keju* had deep penetration both cross-sectionally in society and across time in history. It was all encompassing, laying claim to enormous investments in time and effort by a significant proportion of the Chinese population. It was an incubator of values, norms, and ideas, and so influenced the ideology and epistemology that lay at the foundation of Chinese minds. It was a state institution designed to augment the power and the capabilities of the state. Directly, the state monopolized the very best human capital; indirectly, the state deprived society access to talent and preempted *organized* religion, commerce, and intelligentsia. The Chinese state in history and today is an imprinted version of this *Keju* system.

The Chinese state is strong because it reigns without a society. Society here means a society that is organized, has its own identity, and is considered separately legitimate from the state. *Keju* may not be the only cause, but it is a significant cause in decimating or preempting collective action—the essential feature of a civil society. *Keju* was fiercely competitive. It vaulted triumphs achieved in small and isolated examination cells while it harshly punished collaboration, otherwise known as cheating in a *Keju* context. Think of the vibrantly individualistic Chinese entrepreneurs on the one hand and their collective powerlessness vis-à-vis the CCP on the other. Think of the lockdown order in Shanghai lasting for several months. Even if a fraction of the 25 million Shanghainese acted in concert, either overtly or tacitly, in resistance, the state would be powerless no matter the size of its police force.

In my mind, these are some intriguing conjectures; others may say that they are fanciful. There may be criticisms of, for example, my broad topical coverage. EAST here is not geography; it is the four topics I explore. And I go back and forth between history and today. The book is admittedly broad and self-consciously ambitious.

The usual academic format is to drill into one topic in great depth. My view is that books give us a way to tackle big topics that we are no longer able to take on in refereed journals. Very specialized and technical papers have their rightful places, but one casualty of increasing specialization and the extraordinarily high—and highly varied—hurdles to publication in academic journals is a suboptimal supply of big ideas. Books are one of the few ways to go big. I leave it to the readers to judge whether I have succeeded. My intention is to propose a few scaffolding ideas by which we make sense of some historical and contemporary facts and events.

And there are big topics in front of us. The COVID protest is, I believe, a game changer in the sense that hundreds of millions of people shared a deeply felt experience. The tenacity of imperial regimes and of the CCP derived in no small measure from an ability to compartmentalize and isolate people and preempt collective actions. Will the COVID protests presage a turning point, and what will be the long-term consequences especially amid the rising anxiety and fear in Chinese society? At the time of this writing, some of the issues and situations are still fluid and evolving and I may get them wrong. Or I may not have pinned down all the precise channels and mechanisms. I hope that this book may open further debates and discussions.

I presented parts of the early draft at seminars and panel discussions at the Academy of Management Annual Conference, Annual Political Science Association Conference, Asian Historical Economics History Annual Conference, Columbia University, Georgetown University, Harvard

University, Hong Kong University, Illinois Institute of Technology, Johns Hopkins University, Princeton University, SOAS University of London, Stanford University, University of California at San Diego, University of Pennsylvania, University of Southern California, University of Victoria, University of Washington, Western Michigan University, World Interdisciplinary Network for Institutional Research Annual Conference, and others.

Over the years, I have held conversations with friends and colleagues on wide-ranging topics; several ideas from unexpected quarters made it into the book. Some people commented on my early work on *Keju*; others probed me at seminars; still others wrote books that inspired me to take on this project and to frame discussions the way I did. I acknowledge some of them here: Sizi Chen, Donald Clarke, Jacques deLisle, Patricia Ebrey, Francis Fukuyama, Jack Goldstone, Joseph Henrich, Chang-Tai Hsieh, Ruixue Jia, Bill Kirby, Joel Mokyr, Ian Morris, Barry Naughton, Richard Nisbett, the late Rod MacFarquhar, Fiona Murray, Sonja Opper, Minxin Pei, Elizabeth Perry, Meg Rithmire, Tony Saich, Walter Scheidel, Susan Shirk, Lily Tsai, Ashutosh Varshney, the late Ezra Vogel, Yuhua Wang, Clair Yang, Madeleine Zelin, and Ezra Zuckerman. I also sent out the book manuscript to other colleagues but because of the compressed publication schedule under COVID-19, I was not able to incorporate their comments before the book went into copyediting. I thank them for reading the manuscript.

There are a number of scholars in China who helped me to acquire historical knowledge and historical data, but they have nothing to do with the broader ideas or the contemporary portion of this book. None of them read this book manuscript. Because of the current political circumstances in China, let me err on the cautious side by not thanking them by name. The same applies to a number of student research assistants who helped with database construction, literature reviews, and fact-checking.

Many people helped me along the way. Nancy Hearst at Harvard's Fairbank Center library has helped me with each of my book projects. She has edited earlier versions and corrected my mistakes, some of which I have made repeatedly. Even in this digital age, her library has unrivaled resources on contemporary China. I am very grateful to her. I began to work on this history with a project on *Keju* and many of us working on this topic benefited from the database projects supervised by Peter Bol of Harvard University. Professor Bol kindly took the time to walk my coauthor and me through the database's design and scope, helping us to make the most of this vital resource. I am extremely grateful to several people at Yale University Press who helped me so much in the production of this book. I especially thank Seth Ditchik, Amanda Gerstenfeld, and Julie Carlson for their attention to my book, quick turnaround time, and excellent editorial assistance. The usual caveat—that the author alone is responsible for the remaining errors in the book—applies.

# THE RISE AND FALL OF THE EAST

# Unpacking the EAST Formulation

When your scope for action is greatest, the knowledge on which you can base this action is always at a minimum. When your knowledge is greatest, the scope for action has often disappeared.

—HENRY KISSINGER, 1970

THE QIN DYNASTY (221–207 BCE), China's first dynasty, is the defining and consequential period of Chinese political development.[1] All the imperial progenies of the Qin as well as their republican successors, the Nationalist government and then the People's Republic of China (PRC), carried on many of the salient features of the Qin dynasty, such as its unitary autocracy, top-down rule, impersonal nature, meritocracy, and repressiveness. The Qin dynasty gave birth to political China.

There are, however, two unusual features about that dynasty. One is that for a dynasty with such a long shadow on Chinese polity it was extraordinarily short, lasting for only fourteen years, the shortest of all major dynasties. The other is that the seemingly mighty Qin, which built the Great Wall and terracotta soldiers, standardized measurements and roads, and created a national bureaucracy, was toppled by nothing more than a ragtag gang of peasants-turned-rebels armed with wooden sticks. This is known as the Dazexiang Uprising.

The story line is familiar to all school-age children in China. In 209 BCE, Chen Sheng, Wu Guang, and nine hundred conscripts were ordered to garrison in Yuyang, near present-day Beijing. Severe flooding delayed their journey, but under Qin law, conscripts who failed to reach their destination on time would be executed. This pushed Chen and Wu into a corner: if they were to continue, they would surely die upon arrival; if they were to rebel, they had a fighting chance to be alive. Chen and Wu rebelled. This was the first peasant rebellion in Chinese history, setting a precedent for many subsequent rebellions.

Chinese history textbooks use this episode to teach students about the harshness of Qin rule. The real lessons, however, are much deeper. One lesson is about incentives. From the earlier account, one can easily see that the flaw and the poor design of Qin rule led to the unintended consequence of encouraging the rebellion. But this interpretation sits uncomfortably with our knowledge about the Qin. The Qin espoused Legalism, a doctrine that prized incentives above all else. Other dynasties may have made this incentive error, but probably not the Qin.

A Chinese writer provides what I think is a far more convincing explanation. In his book *The Elegy of the Qin*, Zhu Zhuofeng speculates that the conscript-destination rule was designed for the smaller Qin kingdom, the predecessor to the Qin dynasty. The Qin kingdom unified China in 221 BCE by defeating and amalgamating six other kingdoms. It was small, only a million square kilometers, compared with the later Qin dynasty, which was three times as large. In the Qin kingdom, the conscript-destination rule could be realistically met, but not in the larger Qin empire. Figure I.1 shows the Qin kingdom in the top panel and the Qin empire in the bottom panel. In terms of both the altitude and latitude dimensions, the Qin empire was more expansive than the Qin kingdom.

The larger size of the Qin empire increased the heterogeneity of conditions. A small region is more homogenous in topographical, climate, and environmental conditions. The Qin kingdom was located in the arid northwest region of China, where there were low variances in meteorological conditions. The Qin empire encompassed far more diverse settings. Its territory stretched from the southeast to the north. Flooding might not have been a frequent occurrence in arid north China, but it was common in southeast China. Dazexiang and Yuyang are in two different climate zones, and both places are situated outside of the original Qin kingdom. The decision makers who created the time-bound rule probably had no idea about these heterogeneities on the ground and they failed to take into account the added complexities of a larger empire.

The tensions between homogeneity and heterogeneity—I also call them scale and scope—are an underlying theme in Chinese history and

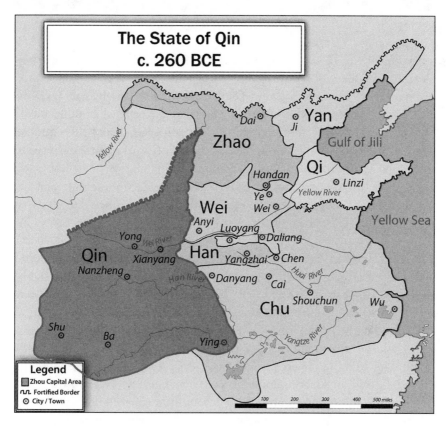

Figure I.1. From the Qin Kingdom to the Qin Empire. *Top*, the Qin Kingdom (897–221 BCE), *bottom*, the Qin dynasty (221–207 BCE). *Source:* Wikipedia; reprinted under the Creative Commons License.

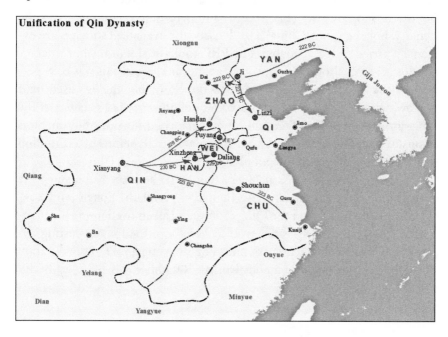

today. What the Dazexiang Uprising shows is that you ignore the complexities of scale and scope at your own peril. The Chinese rulers have resolved these tensions often in favor of homogeneity. In ideology, one idea, Confucianism or Communism, gained at the expense of other ideas. In politics, one ruler, an emperor or a general secretary of the Chinese Communist Party (CCP), dominated other centers of power. In bureaucracy, one type of human capital, Confucian mandarins or technocrats, edged out other types of human capital.

As China homogenized, it also became larger.[2] The Han dynasty (202 BCE–220 CE) covered an area of six million square kilometers.[3] (The figures are estimates and refer to the size of the dynasties at their peak.) The Tang dynasty (618–907) doubled it, to about 12 million square kilometers. In the Song dynasty (960–1279) the size of China shrank, to only 2.8 million square kilometers, but thereafter China began an expansion spree. At its height, during the Yuan dynasty (1271–1368), China occupied an area of some 34 million square kilometers, much bigger than Russia (at 17 million square kilometers), the largest territorial country on earth today. The Ming (1368–1644) and Qing (1644–1911) dynasties stood at 10 and 13 million square kilometers, respectively. The People's Republic of China (PRC) occupies an area of 9.6 million square kilometers. (For comparison, the United States spans 9.1 million square kilometers.)

Along with this increase in the size of its territory, China also scaled up its bureaucracy. During the Tang dynasty, bureaucrats comprised 0.02 percent of the population; this figure rose to 0.06 percent during the Southern Song dynasty (1127–1279) and 0.18 percent during the Ming dynasty. For the Qing, China's last dynasty, the available estimates are extremely varied and less reliable. The PRC took the size of the bureaucracy to another level altogether. In 1982, the number of officials was 0.08 percent of the population, comparable to the Song, but this is based on a narrow definition of the state.[4] A broader definition would encompass the rank-and-file CCP members who often perform governmental functions upon instructions from the CCP. Today, the CCP stands at 96 million strong, or 6.6 percent of the population.

The later dynasties are also very durable. The Yuan had a short life span, lasting only 97 years, but the Tang (289 years), the Song (319 years), the Ming (275 years), and the Qing (266 years) all enjoyed impressive longevity. The Han dynasty is believed to have been the longest-lasting dynasty in China, lasting 414 years, and roughly comparable to the duration of the partially contemporaneous Roman Republic (509 BCE–27 BCE).

But this comparison is debatable. The Han can be thought of as comprising two distinct dynasties, the Western Han (206 BCE–9 BCE, 214 years in duration) and the Eastern Han (25–220, 195 years in duration).[5] The founder of the Eastern Han, Liu Xiu, was a descendant of the imperial clan of the Western Han dynasty, but he was not in the direct line of succession. His ancestors had been generations of landlords in the provinces. It took Liu Xiu some ten years to vanquish eleven other claimants to the throne, a reenactment of a new dynastic creation. If we view the Western and Eastern Hans as sufficiently distinct from each other, dynastic longevity emerges later.

Now let's turn to the PRC. It will be a while before it catches up with the 319 years of the Song dynasty, but its longevity is still impressive. Consider the following attributes of the PRC:

- It is one of the only five manifestly Communist countries still remaining in the world;
- It has withstood catastrophic upheavals, such as the Great Leap Forward, the Cultural Revolution, and the 1989 Tiananmen crackdown;
- It has survived and even prospered from many crises that have toppled lesser regimes (such as Indonesia in 1998). Some of these crises originated from external sources; others were on account of the culpability of the Chinese leadership. These include the 1998 Asian Financial Crisis, the 2008 Great Recession, the 2015 stock market crash, the 2003 SARS epidemic, the 2008 melamine scandal, many days of "Air Apocalypse" in major Chinese cities, and the COVID-19 pandemic;
- It has been able to implement both economic and political shock therapies with apparent impunity: the draconian one-child policy (1980–2015), the massive layoffs of as many as 30 to 50 million workers in state-owned enterprises (SOEs) in the 1990s, the extraction of agricultural surpluses both during the Mao era and, far less well known, during the 1990s, control of the spread of COVID-19, zero-COVID lockdowns of multiple cities between 2020 and 2022, a massive purge of political and economic elites on charges of corruption under Xi Jinping, and the abolition of the two-term limit for the presidency in 2018.
- It has survived the supposedly liberalizing effects of a growing middle class and private sector, globalization, and the rising

living standard, defying the expectation that economic development would lead to democratization of the country.

On October 1, 2023, China will celebrate the seventy-fourth anniversary of the founding of the People's Republic, superseding the longevity of the world's first Communist country, the Soviet Union. That, of course, presupposes that the CCP does not collapse before then, fulfilling the predictions of a long line of Western observers, most famously, Gordon Chang. His book, *The Coming Collapse of China*, was published in 2001. It seems, more than twenty years on, that "coming" is a relative term.

Chang follows venerable footsteps in misjudging the staying power of a Chinese regime. In the 1850s, Marx forecast an imminent collapse of the Qing dynasty.[6] Instead, laboring under enormous pressures from popular rebellions and foreign invasions, the Qing muddled on for another sixty years, outliving Marx himself. Hindsight is 20/20, and world politics is complicated enough that we hesitate to judge forecasters who get it wrong. But the upending by both imperial China and its Communist successor of the forecasts of their life span is worth noting because it has happened so frequently and so repeatedly.

More knowledgeable China hands do not rush out predictions about the demise of China. On imperial China, Eric Jones remarks, "China's uniqueness lay in retaining an empire and a culture for an immense span of time." Political scientist Andrew Nathan noted the "authoritarian resilience" of China in the aftermath of the Tiananmen crackdown, contradicting the view held by many that Tiananmen dealt a fatal blow to the legitimacy of the CCP.[7] In the early 1990s, analysts began counting the actuarial table of Deng Xiaoping, predicting that his death would precede the death of the regime itself. (Deng died in 1997.)

I participated in this debate and happily ended up on the correct side of history. In 1995, publishing in *Foreign Policy* "Why China Will Not Collapse," I argued that after the death of Deng, China would not revert to the chaos of 1976.[8] The reasons I listed were the greater economic integration among Chinese regions as a result of economic growth and the rise of nationalism in the CCP's framing of its ruling ideology. These two observations have stood the test of history well.

The PRC under Mao experienced bouts of power struggles. During the reform era since 1978, the power struggles have waned considerably. There have been large-scale popular protests, notably the demonstrations in 1989, but by and large, these popular rebellions have been brought under control without substantial damage to the overall architecture of the Chinese state. CCP membership rose in the years following the Tiananmen crackdown, along with tax revenue, the economy, and the material welfare of Chinese citizens. Meanwhile, the political system has become noticeably more authoritarian over time. The return to a form of a personality cult and a one-man dictatorship under Xi Jinping is so far out of the norm that few China scholars saw it coming. Many—myself included—predicted persistence back in 2012.

Chinese autocracy seems "stickier" than autocracies elsewhere. Recall the spark that lit up what eventually became the "Arab Spring." The catalyst was an act of self-immolation by a Tunisian street vendor, a protest against the confiscation of his assets by a municipal official. By contrast, street vendors in China are routinely harassed, beaten, and have their assets confiscated, and China's urbanization projects have led to numerous evictions of property owners. None has fazed the CCP. The 2022 COVID protests, a potent threat to be sure, is unlikely to derail the CCP on its own—without significant fissures within the top leadership and significant economic hardship.

My book grapples with this big question of the staying power of the Chinese political system and other related questions in their historical and contemporary contexts. And puzzles abound. How has China managed to achieve a larger size *and* more regime durability over time? What are the tools and instruments used to achieve this outcome? Another big question relates to the rise and fall of Chinese technologies and the relationships between political and technological developments. How has the CCP, one of the world's fiercest autocracies that stifles free speech and inquiries, managed to make advances in science and technology? And in ways that eluded the Soviet Union and its own imperial former self: these advances are achieved on the back of vibrant entrepreneurship and commercial applications. They are not *Lonely Ideas*.[9]

I want to probe what holds together the CCP, a mammoth organization of 96 million members, bigger than many countries, and how the CCP system empowers enough individual agency to enable growth but not enough to generate a systemic breakdown. The last part of the book is future oriented. I explain the path to Xi Jinping and explore the broader implications of Xi's momentous reversion to extreme autocracy.

In the rest of this Introduction, I will present a framework illuminated by the Dazexiang Uprising: a nation often struggles between scale and scope, and successful ones get the balance between them right. I will frame the four topics of this book, examination, autocracy, stability, and technology, in terms of how these tensions are resolved. I conclude the Introduction with an outline of the book to help a reader navigate the concepts, factual narratives, and development of ideas presented in the book.

## Balancing Scale and Scope

A large nation is both blessed and cursed. In their book *The Size of Nations*, Alberto Alesina and Enrico Spolaore explain many of the tensions and trade-offs between the scale of a nation and its scope.[10] A large scale can result in savings in the form of scale economies, but a large scope can sow discord and incoherence. The two economists recommend identifying an optimal zone between these two opposing forces to maximize the benefits of both scale and scope.

Easier said than done. Let me illustrate by contrasting two historical polities, the Roman system of government and imperial China. From the founding of the republic in 509 BCE to the deposing of the last Roman emperor in 476, the Roman system of government is comparable in length to that of monarchical China (221 BCE–1911 CE). But it is not a perfect comparison, on two counts. One is that the Roman Empire was preceded by the Roman Republic (509 BCE–27 BCE) and the transition in the "regime type" under the Roman Empire (27 BCE–476 CE) contrasted with the regime immutability of imperial China (not to mention the era of Communist China). The monarchical phase of the Roman system is only a fraction of the duration of monarchical China.

The other difference is that Roman Empire was split into Western and Eastern halves. The empire was already fractured before 476 when Europe "escaped" from Rome.[11] This is an explicit acknowledgment that the empire had trouble scaling itself and it was too big to be run as a single administrative unit, having to settle for a compromise between scale and scope. Not only that. After the fall of Roman Empire, there were multiple attempts by ambitious rulers and military commanders to reunify Europe in the image of Roman Empire. They all failed.

Imperial China occasionally fell into disunity, but the disunity was de facto, never de jure, and in the sixth century China reconstituted itself as a unified country and it has never looked back. It then embarked on an expansion spree and scaled itself both spatially and temporally. Today China under the CCP is very much a continuation of its imperial former self—tyrannical, unified, and durable against all odds.

There are a myriad of differences between the Roman Empire and imperial China, but let me single out one factor for emphasis. Imperial China invented a tool that enabled it to scale by reducing its scope. That tool is the first letter in our EAST formulation—examination, civil service examination to be exact, which was invented in 587. The Roman Empire never invented a scaling tool as powerful as China's civil service examination and the fierce, resilient heterogeneities derailed all the unifying campaigns. As a collection of sovereign states, Europe today is a legacy of that scaling failure.

This is not to say that Europe could not scale. It scaled outward through imperialistic expansions and its powerful corporations scaled their operations through market and private initiatives. But as an approximation of a single political unit, Europe successfully scaled only after it invented a scaling instrument—democracy. The official website of the European Union (EU) proclaims, "The EU supports democratisation and fundamental freedoms in partner countries by encouraging broad participation in political decision making and local ownership of sectors that are key to sustainable development." All the members of the EU are democracies. This is an eligibility requirement for joining the EU.

Democracy and autocracy resolve conflicts between scale and scope in fundamentally different ways. Autocracy suppresses scope, through coercion, information controls, ideological indoctrination, and value incubation. Democracy preserves scope, but not scope on all issues. Democracy converges ideas, values, and state actions on just a few things, such as sanctity of elections, rights, and rule of law. The EU does not allow any heterogeneities on regime type—they all have to be democracies. The ingeniousness of the democracy is that it restricts scope on a few dimensions so that scope on other dimensions—such as political, religious, and sexual orientations—can be preserved and can flourish. For democracy, getting scale and scope right involves more than a balancing act; it entails reaching an ironclad consensus on a few key, foundational issues. Autocracy, by contrast, treats scale and scope as diametrically opposing values. More than any other autocracies in the world, the Chinese autocracy has vaulted scale at the sharpest expense of the scope. Its absolute insistence on convergence, conformity, and uniformity is reinforced by the Communist ideology, but it is also deeply embedded in its history and tradition. This is the central theme of this book.

This book is admittedly and uncomfortably broad. It spans four big topics, the EAST formulation in the title of the book. To make the discussion analytically tractable, I will use two simple concepts, scale and scope, as a scaffold to frame the discussion. In my telling, each component of the EAST formulation resolves or is affected by the tensions between the scale and the scope conditions of China.

## *Tensions between Scale and Scope*

The dictionary definition of scale is "the relative size or extent of something." It comprises two concepts—size, and size of a particular dimension. Canada is a sizable country in terms of its geographic area: at about 10 million square kilometers, it is the world's second largest country and about 4 percent larger than China. But in terms of population, it is a dwarf, with only 38 million people. One Chinese city, Chongqing, has 32 million people.

Size can refer to a physical dimension—the size of the territory and/ or the size of the population of a country. My main interest, however, is not using the term to refer to a physical condition, an immutable situation, or a natural state of affairs, but using it in a way that denotes action and agency. In the example I provided earlier—in which the China of the Han, at six million square kilometers, grew to be the China of the Qing, at 13 million square kilometers—my interest is to understand that process of expansion rather than the static physical size of China during the Han and the Qing dynasties. I deploy the term in its political dimension—the size and homogeneity of bureaucracy, the uniformity of ideology, and/or the magnitude of intangibles, such as the political commitments of the state.

The dictionary definition of scope emphasizes a "range," a range of motions, of activities, of thoughts, or of operations. Scope comprises multiple dimensions and denotes heterogeneity, which is how the word is used in economics. Economy of scope refers to the cost savings from utilizing common inputs in the production of two or more distinct goods. By contrast, economy of scale refers to the cost savings from producing a large quantity of one good. Unless otherwise noted, I use scale and scope as relative dimensions. A scale expansion means an expansion relative to scope rather than necessarily an absolute increase of scale. An increase of scale can increase that ratio, but so does a decrease of scope when holding scale constant.

Polities and economies can be described in terms of their scope conditions. A polity with scope has more than one political party, more than one ideology, and more than one center of power. One instantly recognizes a democracy in such a description. Multi-party competition, a diversity of opinions, judicial independence, a bicameral legislature, and checks and balances are features of a democracy that meet our scope criterion. Within a democracy, scale to scope ratio can also vary across political organizations. For example, the modern Republican Party arguably boasts a substantially elevated scale to scope ratio in comparison to the Democratic Party.

For me, categorizing political systems along their scale and scope dimensions rather than by a simple binary divide between a democracy and an autocracy is helpful. It recognizes that a democracy possesses scope conditions but it may not monopolize them. This is a central issue I will explore—how Chinese autocracy has varied in its scope conditions. "Autocratic scope" is often hidden, a fundamental difference with a democracy. Scope conditions in a democracy are out there in the open, are legislated, and specified. They are articulated and touted. Scope conditions in an autocracy are de facto, functional, informal, or occasionally delegated. They can be residues from an unfinished scaling project and they manifest themselves as frictions in the system, as sands on a path of an autocrat. Autocratic scope, however, lacks permanence and irreversibility. It often hangs by a thread and is fragile.

Scope can also describe an economy. An economy with multiple ownership types of actors is an economy with scope; an economy that only has one type of ownership—such as state ownership under central planning—is an economy without scope. An autarkic economy that closes itself off to international trade and capital has less scope than an open economy. The Chinese regimes of the dynastic and Communist eras vacillated between open and closed economies and therefore varied in their scope conditions.

A moral from the Dazexiang Uprising is the hazard posed by the heterogeneity of climate conditions and how failing to take into account that heterogeneity can be disastrous. To the pre-modern rulers, scale and scope presented multiple challenges and their interactions produced unanticipated complexities. Long distances increased communication costs and rulers lacked timely and accurate information, hampering efficient decision making. In the late Qing, when the Taiping rebels captured the city of Wuchang, about 1,200 kilometers away from Beijing, it took eight days for the news to reach Beijing.[12]

The ability of the Chinese state to rule over a large territory and over a long span of time during an era without modern communication technologies is a non-trivial achievement. Ancient Europe was unable to do it; China, by contrast, reconstituted itself into a unified polity in 581 and has remained a cohesive political unit ever since. This accomplishment and its upside, as well as its downside, deserve our attention, appreciation, and explication.

## *Democratic Solution to the Scope Problem*

*The Size of Nations* by Alberto Alesina and Enrico Spolaore is a modern formalization of deep-seated tensions long recognized by thinkers and philosophers from the eras of antiquity. Aristotle, Cicero, Machiavelli, Rousseau, and Montesquieu maintained that "republics were delicate flowers that could only be cultivated in small gardens."[13] They all worried about the corrupting influences of increasing size and scope.

Montesquieu believed that "virtue"—a quality that brought benefits greater than to oneself—was constantly threatened by "a thousand considerations" and that vastness and virtue necessarily contradict each other.[14] At the Constitutional Convention of 1787, delegates noted the impressive size of the Spanish empire but also the imposing size of its despotism. It was James Madison who turned around the debate by redefining virtue. Diversity was a virtue and the solution to the downside of the diversity was to spread factions, interests, and passions thin and wide, and to have them check and balance each other.

A system of checks and balances, along with rule of law, free and fair elections, and an independent judiciary, is a democratic solution to the underlying tensions between scale and scope. Today, all large countries, except China, have some democratic components in their political system. (Some, such as Russia, are electoral autocracies.) This is an enduring strength of a functioning democracy, its ability to scale while maintaining scope, whereas autocracies can only scale at the expense of scope. In ancient times, it was the other way around. According to Stasavage, early democracies were small whereas there were sizable early autocracies.[15] It is a miracle that large democracies such as the United States and India, with their ethnic, religious, political, and socioeconomic heterogeneities, can exist as single political entities and can function and deliver economic growth and public services. Many ancient thinkers were pessimistic that large democracies could succeed.

Take India. Winston Churchill once quipped that India is "no more a united nation than the equator."[16] Yet one need not take the words of Churchill at face value to agree with him about India. (Churchill is known for his racist views on India.) We can invoke an adage by a left-wing economist and humanitarian, Joan Robinson, to reach the same conclusion. As recounted by Amartya Sen, Robinson remarked, "The frustrating thing about India is that whatever you can rightly say about India, the opposite is also true."[17] (To be sure, Robinson got quite a few things wrong, in fact, spectacularly wrong, about Maoist China and North Korea.) In a paper mapping the countries of the world by "ethnic fractionalization and cultural diversity," India scores high among the major countries. Its cultural diversity score is 0.667, compared with a score of 0.154 for China.[18]

India has struggled mightily to balance scale and scope, often trading off scale to preserve scope. Its multiple languages, many ethnicities and religions, complex and immobile castes, and extreme variances in human capital—India has some of the world's best computer scientists, yet some of the world's worst primary-school pupils—have impeded many important economic scaling projects. Take manufacturing production. Remarkably, for a country growing more than 6 percent a year between 2008 and 2017, the manufacturing share of GDP remained stubbornly stagnant, at around 16 to 17 percent. A study shows that Indian manufacturing firms are undersized compared with those in other countries. Micro and small firms accounted for 84 percent of all manufacturing firms, as compared with 24.8 percent in China, 27.5 percent in Malaysia, and 69.6 percent in the Philippines.[19] This is due either to the outsized vigor of Indian entrepreneurship or to the fact that Indian firms have trouble scaling to size. The latter is more likely to be closer to the truth.

India has one incredibly effective scaling tool—elections. Indian electoral turnouts at the national level are high, sometimes more robust than those in the United States. By most accounts, Indian elections at the national level are free and fair. English is another scaling tool, at least among Indian elites. In recent years, under Prime Minister Narendra Modi, a man who pursues scale more avidly than India's past leaders, the Indian state has developed a suite of tools that will increase the scale to scope ratio. One of the most controversial efforts was to craft a common identity by attenuating the Muslim component of Indian identity. Not surprisingly, such moves have provoked protests and backlashes. In a scope-rich and scope-entrenched nation, homogenizing religious identity is a risky and counterproductive move.

Prime Minister Modi has rolled out some technocratic tools whose immediate objectives are not to scale, but they are more promising in delivering a scaling effect down the road. The world's largest biometric ID project, "Aadhaar," was made mandatory by Modi. It had been an "opt-in" project under the previous administration. Another consequential accomplishment under Modi is the Goods and Services Tax (GST). The GST unified tax rates across regions and reduces double taxation on goods falling under different tax jurisdictions. GST will foster more internal trade and more regionally integrated supply chains. As Arvind Subramanian, an economic adviser to the Modi government, remarked about the GST in his 2018 memoir, "we should not forget the magnitude of the GST achievement: thirty or more regional governments coming together, giving up their sovereignty for the larger common good of creating one market in India; improving tax compliance; creating a robust revenue base for the country; and creating the fiscal environment for higher investment and growth."[20]

Similar mechanisms exist in the United States. The United States has incredible scope in terms of ethnicity and socioeconomic conditions and in terms of diversity of opinions. To some, wearing masks is a commonsensical public health measure; to others it is an instrument of oppression. Scientists blame global warming for the forest fires in California, but the same fires were also blamed on an inadequate sweeping of the forest ground, according to Donald Trump. One of the threads that such an opinion-rich nation can hang on to is the strength of its election system and its ancillary institutions, such as an independent court and media. This is why Donald Trump's challenging of the legitimacy of the 2020 election posed an existential threat to America's functioning as a nation and as a democracy.

For a democracy to scale while preserving scope, it has to scale on the required dimensions and achieve homogeneity on them. It is critical to have a broad agreement in the society and a complete agreement among political elites on the sanctity of elections and the rule of law. One does not agree to disagree on these issues; one agrees to agree. To secure this "agree-to-agree" homogeneity, democracies have set up multiple mechanisms to ensure free and fair elections, including election observers, vote counting transparency, court challenges, etc. These are all investments in the credibility of elections. Without this democratic consensus, a society is at risk of defaulting to autocracy, or anarchy.

The challenge for democracy is determining that minimum scale, enough to enable the political system to function but not so much to trip over to an autocracy. Democracies can and do entertain a wide variety of views on religion, sexual orientation, climate change, preferences for political parties, and many other matters, the kind of heterogeneity that is unthinkable in an autocracy and the kind of heterogeneity that often baffles visitors from autocratic countries who intuitively equate uniformity with scale. Democracies can afford plenty of room for scope precisely because they are successful in homogenizing the idea and the norm of the democratic process.

We can apply a similar perspective to academic democracy. Academia has rich scope, as anyone who has attended a seminar can attest, but that has not stopped the expansion of the modern research enterprise. Researchers congregate at large universities rather than being segregated at individually homogenous small silos. Peer reviews and consensus formation, which all academics subscribe to, resolve conflicting opinions and conclusions on decisions such as promotion and tenure. Academia scales by a common methodology—knowledge in the public domain, deference to domain expertise, external reviews, and the ways to evaluate impact.[21] Like democracy in the real world, academic democracy can be messy, sometimes acrimonious and occasionally erroneous, but it is probably a better system than all the conceivable alternatives.

## Chinese Autocracy—Scale over Scope

In the model developed by Alesina and Spolaore, citizens in large nations hold heterogeneous preferences, making it difficult to formulate consistent policies and programs. The referendum movements in Scotland and in Quebec suggest that Great Britain and Canada may operate at the edge of an invisible optimal zone between scale and scope. The preferences, cultures, and historical legacies may be too diverse to be accommodated under a single political framework.

This is where autocracies and democracies sharply differ from each other. The autocrats in my book do not sit idly by, agonizing over and feverishly identifying ways to optimize scale and scope and trying to strike an appropriate balance between the two. They undertake actions to directly crack down on differences of opinion and forcibly revise and induce changes in citizens' preferences. Think of the re-education camps during the Cultural Revolution, the National Security Law in Hong Kong, the metric-driven management system of the CCP, and the gathering dominance of Confucianist ideology that has emerged since the sixth century. All are designed to modify, attenuate, or eradicate existing heterogeneities of ideas and conduct.

Autocrats proactively homogenize their countries rather than taking heterogeneity as given. Their success depends on the development of effective homogenization tools. Imperial China since the sixth century and the CCP today have developed some very effective tools at their disposal. Unlike many other books, I do not focus on the substantive claims of Confucianism or Communism. I take it for granted that Confucianism and Communism brook no dissent among their followers, but their effectiveness requires implementation and implementation tools.

A central point of this book is that Chinese autocracy is entrenched, deeply embedded, and enduring because it has developed an incredibly effective implementation mechanism. The first letter of the EAST formulation, civil service examination and meritocracy, features centrally in my account of the invention, expansion, and maturation of that implementation tool in the hands of generations of Chinese autocrats.

Chinese autocracy is lopsided on the scale side of the equation, even compared with other autocracies with an impressive scale-to-scope ratio in their own right. Take Russia as a comparison. Russia is an illiberal democracy and Vladimir Putin's regime is repressive, but it has richer scope conditions than China. During the run-up to Russia's invasion of Ukraine in February 2022, a survey conducted by Western researchers showed that only 8 percent of the Russian citizens supported sending troops to Ukraine.[22] It is unimaginable that Western researchers could conduct similar unimpeded surveys in China, let alone on the eve of a major military operation.

There are other examples. Google is banned in China, but it could operate in Russia, although under heavy censorship. The very fact that Vladimir Putin has poisoned so many of his critics is because he has so many critics who can speak out openly against him. Harassed and targeted by the state, opposition parties are still legal and tenuously legitimate. Some of Putin's critics command a sizable following. Contrast this with China. Since 2013, against the increasingly dictatorial Xi Jinping, there have been three prominent critics of Xi and they were dispensed with quickly. Unlike Putin who has to rely on extra-legal means to silence his critics, suggesting some formal constraints on him, Xi directed the full apparatus of the Chinese state to go after his critics. The Chinese court sentenced Ren Zhiqiang, a businessman, to eighteen years in prison, and Tsinghua University promptly fired Professor Xu Zhangrun, a law professor who wrote an open letter criticizing Xi. On the eve of the CCP's Twentieth Party Congress, a man unfurled on a Beijing bridge a banner calling for removing Xi Jinping. He was quickly detained. Ren, Xu, or the man now known as the "Bridge Man" had no formal political organizations behind them. There are more scope conditions under an illiberal democracy of Putin than exist during the most liberal moments of Chinese autocracy.

The CCP is more authoritarian than even its Communist brethren, the Soviet Union. Russia had a long tradition of an independent intelligentsia, a tradition that tenuously persisted into the Soviet era. There are many well-known Soviet dissidents: Andrei Sakharov, Aleksandr Solzhenitsyn, Natan Sharansky, and countless others. Wikipedia used to have an entry, "List of Political Dissidents," grouped by countries. Under China, six dissidents were listed, but under Russia/Soviet Union, there were 176 names.[23] Omissions and classification methodologies may explain some of the differences between the two countries, but they are not likely to explain all of them. Chinese police told Hu Jia, a dissident, that there were only two hundred people in the whole country who agreed with him.[24] In the language adopted for this book, the Soviet Union had more intellectual scope than Communist China. (One reason could be ethnic. Many Soviet dissidents were Jewish, giving rise to the "Refusenik" movement. This is a dimension entirely missing in the homogenous China.)

In recent years, a de facto scope has emerged in China, giving hope to those who wish to see democracy and rule of law in China. This de facto scope is China's private sector, which now generates more than 60 percent of GDP and accounts for 80 percent of urban employment. But this de facto scope turns out to be no match for the absence of legislated scope. Xi Jinping has taken a series of actions to put the private sector in its place. Just a few days before the biggest initial public offering (IPO) in history, the IPO of Ant Group, a fintech subsidiary of Alibaba, Xi cancelled the scheduled stock debut. Jack Ma was often viewed by others, and he probably made the error of viewing himself, as politically untouchable. Not so. The usually visible and outspoken Jack Ma then completely disappeared from public view.

## *The EAST Formulation*

A reasonable premise is that all Chinese autocrats want to impose homogeneity, but they vary in their capacity to do so. Autocracies may thus end up with some residual scope conditions on their hands and some autocrats will face more frictions than others in the pursuit of their agenda. This is true in Chinese history as well as in China today. The question is, "What scaling tools do autocrats employ?" One simple method is killing the people who disagree with you. A joke from the Soviet era goes like this. On his death bed, Lenin calls in Stalin and asks, "After you succeed me, are you sure other comrades will follow you?" "No problem," Stalin replies, "if they do not follow me, they will follow you."

Qin Shi Huang, China's first emperor, the man who unified China in 221 BCE, famously buried many Confucian scholars. He adopted Legalism as his ruling ideology, and he went after the root of his problem by killing the proponents of Confucianism. Joseph Stalin also killed many of his perceived political opponents during the Great Purge, as did Mao during the Cultural Revolution.

But these were Pyrrhic victories for dictatorships, and even for the dictators themselves. Known for its cruelty and coercion, the Qin was a short dynasty, lasting a mere fourteen years. The family name of Qin Shi Huang is Ying (嬴), a rarity in China today, which one account attributes to the genocide of the Ying clan after the demise of the Qin dynasty.[25] Stalin purged and killed so many of his generals that when Hitler launched "Operation Barbarossa," Stalin's army was caught initially unprepared. Nor did Mao fare well. Just several weeks after his death, his wife and his ideological followers were arrested, and his policies were cast aside by a man who, according to an urban legend, always sat himself at the Politburo meetings in such a way that his deaf ear would face the chairman—Deng Xiaoping.[26]

In Chinese history, the largest killing spree of political elites probably occurred under Zhu Yuanzhang (1328–1398), the founding emperor of the Ming dynasty. He killed over a hundred thousand of his own court officials and their associates.[27] Similarly, during the Qing dynasty, "literary inquisitions" killed an untold number of writers, poets, and scholar-officials. My immediate reaction to these numbers is, "The emperor had so many elites to kill!" This was in pre-modern times. To kill 100,000 Ming bureaucrats and still have some leftover bureaucrats to run the country implies a massive bureaucracy in the first place.

That is the first order of our explanatory business—the size of China's imperial bureaucracy. How did China manage to create such a large literate and literary managerial class hundreds of years before universal education? The CCP's surveillance project to scan faces requires an explanation of the country's ability to collect massive quantities of data and to integrate data across multiple domains. The Chinese autocracy has always been coercive, and sometimes even toward its own elites. Coercion might have helped China homogenize its ideology on the margin by getting rid of elite dissent, but the main instrument to scale the bureaucracy and to rule a large and a growing territory with consistency and standardization was its ability to homogenize ideology. This is China's secret sauce and its scaling instrument.

It is a non-trivial task to homogenize ideas and incentives of ruling elites. It requires design, purposefulness, and massive investments. This is where the examination component of my EAST analytical framework comes in. In this section, I will give a brief rundown of the EAST formulation in history and today, as well as offer a speculative idea about its future.

## *Imperial China*

The foundational institution of political China is *Keju* (科举), the imperial civil service examination. *Keju* means "subject recommendation" and it was instituted in 587 by the Sui dynasty (581–618), a pivotal dynasty in Chinese political development. *Keju* encapsulates an effect that Henry Kissinger posited, which I cited at the opening of the Introduction. It maximized knowledge and reduced scope for action. The "knowledge" is a specific kind of knowledge—memorization, cognitive inclination, and a frame of reference all bound to an exceedingly narrow ideology known as Neo-Confucianism. *Keju* drilled this knowledge into the minds of a large swath of the Chinese male population over a millennium. The scope for other ideas disappeared. *Keju* homogenized Chinese human capital.

Now put yourself in the position of an autocrat in possession of this incredible tool. You will use it to enhance your capabilities, to maximize loyalty, and to design and calibrate human capital to monopolize and maintain power. *Keju* decimated society by denying it a vital nutrient— human capital. Through *Keju*, the imperial state crowded out everything else that would have stood in the way of an absolutist state. No independent intelligentsia emerged, despite high literacy. (Think of the contrast with Russian autocracy here.) Commerce was overshadowed. Organized religion never had a chance. All of these autocratic effects are on top of the deep cognitive biases in favor of autocratic values incubated by *Keju*.

The most powerful state is one without a society. (By society I mean organized society.) Imperial China—and its CCP successor—qualifies as that state. Stability ensued in the aftermath of the autocratic entrenchment. This is in part because the powerful imperial bureaucracy marginalized the aristocracy and landed gentry; it is also because the *Keju* system successfully defused one vulnerability that afflicts all autocracies— opposition from elite insiders. After the sixth century, China experienced fewer and fewer elite rebellions and almost no unconstitutional seizures of power. China was trapped in a splendid political homeostasis.

In this book, I will make frequent references comparing imperial China with Europe. In the realm of technology, the comparisons and contrasts are especially fitting. If we have to credit our modern world to one thing, it is the failure of historical Europe to scale itself. The polycentrism of fragmented Europe in the aftermath of the Roman Empire seeded ideological and political modernity and unleashed technology and economic growth.[28] *Keju* scaled China and created an antipode to post-Roman Europe. Political and territorial competition collapsed. Ideological space contracted. China's exalted technological lead dwindled, forfeiting the optionality of its own Industrial Revolution. China fell behind.

## The CCP era

According to the website *Our World in Data*, China is the only autocracy with more than 100 million in population. Large countries find it easier to accept rather than eviscerate a given level of heterogeneities. The CCP has opted for a different approach. At 1.4 billion in population and over a diverse economy and society, the CCP still insists on homogenizing ideas, values, and conduct. The CCP has been stable in that it has been successful in self-preservation. In recent years, unlike imperial China, the CCP has delivered on stability and technological development simultaneously.

Partisans of this system, including the CCP itself but also foreigners who have pontificated on the subject, describe it as a meritocracy.[29] Meritocracy is the most natural point of connection between the CCP and imperial bureaucracy. Meritocracy is a controversial concept and readers will naturally read into the term the various connotations that are implied and embedded. To avoid any confusion, let me explain how I use the term in this book. I will use meritocracy to mean that it is a metric-driven system. Unlike the partisans of this system, I make no claims about the meritoriousness of the metrics and their welfare impact. It can produce good outcomes, such as GDP growth (for the most part). Alternatively, it can pursue population controls to an extent that harms the welfare of the Chinese citizens and prospects of the Chinese economy. Or it can banish a fixed proportion of Chinese intellectuals to the labor camps as rightists.

The CCP system is beset with many problems, such as corruption, inequality, power struggles, human rights violations, and policy hubris of immense proportions. This is not all an immaculate system. That said, the autocracy of the CCP is a far more sophisticated and productive organization than that blueprinted by *Keju*. More than the imperial system, the reformist CCP recognizes the severe constraints on its ability to monitor the functionaries of the system and it leans heavily on incentive alignment to induce the desired outcome and conduct. (For the purpose of this book, I define the "reformist era" as from 1978 to 2018—with 2018 being the year that the presidential term limit was abolished.) Compared with the imperial system, the reformist CCP is less absolutist in ideological alignment. Economic growth is weighted heavily in the metric-driven assessment even though it requires scope expansions, for example, endorsing private ownership, foreign capital, limited autonomy to civil society, research collaborations with the West, and substantial freedom of action on the part of the bureaucratic functionaries. The CCP has never let go of the economy and society, but it has delegated a lot of autonomy to them. This amount of delegated scope, I argue, contributed to the economic and technological achievements under the reformist CCP.

The reformist CCP has delivered the paired accomplishments of both technology and stability. There is built-in stability, which is due in large part to the cognitive legacies of *Keju*—pro-autocratic values and deference to authority—and the bequeathal from history of a society-free polity. There is also stability that is managed, and this is one area where the CCP is guaranteed to underperform against the imperial state—transition of power from one leader to another. Imperial successions were rule-based—male primogeniture; by contrast, CCP's successions are open-ended. Succession conflicts have plagued the CCP throughout its history but so far they have not escalated into a systemic breakdown. This is either due to fortuitous circumstances or to the institutional guardrails that the reformist CCP has put in, such as term limits. But things changed under Xi Jinping.

## *Future of the EAST Model*

All Chinese leaders are unabashed autocrats, but during the reform era since 1978 some of them have faced more frictions and constraints, often emanating from their own peers. The watershed political moment was the 1989 Tiananmen crackdown. The CCP gradually moved toward the scale end of the spectrum and under Xi Jinping it has accelerated the pace. The CCP in 2023 is a frictionless autocracy, an autocracy without any significant scope conditions.

Between 1978 and 2018, the CCP manufactured a rare feat of delivering on both growth and stability. Chinese history swings between the extreme ends of these two accomplishments. The Han-Sui Interregnum (220–581) exceled at technology but it was riven with conflicts and disunity.[30] The Qing dynasty had the opposite combination: its stability was stellar, but the dynasty marked the nadir of Chinese technological development. The Tang might have landed inside that optimal zone. It enjoyed political longevity and some technological accomplishments, although on technology the Tang paled in comparison with the previous eras, when China was less unified politically. During the contemporary era, the reformist CCP got the balance right more often than not, but the CCP under Xi is tipping China again toward extreme scale. The zero-COVID lockdowns, which ignore the science and the changing circumstances surrounding the virus mutations, are an apt illustration of this development.

The CCP is an autocracy, and it has a built-in gravitational pull toward homogeneity. The corridor is narrow to get the balance right, to borrow from Acemoglus and Robinson.[31] The CCP under Xi Jinping has reverted to China's long-run autocratic mean. And it did so at its most confident moment. It emerged from the initial COVID-19 pandemic relatively unscathed compared with the richer and technologically advanced democracies. The chaos that marred the transition of power from Donald Trump to Joe Biden was taken to confirm a long-standing view of the CCP and of the ordinary Chinese—that autocracy is conducive to stability. Amplifying this view of the CCP is the narrative of China as an AI superpower and as "a full-spectrum competitor" in the Western discourse on Chinese technological dominance, further boosting CCP's priors about itself.[32] In 2021, Xi Jinping proclaimed that "the East is rising, and the West is declining," his vision of a new world order.

Xi has turned the Chinese autocracy into a prescriptive model. To the CCP, the rising East is all about scale, and the declining West is all about scope. A careful review of evidence marshalled in this book directly contradicts this perspective. The lesson from Chinese ancient and recent history is clear: a country needs to strike an optimal balance between scale and scope to get things right. The Qin dynasty literally destroyed itself by getting the balance wrong; the Sui squandered China's technological lead by eviscerating its scope conditions. By decimating the myriad heterogeneities of the reform era, Xi is repeating the mistakes of prior eras and is damaging China's economy and technology.

There is a looming threat on the horizon to one component of CCP stability—leadership succession. In this area, the CCP is completely on its own and it cannot draw from the repository of knowhow, ideas, and methods from hereditary imperial China. During the reform era, the succession stability held because of the term limits. In 2018, Xi rescinded term limits. We will only appreciate the full impact of this action when a future succession is resolved in their absence.

I believe that China is entering into one of its most uncertain and perilous periods. I do not have a crystal ball, but a reasonable conjecture is that the EAST formulation as configured during the reformist era of the CCP may be on the verge of breaking down in one way or another. China may retrench further to extreme and potentially militaristic autocracy by getting rid of all or a substantial amount of de facto scope, such as private sector, foreign capital, and economic decentralization. Or it may break away from the current EAST formulation by recognizing, legislating, and expanding its extant scope. The EAST formula is no longer a stable equilibrium.

## Outline of the Book

This book is broad and ambitious, spanning both historical times and the present day. Historians may object to my sweeping treatment and social scientists may take issue with the topical expansiveness of my approach. These are legitimate criticisms. My defense is threefold. One is that my topical expansiveness is bounded by the scale and scope framework. The four components of the EAST formulation are analyzed through the prism of these two opposing forces rather than being treated as unconnected topics. There is a thread that ties otherwise disparate topics together and I leave to the readers to judge how successfully I tie the thread.

The second defense is that my invocations of history are mainly meant to shed light on the present times. I am making a relatively uncontroversial point that today's China is rooted in its past. That may sound obvious, but going beyond this broad statement and identifying specific connective tissues and sinews between history and the contemporary era is not as obvious. For me, it is the exam-based meritocracy that transmits the autocratic genes across Chinese political eras, although I recognize that there can be other channels of connections. Finally, it is not so much a defense but a plea for forbearance. Scholarship on China is famous for its orientation toward details and rich narratives. An addition to that literature with a bit of reductionism is unlikely to be too ruinous.

The apportionment of my treatment is unbalanced between history and the contemporary era. My historical account covers some two

thousand years of Chinese history whereas my contemporary account focuses on the period since 1978. The only justification is that I will touch
on a few really salient features of the Chinese history and do it with the
aid of data. Chinese history is a vast topic, and I am writing this book with
a decisive disadvantage of not being a historian. My purpose, however,
is not to uncover new historical knowledge but rather to construct and
infer patterns from history at a high level. Doing so is more feasible now
as historical data have become available, supplementing the rich stock of
knowledge that historians have created.[33]

My historical narration draws heavily from newly created databases
on historical technology and on imperial politics. In the past six years I
have overseen two major data construction projects. One is a comprehensive database on Chinese inventions in history; the other is a database on a
variety of attributes of Chinese emperors and senior court officials. Using
data to analyze history allows us to get away from what I label as a 2Q
problem in Chinese historical research. Social science research tends to
focus on the bookends of Chinese dynastic history, either the Qin or the
Qing. With data, we can delve into the dynasties in between. We may lose
some textual and narrative granularities, but hopefully we can gain from a
more holistic view of China's historical trajectory.

I also want to write this book for a general audience. Although the
ideas and the empirical findings are based on and distilled from my work
and the work of others, my writing style does not always follow a rigid academic format. China is no longer an exclusive domain of China scholars.
The policy toward and the perception of China are increasingly shaped by
discussions and discourses that are tangentially rooted in knowledge about
the country. I hope my book can contribute to the richness and informa-
tiveness of these public discussions and perspectives. The book is meant
to be broad rather than focused on one or two themes as is the usual style
for academic books. It draws from history, but also eclectically from economics, political science, and psychology. Where appropriate, the book
offers conjectures, speculations, and normative ruminations while fully
acknowledging things we do not know and complexities that defy simple
linear projections.

I draw policy implications in the book. For the policy community in
China, I hope they are open to the idea that too much autocratic stability
is detrimental, and that this conclusion is not based on "Western" values
and ideology but on China's own history. While there are unique Chinese characteristics, China's technological development and its broader

economic takeoff are a product of an optimal combination of scale and scope conditions. This is not a perspective one often hears in official accounts of Chinese development. Scope-contraction moves, such as curtailing China's private sector or undermining the autonomy of Hong Kong, are economically, and possibly politically, damaging. For the policy community in the United States, I point out flawed assumptions of a policy approach known as "engagement" and I propose an approach that may have a better chance of nudging China toward more political openness.

Finally, I hope to provide some food for thought to anyone who is willing to ponder an alternative political future for China. Many academic books shy away from a normative orientation. We seek to explain and make sense of the world we observe rather than imagining or advocating a world we want to see. In case there arises an inflection moment for China to contemplate an alternative future for the Chinese political system, I hope that some of the ideas I propose here can be helpful. For now, I will engage in it as a thought experiment and not give much consideration to its utility.

The book has five parts, and in the first four empirical parts the content is roughly split between history and the PRC. After this Introduction, two chapters in Part I deal with the E component of the EAST formulation. One is devoted to *Keju*; the other is devoted to the organizational architecture of the CCP. In Part II one chapter shows how the imperial autocracy was entrenched by *Keju* and another chapter traces the evolution of autocracy during the reform era and shows how the 1989 Tiananmen crackdown laid down the path to Xi Jinping.

Part III analyzes the stability of regimes during the two eras. Imperial China attained stability, measured in the length of the emperor's rule, as it scaled its bureaucracy. During the reform era, the CCP has maintained an impressive record of regime stability and has benefited by tapping into traditions, norms, and practices from history. There is, however, one prominent exception—leadership succession. In this area, the CCP has had to improvise. The track record of the CCP in peaceful transfers of power is not encouraging, and the direction that Xi Jinping is taking the CCP is worrisome. Part IV tackles technology. One chapter in this part grapples with the "Needham question"—the famous puzzle posed by Joseph Needham as to why Chinese technology collapsed; the other chapter argues that the technological advances under the CCP result from an adroit collaboration of China's scale advantage—what I label "Republic of Government"—with the West's scope advantage, which is known as "Republic of Science."[34]

Part V opens with a chapter on Xi Jinping. (The previous chapters on the PRC era are mainly focused on the period leading up to Xi.) The transformative impact of Xi is reverberating in China and globally. The final chapter is an assessment of the future of the EAST model. There is a lot we do not know, and the track record of China analysts making predictions about the future is not stellar. Knowing the minefield in front of me, I approach this topic with humility and caution.

# PART I

# Examination

CHAPTER ONE

# *Keju* as a Scaling Instrument

Nowadays, I personally preside over the exam, and decide who can pass the exam. This can completely eliminate the ills of the old system.

—SONG TAIZONG, second emperor of the Song dynasty

THE IMPERIAL EXAMINATION MUSEUM in Nanjing offers a glimpse into what it must have been like to take a *Keju* examination during the Ming dynasty (1368–1644). Nanjing was the capital of the Ming during its early years. The museum is a replica of the Jiangnan Examination Hall built for the "provincial exam," the first of the three *Keju* tests. The venue is massive, covering an area of some 300,000 square meters—making it larger than Gillette Stadium, home of the New England Patriots football team. Inside are twenty thousand examination rooms, with each room designed to hold one *Keju* candidate. The provincial exam, administered by the central imperial court, was held in each of the fourteen provincial capitals.

The replica of Jiangnan Examination Hall depicts both the grandeur of the *Keju* exam and the utter misery it caused. During the exam, the twenty thousand candidates were forbidden from leaving the site, each crammed in a cell that was only four feet long and three feet wide. What's more, the exam was held during the hottest month of the year, in August, in the oppressive and humid climate of Nanjing, known as one of China's three "big furnaces."

Out of this experience of misery, *Keju* scaled imperial bureaucracy, but as a scaling instrument it itself had to be scaled first. In this chapter, I will trace its history and in that telling I will feature three autocrats who played a starring role. There are some fascinating details about them, including the fact that two of them are known—and the third is rumored—not to have adhered to an ideology that came to serve as the operating software of the *Keju* hardware, Confucianism. They were disruptors in some ways, but they also entrenched China's political system in other ways. The history of *Keju* is a long and complicated story; in brief, there were two milestones of this remarkable institution. One is that *Keju* became progressively more systematized over time. By the eleventh century, *Keju* had acquired a degree of formality that American college-entrance exams lacked as late as the nineteenth century. The other is that *Keju* evolved from scope to scale, sacrificing diversity in order to attain scale. That evolution is also the evolution of China's political system writ large and it is in that sense that *Keju* anchored political China.

## The Rise of Meritocracy

The *Keju* system was hugely influential, not only in China during ancient times, but also across Asia and into the modern era. It was emulated by neighboring Asian countries, such as Vietnam from 1075 to 1919, Korea from 958 to 1894, and to a lesser extent, Japan from the eighth to twelfth centuries.[1] *Keju* also provided a blueprint for the meritocratic systems in the West, first in Prussia and then in Britain and the United States.[2] Today, China's college-entrance examination, the *Gaokao*, is closely modeled after *Keju*.[3]

As far as I know, no one has yet offered a compelling explanation for why an examination approach—as opposed to other assessment techniques—featured so early and so centrally in Chinese statecraft. Perhaps the examinations had what psychologists call an "imprinting" effect—the learning and internalization acquired during a critical early stage of cognitive development. The examination, as an idea, methodology, and practice, shaped the formation, development, and maturation of the Chinese state.

### A Brief History

The *Keju* exams screened human capital and recruited it into the ranks of the imperial state. To understand this basic function of *Keju*, we must first review the other methods that the imperial system employed to perform these same functions. There were two. The most primordial mechanism was the family, that is, using bloodline as the pipeline—or, as an extension, drawing recruits from nobility. It is here that China sharply diverged from the West. Other than hereditary successions to the Dragon Throne, the Chinese had long steered clear of running the country on the basis of bloodlines, in principle if not always in practice. The rise of *Keju* dealt a fatal blow to the nobility and aristocracy as the supply base of political human capital.

The other mechanism was a reliance on elite judgment—recommendations from the heads of local governments or regional aristocracies. *Keju* undermined this mechanism as well. Although the Qin dynasty had launched a first salvo against the power and legitimacy of governance by nobility, local aristocracies managed to survive this initial assault. They then experienced a revival during the Han dynasty, the successor to the Qin, which crumbled as a result. Up until the Sui dynasty, powerful regional families had remained entrenched and strong.

Starting in the Sui dynasty, *Keju* examinations came to gradually eclipse the recommendation route, although they did not displace it instantaneously. Between the Sui and the Ming, the pool of examinees was widened, and male commoners began to gain entry into the imperial civil service. (*Keju* was open only to the male population.) This dilution effect did not happen organically and spontaneously. Rather, it was deliberate and designed from the top. The curriculum became standardized, and the imperial court provided the necessary resources for administration and enforcement. Such formalization and systematization then produced secondary—and for the imperial court, first-order—political effects: they strengthened the imperial autocracy and narrowed the ideological space in China.

The Sui dynasty drew from an extraordinarily rich Chinese tradition that favored assessments based on constructed metrics, known in the modern era as key performance indicators. An examination is an ancient Chinese idea. There are references to exams in classical texts as early as the Zhou period (1027–221 BCE).[4] If such references are to be believed, the practice of examinations predates the creation of the Chinese polity.

There is documented evidence of exam practices during the Han dynasty. The Han had a sequential arrangement whereby candidates for central government service were first recommended by the heads of local prefectures, then were examined by central ministers.[5] The formal name for the recruitment system under the Han was *chaju*, or observation and recommendation. First the emperor would issue "employment notices," then officials from all levels of government would make recommendations. The desired criteria for candidates were vague, such as filial piety and integrity.[6] The recommendations were followed by oral exams, much like interviews by company recruiters after they have reviewed résumés. The purpose was to solicit the opinions of the candidates rather than test them on their technical skills. These oral examinations were followed by another round of recommendations—from the ministers to the emperor. This was a labor-intensive process, and in all likelihood, the evaluation process was subjective. Although the examinations were but "a minor element in the system for selecting officials," in the opinion of Ch'ien Mu, a prominent historian, one onerous objective standard had to be met.[7] Those wishing to obtain clerical positions in government were required to take literacy tests. The hurdle was high: a mastery of nine thousand characters.[8] For comparison, according to a 1988 standard promulgated by the Chinese State Council, literacy for a rural Chinese person is defined as the ability to read 1,500 characters and for an urban resident, the ability to read 2,000 characters.[9]

The Han dynasty invested heavily in the cultivation of its political elites. In 124 BCE, under Emperor Han Wudi, an imperial university was established to teach the Confucian classics.[10] It taught a "professional education" rather than a foundational education, similar to the Central Party School today. The imperial university had fifty to a hundred students by 80 BCE, then two hundred students by about 60 BCE, and three thousand students by 10 BCE. According to *Guinness World Records*, the oldest university in the world is the University of Karueein, founded in 859 in Morocco. China beat that record easily.

Contrast this Chinese fixation with the literary type of human capital with the Roman Empire's obsession with promoting generals who climbed to the top by their feats on the battlefield. Throughout Chinese history, the military has been relegated to a station inferior to that of "scholar-officials." For whatever reason, Chinese rulers have long privileged mental capabilities over physical prowess among those whom they wanted to recruit into leadership positions.

Physical capabilities are directly observable and can be assessed in the real world, on battlegrounds or in a coliseum. Assessing mental capabilities, by contrast, requires constructed metrics. That was the idea of an exam and it is a remarkable idea. Chinese purposely eschewed outcomes in the real world as the basis for making personnel decisions. Constructing metrics was a costly and design-intensive endeavor. Rules and protocols needed to be devised to ensure that selections would lead to the desired attributes and to safeguard the informational value and sanctity of these metrics. It was a leap of faith that performances on these constructed metrics were predictive of the desired real-world outcomes. In some ways, this process-oriented thinking is similar to the faith that we have in democracy and rule of law. If we take care to set up the process correctly, good things will happen.

During a period between Han and Sui when China fell into disunity (220–581), the examinations were discontinued, and recommendations became the only basis for making appointment and promotion decisions. (This period, which I will call "Han-Sui Interregnum," features prominently in the history of technology; see Chapter 7.) Not coincidentally, during this period there was a resurgence of rule by local nobility. A system known as the "nine-grade referees" arose to replace the "observation and recommendation" process. The referees, who were further divided into senior and junior referees, evaluated the candidates in their respective regions according to a registration form devised by the reigning emperors of the kingdoms. The registration form classified the evaluation criteria into nine categories. The referees would complete these forms, then submit the evaluations to the superior bureaus for further consideration. No formal examination was involved.

During the Northern Song dynasty (960–1127), *Keju* acquired and developed its famous features: a triennial schedule comprised of three tournament tiers, a preparatory channel, and possibly, anonymization. During the initial years, the exam was held irregularly and sometimes not at all. During the Tang dynasty (618–907), it was only one of several recruitment channels for the imperial bureaucracy, but by the Song, *Keju* was beginning to crowd out other mobility channels. On a per capita basis, *Keju* reached its apex during the Song, when it was the recruitment vehicle for about 90 percent of ministerial positions, compared to a range of 50 to 70 percent during the Ming.[11] Some two hundred *Jinshi* degrees (the highest degree possible) were granted in every *Keju* round.[12] Candidates with humble backgrounds began to populate the *Keju* candidacy. In the late Tang, 76.4 percent of those who passed *Keju* were from noble families, but this percentage dropped to only 12.8 percent during the Northern Song, marking the dawn of China's meritocratic age.[13]

The rising importance of *Keju* was accompanied and enabled by its systematization. In 1067, an imperial decree set *Keju* on its triennial schedule. Protocols and processes were established to ensure the integrity and accessibility of the *Keju* platform. During the Song, the curriculum for *Keju* was still quite open-ended, but then it was standardized and the format became defined and scripted. The multi-channel system of the Tang began to give way to the single-channel system of the Song.

During the Yuan dynasty (1270–1368) *Keju* encountered some headwinds.[14] Officials initially suspended it and although it was reinstated in 1315 by Ayurbarwada, the Yuan's fourth emperor, the scheduling became irregular and recruitment from *Keju* was restricted to lower-level positions. The Yuan rulers, however, implemented a consequential change: they adopted specific annotations from the Confucian classics as the *Keju* curriculum. These annotations were based on Neo-Confucianism, an interpretation of the Confucian classics attributed to Song-era philosopher Zhu Xi. One of the greatest Chinese philosophers, Zhu Xi was a nuanced thinker, but his streamlined version of Neo-Confucianism adopted and adapted for the *Keju* curriculum was textually tight, deeply conservative, expositionally homogenous, and narratively unambiguous. Interpretations of the *Four Books* and *Five Classics* were no longer at the discretion of the *Keju* candidates. Instead, the instructions were preset and preprogrammed.

Neo-Confucianism is more unabashedly autocratic and statist than original Confucianism. It exalted eliminating human desires and a complete subjugation of the self. Summarizing a common view among historians, Peter Bol observes that Neo-Confucianism "provided a justification for seeking external authority in the ruler" and stipulated that the emperor alone was responsible for transforming the world.[15] Remarkably, Neo-Confucianism extricated morality from consideration, instead advocating "absolute and unqualified" subordination to the ruler, "however idiotic or amoral he might be," according to sinologist Arthur Wright. Wright further asserted that "the new Confucianism was more totalitarian in intent than the old had been, in that it gave the monarch authority to police all private as well as public morals and customs, to extirpate heresy."[16] This political rigidity spilled over into the social arena. Women were completely subjugated—with widows, for example, forbidden to remarry. The idea was that fidelity to her husband should endure beyond his lifetime. Foot binding of women was introduced. No wonder the Mongols embraced Neo-Confucianism.

One unique aspect of *Keju* during the Ming dynasty was its regional quota system, which the Ming introduced in order to curtail representation from southern China, the center of Chinese economy and trade. In particular, the Ming sought to prevent the economic elites from capturing too much political power. This motif—the political center of the north vis-à-vis the intellectual and economic gravity of the south—can be seen throughout Chinese history. *Keju* served as an instrument to calibrate the balance between these two forces to the satisfaction of the emperors.

*Keju* experienced some decay during the Qing dynasty (1644–1911), in two ways. One is that educated Han Chinese initially resisted the Manchu rulers of the Qing dynasty. The Qing was established by the Jurchen Aisin Gioro clan of Manchuria, a vassal of the Ming court. Many Chinese viewed the Manchus as alien invaders; consequently some educated Han Chinese boycotted *Keju* organized by the Qing emperors.[17] A second development during the Qing was the auctioning off of both government positions and *Keju* degrees, a move that attenuated the meritocratic nature of the *Keju* system—even if the practice was not technically corruption, because it was an official policy of the Qing. The Taiping Rebellion (1851–1864) created a desperate need for revenue to fight the rebels. The Qing began auctioning off government positions at an unprecedented level. According to Ping-ti Ho, in 1764 and 1840, purchases accounted for 22.4 percent and 29.3 percent, respectively, of the qualification backgrounds of local officials; the rest was mostly accounted for by *Keju* degree holders. But by 1871 and 1895, purchases had risen to 51.2 percent and 49.4 percent, respectively. Meritocracy had lost some of its luster long before the Qing formally abolished *Keju* in 1905.

## Keju's *Heyday*

At its pinnacle during the Ming dynasty, each *Keju* round consisted of three separate and sequential examinations. The first, typically held in August of the year in which *Keju* was offered, was called a provincial examination, and was preceded by a series of qualifying tests. Those candidates who were successful on the provincial examinations were bestowed a title called *Juren*. Candidates with a *Juren* title then moved on to the next stage of *Keju*, called a metropolitan examination, which was typically held the next February. The Chinese word for the metropolitan examination is *Huishi*, which means "meeting in one place for the examination." The metropolitan examination was held in the national capital.

Those lucky few who passed the metropolitan examination were granted the title of *Gongshi*, and they moved on to take the final stage of *Keju*, the palace examination, in March. The candidates who passed this third and final examination, which was held at the palace, were conferred the highest imperial academic honor, called the *Jinshi*, sometimes translated as "presented scholars." This meant that they could be selected for positions in the inner sanctum of the bureaucracy—the eye of the prize in imperial China.

Those who passed the palace examination were ranked. The top three were conferred a "first-class honor," while those who earned between the fourth and—usually—the fortieth top scores were conferred a "second-class honor," similar to the summa, magna, and cum laude honors that are bestowed at some American universities today. The top performers were recruited into Hanlin Academy, an elite academic institution established during the Tang dynasty to perform tasks for the court, and would design the questions and evaluate the answers in future *Keju* rounds.

Elaborate protocols governed every detail of *Keju*'s administration. Before being locked in the small exam cell, each *Keju* candidate was body-searched and provided with three candles to help him perform his intellectual—as well as biological—functions with some light. The Chinese deserve credit for inventing the double-blind review process that is used widely today in academia. According to the rules of *Keju*, both the examiners and the examinees were anonymized. There is some dispute about when this anonymization procedure was introduced: it may have been under Wu Zetian (662–716), or later, under Song Taizong (939–997). In Chinese, this procedure is called *huming* (糊名), literally "covering the name." Under the rules of *huming*, the names and birthplaces of the candidates were concealed from the examiners, and each candidate was assigned an identification number to obscure his identity. Court documents stipulated, in meticulous detail, the procedures and protocols used to anonymize the individual identities of the *Keju* examinees. For each metropolitan exam, sixty-eight court clerks were employed to ensure the sanctity of the anonymization process.[18]

The *huming*, however, did not obscure the handwriting of a candidate, which could reveal information about his identity. The Song took care of that problem—requiring that all examination papers be copied by hired scribes to conceal the handwriting of the examinees. A Bureau of Examination Copyists, which employed two hundred to three hundred copyists, was established in 1015 to supervise this task. The examiners would then evaluate and grade the transcripts of the examination papers. Even a blank page could be interpreted as a signaling device and would trigger automatic disqualification. Elman remarks, "The process inside the examination compound temporarily stripped examinees of their names, family, and social rank. Each was presumed to be unknown and thus equal in the eyes of the examiners."[19]

The chief and deputy examiners were directly appointed by the central imperial court, which administered the entire chain of *Keju*, thereby preventing any local ties. Care was also taken to separate two types of examiners, those who proctored the exam and those who graded the exam. The two groups, housed in separated quarters, were prohibited from communicating with each other.

The Ming court required *Keju* candidates to take the exams in their native provinces, thereby necessitating an additional step to verify the regional identification papers. (By the way, the CCP has retained the same requirement. Rural migrant children, regardless of the duration of their urban residence, must take college-entrance exams in their home provinces.) The imperial court enacted regional quotas on the number of candidates for the metropolitan round of *Keju*. This was to balance the perceived regional inequalities in education, principally between the more developed southern China and the less developed northern and central China. The regional quotas for the metropolitan examinees were 55 percent from south China, 35 percent from north China, and 10 percent from central China.[20]

Contrast *Keju* with the state of college-entrance exams in the United States as late as the nineteenth century.[21] In the United States during this early era, there was no standardization. Each college wrote its own entrance exam, and individual faculty members could decide on their own exam formats and content. Harvard and MIT, two universities located in close proximity, administered entirely different exams. Some colleges would administer their exams only two weeks prior to the start of the classes. In terms of developing a formal, systematically administered testing procedure, China was way ahead of the West. China invented standardized testing.

## How Real Was the Meritocracy?

Scholars characterize the impersonalization of the Chinese bureaucracy as "precociously modern," a view rooted in the Weberian notion of bureaucracy.[22] But this precociously modern view of the Chinese bureaucracy demands a prior question about bureaucratic recruitment: was *Keju* truly meritocratic?

There are many reasons to be skeptical. The incentive to cheat was massive. For the candidates, the upside of success was considerable, and for those already inside the bureaucracy and in charge of *Keju*, there were political advantages to stacking the deck. Navigating imperial court politics required allies, and insiders were motivated to recruit political as well as human capital. This is simply human nature. The current scholar-officials sought to cultivate allies among future scholar-officials and they naturally turned to those *Keju* candidates with shared ties, such as common regional origins or family connections. There were technical challenges as well. The *Keju* scale was enormous, giving rise to informational and monitoring problems.

Tales of cheating and gaming abound. In 1404 the chief examiner, Xie Jin, of Jiangxi province, offered to help Liu Ziqin, an exam candidate from the same province. Liu rebuffed the offer, believing that he could succeed on his own. He was wrong. That year, Liu finished in fifteenth place, compared with the first candidate Zeng Qi, also from Jiangxi. It turns out that Xie Jin had leaked the exam questions to Zeng. The difference between first and fifteenth places meant a huge gap in their respective career paths. For Zeng, connections clearly paid off.

The rankings could also be meddled with. In the fifteenth century, Shang Lu abused his position as chief examiner and manipulated examination rankings to protect his place in history.[23] As a *Keju* candidate, Shang Lu had achieved the rarest of rare distinctions—he had scored "three firsts," first on the provincial exam, first on the metropolitan exam, and first on the palace exam. In 1477, Wang Ao was on the verge of matching Shang Lu's accomplishment—having scored first on both the provincial and metropolitan exams. After Wang's essay was initially ranked first, Shang intervened and had Wang demoted to third place.[24]

For a system of this scale and without our modern record-keeping and monitoring technologies, a reasonable question is not whether it was problem-free, but whether the problems were so crippling that the whole system was incorrigibly corrupt. Anecdotes of individual infractions do not settle the issue. Also *Keju* itself had some guardrails. In one instance, a powerful eunuch secured a larger metropolitan examination quota for his own province and supplied a list of fifty people whom he wanted to be seated as *Jinshi* recipients—but only a few people on his list succeeded in attaining the desired degree. Furthermore, those who meddled with *Keju* risked severe punishment. In 1657, fourteen officials collaborated with twenty-five candidates to tamper with the results of the metropolitan examination. Once discovered, punishment was swift: seven officials were executed, the intermediaries were exiled, and the chief and deputy examiners were demoted. The exam results were also nullified. After a retest, however, among the original 190 degrees granted only eight failed, suggesting that the vast majority of the original cohort were qualified in their own right.

Meritocracy is a fuzzy concept. That commoners succeeded on *Keju* is not itself proof of meritocracy at work. Consider an often-cited data point in Ping-ti Ho's *Ladder of Success in Imperial China*: more than half of those who obtained the *Juren* degree were first-generation, that is, none of their ancestors had ever attained a *Juren* status. This descriptive data is helpful but it is less than complete proof. After all, an absolute majority of men in imperial China did not have *Keju* credentials in their family trees.

Rather than asking whether *Keju* contributed to mobility for commoners, we can ask whether *Keju* worked in the ways it was designed to work. Anonymization was designed to protect the integrity of the exam and to reduce the importance of connections. Anonymization should attenuate the importance of family wealth and background. This is a question that research can answer: did anonymization shield *Keju* from the effects of family wealth and background? Answering that question, however, requires a statistical approach.

As revealed in the 2019 college-admissions scandal in the United States, family wealth has been used to buy admissions into some of the nation's most elite colleges. Contemporary research shows that family background explains a substantial portion of a child's performance on admissions-related tests.[25] There is no reason to believe that imperial Chinese did not succumb to the same afflictions. That said, many of the most egregious American scandals have revolved around extracurricular activities rather than the applicants' core academic performance. High-school transcripts were not faked because the parents were rich and famous. Rather, the discretionary portions of the college-admissions process are the parts that are prone to manipulation and influence peddling. This is consistent with our findings that the more discretionary palace examination was susceptible to considerations that went beyond academic performance.

*Keju* involved multiple steps. It bears some resemblance to faculty recruiting at American universities. The U.S. faculty search process begins with receiving and reviewing published academic papers and books, letters of recommendation, and a CV, then drawing up a short list of candidates. That process is relatively impersonal and objective. Then a job talk, meetings with individual faculty members, and a nice dinner at a local restaurant function to provide clues about a candidate's more subjective traits like her temperament, quick-wittedness, and collegiality.

The palace exam was the imperial equivalent of a job talk. Is it possible that during this stage *Keju* was more subjective than the anonymized and upstream stage of *Keju*? Remember that *Keju* had three tiers—the provincial exam, the metropolitan exam, and the palace exam. The palace examination was not anonymized and it allowed for some scope of ideas and opinions. Candidates wrote more open-ended policy essays that made allowances for a smattering of subjectivity and creativity—though of course, by this point in the process, those candidates who had "survived" into the palace examination had proven themselves to be consummate conformists already.

Armed with this set of facts, we can examine more systematically our earlier question of whether *Keju* worked in the ways it was designed to work. There are two hypotheses to test: (1) the backgrounds of the *Keju* candidates will not affect the exam outcomes during the anonymized stage of *Keju*, but they may have an influence during the non-anonymized stage, and (2) during the anonymized stage, the exam outcomes may be affected by the portion of the candidates' backgrounds that was known to the examiners. Exam outcomes here refer to the rankings that the *Keju* candidates achieved on their exams.

My coauthors and I found evidence to support these two hypotheses. We relied on an extensive database from the Ming dynasty, supplemented by our own data, on some forty rounds of *Keju* exams during the Ming dynasty.[26] In a paper titled "It Is Not Just What You Know," we looked at two background variables that differed in their visibility to the examiner. One was the provincial origins of the *Keju* candidates: we coded an examinee as having a connected background to an examiner if both of them hailed from the same province. (During the Ming, the regional information of candidates was known to the examiner to enforce the regional quotas, discussed in the next section.) The other background variable, which was invisible to the examiner because the name of the examinee was hidden, was the relationship between an examiner and an examinee's father. If the father of an examinee attained his palace exam degree in the same year as the current examiner, then we coded the examiner and the examinee as being connected with each other.

The findings are illuminating. The two variables had very different effects depending on the *Keju* round in question. In our various regressions, during the anonymized stages of the *Keju* exams, the provincial background variable was consistently statistically significant and positive— that is, having a shared provincial origin with the examiner improved the exam ranking of a candidate. By contrast, a connection with an examinee's father had no effect on the exam rankings during the anonymized stages. But on the non-anonymized palace exam the situation changed. During this round, both background variables boosted an examinee's ranking in a statistically significant way. Background factors, and by implication, more subjective and discretionary considerations, clearly mattered at the finish line of the selection process. *Keju* was meritocratic—up to a point.

## Scaling the Scaling Instrument

How did the *Keju* exam go from having only limited influence during the Tang dynasty to being the dominant human-capital pipeline during the Song and Ming dynasties? For China to expand from the physical size of the Han dynasty, six million square kilometers, to the Ming, ten million square kilometers, and the Qing, 13 million square kilometers, a scaling instrument was required. *Keju* was the instrument that augmented state capacity, homogenized ideas, standardized human capital, and nationalized the regional elites. But in order to be that tool, *Keju* itself had to be scaled first.

The scaling of *Keju* required successive generations of imperial rulers to undertake a number of actions. One was to widen the pipeline for the supply of talent. Another was to devise a standardized exam format that could be administered uniformly to a large number of examinees—by the time of the Ming and Qing, millions of test-takers were participating in the qualification rounds. And still another was to create examination protocols that would deter fraud and bias. If the examination protocols were not perceived as fair and impartial, the Chinese imperial system would have been unable to motivate millions of Chinese boys and men to invest large chunks of their time, money, and effort in the *Keju* process.

Scaling *Keju* meant that many existing barriers had to come down and new institutions, such as schools for preparing candidates, had to be created. Scaling also required resources. During the Ming dynasty, there was one preparatory school, on average, for each Chinese prefecture. These schools required massive funding from public coffers. There was a political agenda. The rulers did not maximize meritocracy for the sake of meritocracy; instead they used *Keju* to disrupt, weaken, and decimate the power of the incumbent aristocratic class. It is not a coincidence that *Keju* was scaled most by those rulers who harbored the most ambitious goals.

## *The Sui Dynasty: Consequential but Obscure*

Consider this intriguing observation: Chinese political development was shaped and defined in profound ways by two of its shortest dynasties, Qin and Sui. The Qin lasted a total of fourteen years; the Sui dynasty died at the tender age of thirty-seven. The Qin is well known. It was China's founding dynasty. Many Westerners know about the Qin because of its remarkable terracotta army of warriors. Though obscure, the Sui dynasty is arguably just as consequential. Although the political unification of China began during the Qin dynasty, innovations during the Sui launched an operating system that put this unification on a permanent footing. The short Sui dynasty was beset with palace power struggles, involving a patricide no less, and the system created by the Sui took hundreds of years to take shape, refine, and mature. But the Sui established the blueprint that would configure the level and the composition of human capital formation for imperial China.

Ann Paludan likens the Sui to an "overture to a great opera." By opera, she means the great Tang dynasty (619–907). It is common for historians to treat the Sui as a mere preface to the glorious Tang era. John Fairbank's widely used college textbook on Chinese history, *China: Tradition and Transformation*, devotes a mere page and a half to the Sui dynasty.[27] Ch'ien Mu mentioned Sui only twice in his book on Chinese imperial government, once together with the Tang dynasty in a section on land policy and another time on canal construction.[28]

To the extent he garners any attention, the founding emperor of the Sui, Sui Wendi, does so from an unexpected quarter. As a man who reunified China, Sui Wendi was ranked eighty-fifth—just behind Vladimir Lenin—in Michael Hart's *The 100: A Ranking of the Most Influential Persons in History*.[29] But this ranking is an exception. Chinese historiography tends to tread lightly on Emperor Sui Wendi and treats him unflatteringly. Mao Zedong, a deep and serious student of Chinese history, was dismissive of him. In 1993 the Chinese government published annotations that Mao had made on some books he had read. Next to a description of Sui Wendi as someone who was uninterested in books, suspicious of others, and often took the advice of women, Mao wrote: "This is brewing for trouble."[30]

(Other than the part about books, the two men actually had many things in common.)

The brevity of treatment of the Sui belies its significance. Historians mention the Grand Canal and the reunification of China as the main achievements of the Sui, but the way the Sui shored up the Chinese autocracy warrants far more attention. Preceding the Sui was 360 years of political chaos and disunity, which included, first, the Three Kingdoms period (220–265), when three aristocratic warlords fought with one another to gain control of the country, followed by a long span of fractious political and military competitions and regime transitions. The Sui brought to an end this era of chaos and disunity.

In addition, the unity enacted by Sui was long-lasting, with the PRC today being a legacy and beneficiary of the Sui's reunification project. Prior to the Sui, as a ratio the period of disunity to the period of unity was about 0.81. After the Sui, that ratio shrank to 0.29.[31] Something of a profound and material nature occurred after the Sui: China figured out a way to govern on a large scale durably and in a unified fashion. The Sui invented a system that enabled imperial China to successfully scale both spatially and temporally.

Sui Wendi unified China through a military conquest, but he kept it unified as an institutional project. Contrast the Sui with the Western Jin (265–316). After the demise of the Han, the Western Jin first reunified China in 265 but it did so as a narrow military feat and Chinese unity collapsed along with the Western Jin. Sui Wendi succeeded where the Western Jin had failed. He also accomplished in China what generations of European kings and generals had failed to do in Europe: none of them could reunify and perpetuate Europe in the image of the dissolved Roman Empire.

In 587, the Sui set in motion China's cognitive revolution and political transformation—the prototype of *Keju* was established. Then over time, *Keju* replaced a recruitment scheme that had enabled aristocrats to control the gateways to the imperial bureaucracy. The *Keju* system asserted end-to-end controls over the entire pipeline—nomination, evaluation, and final selections. The path-breaking reform had an awkward name, "submitting materials and self recommendations" (*toudieziju* 投碟 自举), but it captured the essence of the new process. Applicants came with their materials and on their own volition. They no longer relied on recommendations by other people. There were eligibility restrictions but outside of those, the entire male Chinese population was theoretically able to ascend into positions in the imperial bureaucracy. To be sure, not all of these measures were cleanly and instantaneously implemented. Still, few actions in human history can match the transformative potentials of this single move.

## Three Autocrats Who Scaled Up

In their book, *Scaling Up Excellence: Getting to More without Settling for Less*, two Stanford organizational sociologists, Robert Sutton and Huggy Rao, observe that "scaling starts and ends with individuals—success depends on the will and skill of people at every level of an organization."[32] Scaling is difficult. It requires grit, intelligence, persistence, and determination. The two professors quote a McKinsey consultant as saying that scaling requires "moving a thousand people forward a foot at a time, rather than moving one person forward by a thousand feet."

All three autocrats I will profile are imperial versions of these modern and ambitious business leaders. They founded their own dynasties—in one case, forcefully carving and spinning one out of an existing dynasty—and they were determined to imprint their dynasties by eradicating the residues of the previous ones. They were all outsiders. Sui Wendi (541–604) was an avowed Legalist, someone who was "displeased with Confucianism."[33] He, as noted earlier, launched *Keju*. The second on our list is an ultimate outsider, a woman, the only female emperor in Chinese history. This is Wu Zetian (662–716), beguiled by the Confucianists but hailed as a proto-feminist by some modern revisionist historians. The third is the founding emperor of the Ming dynasty, Zhu Yuanzhang (1328–1398). Zhu is not known for his educational pedigree. He came from peasant stock and did not receive a formal Confucianist education. As an emperor, Zhu empowered as many Confucianists as he killed.

History is written by the victors. The Chinese version of this dictum is that history is written by Confucianists. Confucian historiography was unkind to our first scaling autocrat, Sui Wendi, and downright hostile toward our second autocrat on the list, Wu Zetian—a Buddhist and a female ruler, to boot. But let's not take their judgments too seriously. Confucian historiographists were doctrinians rather than consequentialists. They seemed not to recognize that Sui Wendi and Wu Zetian created or institutionalized an apparatus that perpetuated the dominance of Confucianism.

Wu Zetian founded and ruled the short-lived Wu-Zhou period (690–705), though official court historians long refused to grant "dynasty" status to the era when she was China's emperor. She ended up presiding over a period framed as simply an interlude in the glamorous Tang dynasty. This framing understates the significance and uniqueness of this era in Chinese history. Brevity of her rule is a reason for such an understatement but Confucianists' revulsion toward a female—and ambitious—ruler also played a role. When discussing her reign, Confucian scholars often cite her brutality and terror. Probably influenced by this Confucianist narrative, Fukuyama titled a section in his book "Evil Empress Wu."[34] It did not help her reputation with citizens of the PRC when the followers of Jiang Qing, Mao's unpopular wife, glorified Wu Zetian in their tribute to Jiang.[35]

This treatment is patently unfair. Many Chinese emperors were ruthless and brutal but escaped the wrath of the Confucianist historians. Unlike Jiang Qing, who brought China to a verge of collapse, Wu Zetian presided over a period of prosperity and cultural openness. Wu Zetian was her own person, ruling China in her own name. By contrast, Jiang Qing was a lackey of her husband; as she famously protested at her trial, "I was Chairman Mao's dog. Whomever he told me to bite, I bit."[36] After the Gang of Four was arrested in 1976, Jiang Qing was once again compared to Wu Zetian, this time by her detractors, who implicitly reverted to the misogynist Confucian villainization of the empress.

To be sure, Wu Zetian was no shrinking violet.[37] She was a concubine of Tang Taizong, one of the greatest emperors of the Tang dynasty. Tang Gaozong, the ninth son of Taizong, "fell under the spell of his [father's] captivating and ambitious consort." That consort was Wu Zetian, and he had her installed as his empress. Wu Zetian achieved this remarkable feat of rising from a concubine of a father-emperor to an empress of his son-emperor. She did so through cunning and methodical brutality, traits eagerly spotlighted by Confucian historians. She had her own daughter murdered. She framed Gaozong's wife, had her demoted to commoner status, and exiled her. Still not satisfied, Wu Zetian, after becoming empress, had the former queen murdered, with her body dismembered and stuffed in a wine vat.

Wu Zetian dominated imperial politics for half a century, the Wu-Zhou period being the manifest portion of her dominance. While Gaozong was still the nominal sovereign, Wu Zetian began to participate in state services previously reserved exclusively for the emperor. When there was an attempt to remove her in 684, she responded by having some members of the imperial family and aristocrats murdered. She earned her proto-feminist reputation by taking up women's causes. In 666, she led a procession of women to perform a sacred rite on Mount Tai, and she founded an institute to write a *Collection of Biographies of Famous Women*. She also sought support from and advocated Buddhism, which, in sharp contrast to the misogynist stance of Confucianism, recognized the importance of women. In fact, Buddhism may help explain the coincidence of female power during this period in East Asia. A half-dozen female rulers in Japan, Silla, and Linyi ruled between 592 and 750.[38] In China, under Wu Zetian and at this time of ascendant Buddhism, women gained power, stature, and recognition.

Wu Zetian eventually took over the throne. She allegedly poisoned the direct heir, deposing her two sons along the way. The first son, Zhongzong, was in power for only six weeks in 684. The second son, Ruizong, lasted for six years between 684 and 690. He reigned but never ruled. Kept as a prisoner, he did not inhabit the imperial quarters nor did he appear at state functions. In 690, he asked his mother to formally take power. After "the customary triple refusal," she did. (After the abdication of Wu Zetian in 705, the two sons launched what Paludan describes as "a sorry replay of the reign."[39])

It is ironic that Wu Zetian played a pivotal role in entrenching Confucianism in the long run, a deed that went unappreciated by the Confucianists. She went after the aristocracy. Sui Wendi had converted imperial recruitment from nomination to application, though he had also imposed many restrictions on eligibility. Some of these restrictions were de jure; others were de facto. On the de jure side, the Sui had instituted restrictions on merchants, which Empress Wu, now acting as the sovereign ruler, partially lifted. Another restriction, apparently resurrected by the Tang, was the requirement that candidates had to be recommended in order to take *Keju*, a requirement that Wu Zetian waived.[40] But even a proto-feminist had her limitations. She never extended the franchise to women.

The greater changes occurred on the de facto side. When *Keju* was first established, most of the candidates were drawn from the capital city and its vicinity, and from elite aristocratic families. Wu Zetian, who had experienced pushback and resistance from the elites, broke their monopoly.[41] She did what a smart politician in her position would do—she diluted the existing powerholders by expanding the *Keju* pipeline to outsiders and newcomers.

Her method was both nuanced and direct. She increased the number of *Jinshi* degrees. In 655, for instance, there were forty-four *Jinshi*-degree graduates, but during the following seven years, fifty-eight graduates per year, on average, achieved this honor. Wu Zetian also made the curriculum less Confucianism-centric. She abolished the Confucian schools and sidelined the establishment Confucianist scholars. She assembled a group of independent scholars, called the "North Gate Bachelors" (北门学士 or *beimenxueshi*), as her core advisers.[42] She applied a spatial strategy to dent the power base of the incumbents. She moved the capital from the aristocratic stronghold of Chang'an to Luoyang, a region populated by commoners.

The nuance in her method was the elevation of the *Jinshi* examination over the *Mingjing* examination. The *Mingjing* examination tested memorization of classical texts, whereas the *Jinshi* examination of the Tang vintage focused more heavily on essay composition and poetry writing. These two categories of examinations sorted candidates according to different capabilities. While the *Jinshi* examination selected for innate talent and creativity, the *Mingjing* examination prized sheer memorization. By elevating the *Jinshi* examination, Wu Zetian nudged the selection process to favor creative talent, to the detriment of those rich households who possessed intellectual assets, such as books and classical texts. Wu Zetian helped to level the playing field between candidates from lower socioeconomic commoner classes and those from rich aristocratic households.

Wu Zetian also pioneered a technique known in the advertisement industry as "brand ambassadors." She elevated the visibility and prestige of *Keju* by becoming an examiner herself. This did not happen by coincidence. Emperor Tang Taizong relished presiding over the exam, and as his onetime consort, Wu Zetian might have learned from him the real purpose of the palace exam—to give aspiring scholar-officials a ritualized way to acknowledge the emperor's authority.[43]

As an ultimate outsider, Wu Zetian needed that acknowledgment. By presiding over *Keju*, she conferred her imperial imprimatur on the exam, and sent an unmistakable signal that she would select people she trusted. *Keju* began to attract tens of thousands of examinees, as compared with about two thousand examinees under the Tang. She formalized and routinized the palace examination, but unlike its Ming namesake successor, the palace examination under Wu was held in parallel with other parts of *Keju* rather than as a final stage in a sequential process. Anyone could show up and take it. The improvised nature of the reformed *Keju* broadened the pool of the *Keju* candidates and democratized bureaucratic recruitment.

Wu Zetian is also believed by some to have introduced an anonymization protocol for *Keju*, in 690, the very first year of her reign.[44] (The anonymization protocol has also been attributed to the Song dynasty.)

Research shows that reviewers are stricter and more critical under a double-blind review process.[45] Our own research—reported earlier—shows that the anonymization protocol worked as intended. This was a momentous milestone in the development of *Keju*. The vaulted impartiality feature strengthened the legitimacy of the autocratic meritocracy by making *Keju* at least seem objective.

Trailblazing emperors scaled up *Keju* for another reason. They needed to replenish the depleted stock of human capital in the bureaucracy. A common method used by Chinese emperors to break up the status quo was to eliminate physically a large number of the incumbents. Although this method of elimination solved one problem, it created another one. The decapitated bureaucracy had to be replenished with new blood, pun intended, often in a hurry. All the Chinese emperors were killers, but the more an emperor killed, the more he needed to recruit. You need a flow solution to solve a stock problem.

Our third trailblazing emperor, Zhu Yuanzhang, got himself in that situation. Zhu, the founding emperor of the Ming dynasty (1368–1644), was fiercely anti-incumbent and slaughtered so many bureaucrats that he had to quickly expand the human-capital pipeline in order to make up for the shortfall. He recruited eunuchs into the imperial ranks, paving the way for later clashes between eunuchs and Confucianists. For a time, he also revived the recommendation practice.[46] Zhu Yuanzhang was firing on all cylinders.

Zhu had a lofty agenda when he decimated the bureaucracy—stopping corruption.[47] (Xi Jinping is thought to have taken a page from Zhu Yuanzhang in his anti-corruption campaign, down to the detail of culinary specifications. In 2013, during the first days of his administration, Xi let it be known that he favored a relatively modest "four dishes, one soup" menu, which Zhu Yuanzhang had insisted on during his own early reign.) Zhu also stipulated civil servants' pay, and punishments for corrupt officials, in a document hailed as China's "first textbook on anti-corruption."[48] The manual prescribed some macabre methods. Corrupt officials who had received bribes worth sixty silver tael would be beheaded. Their skin was sewn into their office chairs, as a gruesome warning to the future occupants of those chairs. Maybe this was Zhu's version of "having skin in the game."

Zhu's anti-corruption campaign devastated and hollowed out the imperial establishment.[49] Zhu ordered over a hundred thousand executions, including of bureaucrats and their family members. Of the sixty-four ministers who assisted Zhu during his rebellion, twenty-eight were executed, one committed suicide, and two were stripped of their titles. Among the rest, thirty-three sons of theirs were punished, with twelve executed and seven stripped of their titles. Just as during Stalin's terror, every morning the Ming officials would "bid their wives adieu as if this was their last" and congratulate themselves in the evening for having made it to another day. In some ways, Zhu's killing sprees reflect prior emperors' success in wiping out aristocrats: there were so few of them left that it was the bureaucrats' turn to pose a threat, real or imagined.

Zhu faced a geographic imbalance similar to that which had troubled Wu Zetian. His bureaucracy was dominated by southerners, who lived close to Nanjing, the national capital. (The third emperor of the Ming would move the capital north, to today's Beijing.) The political, economic, and intellectual schisms between the north and the south escalated under Zhu's reign. His solution? Micro-managing *Keju*. In 1371, Zhu, dissatisfied with the 120 top *Keju* candidates, suspended two rounds of the examination. He then screened the texts used to prepare for *Keju* and expunged eighty-five of the required 260 chapters of Mencius he deemed offensive. (An example: "The people are the most elevated, next comes the state, the sovereign comes last.") He supposedly said about Mencius, considered to be the second Confucian sage: "If that old guy were alive today, he would be punished." Preceding Chairman Mao, Zhu ordered that his own instructions be taught in all the *Keju* preparatory schools.

In the 1397 round of *Keju*, Zhu found the outcome disagreeable: all fifty-two successful candidates on the metropolitan exam came from southern China. He suspected favoritism by the *Keju* examiners, most of whom also hailed from the south, so he ordered an investigation. His examiners reported back that the initial results were accurate and that there had been no wrongdoing. Not a smart answer. Zhu decreed that some twenty persons involved in administering the exam be sliced to death. The emperor then reread the examination papers himself and ordered a retake. This time, miraculously, all sixty-one successful candidates hailed from the north. This episode is known in Chinese history as the "South-North List" event.

But Zhu would not settle for meddling in just that round of the exam. He institutionalized a permanent cap on *Keju* candidates from the south, imposing a quota of 55 percent on southern candidates. The quota system went into effect in the 1427 round of *Keju*, formalizing the fusion of politics and meritocracy. The spirit of this regional quota system has persisted to this day. College applicants in some Chinese provinces face a higher *Gaokao* threshold than those from other provinces. The CCP is retrogressive compared with Zhu Yuanzhang. The admission cutoff level is often set higher for college applicants from rural provinces, an affirmative policy in reverse.[50]

## A Confucian Technicality

If we compare *Keju* to a computer, then its operating system is Confucianism. The *Keju* exam tested one subject only: mastery of the Confucianist texts and knowledge of the great Four Books (*Great Learning, Doctrine of the Mean, Analects,* and *Mencius*) and Five Classics (*Book of Odes, Book of Documents, Book of Rites, Book of Changes,* and *Spring and Autumn Annals*). No other subject matter was tested, not even the other great traditions and thoughts of ancient China, such as Daoism and Legalism.

Why did Confucianism dominate the curriculum? The mystery deepens because some of the architects of this Confucianist operating system were not Confucianists themselves. Of the three scaling autocrats, Sui Wendi was a Legalist and Wu Zetian was a Buddhist. There is some speculation that Zhu Yuanzhang followed an Islamic faith, although this is unproven.[51] *Keju* reached its apex during the Ming, but at least five Ming emperors were Buddhists. Emperor Yongle, who dispatched Zheng He on six ocean voyages (see Chapter 7), was a Daoist. The heterogenous Tang elevated Confucianist texts as the main test subjects on the *Keju* exam. The Chinese imperial rulers stuck to the institutional, public faith of Confucianism, even though they had a private penchant for other beliefs.

Outside of the *Keju* curriculum, the Confucianists were not categorically averse to other ideas. They are known for invoking Legalism from time to time. Zhang Juzheng, the Confucian grand councilor of the Ming, incorporated the statecraft of the famous Legalists, such as Shang Yang and Han Fei, into his teachings.[52] And although Confucianism is an autocrat's ideology, championing obedience and hierarchy, Legalism is hardly "a weapon of the weak." Legalism also champions obedience—although not through indoctrination, but by imposing penalties. The Chinese imperial autocracy ruled and operated on a fusion of Confucianism and Legalism rather than on the basis of Confucianism alone.

So why did the *Keju* exam feature only Confucian teachings? I think Confucianism was favored over other ideologies because of a technicality: Confucianism is challenging to master. The Confucianist texts tested on the examinations were dense and extraordinarily difficult. Much of *Keju* consisted of sheer memorization, and Confucianism offered a lot to memorize. Just as SAT vocabulary words are famously obscure and tricky, Confucianism offers a dense and vocabulary-rich ideology. It makes for an excellent screening device. Legalism, by contrast, is linguistically econom-ical and structurally straightforward. It consists of a series of dicta rather than lengthy treatises and doctrinarian elucidations. Legalism operates on a "negative-list" principle, specifying what you shall not do. It proscribes rather than prescribes. A Legalist curriculum would be akin to a recitation rundown of the "Ten Commandments." As a curriculum, the bar would have been set too low.

So how high of a bar did Confucianism set? Beyond offering a tex-tually rich ideology of indoctrination, persuasion, and cultivation—in other words, a rich vocabulary perfect for binding together the ruled and their rulers—Confucianism is very wordy. There are approximately four hundred thousand characters and phrases in the Four Books and the Five Classics, according to Elman.[53] How does that compare with other ideol-ogies? A handy tool in this comparison is the website Chinese Text Proj-ect, "an online open-access digital library that makes pre-modern Chinese texts available to readers and researchers all around the world."[54] The website organizes texts by their ideology, and the paragraphs of the texts are numbered. For example, one chapter of *Analects*, "Xue Er," contains sixteen paragraphs. By comparing the number of paragraphs of Chinese ideologies we can get a sense of their differing technical hurdles.

Confucianism is paragraph rich. Of texts created before and during the Han dynasty, Confucianist texts contain 11,184 paragraphs; Legalism has 1,783 paragraphs; Daoism has 1,161 paragraphs; and Mohism has 915 paragraphs. No other ideology comes remotely close to Confucianism in terms of textual richness and fecundity and thus in its suitability for a stan-dardized test. Could it be that the entire ideological apparatus of China ran on Confucianism due to this technicality?

———

*Keju* started out as a multi-plex system that evaluated candidates' mas-tery of many subjects. In its formative centuries, the curriculum of *Keju* was vague, broad, and ad hoc, and *Keju* coexisted with other recruitment mechanisms, such as recommendations. Scope prevailed within the exam itself. After the Song dynasty, however, the balance tilted toward scale at the expense of scope. Exam subjects were dropped over time until, by the Ming, the only remaining subject was "knowledge of classics, stereotyped theories of administration, and literary attainments."[55] The Ming's adoption of the highly scripted essay format known as the "eight legs" was the final nail in the heterogeneity coffin of *Keju*.

Historian Ch'ien Mu describes the "eight-legged essay" as "the greatest destroyer of human talent." There is, however, a rationale for such a format. The idea was to manufacture objectivity out of intrinsically subjective subject matter. And when the pool of applicants is large, a standard format becomes essential. Scaling requires standardization.

The evolution of *Keju* mirrors what happened in American higher education in the twentieth century.[56] In 1950, Harvard's acceptance rate was 76 percent. The "Big Three" at the time, Harvard, Yale, and Princeton, were boutique operations, drawing their applicants from the northeast corner of the United States and from a homogenous pool of white, Anglo-Saxon, Protestant families. In 2021, by contrast, Harvard's acceptance rate was a miserly 3.4 percent. Harvard did what *Keju* had done many centuries earlier—scale the applicant pool and increase access by weighting academic performance more heavily than the socioeconomic features of a particular demographic group.

This transformation was aided by standardization, or to be precise, by the SAT. Standardization opened Harvard to a nontraditional demographic cohort—first Jews and then Asians, who excelled in vocabulary and quantitative reasoning. Today Harvard, Princeton, and Yale draw applicants from across the globe and from all socioeconomic backgrounds. Yet although their student bodies are far more heterogenous than they were in 1950, there is more uniformity on one dimension: their IQ scores are tightly clustered.

The "Big Three" could not have scaled simply by admitting more white, Anglo-Saxon, Protestants. Similarly, *Keju* could not have scaled just by drawing in more aristocrats. The ratio of aristocrats to commoners was always small. To scale any human system requires scaling it on universal human capabilities and potentials. *Keju* is derided for its destructive effects on creativity, but it is also praised for advancing Chinese literacy. These two effects go hand in hand. Scaling requires standardization; there is no other way, but it is also true that standardization is not about achieving homogeneity across the board. It achieves homogeneity on targeted dimensions while resulting in heterogeneity on other dimensions. *Keju* increased scope in one dimension—there were more commoners than before—but it reduced heterogeneity in the mastery of Confucianist texts and in the adherence to Confucianist ideology. That is the homogeneity the rulers wanted and valued.

*Keju* accomplished for imperial China what the SAT did for Harvard. It increased access to the imperial bureaucracy, made recruitment extraordinarily cutthroat, and homogenized imperial bureaucratic recruits on metrics that were designed and constructed. Its effects were remarkable and significant. "The Chinese imperial state," Fu remarks, "was a product of conscious design and planning."[57] Autocracies are often dismissed as nepotistic, personalistic, arbitrary, and capricious. China may be an exception that proves that rule. Let's take a look at arguably the world's most formidable autocracy today, the CCP, next.

CHAPTER TWO

# Organizing China—and the CCP

This is an organization bent on world domination.

—JOHN MICKLETHWAIT AND ADRIAN WOOLDRIDGE,
*The Fourth Revolution*

THE CHINA EXECUTIVE LEADERSHIP ACADEMY (CELA), run by the Chinese government, provides executive education to its civil servants. Housed on forty-two acres in Pudong, Shanghai, it is picturesque, featuring lakes, gorgeous forested grounds, tennis courts, a gym, and lecture halls. One is forgiven for mistaking it as a country club if unfamiliar with its heavily Marxian curriculum. When John Micklethwait and Adrian Woolridge with the *Economist* visited CELA, each Chinese civil servant was required to undergo training for about 133 hours a year, and CELA's courses were frequently oversubscribed.

In their book, Micklethwait and Wooldridge implored the West to take the Chinese system seriously and draw inspiration from it. They quoted a view conveyed to them by their CELA interlocutors: the Chinese invented meritocracy 1,300 years ago. After the West stole it in the nineteenth century China suffered a setback, but now the Chinese are getting it back, and China's rise is unstoppable.[1]

History is more complicated than that. In Chapter 7, I will show that China's technological leadership collapsed soon after the Chinese introduction of meritocracy in the sixth century. The logic is also flawed. Un-

54

like a battleship, meritocracy is non-rivalrous. The Western "stealing" of it did not subtract from its continuous deployment in China. It may explain the rise of the West, but it could not have possibly caused a Chinese decline. This is not to mention, as I will in Chapter 3, that the Western version of meritocracy is totally different from its Chinese counterpart.

But Micklethwait and Woolridge's Chinese interlocutors got one thing absolutely right: the Chinese are bringing it back. "It" means *Keju* and its spawned methods, practices, and ideas. The recognizable successor institutions to *Keju* are the *Gaokao*, China's college-entrance exam, the Chinese Communist Party (CCP) school system, training academies such as CELA, and the oversubscribed civil service exam. These institutions cast an ideological homogenization effect on the Chinese population in general and on the pipeline up the CCP hierarchy in particular. But *Keju*'s influence extends much further than recruitment methods. A significant feature of *Keju* was its systematization—such as its tiered competition, anonymization, metric-driven qualities, and standardization. The CCP inherited and expanded on the principles and the practices of that systematization.

Francis Fukuyama credits the Chinese with having invented the modern state, "a state that was centralized, bureaucratic, and had aspirations to be impersonal."[2] A feature of a modern state is systematization. Imperial China had a "Weberian" system, rational, procedural, and process oriented. The Chinese invented the Weberian system long before Max Weber did.

The CCP system I will portray in this chapter is "Weberian" in some critical respects, but I am not going to rely on the operating manual of the CCP to make this point. What I will show is that a set of organizational practices by the CCP can be plausibly constructed as rational solutions to common problems of running a large organization. This is the systematization aspect of the CCP bequeathed by the *Keju* system. This systematization distinguishes the CCP and its imperial ancestors from the personalistic autocracies prevailing elsewhere in the world.

The label the CCP gives itself is a meritocracy, a system of government that the CCP insists is neither an autocracy nor a democracy. The concept of meritocracy is controversial and what constitutes a "merit" is malleable. For the expositional purpose here, I adopt a definition of meritocracy that allows for the CCP's proclamation about itself to contain an element of truth, while not validating the CCP's broader claims about its "meritoriousness." Under that definition, merit is determined by

a top-down authority, and there is an established, regular, and widely accepted mechanism based on peer competition to demonstrate that merit.

This is a mechanical and process-oriented definition, and it is entirely
silent on what a merit is. It is closer to the Weberian conception than
to the original idea of meritocracy as formulated by Michael Young, the
man who coined the term.[3] (Lost to many who invoke that term, Young
wrote his book as a satire, and he viewed meritocracy as a dystopia.) Both
the CCP system today and the *Keju* system of imperial China fit with
this definition. They are top-down, and they have instituted established
vetting and evaluation protocols and processes—the tiered exams in the
case of imperial China, and the personnel management system in the case
of the CCP.

Let me be clear: calling the CCP a meritocracy in no way validates its
claims of meritoriousness. During the era of Mao Zedong, merit was specified as loyalty to Mao. That merit led to exiles of intellectuals during the
Anti-Rightist Campaign and the madness of the Great Leap Forward. Career competition in such a context can be ruinous. James Kai-sing Kung
and Shuo Chen show that those officials at the cusp of promotion, for
example from alternate to full members of the Central Committee, pro-
cured more grain from peasants during the Great Leap Forward, exacer-
bating famine and causing excess deaths.[4] There is nothing commendable
about these outcomes. During the reform era, merit has been redefined as
GDP growth. While this merit is more worthy than the class struggles of
the Cultural Revolution, the pursuit of the GDP has also led to environmental degradation and large-scale corruption.

The CCP and imperial meritocracies differ in three crucial aspects.
For the CCP, merit is determined by metrics that are far more varied
than an exam score. The CCP also changes its merit frequently and often
pursues competing merits. The other difference is that the CCP system
of vetting is far more extensive, complex, and methodical than the *Keju*
system. *Keju* was the pipeline to the imperial state. The personnel pipeline
is important to the CCP as well, but it is only one of its many components.
Personnel management of the CCP consists of personnel selections, appointments, promotions, evaluations, and a host of other vetting procedures and processes.

The third difference is complexity. The meritocracy of the reform-era
CCP recognizes the complexity of the goals of the state and the complexity of human motivations and conduct. Delivering GDP growth cannot
be accomplished by rote memorization of classical or Marxist texts (or for

that matter of neoclassical economics texts). It requires experimentation, trial and error, and some tolerance for unorthodox ideas and actions. In other words, a scope of action and degree of autonomy must be a part of that system. The CCP also recognizes uncertainty. Not all the contingencies can be mapped out beforehand and while they can be modified by ideology, human incentives cannot be eliminated. The CCP wants to channel or harness incentives for its own goals.

Notice the apolitical language, drawn from organizational theories, that I use to describe this CCP system. There are some genuinely fascinating regularities of that system. For example, of the six heads of the CCP since Mao Zedong, five came from regional leadership backgrounds. When a provincial governor leaves his post, he is far more likely to be replaced by an official from another province, but a departing minister is more likely to be replaced by someone in the same ministry. Why do regional leaders get to rule China? And how are these personnel patterns related to the overall performance of the CCP?

Here I approach the CCP as an organization, not as a polity. As an organization, the CCP is quite advanced and armed with strong norms and clear processes. Compared with party organizations in other autocracies, the CCP comes closest to that Weberian organizational ideal. Most autocracies in the world are personalistic and idiosyncratic. The late Lucian Pye, an expert on political culture, was fond of saying, "China is a civilization pretending to be a state." To paraphrase Pye, China is an organization pretending to be a polity.

The title of this chapter is borrowed from Harry Harding, one of the preeminent sinologists in America. His book, *Organizing China: The Problem of Bureaucracy, 1949–1976*, is about the formative era of the CCP's bureaucracy under Mao Zedong.[5] The Chinese tradition of recruiting officials based on ideological conformity influenced the thinking of Mao and his colleagues, but one of the fundamental differences between the CCP and the imperial court is that the CCP is transformative, whereas the imperial regimes sought to preserve the status quo. During the Mao era, the radical aims of the CCP and of Mao relied on "mass campaigns." The bureaucracy was either a sideshow to the mass campaigns, as during the Great Leap Forward, or it was a victim of them, such as during the Cultural Revolution.

Since the end of the Cultural Revolution, the mass campaigns at the stratospheric level of the Great Leap Forward and the Cultural Revolution have mercifully come to an end. (So far.) Rather, the CCP's agenda is, for the most part, technocratic—designed to generate economic growth. While the CCP has periodically mobilized society to implement some of its objectives, it has done so within highly structured and orchestrated channels. Organizing China requires getting the CCP to itself be well organized, on the basis of the meritocratic principle in the sense that I defined earlier.

And there is a lot to organize. At the time of this writing, the CCP boasts some 96 million members. In pre-modern China, the state never extended its reach below the level of county. Today, by contrast, each village in China has a CCP branch headed by a party secretary who is accountable to his superiors in the CCP hierarchy rather than to the villagers themselves. And under Xi Jinping, the CCP has escalated its organizational reach. Private businesses are required to establish CCP branches; even the affiliates of multinational corporations are not spared. Many Chinese business partners have asked their foreign joint-venture partners to revise company charters so that CCP branches could be established. The revised charters have given the CCP branch more say over management, including personnel issues and reimbursement of the CCP branch's overhead expenses.

I rely on two social science theories to help frame and articulate the organizational logic and operations of the CCP. One is the theory related to multi-functional and unitary forms of corporations and the other is organizational economics. These two schools are related but also distinct. The first focuses on the structure of an organization; the second is concerned with the incentives of the agents in an organization. The two combined, I believe, yield a good approximation of how the CCP organizes itself and how it operates.

We can start with a general idea: organizations struggle between control and autonomy. Too much control stifles initiative and innovation. The old IBM was often cited as an example of over-centralization. So was the defunct Wang Labs. Yet too much autonomy can also lead to business failures. Lehman Brothers and Enron were led by aggressive CEOs who incentivized unsupervised internal competition. The lack of discipline, among other maladies, led to reckless business practices and to the companies' eventual doom. The CCP, too, struggles with these two opposing forces. Excessive stratification dampens incentives for growth at the local level and undermines the CCP's paramount goal of economic growth. But too much autonomy leads to centrifugal forces that pull the country apart or, as in the 1980s and the 1990s, feed inflationary pressures. Striking the right balance between control and autonomy is not easy and it relies on the norms and methods inherited from history, organizational processes and procedures, and the political preferences of Chinese leaders.

Between 1978 and 2018, the reformist CCP found that balance. The reformers granted a substantial degree of autonomy to its regions, enabling competition and entry of new firms, in a setup known as a "M-form economy." But the reformers were also mindful of the potential risks of too much regional autonomy and they encapsulated the M-form economy within the confines of CCP's centralized personnel management. The resultant system empowers but it also constrains autonomy, and it shapes and structures the incentives of the agents operating in that system.

This is why analysts such as Gordon Chang got it so wrong about a coming collapse of China. They failed to appreciate that the CCP system is embedded with autonomy but also control—at least prior to the retrogressive policies of Xi Jinping—and that it is able to deliver both growth and stability. In the words of organizational economists, agency problems have not been permitted to fester. This less heralded aspect of the reformist CCP explains why the Chinese economy was able to take off in the 1980s and 1990s and why the reformist CCP succeeded in implementing reforms through experimentation and bottom-up initiatives.

## The M-form Economy

In 1993, Yingyi Qian and Chenggang Xu wrote one of the most influential and insightful papers on Chinese economy, "The M-Form Hierarchy and China's Economic Reform." The two economists applied an insight from Oliver Williamson's theory of U-form and M-form corporations to explain how the Chinese economy took off in the 1980s.[6]

### Theory of M- and U-form Corporations

Williamson explains his theory in his 1975 book *Markets and Hierarchies*, where he classifies corporations into two types. One, which he calls a unitary-form corporation, or a U-form corporation, operates based on functional specialization.[7] Such corporations are divided into functional lines such as sales, finance, manufacturing, and so on. A great advantage of a U-form corporation is its ability to reap efficiency gains from scale economies. In contrast, M-form, or multi-functional corporations, are organized along divisions, such as brand names or geographic branches. An M-form corporation consists of several scaled-down U-form corporations, with each division heading the specialized functions like manufacturing, finance, or sales.

Until the early 1920s, the dominant corporate structure in the United States was the U-form corporation. These corporations had a single product line, such as meat packing, tobacco, or oil. Starting in the early 1920s, however, pioneered by General Motors and DuPont and followed by Goodyear, General Electric, IBM, Ford, and Chrysler, large firms began to organize their activities along the lines of M-form organizations. By the 1960s, M-form corporations became dominant among American corporations.

Alfred Chandler and Oliver Williamson argue that M-form corporations were better able to overcome "information overload."[8] Firms face information overload when they expand in size and into new markets. Because U-form corporations place strategic planning and inter-functional coordination in the hands of a general office, they experience increased stresses during expansions. Coordinating sales with finance, for example, becomes increasingly complex as the size of the firm grows and requisite knowledge becomes highly specialized. Corporations respond by first including functional managers in strategic decision making, but this solution leads to advocacy and representation of sectional interests. Decision making becomes politicized.

M-form corporations possess several advantages. Each operating unit of an M-form corporation carries out its own inter-functional coordination, relieving the general office of these tasks. The general office can then focus on strategic decision making and planning, leaving micromanagement to the regional operating units. Information overload is less severe and decision making is less politicized. The M-form corporations gain in efficient information and expertise management, even though they experience losses such as diseconomies of scale. Corporations always face trade-offs among different kinds of efficiencies. In the case of M-form corporations, their strategic, informational, and managerial efficiencies outweigh any static scale inefficiencies.

## The Chinese M-form Economy

Qian and Xu use this organizational dichotomy to explain why the Chinese economy took off while the Soviet economy stagnated. Their argument boils down to the following basic proposition: the Soviet Union was a U-form economy, whereas China was an M-form economy.

The M-form Chinese economy enjoyed two advantages that eluded the U-form economy of the Soviet Union. One is that an M-form economy permits, and encourages, the entry of new firms, including private firms. The other is that an M-form economy is constantly engaged in experimentation. To achieve both of these advantages, the Chinese regions—equivalent to the operating units in an M-form corporation—are given substantial autonomy.

China is not only an M-form economy; it is an extreme M-form economy. Its general office is the central government. Below the central government there are four divisional tiers—provinces, prefectures, counties, and townships. There is one Russian feature to this otherwise very Chinese system: the recursive structure of a Russian doll. Each of the operating units encases several of its operating sub-units, and each encased sub-unit replicates the same characteristics of the encasing one, such as operating autonomy, inter-functional coordination, self-sufficiency, and so on.

The M-form economy solves one of the biggest problems of a planned economy—soft budget constraints. At the lowest level of this structure, townships do not receive investment allocations from superior levels, which means that local governments are forced to generate growth through other means, including by wooing businesses such as private firms. Bureaucrats in the U-form Soviet Union had no equivalent incentives because they depended on allocations from their superiors.

The other advantage is experimentation. Experimentation is more likely to occur and more likely to be successful, because micro-management by bureaucratic overlords, who typically stamp out any policy innovations, is absent. And because inter-regional interdependence is low, experimental failures in one unit do not instantly cascade into catastrophic and systemwide consequences. This safety feature eases the concerns of central planners who are typically risk averse and ideologically conservative. And finally, successful experiments are more likely to be adopted because the conditions among operating units are similar.

It is important to recognize the cost of the M-form economy, which is the cost of forgoing the benefits of regional economic integration. Study after study shows that the Chinese economy during its takeoff period was highly autarkic. China is known as the "factory of the world." True, but China is more a factory of the world than it is a factory for itself. In the 1990s, Chinese provinces traded with foreign countries more than they traded among themselves. Inter-provincial trade in China was smaller than the interstate trade among members of the European Union. In the 1980s and the 1990s, the M-form autarky increased. Between 1986 and 1991, for seven broad categories of consumer goods, regional variations in prices increased.[9]

As we have seen elsewhere, scale and scope conditions often trade off against each other. A case for the M-form economy, then, requires that the dynamic efficiencies of an M-form economy outweigh the costs of its static inefficiencies. Chinese regions widened their scope to welcome private entrepreneurs and foreign investors. Efficiency gains from competition, entry of private firms, and policy innovations through experimentation exceeded the benefits of simple scale economies. This is how the Chinese economy took off.

The M-form economy also aided reform politics. Unwittingly, the M-form economy attenuated the decision rights of the conservative planners. In the 1980s, as powerful as conservative leaders were, they mainly operated in the background, removed from the day-to-day economic management. (More on this in Chapter 4.) Their interventions were often ex post rather than ex ante. Several times, the leaders of Guangdong received stern lectures from Chen Yun, China's top central planner and the head of the Central Discipline Commission, about the contaminating effects of foreign capital and trade.[10] But reversing a fait accompli is more costly than preempting a proposed course of action, and the local autonomy embedded in the M-form economy brought about many instances of fait accompli.

## Overcoming Information Overload

Central planning fails because it can never match a market economy's efficiency in collecting and processing information and knowledge, as Friedrich Hayek explains in his 1945 paper "The Use of Knowledge in Society."[11] By extension, centralized planning fails more than decentralized planning because it is more information-intensive to run. An M-form corporation is less burdened with information overload.

The Chinese economy began to outperform the Soviet economy even before the two countries began to undertake reforms. In the 1970s, the Chinese GDP growth rate was comparable to or even possibly faster than that of the Soviet Union. (The quality of the data from that period is not high.) This is especially impressive considering that during those years China was engulfed in the chaotic and destructive Cultural Revolution. While the entry of new firms enabled China to grow quickly during the reform era, the superior growth in the 1970s occurred because Chinese planning was more efficient than Soviet planning. The decentralized Chinese economy incurred lower informational costs. Most allocative decisions were made intra-regionally rather than inter-regionally, creating an element of redundancy. The central government had limited allocative functions and the sectoral central ministries were not that intrusive. This was stabilizing at a time when the central state was paralyzed by raging ideological and power struggles.

The Chinese central planning apparatus, decimated by the Cultural Revolution, was extremely bare. As of 1976, the number of Soviet statisticians in the central government outnumbered their Chinese counterparts by a factor of nine hundred. At one point in the early 1970s, the Chinese State Planning Commission (SPC) had only fifty staff members. After the Cultural Revolution, China began to build up its central planning capacity, but it never reached the Soviet level. In 1987, the number of staff at the SPC climbed to 1,255 persons, still only about one-half the size of Gosplan, the Soviet central planning agency.

To their credit, the Chinese leaders chose to delegate decisions rather than insist on running things from Beijing. What happened when the Chinese leaders ignored the information overload problem and attempted a U-form approach? In my 1994 paper "Information, Bureaucracy, and Economic Reforms in China and the Soviet Union," I delved into a little-known episode in Chinese economic history when that occurred.[12] I found that market reforms unfolded in China not because Chinese leaders bought into the idea of market economy, but because they had lost the capacity to execute central planning.

The Chinese reforms are described as "post-Mao," but this is imprecise. Mao died on September 9, 1976, but the agricultural reforms did not commence until the end of 1978. What happened during this two-year interregnum? The Chinese tried and failed at central planning. It is important to get the historical sequence right rather than blithely accepting the *post hoc ergo propter hoc* of "problems, therefore reforms" so common in writings about the Chinese reforms. In 1976, the Chinese leaders did not interpret the Cultural Revolution as a failure of central planning but rather as a failure to properly *implement* central planning.[13] The prevailing policy objective at the time was to restore the Chinese economic system to that which existed prior to 1957. That was not a clarion call for market reforms; it was a call to resuscitate the Soviet system.

The central planners made the mistake of launching an ambitious industrialization drive on the presumption that the requisite planning and execution capabilities were in place. Sizable contracts were signed with Japanese companies to import turnkey projects and ambitious plans were formulated to increase steel production.[14] This was China's "Great Leap Outward," implemented without even rudimentary inter-sectoral coordination, input-output analysis, or budgetary forecasts. In other words, the planners attempted a U-form feat on an M-form infrastructure. Large-scale economic dislocations ensued. Trade and budgetary deficits exploded. The economic bureaucracy was thrown into chaos. The debacle forever tarred the reputation of Hua Guofeng, Mao's successor, and discredited the central planners. One faction of the CCP, however, gained from this economic fiasco: the reformist faction headed by Deng Xiaoping. The rest is history.

## The M-form Organization

Qian and Xu provide a convincing framework to explain the effects of the M-form economy, but their paper is entirely silent on the factors that have enabled the Chinese economy to function in this way. Let me make up the shortfall here. China's M-form economy functions under an organizational architecture, which I call an "M-form organization," a system that both empowers and constrains Chinese regions.

It has three important elements. One is that the M-form organization not only empowers regional governments but also constrains central ministries. Second and relatedly, the Chinese regional leaders seem to be given the right to rule China ahead of their ministerial colleagues. A third feature is the heavy reliance on GDP as an evaluation metric. The GDP metric expanded regional autonomy but also furnished some discipline to the exercise of that autonomy. The Chinese officials are still subordinate functionaries in a top-down autocracy, but they have acquired a degree of action and decision agency only in this specified domain. An even more consequential effect is that the GDP as a metric and as a policy goal orients the central leaders away from some terrible alternatives that the CCP has pursued on a customary basis, such as class struggles, mass campaigns, a cult of personality, and so on. It has a moderating effect on Chinese politics.

### Empowering the Regions

It was the year 2007, and a large crowd gathered expectantly in a cavernous atrium of China's Ministry of Commerce. On one side of the wall hung a huge banner, "Go and create another glory." The crowd was there to bid farewell to their departing minister, Bo Xilai. Bo, tall, handsome, and utterly assured of himself in ways only a princeling could be, made an impromptu speech—which he twice interrupted with his own spontaneous singing—lauding his achievements at the ministry and expressing his excitement about his next appointment, party secretary of Chongqing municipality.[15]

Bo was leaving his post as minister of a powerful central ministry to assume a regional post. As CCP chief of Chongqing, Bo would be elevated into the country's penultimate center of power, serving concurrently as a member of the CCP's Politburo. (The Politburo Standing Committee, PBSC, is the ultimate seat of power.) But in 2012, he was arrested, charged with corruption, and sentenced to life imprisonment.

The travails of Bo Xilai show that the currency of power in China is regional, not ministerial. The reason he fell hard is because he had climbed so high. No other fellow ministerial colleagues ascended to that height of the Politburo membership. Significantly, his fall from power paved the way for the rise of a fellow princeling, Xi Jinping. The entanglements of Bo in the dynamics of leadership succession—which include a lurid murder, defection, and love affairs—are the stuff of Chinese political legend, and expose successions as an Achilles' heel of an autocracy (more on this in Chapter 6).

For our discussion on China's M-form organization it is important to understand that Bo's move from the Ministry of Commerce to Chongqing was not a demotion. In the Chinese political system, a ministry and a province have the same bureaucratic rank. (And Chongqing, although a municipality, has a provincial rank.) Others made similar lateral moves in their political careers. In 1985, Jiang Zemin left his post as Minister of Electronics to become mayor of Shanghai. (Shanghai, like Chongqing, has a provincial rank.) And in 2000, Tian Fengshan was appointed Minister of Land and Resources from his position as governor of Heilongjiang province, until corruption charges led to his downfall in 2003.

This rank equivalence is an intentional feature of the Chinese system. At one point in the history of the PRC, the CCP decided to grant decision-making rights and operating autonomy to the regions and to place prohibitions on the power of central ministries. For example, central ministries can provide input, but in most cases the provincial governments control personnel decisions in the provincial bureaus of the line ministries. Central ministers issue instructions to their provincial subordinates only with the consent of the governors.[16] This arrangement formally constrains the central ministries from intervening in provincial affairs. The M-form economy functions in this context.

## *Why Regions Rule China*

In 2012, Bo Xilai, the CCP chief of Chongqing, put himself in contention for a seat on the PBSC. History was on his side. Regional officials often climb to the top. Of the six heads of the CCP after Mao died, five—Hua Guofeng, Zhao Ziyang, Jiang Zemin, Hu Jintao, and Xi Jinping—had experience in regional leadership. (Sun Zhengcai, once viewed as a likely successor to Xi Jinping before he was purged in 2017, was the CCP chief of Chongqing.) The lone exception is Hu Yaobang, who ruled from 1982 to 1987. Throughout his career, Hu mainly worked in the central CCP apparatus, such as the Communist Youth League and the Department of Organization.

There is a simple explanation for this phenomenon: governing a Chinese province is good training for governing China as a whole, since a province is in many ways a political microcosm of the nation. Before we accept this simple explanation, let us consider the following anomaly: a departing provincial official is typically replaced by an out-of-province official.[17] In 2012, for example, 80 percent of the provincial party secretaries and governors were outsiders.[18] This is at odds with an expertise argument, albeit expertise of a different kind. Presumably, regional expertise is also expertise (and this is why many universities in the West have China scholars). Shanghai is as different from Guizhou as the Ministry of Foreign Affairs is different from the Ministry of Finance.[19]

For insight, let's look at the Soviet Union, the country that tutored Mao Zedong, Liu Shaoqi, Zhou Enlai, Deng Xiaoping, and Chen Yun in its political and economic ways. The Soviet Union had compelling reasons to draw its ruling elites from its territorial ranks. It was larger and more diverse than China, spanning 22 million square kilometers and eleven time zones, compared with China's 9.6 million square kilometers and five time zones. It was also more ethnically varied: Slavs constituted 70 percent of its population, compared with China's dominant ethnic group, the Han, which made up 94 percent of the Chinese population. The country had no fewer than thirteen officially recognized languages in addition to Russian, the official language. An intimate knowledge of the regions would have been extremely beneficial.

But that was not how the Soviet system selected its leaders.[20] Of the five leaders of the Soviet Communist Party after Joseph Stalin, only two, Nikita Khrushchev and Leonid Brezhnev, came from top regional government backgrounds.[21] ("Top" here means leading one of the fifteen union republics, the Soviet administrative unit that was comparable to a Chinese province.) Khrushchev held the top party position in Ukraine and Moscow before ascending to his central leadership positions, whereas Brezhnev came from Moldova and Kazakhstan. By contrast, the other Soviet leaders—Yuri Andropov, Konstantin Chernenko, and Mikhail Gorbachev—had modest or no background in regional government.

Moreover, the regional credentials of Khrushchev and Brezhnev pale in comparison with those of the top Chinese leaders. Consider Xi Jinping and Li Keqiang, China's premier from 2013 to 2023. Xi spent a combined total of nine years as the party secretary or the governor of Shanghai, Zhejiang, and Fujian, while Li Keqiang spent five years in two provinces, two in Henan and three in Liaoning, as party secretary. By contrast, Khrushchev and Brezhnev spent only three years in the union republics. (Granted, Khrushchev's Moscow career was longer, but it is difficult to disentangle his career in Moscow from his overlapping career in the central government.)

Aside from Jiang Zemin, whose regional portfolio consisted of only Shanghai, all the other Chinese leaders moved through multiple provinces before assuming top national positions. Hu Jintao was first party secretary of Guizhou and Tibet. Zhao Ziyang, China's premier and later its general secretary, had been party secretary and governor of Guangdong and Sichuan. The regional dominance of Chinese ruling elites shows up in the membership composition of the PBSC. Of the seven members of the PBSC of the Nineteenth Central Committee (2017–2022), only one, Wang Huning (ranked fifth), did not have any significant regional leadership experience. In the PBSC of the Twentieth Central Committee, newly constituted in October 2022 with a five-year term, Wang remains the lone exception among the seven members without any regional leadership experience. Ding Xuexiang, a new addition to the PBSC, has a slightly heavier experience in the central government. In 2013, he was appointed as the chief of staff for Xi Jinping after having spent a long career in the Shanghai government.

Equally striking is the absence of the technocratic, ministerial backgrounds at the highest level of the Chinese political hierarchy. Only Wang Yang, one of the seven PBSC members of the Nineteenth Central Committee, ever held a technocratic position at the ministerial level. And it barely counts. He was a deputy director, not the head, of the State

Development and Planning Commission between 1999 and 2003. Not a single person on the PBSC of the Twentieth Central Committee ever worked in a ministry at a senior level. Foreign observers marvel at China for being a technocracy. Except at the very top. The top leaders of China have a background of running the CCP apparatus at the regional level. The promotional odds are stacked heavily in favor of political generalists rather than technocratic specialists.

Two other details reveal a fundamental difference between leadership incubations in China and the Soviet Union. Some of the Chinese leaders first spent time in the central government and then were dispatched to the provinces, only to be recruited back to the Center thereafter. In contrast, the Soviet leaders had a unidirectional career trajectory. They started out in the union republics, then climbed up to reach their terminal positions in the central government. There was no back and forth between Moscow and the regions.

Consider Mikhail Gorbachev. From 1970 to 1977, he was the first party secretary of Stavropol, a regional government under the Russian Union Republic. According to the 1989 census, the Stavropol region had a population of 2.4 million, about 0.8 percent of the Soviet population. From this perch, Gorbachev went on to a central government post that put him in charge of the entire country's agriculture.

In the Chinese system, it would have been inconceivable to catapult a person of this diminutive stature to such a prominent national position. The Chinese launchpads to a national career are the likes of Shanghai, Guangdong, and Zhejiang, all economic powerhouses—or Sichuan, one of the most populous provinces in China and its major agricultural producer. In 1980, Zhao Ziyang left Sichuan to become China's premier after engineering an agricultural miracle in the province: he increased output by 25 percent within three years. Sichuan had 98 million people in it as of 1980, accounting for 10 percent of the Chinese population. A Chinese saying at that time, which rhymes in Chinese, was "If you want to eat, go and look for Ziyang."

## The GDP Metric

Pierre Landry refers to Chinese local officials as a "colorful mosaic."[22] This is an apt metaphor of the CCP during its M-form era. At the local level, the Chinese officialdom is not uniform. Economic autarky and local protectionism run rampant. Provincial officials, as mentioned before, are not outranked by ministerial officials. So how does the CCP hold all these discordant pieces together?

The integrative mechanism is the CCP's personnel system, which, in sharp contrast to the Chinese economy, has remained extremely centralized.[23] At the end of the day, as powerful or as charismatic as Bo Xilai was, he was still subject to regular, often rigorous vetting and evaluation (if pro forma and with considerable leeway accorded to a person of a princeling status, such as Bo). This is the control side of the picture. The M-form autonomy only goes so far and it is bounded by the parameters laid down by the personnel system. I will focus on two aspects of that system. I will consider the metric on which the reformist CCP has relied heavily to do its vetting and evaluation; and I will hypothesize that a function of some of the personnel practices is to preempt the unwanted behavior of the regional officials.

In Chapter 1, I postulated that Chinese imperial state scaled based on the performance on the highly formatted *Keju*. What is the contemporary meritocratic equivalent of that *Keju* performance? It is GDP. Here the two bodies of the literature, personnel controls based on a single metric of GDP and M-form economy, come together. The former requires the latter.

Let's first imagine applying a single metric to a U-form type of economy. In that system, the ministers hold all the power and, as in the Soviet Union, they rule the country. But how do you compare the performance of two ministers, say, the minister of metallurgy and the minister of agriculture? Who is more capable, the minister who churned out more tons of steel, or the minister who churned out more tons of wheat? You can make an argument on either side, but there is an inherent ambiguity. In other words, applying a single metric to a U-form economy is difficult because ministerial outputs are different from each other.

An M-form economy has a reductionist edge. It can alleviate what Williamson calls a commensurability problem, or what we might call the problem of comparing apples with oranges.[24] Under the M-form system, each region is a "profit center" and the central human resource managers can compare the GDP performance of Shanghai with that of Chongqing more easily than they can compare the steel and wheat outputs of two ministries. Under the right assumptions (such as market-based exchange), a profitable unit is considered more beneficial to the organization as a whole than an unprofitable unit.

The M-form organization does not make the commensurability problem go away, but it forces the resolutions of that problem downward in the organizational hierarchy. Keep in mind that an M-form organization has a recursive structure consisting of divisionalized tiers. The resolutions of the relative worth of apples and oranges take place at lower tiers of an M-form organization, relieving central decision makers of the burden of solving this commensurability problem. The central government can instead focus on bigger things, such as strategy and development goals.

Now we come to the well-known Chinese reward system, which is based on officials' GDP performance. Landry provides a detailed catalogue of the thirty-three performance indicators for 104 municipalities in China.[25] These indicators are broken down into five broad categories— economic development, human capital, quality of life, environmental protection, and key infrastructure—and within each category there are subcategories. For example, economic development comprises six indicators: GDP per capita, share of nonagricultural sectors in GDP, share of services in GDP, contribution of technical progress to GDP, share of trade to GDP, and degree of urbanization. The indicators are weighted, with economic development given the largest weight, at 28 points (out of 100), human capital given 17 points, quality of life 22 points, environmental protection 18 points, and key infrastructure 15 points. (There were other metrics, such as population control and stability, but fulfilling them did not necessarily lead to promotions. Failing to meet them could lead to demotion.)

It is likely that the system operates in a far more brute-force manner than portrayed here by Landry. Many of the component metrics are highly ambiguous. How does one accurately estimate the contribution of technical progress to GDP? What exactly is "technical progress"? Some of these indicators are correlated with each other, so assigning them separate weights makes little sense. Other indicators can work against each other. For example, given a particular state of technologies, GDP growth can degrade the natural environment.

The Department of Organization, however, is not giving a seminar on econometrics. The point of the metric management is to make it seem like the CCP's decision making about promotions is guided by objective metrics. I write "seem" because the metrics are clearly not as objective as they sound, and any metric-driven assessment is subject to manipulation and corruption. Academic research is also mixed on whether GDP truly explains the promotions of Chinese officials.[26]

But none of the CCP officials have read these academic studies. What matters is that the CCP explicitly laid out GDP as an evaluation metric. As in the case of *Keju*, the perception of objectivity is important, because perceived objectivity lends itself to an aura of legitimacy and to a shared sense that the system is not arbitrary. Under a one-party system, this is an extraordinarily valuable function because the system does not have many ways to generate legitimacy.

Running China on a GDP metric produces massive pathologies. Environmental protection was given 18 points, but that is hardly evident in China's environmental performance. China has suffered from many years of "air apocalypse" and 1.25 years have been shed off the population's average life expectancy.[27] There is also corruption, both financial and statistical. Yet in a variation of Churchill's famous quip about democracy, we might say that GDP is the worst metric except for all its alternatives. A top-down system is compelled to come up with a metric. During the Cultural Revolution, China defined class struggles as its metric and increasingly under Xi Jinping, it is personal allegiance to him. You can take your pick, but in my opinion, GDP is clearly superior to these unsavory alternatives.

The GDP metric ties the autonomous regions together in a standardized way that is reminiscent of the eight-legged essays of *Keju*. It orients the CCP toward a more productive, objective function and away from the destructive ones it has pursued before. GDP is more grounded to reality (even though its statistics can be manipulated), and it is less subjective than other unappetizing goals of the CCP, such as personality cult, class struggles, and political purges. It is more encompassing than the performance on the *Keju* exam, yet it is not so broad and amorphous that implementing it is meaningless. An autocracy lacks a way to aggregate preferences of its citizens and in that context, the GDP metric aligns the interests of society with those of the autocracy better than any other customary metrics of the CCP.

## The Organizational Economics of the CCP

On November 15, 1979, an oil rig capsized during a storm in the Bohai Sea, off the east coast of China. Seventy-two lives were lost.[28] Song Zhenming, the minister of the petroleum industry, was held responsible for the incident and was sacked. His replacement was Kang Shien, another oil man and Song's predecessor at the ministry. In 2011, Liu Zhijun, minister of railways, was dismissed on charges of corruption. Liu was replaced by Sheng Guangzu, director of the General Administration of Customs. Sheng, a 1974 graduate of Shanghai Institute of Railways, was a veteran in the Chinese railway system and was its vice minister until 2000.

In 1987, a corruption scandal led to Ni Xiance's removal as governor of Jiangxi province. His successor was Wu Guanzheng, who had been the mayor of Wuhan of Hubei province. In 2006, a corruption charge sank Chen Liangyu, the party chief of Shanghai. An outsider was called in: Xi Jinping, party secretary of Zhejiang province. Both Wu Guanzheng and Xi Jinping then rose rapidly in national politics. From 2002 to 2007, Wu was a member of the PBSC, making him one of the most powerful leaders in the country. Xi, of course, is China's paramount leader today, probably the only leader who matters.

What explains the replacement by an insider at a ministerial post and the replacement by an outsider at a provincial post after similar ignominious fates of their predecessors? Is it purely a coincidence that provincial leaders such as Wu Guanzheng and Xi Jinping ascended to the apex of Chinese politics, whereas ministerial officials such as Kang Shien and Sheng Guangzu languished in historical obscurity? And with so much autonomy and decision rights, why have the Chinese regions not gone "rogue?" How does the CCP maintain autonomy and control at the same time? A partial answer lies in the fact that so many regional leaders get to rule China.

## An Organizational Economics Perspective

A successful organization must maintain a balance between control and autonomy. The M-form economy supports the autonomy side of the equation in China. Let me use insights from organizational economics to analyze the control side of the CCP.

Organizational economists study activities that take place within organizations (as opposed to exchanges that occur across organizations).[29] They often start with a list of control problems in an organization. A control problem is a situation in which the subordinates of an organization behave in ways that are inconsistent with the interests of the organization as a whole. For example, as Michael Jensen and William Meckling explain:

> If both parties to the relationship are utility maximizers, there is good reason to believe that the agent will not always act in the best interests of the principal. The principal can limit divergences

from his interest by establishing appropriate incentives for the agent and by incurring monitoring costs designed to limit the aberrant activities of the agent. . . . However, it is generally impossible for the principal or the agent at zero cost to ensure that the agent will make optimal decisions from the principal's viewpoint.[30]

Control problems arise when there is an "information asymmetry" between the owner and managers. Managers, in general, have superior information about the tasks assigned to them, either because they have expertise in the associated technical details or because of their proximity to the tasks at hand. Because of this informational advantage, they may be prone to behave opportunistically. They may maximize their own interests, whether by consuming excess leisure or by engaging in non-pecuniary consumption, at the expense of shareholders' interests. And they may try to avoid uncertain, albeit potentially profitable, ventures because they are unwilling to sacrifice their leisure, time, and effort.

Organizational economics prescribes a number of solutions to these control problems. One is direct supervision and performance evaluations that are designed to reward or punish specified behavior. If a manager consumes excess non-pecuniary benefits, he can be demoted, or his compensation can be reduced.

Direct controls presume an ability to specify all future contingencies, a difficult task in complex organizations. An example from Soviet planning practices describes this problem vividly, as told by Nove:

Long ago Krokodil published a cartoon showing an enormous nail hanging in a large workshop: "the month's plan fulfilled," said the director, pointing to the nail. In tons, of course. It is notorious that Soviet sheet steel has been heavy and thick, for this sort of reason. Sheet glass was too heavy when it was planned in tons, and paper too thick.[31]

Organizational economists propose processes and compensation packages to minimize these control problems. Two of these—promotions and stock options—are all about incentive alignment. Career pathways are a form of "implicit incentives" and they can be designed to induce employees' efforts and contributions.[32] One practice observed is to restrict the number of entry-level hires to a low level relative to what can be justified by objective business needs. This creates some tautness in the supply of candidates for upper-level positions and so adds a reasonable expectation of promotion for current employees, who are more inclined to stay and work hard. In this framework, promotion is more than rewarding "the right performance" ex post; it is also used to align incentives ex ante.

Stock options also align incentives. Executive managers are often given stock options—the right to own stocks during a stated period with attached conditions—as a non-trivial portion of their total compensation. This encourages managers to take risks, since their future stock profits will depend on their undertaking those risk-taking activities that increase the overall value of the firm.

## Incentive Alignment in the Chinese System

A key insight from organizational economics is that incentive alignment is particularly relevant when direct monitoring and controls are problematic. Let me apply this reasoning to the CCP system, in particular to explain why the regions rule.[33]

China scholars distinguish between two kinds of officials in the Chinese system: generalists and specialists.[34] Territorial officials are generalists. Their portfolios cover a wide range of tasks—industry, agriculture, education, and so on. Ministerial officials, by contrast, are specialists who perform dedicated tasks in one sector. An electronics minister, for example, runs the electronics industry; a foreign minister handles China's relations with the world. This is all relative, of course, but it is true in an overall sense.

Both ministerial and territorial officials are "agents" in the sense employed by the organizational economists. They are hired managers serving at the behest of their principals—the general secretary of the CCP, members of the Politburo, and the premier of the State Council. And because they are agents, they are prone to the kinds of agency problems that organizational economics warns against.

A non-technical expression of the agency problem in the Chinese context is "The mountain is high and the emperor is far away." For ministerial officials working in Beijing, the mountain is not that high, and the emperor is right in your face. For them, as specialists, the monitoring costs are lower and direct controls are feasible, such as through the issuance of instructions, the evaluation of job performance, or demotions in the case of significant performance failures. Contingencies are also easier to specify within a single sector than across multiple sectors. This may explain why not many ministerial officials rise to the top. A promotional incentive is less necessary to induce desired behavior.

Provincial officials, the generalists, require more in the way of incentive alignment. Imagine yourself as a provincial official, with a high mountain separating you from a far-away emperor. The temptation to engage in self-serving activities at the expense of the central government is strong. The temptation that pulls you away in the other direction is a reasonable expectation of being promoted to the Center and the knowledge that this option is not always snatched up by those in the proximity of the central decision makers—that is, the ministerial officials working in Beijing.

As is often the case, the real world is more complicated. For example, perhaps we are observing an assignment effect. Imagine that, for whatever reason, you are being considered for a top position in the central government. The compelling factor could be your princeling background, as in the case of Xi Jinping. Or it could be a connection with the Youth League faction, as in the case of Li Keqiang. Then you are assigned to the provinces to be groomed for a central leadership position. But the mystery does not go away. The question is, "Why does this assignment effect work so often through a provincial channel rather than through a ministerial channel?" We are trying to explain why regional officials as a whole are more likely to make it to the top than ministerial officials as a whole, not why particular individuals, such as Xi Jinping or Li Keqiang, made it.

Another incentive alignment tool is a stock option. Government officials cannot be issued stock options, such as a share of the fruits of GDP growth. At least, no government official I know of has done this openly and legally. But the underlying idea behind stock options—to convert an agent into a principal—can be applied to the CCP situation. Within the current Politburo, which has twenty-four members, there are two hierarchical tiers. The PBSC, with its seven members, represents the apex of the Chinese political system and it acts like an executive committee in a company management structure. The PBSC has responsibility for day-to-day operations and has the right to make all final decisions. The non-executive members serve more as a pipeline to the next term of the PBSC rather than as decision makers themselves. (Bo Xilai was a non-executive member of the Politburo.)

Of the eighteen non-executive members of the Politburo of the Nineteenth Central Committee, six were serving concurrently as provincial party secretaries. This number has increased to eight on the new

Politburo elected by the Twentieth Party Congress in October 2022. The non-executive seat is like a political stock option. It gives these provincial officials a status of a partial political principal and aligns them with the policy preferences of the PBSC, but without granting them the same decision-making rights as the PBSC members. As other scholars and I have found, provincial officials with a status of a partial principal are the most observant of central policy edicts to curb inflationary investment activities.[35]

We can think of this arrangement as a solution to the agency problems in three ways. First, the provincial officials on the Politburo are given some of the political residual rights, so to speak, so they will calculate that their long-term career prospects lie with the Center, not just with their respective provinces. Second, this is a bundling arrangement—one pursues one's own interests along with the interests of the entire political system. And third, the costs of noncompliance increase as participants' actions become more observable to the PBSC members. A non-executive seat on the Politburo brings the emperor a little closer to the province.

Of the seventeen non-executive members on the current Politburo, there are four individuals who serve concurrently in a ministerial capacity, compared with eight provincial leaders. This pattern holds true historically. Data from the 1980s and the first half of the 1990s show that provincial party secretaries were between two and five times more likely as ministers to simultaneously serve as non-executive members of the Politburo. If anything, this disparity has only grown over time. There were more ministers on the Politburo of the Thirteenth Central Committee (1987–1992) than on the Politburo of the Nineteenth Central Committee (2017–2022).

## *Control Instruments*

If regional agency problems are more severe than ministerial agency problems, more attention is required to ensure the incentive alignment of regional officials, including greater promotional odds and greater availability of seats on the Politburo. Managing regional agency problems necessitates more frequent applications of control instruments on regional officials. Going back to imperial times, the Chinese system has developed a suite of time-tested control instruments, some of which the CCP has adopted and adapted.

The rule of avoidance, for example, was created by the Han dynasty to prohibit magistrates from being appointed to their places of birth.[36]

Over time, this rule was extended to the relatives of central court officials, who were banned from serving in regions closest to the capital in order to deter their collusion with local officials. During the Qing dynasty, possibly because of schisms between the Manchus and the Chinese, concerns escalated and the prohibitions were extended: fathers, uncles, brothers, grandparents, nephews, cousins, and in-laws of court officials were not allowed to serve in the court.[37] Confucianism is hailed as pro-family, but its political implementation is fiercely anti-family.

According to the logic of organizational economics, these control instruments should be applied more frequently to regional officials than ministerial officials. This does appear to be the case. In a study published in 2002, I examined several dimensions of personnel management based on the appointments and promotions of Chinese bureaucrats during the first forty-five years of the PRC.[38] I found that provincial officials indeed had shorter tenures than ministerial officials, and that the tenures of both provincial and ministerial officials declined during the reform era (which was defined for that study as 1977–1995) compared with the era of Mao Zedong (1949–1976). (My calculation excludes periods of unusual political events, such as the Cultural Revolution when almost all the officials were purged.)[39] On average, before 1977, ministers served 23 percent longer than provincial party secretaries and 19 percent longer than provincial governors, while after 1977, these two figures are 10 percent and 16 percent, respectively. A comparison of the same periods shows that the average duration of tenure declined by more than 30 percent for both ministerial and provincial officials, including among lower-level officials. The declines have continued. In 1990, for example, Chinese mayors averaged about three years in office; by 2001 they averaged only 2.5 years.[40]

We can use organizational economics to explain these patterns. Each appointment decision is an intensive process that requires soliciting and collating information and peer opinions and performing due diligence on a candidate. The central Department of Organization runs the appointment and promotion process for the ministerial and provincial-level cadres. A higher frequency of appointment decisions on provincial officials indicates more intensive vetting on provincial officials. At a minimum, the centralized appointment procedure filters out undesirable candidates.[41]

The same logic explains the across-the-board shortening of tenures over time. The policy agendas of Mao Zedong and Zhou Enlai were simple and straightforward: there was no competition for fiscal resources and foreign capital, and there were no debates over the direction of reforms, priorities of industrial policy, trade wars, and making concessions for the World Trade Organization. During the reform era, by contrast, the scope conditions have expanded, while the homogenizing effect of ideology has weakened, all of which has escalated tensions within the Chinese political system. A rational autocrat needs an additional tool to resolve these conflicts. Personnel management is such a tool.

Another approach, also inherited from imperial times, is to rotate officials among agencies and across regions. Take Li Keqiang, for example. He was the party secretary of Henan between 2002 and 2004, then was sent to Liaoning to serve as the party secretary there. A rotated official is not allowed to bring his entourage to his new position; instead, he must build his new political base from scratch.

Rotation deters network ties that might compete with the CCP's formal command structure. The Chinese system of both dynastic and CCP eras has invested heavily in the vertical portals of power and information flows and it has actively curbed horizontal ties and the exchange of resources. Network ties are derided as "factionalism," a serious offense in the CCP rulebook. In 1982, Chen Yun, who ran the personnel affairs of the CCP in the 1940s and who helped shape the personnel norms, commented: "The rotation system is good. It is not good to have an official work in a locality for a long period of time because it gives rise to factionalism."[42] We can think of rotation as a super control instrument. It achieves the regulation effect of a regular appointment decision but it also uproots an official's accumulated network ties and political base.

Factionalism is an agency problem, and a method designed to deter factionalism should be applied more aggressively to regional officials than to ministerial officials. Evidence bears this out. Of the seventy provincial party secretaries appointed between 1985 and 1995, eleven of them, 15.7 percent of the total, had served as party secretaries or governors in other provinces immediately before assuming their rotated posts. For governors, the percentage is lower, around 6.5 percent.

By contrast, rotations are seldom applied to ministerial appointments. Of the sixty-five new appointments between 1984 and 1995, only one minister, the governor of the People's Bank of China, had come directly from another ministry.[43] Recall Song Zhenming and Liu Zhijun, two ministers who were removed on charges of dereliction of duty and corruption. Both were replaced by ministerial insiders, in contrast to the two disgraced provincial officials who were replaced by officials parachuted in from the outside. This insider control of the ministries fits with a broader pattern I have portrayed here, of less frequent turnovers and rotations of ministerial officials as compared with provincial officials. If we add to this pattern the fact that provincial officials are more likely than ministerial officials to rise through the ranks and rule China, and that they do so in the context of an M-form economy, a plausible narrative emerges for how the CCP meritocracy both empowers and curbs regional power.

===

The CCP system of the reform era is more ingenious than many of us have given it credit for. It is systematic and attentive to incentives. It benefits from the historical legacy of *Keju*, but it has also modernized many features inherited from the imperial past. There is, however, a critical prerequisite—the autocrat in power has to be on board with it.

Autocrats come and autocrats go. The M-form economy is not legislated; it is delegated, and different autocrats have different views on the wisdom of that delegation. Deng Xiaoping sanctioned the M-form approach, but Xi Jinping has sharply curtailed the incentive and autonomy aspects of the CCP meritocracy. He has redefined "merit" toward politics at the expense of economics. Autocratic meritocracy is inherently fragile. How "merit" is defined and constituted in that system is subject to the wisdom of the wise autocrats as well as to the whims of the whimsical autocrats. In Chapter 9, we will take a detailed look of how Xi has upended Deng's innovative meritocracy—with grave consequences for the Chinese economy and politics.

PART II

# Autocracy

CHAPTER THREE

# A State without a Society

If this salary formula [in favor of civil servants] can draw out
higher-quality men into politics, whatever their motivations,
I say, let us have them. It is better than the Opposition we
now have.

—LEE KUAN YEW, former prime minister of Singapore

IN THE SUMMER OF 1582, the Ming had reason to celebrate: their emperor,
Wanli, had become a father to a son, Changluo. In keeping with Confucian tradition, it was expected that Changluo would be anointed the crown
prince.[1] But years passed and Wanli kept postponing the anointment decision. It turns out that he had another idea. He wanted to anoint his third
son, Changxun, rather than Changluo. Changxun was the son of Lady
Zheng, an imperial concubine and the love of Wanli's life. It was a desire
from his heart.

Wanli's wish ran into anxious and determined opposition from the
Confucian Mandarins. Skipping the first-born son was a blatant violation
of the rule of primogeniture. It was against the basic tenets of the morality
proclaimed in the *Four Books*, which state that the old should command and
lead the young.[2] One after the other, the Confucian bureaucrats pushed
Wanli to anoint Changluo, but in that system bureaucrats proposed and
the emperor disposed. First a grand secretary, one of the highest officials

in the court, Shen Shixing, spoke up, but Wanli ignored him. Then two officials from the Ministry of Personnel each submitted investiture petitions. Wanli reacted by demoting both. The pleading continued. One official from the Ministry of Rites even filed a formal remonstration that accused the emperor of being negligent of his duty as the Son of the Heaven. In return, he earned sixty lashes.

The weight of morality and precedent was clearly on the side of the Confucian bureaucrats, and the best Wanli could do was to procrastinate. He first ordered the Confucian officials to shut up. Failing that, he resorted to delay tactics. He promised to install his eldest son a few years down the road but only if no one would again bring up the subject. He kicked the can down the road to the Confucian Mandarins and decreed that all petitions be reviewed by them without his involvement, thus all but guaranteeing a non-decision.

In the end, after a stalemate that dragged out for more than ten years, Wanli caved in 1601 and installed Changluo as the crown prince. By then, however, he was spent and thoroughly defeated. He sequestered himself in his royal quarters, suspending all his sessions with court officials and refusing to discharge one of his most solemn responsibilities—reviewing and approving personnel decisions. Eventually, he simply stopped ruling.

There are many morals from this tale. One is about the power that the Confucian Mandarins wielded in imperial China. The Confucian Mandarins, also known as scholar-officials, were the pride of *Keju*. They had aced the *Keju* exams in their respective *Jinshi* cohorts. They were steeped in Confucian principles and were considered the guardians of the purity of Confucian morality and immortality.

These scholar-officials got swept up in the succession affair because they had been entrusted with imparting Confucian values to the next emperor, and they wanted to begin tutoring the crown prince as early as possible, while he was most impressionable. Imperial protocol dictated that only the crown prince, not any son of the emperor, was entitled to tutorship from the most erudite Confucian scholars, the academicians at the Hanlin Academy. The Confucian Mandarins were justifiably concerned that a delay in the timing of the anointment would cause the future emperor to be insufficiently schooled in Confucian ideology and nomenclature.

Perhaps more important, the Confucian Mandarins wielded this power because they could. Wanli's personality has been described as "feminine and irresolute." By contrast, the founding emperor of the Ming, Zhu Yuanzhang, who killed some one hundred thousand bureaucrats and their associates, had blithely ignored the principle of seniority and anointed his grandson, Zhu Yunwen, as heir apparent, skipping not one or two of his sons but thirty-five of them! The Confucian morality crumbled in front of the muscle power of Zhu Yuanzhang, as did the lives of many Confucianists themselves.

Notice the dyadic nature of this Wanli affair. All the interlocutions took place between the emperor and his scholar-officials. No priests weighed in to offer a celestial perspective. Nor did any parliamentarians intervene to check if the right process was followed. Lady Zheng stayed silent and so did the empress. The Confucian Mandarins raised one issue, and one issue alone, that of male primogeniture, and the issue did not garner a spirited pushback and a contrary doctrine either from Wanli himself or from his other advisers. That Changxun was not born within the formal wedlock of Wanli did not raise any eyebrows. The name of the game in this episode is simplicity.

Contrast this to the royal succession intrigue that had taken place about seventy years earlier, on the other side of the globe, when Henry VIII of Tudor England wanted to marry Anne Boleyn and install their future child as the heir apparent. Anne was intelligent, and, according to some, scheming and calculating. She mastered French to gain access to the royal household, then she managed to get herself appointed as a lady-in-waiting to the queen. She charmed Henry VIII with her good looks, her poetry, and her romantic tactics.

But Catherine of Aragon, the lawful wife of Henry VIII, stood in the way of the budding romance—and a marriage could be annulled only by someone over whom Henry VIII had no control—the pope. For five years, the pope refused to grant an annulment. Then, in 1532, Anne Boleyn became pregnant, but the child could only be the heir if Anne were to be made a queen before the birth. Henry VIII had to act fast, and act he did. He launched an anti-pope campaign; then, through a series of Parliamentary acts, severed England's ties to the Catholic Church. In 1533, Thomas Cranmer, the Archbishop of Canterbury, nullified Henry VIII's marriage to Catherine of Aragon. Henry VIII married Anne Boleyn that same year.

Although Henry VIII was a strong, even brutal king—one who ordered multiple executions of officials and his opponents, as well as Anne Boleyn—he was constrained by rules and traditions surrounding the British monarchy. Henry VIII had to seek permission to get a divorce, and the pope had the authority to deny that divorce. There were other obstacles. There was a Parliament to deal with, pressure by the supporters of

Catherine of Aragon, and an established standard to judge which sons were "legitimate" and eligible to succeed him. Viewed from Wanli's vantage point, all of this was maddening, bewildering, complex, and inconvenient.

The tale of these two monarchs is that long before the advent of political modernity, China and England differed fundamentally in their politics and institutional configurations. The two sovereigns, Wanli and Henry VIII, both engaged in a prolonged clash over affairs of the heart and of succession. The manner of their clashes, the nature of their interlocutions, and the eventual resolutions speak volumes about the differences in the institutional milieus within which these two rulers operated. The fundamental difference, I will argue, is that Wanli ruled over an organization, whereas Henry VIII presided over a polity.

That difference cast a long shadow over the political trajectories of these two countries. The world of Wanli is a state without politics and a nation without a civil society. The imperial autocracy of Ming was "simpler," not in the sense that it was primitive, but in the sense that authority was hierarchically arrayed; fewer norms and rules complicated and constrained decision making, and the power was undifferentiated. The world of Henry VIII was vastly more complex, more open-ended, more argumentative, and more uncertain. Democracy and rule of law emerged more naturally from the contentious and cavernous polity of Henry VIII rather than from the ordered hierarchical world of Wanli.

This is where the first and second letters of the EAST package are connected. *Keju* contributed to the organizational character of the autocracy of imperial China. Wanli's court was akin to a "private government," a concept proposed by Elizabeth Anderson, professor of philosophy at the University of Michigan. In this conception, hierarchy prevails and it prevails without rights, accountability, and recourse. *Keju* features in this development because it marginalized and preempted all the social and economic forces that could conceivably pose as competition to the state. First, there was a platform effect. *Keju*, simply speaking, was the most advanced and systematic channel of upward mobility. It had an unrivaled level of channel penetration. It was end-to-end, and it was extremely well organized. The evaluation metrics were clearly spelled out. The upside was enormous and visible. Put yourself in the shoes of an average Ming subject, thinking of either going into commerce, political opposition, or preparing for *Keju*. A rational person would choose the *Keju* route.

Second, it starved the beast in its infancy. Religion, political opposition, an independent intelligentsia, and commerce were outcompeted and outmanned. In premodern times, human capital was the only input for economic growth and the development of society. The imperial court monopolized the quality human capital generated by *Keju*. It could have even hoarded rather than fully utilized the talents in its possession. This is precisely the point—to deprive the opposing side of the talents. The political monopoly of human capital resolves a deep puzzle: why did the high literacy in imperial China not generate economic growth as it did in the West? The answer is that literacy was not deployed to deliver growth. It was used to augment autocracy and to shackle society.

There is what I call a "*Keju* puzzle." Evolutionary psychologist Joseph Henrich argues that literacy induced biological changes in European brains and seeded the takeoff of the West.[3] But although Chinese literacy was not insubstantial—at least among the males—*Keju* literacy gave rise to none of the modernizing effects Henrich identified. Why? Later I will go into some detail about the values associated with *Keju* literacy, which are fundamentally antithetical to democracy and individual agency.

Answering this *Keju* puzzle helps resolve the Weberian pessimism about East Asia. Max Weber asserted that Confucianist culture was incompatible with economic growth, a proposition we know to be flatly wrong. But maybe Weber is wrong factually but not analytically. The mistake by Weber is that he falsely believed that Protestantism monopolized work ethics. Any reader who finished Chapter 1 will no doubt agree with me that a lot of work was required to prepare for *Keju*. *Keju* incubated work ethics as well as the capabilities and brain changes that Henrich identified, but their broader economic activations require complementary conditions. Those conditions—enlightened leadership, economic competition, and entrepreneurship—arrived in East Asia after World War II and in China after 1978. Economies basking in the legacies of *Keju* then took off.

Before I tackle all these topics, let us return to the political system of Wanli.

## A Tale of Two Political Systems

On a historical scale, King Henry VIII of Tudor England and Emperor Wanli of Ming China were contemporaries. Henry VIII was born in 1491 and died in 1547. Wanli was born sixteen years later, in 1563. Notwithstanding their historical proximity, the two autocrats lived worlds apart in political terms. The imperial Chinese state arrayed authority relations vertically. There was a single hierarchy, with the emperor at the top. Constraints on the emperor's power, to the extent that they existed, were not formalized and rule-based. They were self-constraints, or they arose from rational calculations of the costs and benefits of observing them. Decision rights were undifferentiated ex ante. They could be differentiated ex post, by delegation, rather than by law and institutional design.

We can extend this organizational perspective downward to analyze the relations between the state and the subjects it governs. Dominance is the reigning principle in such an entity, either directly through an administrative apparatus, or indirectly, through obliging values and norms. We can express the same idea in the familiar social science language on state and society. In that literature, a premise is that society possesses a degree of autonomy from the state.

The strongest version of that idea is Joel Migdal's book *Strong Societies and Weak States*.[4] Migdal identifies a common problem in the developing world—the struggle of the state to emerge as an autonomous and capable entity. The private-government perspective, which I will introduce shortly, turns that view on its head and argues that the state towers over and dominates society. The imperial state, and the CCP today, is a private government writ large. The state is not shackled; society is.[5]

Who is shackling whom depends crucially on "who" came first. In the West, bureaucracy arose after an overall framework of political governance was in place and it was a dedicated technocratic tool to tackle policy problems and to implement domain-specific programs. In other words, bureaucracy arose to perform task-specific functions, such as fighting wars, collecting taxes, administering healthcare, and forest management. It was not meant to perform an overall governance function. That function is instead supplied by a panoply of institutions, ideas, and arrangements, such as a parliament, doctrine of rights, and separation of powers. Bureaucracy was a latecomer to that arrangement, and it was a part of it, but by no means all of it.[6]

In China, by contrast, the imperial bureaucracy arose when the society was embryonic, weak, and struggling. The scaling of *Keju* established the state's dominance over society, and the dominance was both administrative and notional. Historians pointed out that in imperial China, a powerful rural gentry often operated beyond the long arm of the state, and some imperial subjects manipulated government demands and gamed the system to pursue private interests.[7] All true, but notice an important function performed by rural gentry—collecting taxes on behalf of the state, known as tax farming. They were thus a substitute for and not a constraint on the state. And although some imperial subjects manipulated the system, they did so on terms dictated by the state, not by society.

The power of the state was—and is—paramount, and the Chinese system is a watertight system. A watertight system does not break easily. Autocracy has deep roots in China because of its near immaculate design, absence of civil society, and deep-seated values and norms. We can credit this situation to the ability of *Keju* to asphyxiate society. *Keju* anchored political China.

## A Private Government

In his book *The Idea of India*, Sunil Khilnani defines politics "as a necessarily undeterminable field of human agency, a space of constantly competitive, strategic and practical action, undertaken in conditions of imperfect and partial information."[8] Contrast this notion of politics with what Elizabeth Anderson calls "private government." She invites us to

> Imagine a government that assigns almost everyone a superior whom they must obey. Although superiors give most inferiors a routine to follow, there is no rule of law. Orders may be arbitrary and can change at any time, without prior notice or opportunity to appeal. Superiors are unaccountable to those they order around. They are neither elected nor removable by their inferiors. Inferiors have no right to complain in court about how they are being treated, except in a few narrowly defined cases. They also have no right to be consulted about the orders they are given.[9]

Actually, we do not have to imagine. Such a government exists, in China, and that government has existed for two millennia. All the relationships are hierarchical. There are routines, rather than interactions. There are orders, rather than consultations. There are commands to be obeyed, rather than a rule of law to be complied with. There are superiors, rather than equals. There are no rights and no recourse. Norms, in the sense of equal constraints on superiors and subordinates, are absent.

This private-government perspective captures some essential differences between Tudor England and Ming China. The Ming China of Wanli was a private government, whereas the Tudor England of Henry VIII was closer to a modern polity where there is some division of power and where subjects have a degree of autonomy and independence.

Henry VIII operated in a political world in the sense that Khilnani used. He contended with a multitude of actors, over whom he exercised no or limited authority. His actions were constrained by long-standing norms and rules beyond his control. His was also a world of indeterminacy, a more open-ended universe where the outcomes were negotiated and strived for rather than decreed and dictated. He had to contend with not just politics, but thick politics full of drama, surprises, and upsets. The world of Wanli was infinitely more straightforward, hierarchical, ordered, and close-ended. There was still politics in Wanli's court, but it was "corporate politics," fought under the table and often undertaken at great risk due to its lack of legitimacy. The politics was thin, devoid of argumentativeness, procedural maneuverings, and layers of decisions and appeals.

A small but significant detail: The romance between Henry VIII and Anne Boleyn was closer to a real love affair. She courted but also resisted the entreaties from Henry VIII. Anne had some decision rights, buttressed by her family prominence. Her father was ambassador to France. Catherine of Aragon was also not a detached bystander who simply accepted whatever fate fell her way. She came with her own political gravitas, as a Spanish royal. Her father was the king of Aragon, and she had backers in the court and in the region. She took action to thwart Henry VIII's plan. The subjects of Henry VIII had some agency, a voice, and a degree of operational autonomy from the king.

By contrast, Lady Zheng and the empress featured in the succession saga as props onstage rather than as actors. Other than her last name, we do not know much about Lady Zheng. Wanli just commanded her into a relationship. Their "love affair" involved Lady Zheng obeying an order as a subordinate to her boss. No scholar-official appeared to speak on her behalf. This voicelessness of imperial women was by design. Some dynasties even forbade recruiting women of royal backgrounds into the imperial household, thus ensuring a maximum power distance between the emperor and his consorts.

By decree, Henry VIII could not divorce Catherine on his own. He needed a permission slip from the pope. It would never cross Wanli's mind that outside intervention was required for his marriage—the concept of divorce probably did not even exist. To Wanli, spousal decisions were no different from promotions or demotions in a bureaucratic agency, a power he exercised when he elevated Lady Zheng to an imperial consort, a level below the empress. It was a personnel matter, a human resource decision.

A "virtue" of a hierarchical system is its simplicity—at least for the ruler. In Wanli's court, religion did not enter succession deliberations—he was unencumbered by any power dilution and by any religious rules or norms. As a Catholic, Henry VIII was subordinate to the pope just like a commoner was. Even in this pre-modern age, decision rights were already differentiated, and the differentiation was codified. It was also a source of contention. Henry VIII and the pope clashed because the religious affair of marriage and divorce and the political affairs of the state intersected.

There were restrictive rules and norms, but some decisions in the Tudor court were more open-ended than others. In the Tudor court, both female and male lines of succession were permissible, making room for debates, disagreements, discretion, and decisions. Mary, the daughter of Henry VIII and Catherine of Aragon, was eligible to succeed Henry VIII—an idea promoted by supporters of Catherine of Aragon. The complicated norms and rules led to tortured and hair-splitting argumentation. Henry VIII sought to annul his marriage—and make Mary ineligible for the crown—on the grounds that he was never married to Catherine of Aragon in the first place, since she was his late brother's wife.

## Simplicity vis-à-vis Complexity

Henry VIII's contrived argument is a reminder of the complexities of the Tudor court. His marriage to Catherine of Aragon stemmed in part from political expediency—a desire to maintain an alliance with Spain. A dispensation from the pope was needed to authorize the marriage, since marrying your brother's wife was considered problematic. There were also disputations about what did and what did not constitute "legitimacy." Henry VIII wanted a male offspring with Anne to be his heir, but he already had a son, Henry Fitzroy, who was ineligible for the throne because he was the fruit of an affair with a mistress.

In Wanli's court, all of this intrigue and all of these debates would have been inconceivable. Wanli's court was governed by routines, not by complicated and ambiguous norms. The rule of primogeniture simplified and overrode everything. No one cared if the successor was or was not a product of a legal marriage. (Wanli himself was an offspring of a concubine.) There were only two items on the checklist: firstborn and a son. Birth order of the right sex ruled.

As Francis Fukuyama notes, the "assertion of Frederic Maitland that no English king ever believed that he was above the law could not be said of any Chinese emperor, who recognized no law other than those he himself made."[10] This is true, but before we get to the question of rule of law—and of democracy, there is a question about the texture of the British and the Chinese systems. Henry VIII's world was an order of magnitude more complex than the world of Wanli. It was simultaneously more open-ended and more restrictive. More norms and more rules. More decisions and more debates. More disagreements and more decision makers. Henry VIII was a participant, as a first among equals to be sure, but not as an absolutist compared with a Chinese emperor. He had to "campaign" a little bit and to line up his supporters.

Existence of norms is another source of complexity. On an issue of central importance to a human society, unlike in England and many other countries, when it came to marriage and divorce, imperial China developed remarkably few norms.[11] In imperial China, for example, cousins were allowed to marry.[12] (Not until 1981 was this practice banned.) The exception was a marriage between patrilateral parallel cousins, that is, the children of two male siblings. Children of the male siblings shared the same family name, so such marriages were seen as the same as those between siblings, which were considered problematic. (This is a strange view on genetics, but one reason could be that children of two female siblings typically lived apart from each other, reducing risks of consanguine marriages of their children.) Polygyny was widespread, and one-third of elite families in the Song dynasty had concubines.[13] Deciding to have a concubine was a matter of capacity to pay; it was not a matter of morals and morality.

Imperial China is said to have had liberal marital norms, whereas Europe had restrictive norms.[14] I think it is more accurate to say that China did not have many norms. Period. And this normlessness came with political implications. One is that loose ideas about marriage improved the odds of the rich to have offspring. As the nominal owner of the entire empire, the emperor had the greatest capacity to pay, and he was assured of having at least one male heir, reducing the probability of a succession vacuum. According to Yuhua Wang, Chinese emperors averaged 7.57 spouses, 6.97 sons, and 3.12 daughters. In one case, Emperor Huizong of the Song had 148 partners, and another emperor, Xuan of the Chen (530–582), had 42 sons. During the imperial era, 58 percent of the emperors were succeeded by the sons of their wives, and 42 percent of the emperors were succeeded by the sons of their concubines. The legitimacy issue of Henry Fitzroy never arose. Children of the concubines had the same theoretical inheritance status as the children of wives, a legacy that still plagues divorce cases in China today.

The other political consequence is that Chinese emperors gained unbounded power. Of the two rulers, Henry VIII was more forceful. He ordered executions, even of his beloved Anne, and took decisive actions, whereas Wanli just faded away. But if norms constrain both the powerful and the powerless, the lack of norms conferred power on the Chinese emperors. Wanli possessed more nominal power than Henry VIII. Similarly, today Xi Jinping is more powerful than the world's theocrats, who still must answer to their religions.

Henry VIII's world was the kind of politics that Khilnani had in mind. It was a world in which actors of more or less equal power accept each other as they are, and they hammer out their disagreements by haggling, persuading, scheming, or arguing. The world of Henry VIII comprised several equal, independent, and sometimes overlapping hierarchies, including the royal court, the church, the aristocracy, and others. Rules and norms bind the interactions among these hierarchical pyramids.

In the end, Henry VIII resolved the situation by moving England closer to a hierarchical organization. He pulled a Brexit of his era by severing England's ties to the Catholic Church. As historian J. J. Scarisbrick comments in his book *Henry VIII*, he "defied pope and emperor, brought into being in England and Ireland a national Church subject to his authority, wiped about a thousand religious houses off the face of his native land and of those areas of Ireland under his influence, and bestowed on English kingship a profound new dignity."[15] England, however, never rid itself of its other power pyramids, such as Parliament, organized merchant guilds, and independent academia. England is the way it is today because Henry VIII did not, or could not, transform the English polity into a private government.

## A Shackled Society

When I use the term "society," I do not just mean actors and entities that exist outside of the state. Private property, households, and individuals have always existed unattached to the state apparatus, including in totalitarian societies. By society, I mean organized society, with independent hierarchies such as organized religions, autonomous universities, and others that compete with and constrain the state. It is not merely a matter of resources. Even a non-state organization that commands enormous resources and visibility is not guaranteed to be a part of organized society. (If you doubt this, just ask Jack Ma.) A shackled society lacks the legitimacy, status, or wherewithal to challenge the state.

Chinese society is not just weak; it is congenitally weak. It barely exists as even a *notionally* separate and parallel identity to the state. There is no room for society in a private government like China's. Economist Tyler Cowen criticized Anderson's private-government thesis for not recognizing a crucial difference between a government and a company: a company does not exercise the monopoly of power naturally exercised by a government. Companies, for example, compete with each other in the labor market. If one company has a dress code you do not like, you can always decide to work elsewhere. The validity of Cowen's critique depends on the existence of society. What if there is only one company and employees cannot reject its dress code? This is the state without society, the CCP, and China's imperial state from time immemorial.

We saw how the Catholic Church constrained Henry VIII. China, however, never had an organized religion on a scale remotely comparable to that of the Catholic Church. By the early Tang, Buddhist monks, however famous, had to worship the emperor on bended knee. And after the Qin and Han dynasties, emperors supplanted the deity, becoming the "heavenly gods."[16] After the Tang dynasty, Confucianism began to eclipse other ideologies in China, as measured by references to ideologies in official documents.[17]

Another missing civil society actor is intelligentsia—those intellectuals with a separate identity from the state. In the eighteenth century, China had a higher rate of basic numeracy than Tsarist Russia (see Table 3.1), yet it had nothing like Russia's strong tradition of intelligentsia. (The concept of intelligentsia originated from Russia.) Without an intelligentsia, ideas and values that could have dented the ideological monopoly of Confucianism never took root in China. For although imperial China had no shortage of splendid writers, poets, and technologists, they acted in their own capacity. High literacy, numeracy, and vibrant book readership did not launch any Chinese equivalents of the Royal Society of Great Britain or the many learned societies in France. To be a scholar-official was to be more of an official than a scholar.[18]

One institution that left a modest mark is Donglin Academy, a private discussion forum founded in 1111 by Song dynasty intellectuals. The academy languished into obscurity soon after its founders died, a clear sign that it lacked institutional vitality. In 1594, during the Wanli era, the Donglin Academy was revived, but instead of operating it as an academy, the scholar-officials forayed into imperial court politics. They formed a "Donglin faction" that was later brutally put down by the powerful eunuchs of the Ming court, a victim of the perennial power struggles between Confucianists and the eunuchs, who at that moment felt empowered by Wanli's retreat. The second life of the Donglin Academy lasted just thirty-one years, from 1594 to 1625.

## Vertical versus Horizontal Capitalism

The bourgeoisie class is another conspicuous lacuna in Chinese society. Merchants never acquired an identity as a social group, but not because of a shortage of commercial flourishing. During the Song, a vibrant market economy emerged. The state and merchants forged a symbiotic relationship whereby the state benefited by taxing, rather than suppressing, the merchants.[19] The Ming and Qing dynasties should have been heavenly for business development. The Ming and Qing closed China off to foreign trade, creating a protected domestic market. They also loosened controls on businesses. Carpenters, masons, weavers, and potters were allowed to buy themselves out of servitude and become free agents. Taxes were paid in money rather than in kind, freeing up farmers to grow cash crops.[20]

But the state was always wary of the disruptive effects of commerce. Frederic Wakeman noted that as early as during the period of Confucius (551–479 BCE), commerce began to challenge the cherished aristocratic order, and "classical Confucianism scorned businessmen precisely because commerce had played such an important part in Chinese history." Confucius thus conceived of a social pecking order that subordinated business. Successive imperial regimes, as well as today's CCP, have resorted to a version of this social pecking order when they want to denigrate business.

The anti-business stance gave rise to a particular kind of capitalism—what I call "vertical capitalism." It is a capitalism enmeshed with the state, in two formats. One is state capitalism, which involves state ownership and operation. The other is crony capitalism, which entails an alliance between the state and business. The contrast is a horizontal kind of capitalism. Horizontal capitalism thrives by collaborations between business interests and does so through a variety of mechanisms, such as partnerships (rather than single ventures), share capital (rather than proprietor capital), associations (rather than single deals), contractual obligations (rather than cash), and equity (rather than credit). With modifications of details and adjusted for scale, vertical capitalism still holds true in China today.

As Raghuram Rajan and Luigi Zingales observe, pro-business is not the same as pro-market.[21] The Song dynasty was pro-business, but it imposed stringent size and sectoral restrictions on private businesses. Emperor Taizu of the Song sentenced to death any merchant who transported or manufactured products beyond a certain amount or scale determined by the state.[22] The commanding heights were the prerogative of the state. Private capital was allowed only in low-margin sectors such as sewing, clothing, meat, and children's toys.

Crony capitalism thrived. As Han-Sheng Chuan has documented from Song dynasty documents, court officials actively ventured into the business realm. They would use the power of their position to invest public funds as capital, appropriate state-owned commodities or raw materials, use official ships for private trafficking, deploy government labor, use state power to trade or monopolize, and evade taxes. Merchants also got involved in government. One widespread practice during the Qing was venality—sales of government offices. The state obtained revenue from this practice, whereas the wealthy merchants gained access to business opportunities controlled by the state.

But there was more. In an autocracy, officials enjoy more security than commoners. Venality thus provided security of property to the venal merchants and reduced state predations. The solution was individual-specific, even deal-specific. It conferred not "rights"—granted to all—but privileges available only to the few highest bidders. It protected but also excluded, and the venal merchants were held at the mercy of the goodwill of the state. Vertical capitalism is dependent capitalism, not arm's-length capitalism, as generations of autocrats have preferred it.

## A Birth Order Effect

One of my favorite TV shows is *Yes Minister*, and its sequel, *Yes, Prime Minister*. From my own political upbringing in China, I thought the show would be about politicians commanding obedience and sycophancy from bureaucrats. It is anything but. The permanent and private secretaries frustrate and obfuscate the agenda of the British politicians all the time, and dominate them intellectually. They show off their OxBridge pedigrees, snickering about the LSE education of their politicians. They burst into long, complicated, and coded sentences peppered liberally with quotes from Homer and other Greek classics. They periodically plunge into long orations, in Latin, no less.

Bureaucracy in a Western democracy is a nested institution. It is a vitally important part of the political system, with components that are sometimes in tension with each other and sometimes collaborative. Despite the claim of a "deep state," Western bureaucracy is not an all-encompassing organization single-handedly carrying out its own agenda. Nor does it blindly enforce the ideas of the ruler of the country. It is a contending force in a setting of political, social, and ideological pluralities. Recall the comment by the Chinese official that the West "stole" meritocracy from China. If so, it was a piecemeal and tailored theft rather than a wholesale transplant.

The phrase "laissez faire" is reputedly Chinese in origin. François Quesnay, an eighteenth-century French economist of the Physiocratic school, invented the term. An admirer of the *Keju* system, Quesnay believed that Chinese emperors conferred maximum autonomy and freedom on scholar-officials, who attained their positions due to merit, not the blessings of the emperors. The meritocrats were left alone to run the state and the economy. Hence "laissez faire."[23]

This particular attribution may or may not be true; what is true is that *Keju* enjoyed a substantial following among Western enlightenment thinkers, including Montesquieu, Rousseau, and Voltaire. *Keju* exerted a powerful influence on the state of Prussia, the first European state to establish a modern bureaucracy, under King Frederick William (1620–1688). According to Fukuyama, Frederick William inherited a patrimonial arrangement.[24] He had to share power with the estates and those representing "the landed nobility who were effectively sovereign on their own lands and needed to be consulted in matters of war and taxation." But Frederick William wanted to centralize power. He maintained a standing army, whereas the prevailing practice at that time was to disband the army during peacetime. To fund this standing army, he centralized state finances by taking over the fiscal powers of the estates and disbanding the independent militias. A powerful bureaucracy was created to host all these powers. There was a civilian bureaucracy and there was a military bureaucracy.

There was a Chinese connection to these modern political reforms in Prussia.[25] Frederick William was an avid student of China. He collected many books in Chinese, and he patronized the "China specialists" of Prussia, hoping to establish direct relations with China. When his professionalization of the Prussian state created a demand for new personnel recruitment, he held the first written civil service examination in Europe, in 1693. His son, Frederick the Great, was less enamored of China, although his close advisers were. One of these advisers was Gottfried Wihelm Leibniz, a co-inventor of calculus, as well as a philosopher and technological enthusiast. In a 1697 publication, Liebniz refers to *Keju* as "'the mandarins' examinations on the basis of which distinctions and magistracies are granted.'"[26] Privy Councilor Samuel von Pufendorf was also a fan of *Keju*, stating:

> Yet in some states little heed is given to birth, and every man's nobility is derived from his own virtue, and what he has done for the state in private and public capacity. . . . This nation accords no nobility to mere family lineage. . . . Now such customs may be abhorrent to ours, and yet wise men teach that nobles should not depend on lineage alone, but much more upon virtue.[27]

In this respect, the West emulated China, not the other way around. More specifically, Prussia emulated China, Britain emulated Prussia, and the United States emulated Britain. But China and the West developed their bureaucracies differently and under an entirely different sequential order. One difference is that there was never just one civil service in the West: there was a military civil service, a civil service for foreign affairs, one for forestry, and so on. These organizations competed with one another for prized human capital, and together competed for talent with other groups across the private and public spheres, such as political parties, universities, and businesses.

In the United States, the Pendleton Act of 1883 removed the power of Congress and the political parties to control civil service appointments. Before the 1883 act, federal appointees returned a portion of their salaries to the party that had appointed them.[28] The civil service never became completely independent, however. Today, the U.S. Congress wields enormous power and oversight over the bureaucracy, including the power of the purse that funds it.

Another difference between bureaucracy in the West and in China—and this is a big one—is the timing of its development. Chinese bureaucracy preceded and stunted political development; in the West politics developed and matured first, imposing constraints on bureaucracy. The United States introduced bureaucracy in the nineteenth century, after "the two institutions of constraint, the rule of law and accountability, were the most highly developed."[29] Politics came before the bureaucracy, not the other way around. The establishment of a bureaucracy in the West also occurred after the liberating movement of Protestantism was well under way. Martin Luther issued his proclamation in 1517, more than a century before Prussia's bureaucratic professionalization. Frederick the Great gave his imprimatur to religious freedom in the eighteenth century, a century before the Prussian bureaucracy was fully operational. Religious freedom was thoroughly entrenched when Britain and America introduced their civil service.

The Prussian, British, and American civil services emerged in the midst of pluralism and religious and social freedom. The Western bureaucracy did not arise to stifle society; it instead operated within a longstanding milieu of pluralistic forces and societal constraints. The bureaucracy would compete with the church and other social groups for human capital, legitimacy, and resources, not supplant those groups.

In the eighteenth century, according to Polity IV, a widely used historical database on political regimes, Prussia was an autocracy, but compared with imperial China there was substantial religious freedom. The democratic states in America and Britain, meanwhile, were already "a shackled Leviathan" when their bureaucracies emerged.[30] That is, society was strong and the idea of basic rights, if not the actual practice in each instance, was entrenched long before the state ramped up its administrative capacity. The rule of law, the principle of accountability, and the powers of the legislature and the political parties preceded, enabled, but also constrained bureaucracy in the West. The shackled states shackled each other.

## The Platform Effect

Birth order matters. Imperial China's bureaucracy was on the scene first, and engulfed and overwhelmed the kind of politics that Khilnani had in mind. To understand how the Chinese state acquired this encompassing power and its shackling effect on society, we return to the first letter of our EAST formulation. One powerful way the state shackled society is by controlling two critical inputs into the formation of society—time and talent. *Keju* supplied that monopoly function as a programmed and well-organized platform. It also impacted the attitudinal formation of the Chinese population, which then reinforced this platform effect.

As a method for controlling society, *Keju* was extremely advanced for its time. The route to success and the path for preparation were laid out clearly for participants. The metrics were unambiguous and delineated, and in modern marketing language *Keju* had a deep channel penetration—it was accessible to all of the cross-sections of society, including its lowest rungs. All else being equal—and often all else was stacked in favor of *Keju* in any case—a rational person would likely choose *Keju* over other career paths that yielded uncertain payoffs.

An unrivaled advantage of *Keju* was its systematization. It was procedure-oriented and rubric-based. The strict anonymization protocol contributed to its perceived ability to offer mobility regardless of the rank, status, or birth origin of the candidate. *Keju* was open to commoners as well as to sons of official and nobility families. The patterns of both upward and downward mobility, documented by Ping-ti Ho, confirm that *Keju* indeed offered equal opportunities for all.[31]

The *Keju* pipeline extended wide and deep into Chinese society. The imperial regimes built up an infrastructure for the male population that approximated a degree of universal education, with literacy achieved by a large proportion of the male population. This is a non-trivial task even today, let alone in a pre-modern society. *Keju* was a truly mass phenomenon rather than a niche activity for the elitist few. The mobility achieved through the *Keju* was so efficient that it demolished all other mobility channels, such as aristocracy, commerce, religion, intelligentsia, and political opposition.

The view I developed on *Keju* is a departure from the standard perspective that celebrates *Keju* as meritocratic and promotive of social mobility, a view also supported by rigorous modern social science research.[32] I do not disagree with this view in its narrow construction, but in the grand scheme of things, this is true of trees but not of a forest. By decimating everything else in its path, *Keju* was an anti-mobility mobility channel that deprived society of its own mobility channels. Preempting a civil society is a far more consequential effect of *Keju* than the narrow mobility achieved within imperial bureaucracy. It is also a defining difference with bureaucracy and civil service in the West.

## *The* Keju *Infrastructure*

Imperial China built and funded a large-scale educational infrastructure in order to overcome the advantages of wealth and incumbency. During the Song, prominent thinkers such as Fan Zhongyan and Wang Anshi advocated greater access to education, a very progressive idea for their era. Their advocacy led to the establishment of a public school system to prepare students for *Keju*. During the Ming, this basic educational infrastructure was augmented. In 1369, the founding emperor of the Ming dynasty, Zhu Yuanzhang, decreed that the imperial bureaucracy would establish and fund dynasty schools, or preparatory schools, for the qualification rounds.

These preparatory schools provided government stipends and tuition waivers. As a sign of excess demand for school seats when the clearing price was set to zero, the imperial court had to impose admission quotas. The *Keju* preparatory system was massive in scale. The early Ming imperial bureaucracy operated 1,435 administrative units and 1,318 dynasty schools—almost one school per administrative unit.[33] Public education was provided at scale to offset the inherent advantage of wealth.

Did this system work as intended? In a paper I wrote with Clair Yang, we explore this question in detail, examining whether wealth (as measured by the candidate's number of wives) was correlated with stronger performance on the *Keju* exams, all else being equal.[34] Modern social scientists have documented correlations between wealth and high standardized test scores, and this wealth effect may very well have held true for pre-modern China as well. Were *Keju*'s safeguards against this wealth effect—access to education and the anonymity of participants—successful? We found that at the provincial and metropolitan stages of *Keju*, the two stages that were anonymized, the safeguards worked. And at the palace examination stage, where a candidate's background was known, *Keju* in fact discriminated against wealthy candidates (more on this in Chapter 5). This is an unthinkable outcome in the absence of substantial public funding of education and the insulation built into the *Keju* infrastructure. *Keju* counteracted the dreaded incumbency and wealth effects. Apparently, it succeeded.

## Mass Literacy

If the *Keju* infrastructure worked as intended, then imperial China should have widespread literacy. But how literate was pre-modern China? Several historians have made heroic attempts to answer this question. The most thorough study in English is *Education and Popular Literacy in Ch'ing China*, by Evelyn Rawski. (Ch'ing is the Wade-Giles spelling of Qing.)

In this rich and meticulously researched book, Rawski draws from voluminous archival sources, including school records and local gazetteers, and is careful to distinguish between elite literacy and mass literacy. The level of literacy required to successfully attain a *Keju* degree was elite literacy, which was achieved by very few. Some scholars refer to the Qing as an illiterate society without making it clear that they are referring to elite literacy. The more relevant measure, however, is what Rawski calls "functional" or "basic" literacy. Far more people failed at the preparation rounds and at the *Keju* exams than succeeded, but they acquired literacy along the way. Rawski believes that basic literacy during the Qing was far more substantial than commonly assumed. She estimates that in the eighteenth and nineteenth centuries, around 30 to 45 percent of the male population had some form of basic and functional literacy. Literacy for women is estimated to have been between 2 to 10 percent.[35]

Rawski's conclusion is controversial, and much of the criticism has focused on the definition of "literacy" used in the book.[36] Rawski's estimate is based on assessing who had knowledge of a few hundred Chinese characters, but some critics argue that this is too low of a standard. For the purpose of this book, we can set aside this issue and focus on whether the *Keju* infrastructure reached the masses. By definition, "elites" cannot possibly comprise 30 to 45 percent of the male population, so although imperial China did not have universal literacy, its ability to reach 30 to 45 percent of the male population (the only population allowed to be educated) is an extraordinary achievement.

Rawski used the scattered information on teacher capacity and enrollment provided in the local gazetteers to come up with her nationwide estimate. A recent paper using other sources of information has confirmed the lower-bound estimate by Rawski—a 27 to 32 percent male literacy rate during the nineteenth century.[37] There is also qualitative evidence. Rawski depicts a Chinese society saturated with written methods of communication. Emperors communicated to subjects through written notices; the walls of government buildings were plastered with information about agricultural techniques; written registries were used to keep track of tax collection and police functions; and circulating libraries did a brisk business. Foreigners in Canton (Guangzhou in pinyin) debated propositions such as "In China, there are more books and more people to read them than there are in any other country in the world." One foreign estimate was that the population of Guangzhou was 80 percent literate.[38]

Indeed, book ownership was widespread in China as early as the Ming dynasty. "More books were available," Timothy Brook writes, "and more people read and owned more books, in the late Ming than at any earlier time in history, anywhere in the world." Jesuits visiting China conveyed the following impression: "More surprising, perhaps, is that complete illiterates may well have been a minority in the late Ming."[39] Because of a potential selection bias, we should not take the words of foreign Jesuits at face value. They might have interacted more frequently with educated Chinese than with average Chinese. But the Jesuit whom Brook cites in his book, Adriano de Las Cortes, notably compared the aristocrats in his own country, many of whom did not learn to read and write, to both the privileged and the poor Chinese. He also conducted "field research" on the dynasty schools that were funded by the Ming court. In his memoir, he wrote that "among the great, of whatever quality, rare is he who does not know how to read or write." He further observed it was uncommon "that a boy, even the son of a Chinese very poor and of low condition, does not learn at least to read and to write their characters."[40] He noticed that far fewer women were literate. In all the schools he visited, he saw only two girls.

Las Cortes's reflections on literacy among the Chinese poor suggests that the *Keju* infrastructure accounted for this literacy achievement. But another theory has been proposed: that functional literacy was fostered by life in a highly urbanized Qing society. Susan Naquin and Evelyn Rawski, for example, attribute the rise of literacy during this period to commercial developments, for which signed, written contracts were important.[41]

This view seems implausible, however. First, consider the sharply gendered nature of Chinese literacy. As a foreigner observed in the 1830s: "Of the whole population of Canton not more than one half are able to read. Perhaps not one boy in ten is left entirely destitute of instruction: yet of the other sex not one in ten ever learns to read or write."[42] Did only males, but not females, participate in urban life and read shop signs? A far more convincing explanation is that a gendered institution explained a gendered outcome. Second, if we accept Rawski's estimate of 30 to 45 percent male literacy, then it cannot possibly be the case that urbanization explains literacy. The Qing's urbanization rate, the urban population divided by the population of the country, was only around 7 percent (compared with, say, 20 percent during the Northern Song).[43] If we assume that each and every urbanite was literate, this still amounts to nowhere near the 30 to 45 percent male literacy rate estimated by Rawski. *Keju* infrastructure, which led to almost every prefecture having a preparatory school, is a more plausible explanation for China's high literacy rate.

## *Monopolizing Talents—and Time*

The best way to weaken society is to starve it of a supply of talent. *Keju* enabled the state to capture all the fruits of the high literacy in imperial China. The Chinese state recruited and kept on staff a huge proportion of the educated, talented people in China, thereby diverting and depriving talent flows from its political as well as economic competition. If we want to understand the self-perpetuating power of Chinese autocracy, this is the place to start.

Earlier, I quoted Lee Kuan Yew's explanation that the ruling regime can siphon off human capital from its opposition by raising civil servants' salaries. A Tang emperor, Emperor Taizong, anticipated the wisdom of Lee Kuan Yew by a few centuries. He proudly proclaimed that through *Keju* he "had all the best of the country within the shooting range of my bow." It is not clear whether he meant he could kill them or that he was in full control of them. Regardless, they would not rebel against him.

*Keju* also kept the Chinese population busy. *Keju* took years of often fruitless preparation and involved cutthroat competition. But the promise of "making it" was intoxicating. Fan Jin, a fictional character penned by Wu Jingzhi (1701–1754), epitomizes this aspect of the *Keju* exam. Fan Jin toiled for twenty years to pass the first tier, the provincial exam. In the process, he generated no income and garnered ridicule from neighbors and relatives. His family often went days without food, and everyone thought that he simply was not cut out for the long days of studying. His father-in-law, a butcher by profession, was not happy about a son-in-law who routinely ignored the welfare of his daughter. He beat Fan frequently.

At the advanced age of fifty-four, Fan at last passed the provincial exam, earning him the title of "recommended man" (*Juren*). His passing came as a total shock, to himself and to everyone else. He lost his sanity in a combination of disbelief and exhilaration. His neighbors implored his father-in-law to use force to bring Fan back to his senses, but this time the father-in-law hesitated, not daring to inflict physical harm on a son-in-law who had just acquired an elevated status.

The *Juren* was the lowest degree in the *Keju* hierarchy. To make it all the way to a *Jinshi*, the ultimate *Keju* degree, Fan would have to take two additional, and progressively more grueling, exams—the metropolitan exam in the capital and the palace exam. Fan never made it that far. As a *Juren*, he was given a position as a minor official, but he was incompetent. The years of toiling to prepare for the exam had left him with great gaps in his knowledge.

Millions of individuals took qualifying tests, often repeatedly, to become eligible to sit for the provincial exam. And millions, including Fan Jin's creator, Wu Jingzhi, never made it. There were both direct and opportunity costs of this endeavor. Fan neglected his family as he spent time studying, and he used otherwise needed family resources to acquire books and study materials. He did not help out in his father-in-law's butcher shop, thus not generating any sales there. Last but not least, the exams were extraordinarily difficult, requiring the candidates to memorize hundreds of thousands of vocabulary words and phrases in classical Chinese, a language not used in day-to-day conversation. The skills required to pass the *Keju* exams were nearly useless in everyday life. Imagine the sense of devastation, accentuated by a sunk cost mentality, when one kept failing these exams—and the exhilaration when one eventually passed them.

Now consider a real *Keju* candidate, Ming dynasty scholar Gui Youguang. Before passing the provincial examination in 1540 at the not-so-old age of thirty-four, he had failed it six times. He then toiled for another twenty-four years for the next stages of *Keju*. In 1565 he finally attained his *Jinshi* degree, near the bottom of his class and at the ripe age of fifty-nine.[44] But alas, Gui only had six years to bask in his exalted status—he died at age sixty-five. Assuming that he had started preparations at age three, a common practice, 95 percent of his life had been spent in some stage of preparing for *Keju*.

This feature of *Keju*—that it could be taken ad infinitum—may be one reason why *Keju* literacy did not spill over into other arenas. Keep in mind the gargantuan task at hand—memorizing some 400,000 characters and phrases. Preparation for *Keju* began early. Boys as young as three, four, or five would begin to practice their memorization drills. *Keju* was their first exposure to the world beyond these boys' immediate families. The imperial state monopolized not only China's talent, but also the lifetimes of its male population.

The infinitesimal odds of success failed to deter the multitudes from participating in this rite of passage. We can use the figures provided by Elman to get a rough sense of the odds. Between two to three million regularly took the qualifying tests during the Ming. Of these, only about four hundred made it all the way to the palace examination, earning a *Jinshi*, the highest degree. Using three million as the base, this would imply odds of 0.00013 to make it all the way from the qualification round to the *Jin-shi* round. To put this number in perspective, it is better than the odds of an American being struck by a lightening during his or her lifetime (0.000065), but far worse than the odds of a middle-age, college graduate becoming a millionaire in the United States.[45]

While reaching the stratospheric level of a *Jinshi* was extraordinarily difficult, during the Ming era about 4 percent, on average, passed the first tier of *Keju*, the provincial exam.[46] This is still more difficult than getting into Harvard in most years, but keep in mind that unlike applying to Harvard, *Keju* was not a one-shot deal. An average Ming subject believed that with hard work and repeated tries, he would eventually achieve the success of landing a minor bureaucratic post. For the autocrat, this belief worked out brilliantly. He captured the truly talented ones who eventually succeeded, and he tied up the rest in a perpetual quest for illusory *Keju* glory. No time for rebellious ideas or deeds.

## *Keju* Literacy

In a fascinating book, *The WEIRDest People in the World: How the West Became Psychologically Peculiar and Particularly Prosperous*, Joseph Henrich sets out to explore the cultural and psychological roots of why the West is so different from other civilizations.[47] The West first became educated, industrialized, rich, and democratic at a time when the rest of the world was mired in poverty and backwardness. How did this come about? Henrich approached this big question from within—within the brains of individuals, their attitudes and ways of thinking.

One particular claim in the book is startling: literacy induced biological changes that eventually led to broad socioeconomic developments. Literacy literally changes a person's brain. Some parts of the brain, the left ventral occipitotemporal region, build and fortify connectivity to the other areas of the brain in response to repeated exposures to reading. "Literacy changes people's biology and psychology without altering the underlying genetic code," states Henrich. Literacy also cultivates capabilities such as "memory, visual processing, facial recognition, numerical exactness, and problem-solving." According to this view, these effects are long-lasting, showing up even centuries after literacy was first introduced. The West rose first in part because it got literate first. (Henrich discussed other factors as well.)

This approach is fascinating, but applying Henrich's framework to China yields a glaring anomaly. A hallmark of ancient China was mass literacy beyond the immediate elite circles of society, but it acquired none of the modernizing effects putatively attributed to literacy. And Chinese literacy was not generative—that is, an initially high level did not plant seeds for further and universal literacy. In my telling, using the EAST formula, literacy did the opposite: it augmented and prolonged autocracy and led to China's technological stagnation.

How is it that literacy, as considered in the EAST and the WEIRD frameworks, induced opposite effects? One might argue that while male literacy was high in imperial China, the overall literacy rate in the population was low. This is true, but it still does not get to the bottom of the issue, since we do not observe Henrich's effects among the literate male Chinese. Another possibility is that these are two different types of literacy. *Keju* literacy incubated an authoritarian deference, whereas the Protestant literacy propagated through the Protestant Reformation promoted liberal values. I think this hypothesis makes a lot of sense, but then the substantive differences between Confucianism and Protestantism would be central to the equation, not biology.

My take on the *Keju* puzzle is that *Keju* and Protestant literacies are fundamentally different in their applications, value orientation, and conjunctional conditions. *Keju* literacy was deployed to augment autocracy rather than to deliver growth, and *Keju* literacy cherished authority whereas the Protestant movement arose as a challenge to authority. The function of literacy is conjunctional rather than singular: other conditions have to be in place for literacy to produce broad socioeconomic effects. Those conditions only materialized in East Asia after World War II and in China after 1978.

## *The* Keju *Puzzle*

Henrich's argument is complicated, and I cannot do full justice to it in just a few sentences. He argues that the Protestant principle of *sola scriptura*—that everyone should have a personal relationship with God—led to the translation of the Bible into vernacular languages, which in turn incubated and propagated mass literacy and so led to beneficial biological changes in human brains. The West rose because the West got literate first.

Universal literacy—defined as literacy of the entire population—happened in the West much earlier than in China. By the late nineteenth century, Great Britain and the Netherlands had attained near universal literacy. In the 1890s, the literacy rate of China's population was low, only 18 percent according to an estimate by Chinese historians, far below the 95 percent that was present in England and the Netherlands.[48]

So why low universal literacy despite *Keju*? Or maybe because of *Keju*? The limitations of *Keju* arose from its gendered restriction and from its classical content entirely divorced from the day-to-day life of an average Chinese. That said, the cognitive effects of literacy posited by Henrich did not so much depend on *universal* literacy but on some forms of mass literacy, that is, literacy reaching beyond a narrow circle of royalty, aristocrats, and clergymen. The timing of the takeoff of the Western literacy is indicative of this point. Let me quote from Henrich. "Suddenly," Henrich writes, "in the 16th century, literacy began spreading epidemically across western Europe."[49] What was the level of European literacy in the sixteenth century? According to the data cited by Henrich, it was 16 percent for Great Britain, 12 percent for the Netherlands, and 16 percent for Germany. This was the level of mass literacy that launched the onset of cognitive developments and value transformation in Europe.[50]

Because of methodological differences between the Chinese and European estimates, these literacy estimates could be inaccurate.[51] So let's take another look, from the perspective of numeracy, which is more consistently defined across countries and better suited for cross-country comparisons. The data come from Our World in Data, an online database maintained at Oxford University.[52] In the historical section of the database, basic numeracy is defined as the ability to state one's age correctly. I present the numeracy data in Table 3.1. Three groups of countries are included: East Asia (China, Japan, and Korea), Europe (Great Britain, France, Germany, and Sweden), and other civilizations (India, Egypt, and Russia). The data are from 1600 to 1950 and are broken down every half-century.

The pattern is striking. Until the nineteenth century, China outperformed every single other country in the graph, including the most advanced European countries such as Great Britain and Sweden. As early as the second half of the seventeenth century, 94 percent of the Chinese population was already capable of basic numeracy, compared with 79 percent for Germany and France. Chinese numeracy dipped during the first half of the nineteenth century, but otherwise it enjoyed near universal numeracy close to the European levels. The two other *Keju* countries, Japan and Korea, also exhibited higher numeracy levels than European countries. Basic literacy and numeracy are likely correlated with each other, at least

Table 3.1. Percent of populations with basic numeracy, 1501 to 1950 (basic numeracy defined as the ability to state one's age correctly). (Our World in Data at https://ourworldindata.org/grapher/share-of-the-population-with-basic-numeracy-skills-by-birth-decade)

| | 1500–1550 | 1551–1600 | 1601–1650 | 1651–1700 | 1701–1750 | 1751–1800 | 1801–1850 | 1851–1900 | 1901–1950 |
|---|---|---|---|---|---|---|---|---|---|
| China | | | | 94 | 99 | 98 | 85.2 | 96.9 | 99.3 |
| Japan | | 81 | | | | | 97.8 | 99.3 | 99.7 |
| Korea | | | | | | | | 99.9 | 99.7 |
| Great Britain | | | 76 | | 93 | 92.6 | 95.9 | 98.1 | 99.4 |
| Germany | 40 | | 78 | 79 | 83.1 | 92.7 | 99.2 | 99.7 | 100 |
| France | | | | 79 | 73.5 | 91.6 | 97.6 | 99.8 | 99.5 |
| Sweden | | | 79 | | | 100 | 99.4 | 99.9 | 99.7 |
| India | | | | | | | 33.7 | 38.0 | 42.3 |
| Egypt | | | | | | 7.8 | 7.7 | 14.8 | 38.5 |
| Russia | | | | 43 | 53.6 | 69.9 | 73.6 | 94.3 | 99.3 |

to some extent. Henrich in fact believes that numeracy is an effect of literacy. The high numeracy of China suggests that its literacy could not be that far behind European countries.

We can pose the *Keju* puzzle as the following question: "Why did China fail to launch?" It is a question of dynamics, not of statics. Rawski's estimate of Chinese male literacy at 30 to 45 percent for the eighteenth and nineteenth centuries meant that China was comfortably within the launching range that Europe had in the sixteenth century. In fact, China might have reached a takeoff threshold even earlier, since the earlier Ming dynasty (1368–1644) was the apex of *Keju*, and book ownership and circulations were already substantial during the Ming. Even during the Song (960–1279), long before the Protestant Reformation, the influence of the *Keju*-induced education was already substantial. Between 997 and 1207, the number of *Keju* applicants increased much faster than did population growth.[53]

Yet Chinese literacy did not spread "epidemically" and it never induced any of the modernizing effects associated with the Protestant literacy in Europe. The initially impressive literacy achievements stagnated both quantitatively and qualitatively. *Keju* literacy never engendered a value transformation, such as gender equality. *Keju* stayed stubbornly a male institution. And it never led to a culture of economic growth—instead, Chinese technology collapsed.

## Legitimizing Statism

According to legend, an emperor in the late Tang dynasty hung on the wall a wooden tablet proudly displaying his *Keju* degree. But the degree was fake. The emperor had it made for himself.[54] This is the legitimating power of *Keju*, so intoxicating that even an emperor coveted its bona fide. (This academic credentialism pervades officialdom today. Many Chinese government officials list advanced degrees, earned or otherwise, on their résumés.) Notice a sharp difference with Protestant literacy, which incubated values challenging authority.

*Keju* promoted statism. One way came through perceptions. *Keju*, as I noted before, was meritocratic during its anonymized stages. The fate of *Keju* aspirants was decoupled from the discretionary power of the emperors. The massive investments in the process—integrity, anonymization, and tiered competition—are investments in perceived impartiality and objectivity. The manufactured objectivity is a subtle, yet alluring, idea from which autocrats stand to reap benefits. By ceding this critical decision right to an ostensibly objective process, the autocrat more than makes up for the loss by earning the right to make other decisions on your behalf. Impartiality and objectivity are the "universal" values with strong appeals to the masses.[55]

The other way was through indoctrination, and the process began early. Starting as early as age three to five, Chinese boys would begin writing characters by copying sayings that were intended to instill admiration and devotion to the ideas and teachings of the master—Confucius—that would eventually be tested on *Keju*. The following is a popular first lesson that would launch a boy's lifelong pursuit of examination glory:

> Let us present our work to father.
> Confucius himself
> Taught three thousand.
> Seventy were capable gentlemen.
> You young scholars,
> Eight or nine!
> Work well to attain virtue,
> And you will understand propriety.[56]

The exposure to *Keju* for male Chinese was at a young, impressionable age. This was dictated by the nature of *Keju*. *Keju* was all about memorization. The young have an innate advantage in memorization. (If you hear from a Chinese parent the mantra, "Do not lose at the starting line," you now know where it came from.) Thus *Keju*, a pervasive information environment for the male Chinese and narrative control, produced what psychologists call "an imprinting effect." This imprinting effect might have been far stronger than the Protestant literacy, which was administered mainly to adults.

*Keju* tilted the balance of power toward the state at the expense of the society. This approach could not have been more different than the way that Prussia and other European countries implemented universal education. Martin Luther called for the state to provide universal education and the state obliged. In imperial China, high literacy was achieved through a top-down mandate, a supply-driven approach. Preparatory schools were established to channel mental efforts and investments in a narrow curriculum designed, tailor-made, and highly customized by the state to satisfy its own needs for human capital. This state-supplied investment force-fed classical literacy to the Chinese population rather than democratizing and propagating the vernacular literacy of the commoners.

From the seventeenth century onward, the European masses were exposed to the anti-authoritarian values of Protestantism, while since the sixth century, the Chinese masses were exposed to the statist values of Confucianism. Protestantism arose to challenge the orthodoxy of the Catholic Church and contributed to religious freedom and diversity. (Today in Germany, Catholics, at 22 million, and Protestants, at 20 million, are roughly equal in number.) Early on, Prussia developed incipient notions of religious freedom. King Frederick the Great declared each individual to be free to find his own salvation. In the language adopted for this book, religious freedom expanded the scope conditions of Prussia. Henrich speculates that Scotland was the birthplace of so many enlightenment intellectuals, such as David Hume and Adam Smith, because of the early spread of Protestantism and the associated notion and practice of universal education. The literacy intermediated through *Keju*, by contrast, churned out reams of "scholar-officials" whose first obligation was to serve the state, not to produce knowledge or new ideas, or to discover truth.[57]

We can draw from the familiar criticisms of standardized tests by modern educational researchers to think about these effects of *Keju*.

Standardized tests cultivate a mental habit of dependency and deference to authority for answers and for value alignment. Standardized tests also devalue what educational scholars believe to be the mental traits vital for navigating successfully in a complex and heterogenous society. These include critical thinking (independence of opinions and reliance on logic and reasoning), recognition of diversity (an acknowledgment that the world around us is heterogeneous), and empathy (an ability to see the world from another person's perspective).[58] *Keju* is a negation of all these liberal values. In keeping with how autocrats prefer to construe their world, its premise rejects the possibility that there could be a heterogenous world of peoples, views, and perspectives.

There is another significant, if subtle, difference. The Protestant principle of *sola scriptura* tacitly undermined the authority of a living and breathing personage—the pope. Its disciples were encouraged to instead develop a personal relationship with an ethereal abstraction, an abstraction with "God" in its name. *Keju* has a more concrete touch. It inculcated a deference not to the autocracy as an abstract concept but to the autocracy as personified by the autocrat, the emperor. The ideological deference was not directed to the authority of Confucianism as a system of ideas but to the philosopher sage. I call this mental framework "*Keju* epistemology," a frame of mind that focuses on the features of powerholders rather than the surrounding institutions. In this framework, bad rule is fixed by a good ruler, and a good ruler is both a necessary and sufficient condition for good rule; the system that enables or constrains autocrats is left out of the equation. Only the ruler registers attention. The cycling and recycling of endless emperors in history and from Mao to Xi are a product of the way the *Keju* epistemology diagnoses problems, assigns causes, and prescribes solutions.

## Preempting Individual Agency

Beyond these explicit values, there is an underlying connection between *Keju* and autocracy. In his excellent book *The Geography of Thought*, Richard Nisbett shows that when asked to recount stories of things and events, East Asians tend to focus on the situational environment; Westerners tend to focus on the individual players in their recounting.[59] This difference in focus of attention is one of the most robustly documented differences between East Asians and Westerners in psychological studies. There is a mental "discount" of individuals among Chinese.

The usual explanation is that Greek civilization placed more emphasis on personal agency and individuality, whereas Chinese civilization placed more emphasis on harmony, relationships, and the collective welfare of the community. This is no doubt true, but it is too general and vague. Arguably, a more fundamental difference is that Greek civilization is more heterogenous than the Chinese civilization. Plato cherished collective values and acts of good, while other Greek thinkers such as Epicurus (341–270 BCE) cherished unabashed virtues of individualism.[60] After the Song dynasty, very few Chinese philosophers and thinkers promoted an explicit theory regarding individuality and individual agency—the notion that individuals matter and can make a difference.

To me, this is a more foundational difference between the East and the West. People steeped in the Chinese tradition are penalized for thinking and acting in their individual capacity, and they naturally turn their gaze away from individual factors. The Greeks had the scope conditions to choose between an individual focus and a group focus; for the Chinese, such a choice did not exist. No one we know of ever attained a *Jinshi* degree by challenging the Confucianist orthodoxy and survived to tell their heroic stunt. During the Ming and the Qing, no one attained a *Jinshi* degree by expressing Confucian orthodoxy through a format other than the highly scripted eight-legged essays. On the *Keju* exams, uniform answers in the correct format were rewarded, not quirkiness, cleverness, or any other creative deviation. Conformity is the winning formula. Is it any wonder that test subjects steeped in this powerful cultural tradition do not focus on individual factors?

This preemption of individual agency lies behind the shackled society. The personal agency effect of Protestantism manifested itself in a movement away from the Latin language and an embrace of the familiar vernaculars of the masses. Protestantism set loose commoners from a remote and alien language that was taken up only on rarefied occasions. The discourse became intimate and personal, enriching conversations and potentially enabling the kind of "discussion democracy"—in the words of Amartya Sen—that existed prior to the establishment of formal democratic institutions.[61] The empowerment came from a facility with one's own means of discourse and expression. It is a capability vital for horizontal communications and potentially for collective actions. Through *Keju*, the autocrat monopolized not only points of view, but also the entire lingua franca of politics.

*Keju* literacy prevented "discussion democracy" by imposing an alien discourse on the population. The Confucianist texts were dense and difficult. Memorizing the language of the ancient texts, and absorbing the authoritarian values in them, were brutal. There was no time or energy to do much of anything else, whether that was exploring new ideas and natural phenomena, delving into mathematics, organizing a political opposition, or developing a crucial trait in the development of liberalism and science—skepticism. The human capacity was already taxed to its very limit.

## Capabilities

Imperial China "overperformed" on the literacy front from an economic perspective. Economically it was in the same league of countries as India, Egypt, and Russia, but as shown in Table 3.1, it had the European level of numeracy. There was a gap between capabilities and economic outcomes, a gap that still persists today. *Keju* literacy probably triggered a rewiring of Chinese brains just as Protestant literacy did in the European brains, and the Chinese also acquired mental processing and work ethics, a feature of Protestantism that Max Weber emphasized.[62]

But here is a crucial difference between China and Europe. The Europeans acquired these capabilities in the polycentric context of post-Roman Europe, whereas the Chinese did so in an autocratic context.[63] Enabled by freedom and explorations, the capable Europeans plunged into science, technology, and commercialization and built sophisticated political institutions. The capable Chinese systemized autocracy (Chapter 1), scaled the size of the territory (Introduction), maintained political unity, preempted intra-elite conflicts (Chapter 5), and launched impressive statist voyage projects (Chapter 7). The single-mobility channel of the imperial bureaucracy crowded out and decimated all other applications of capabilities.

The test of this conjecture arrived when the scope conditions of Europe landed in East Asia. After World War II, East Asia began to reap the cognitive benefits of literacy—the rewiring of brains, numeracy, memory, and work ethics—and applied these capabilities to economic development. First Japan and then South Korea, Taiwan, Hong Kong, Singapore, and finally China rapidly industrialized and grew more prosperous. The legacy impact of *Keju* materialized eventually. For centuries, these modernizing traits quietly lay in dormancy, and they burst out in force when the right conditions and circumstances arrived. This should have been what Napoleon Bonaparte meant when he said, "Let China sleep, for when she wakes, she will shake the world."

Notice that the East Asian miracle occurred under a confluence of cognitive capabilities and scope conditions rather than under one of these factors alone. The capabilities intersected with enlightened leadership, globalization, private entrepreneurship, and competition. This is another illustration of our running theme—a country needs both scale and scope to succeed. Is it any wonder that the same *Keju*-legacy countries, the centrally planned economies of Mao's China and North Korea, are a glaring exception to the East Asian miracle? Is it any wonder that East Asian female labor participation is extraordinarily high, despite the patriarchal culture? Is it any wonder that so many other developing countries embracing economic and political liberalizations but without basic literacy failed to generate long-lasting growth? Henrich and Weber can still explain East Asia, but with a time lag and by adding a conjunctional condition of scope.

China's autocracy has been remarkably long-lasting, sustained by a powerful, mutually reinforcing intersection of authoritarian structure and values. If we set aside some of the factual specifics, the tale of Henry VIII and Wanli already tells us a lot about the deafening allegiance of loyalty that the delegates at the Twentieth Party Congress swore to Xi Jinping and about the noisy insults the members of the Parliament hurl at Rishi Sunak (or whoever occupies 10 Downing Street when this book is in your hand).

The political structure bequeathed by imperial China was simply not accommodating to democracy. Democracy more naturally evolved from the tumult of politics and from a heterogenous and noisy world of "indeterminacy and competition," not from an ordered, clinical hierarchy. Long before the arrival of democracy, Henry VIII had to contend with differentiated powers, contentiousness, and open-endedness, situations in which no Chinese ruler has ever found himself. The Chinese system lived up to an admonition purportedly issued by Confucius, "There cannot be two kings for the people just as there cannot be two suns in the heaven."

China is an organization, not a polity. This is the other limiting condition—China does not have an organized society and the absence of a civil society reinforces the strength of the state down the road. A strong society provides an outside option to those inside the state. In a democracy that option is often derided as "a revolving door," but it has a valuable function. It lowers the costs to those seeking an exit from the state. State functionaries can vote with their feet, as many did during the Trump administration. A strong society raises opportunity costs for the state to recruit and retain human capital. This receptor function is missing in China.

The true miracle of *Keju* is the high mass literacy it cultivated and the related changes in the brain induced by literacy, not that it created a capable bureaucracy. The work ethics, numeracy, and mental processing capabilities of the people powered the economic growth of East Asia and of China when the right conditions materialized. In politics, however, *Keju* produced an opposite effect. It forestalled or delayed modernization and progress. Recall Gui Youguang, who spent an estimated 95 percent of his lifespan in some form of *Keju* preparation. Now imagine an individual diligently studying whatever the state deems important—verbal portions of the SAT, New or Old Testaments, the Koran, Shakespeare—for 95 percent of his or her lifetime. Now further imagine that this has been happening for over a century and a half and for a large segment of the population—you get a sense of how powerful this legacy is.

Let me end this chapter on one key difference I have noted between the worlds of Wanli and Henry VIII: norms. Norms are ideas and ways of thinking that the masses take for granted at their face value. They cast a long shadow not just over a country's past but also its future. The *Keju* norms are pro-autocracy and anti-collaboration. They are incredibly strong and are what psychologists call "sticky priors." Autocracy is not questioned, not second-guessed, and not scrutinized by the population. The state is granted automatic legitimacy. There is an axiomatic deference to authority and absence of skepticism. Any movement away from the current political system of China runs against these prevalent norms.

*Keju* penalized collective actions and its norms impede a path toward Chinese democracy. A paradox is that democratization is often advocated on individual values but it is actuated through collective actions—Protestant Reformation, women's suffrage, the civil rights movement, church, political parties, even bowling leagues.[64] Voting is a tool to coordinate preferences and aggregate collaborative acts. By contrast, *Keju* celebrated hyper individualism, not individual agency. Candidates were pitched against each other in a fierce zero-sum tournament where collaboration was severely punished. They were locked in small, isolated cells, waging competition that is lonely, atomistic, brutal, and on terms entirely dictated by a remote and mythical state. A "society" so individualized ceases to be a society.

Plenty of this dynamic is at work in China today. How does the fierce competitiveness of entrepreneurship coexist with the heavy-handed CCP? Easy. Entrepreneurship thrives on atomistic individualism, while autocracy flourishes from the absence of individual agency. In fact, the CCP actively encourages "political participation" but only in their isolated and uncoordinated silos. Citizens are free to provide opinions to the CCP through surveys, online portals, and petitions. Tyranny is not at all adverse to individualism.

There are no social norms in China today that are remotely powerful enough to compete with autocratic norms. During the lockdown of Shanghai, even emergency care was suspended. Hospitals turned away patients seeking urgent care, resulting in untimely, preventable deaths. There is no Hippocratic Oath that vies with, let alone overrides, the edict of the state. There were protests against the lockdown, but these Shanghai residents protested individually and in isolation from each other. They were like *Keju* exam-takers, given three candles and kept in a small cell until the trial was over. Forever standing alone, they were no match for the awesome power of the state.

CHAPTER FOUR

# Reversion to the Autocratic Mean

My father thinks that Gorbachev is an idiot.

—attributed to DENG XIAOPING'S SON

ONE DAY IN 1980, an audience seated in a Beijing theater waited expectantly for the opening of *What if I Were Real*, a play about the power and privileges of Chinese officials. An announcement came over the loudspeaker announcing a delay due to the late arrival of an official. As the delay grew longer, the audience started speculating about that official's seniority, assuming that the higher the rank, the longer the delay. Finally, the "official" made an entrance and the show commenced. The manufactured delay was a part of the performance.[1]

On May 8, 2011, flight HU7297—operated by the now defunct airline HNA—took off from Ningbo airport, jumping ahead of another plane scheduled for an earlier departure. Chinese flights are often delayed or cancelled without explanation, but this time the airport staff offered one: a passenger on HU7297 was a VIP, defined as ranked at or above the vice-ministerial level, and the airport was required to give priority to high-level officials.

Chinese airport regulations may or may not contain such a provision, but one thing is clear: attitudes toward institutionalized privileges of the state have undergone a dramatic change from the early days of the Chinese reforms.[2] Today, political power is revered. Xi Jinping has yet to command the stratospheric level of the personality cult of Mao Zedong, but he is well on his way. Reverence and deference to power permeate the entire political system. One indication is the monetization of power. Xi's anti-corruption campaign is targeted against both "flies and tigers," but many flies—minor functionaries in the Chinese system—receive tiger-sized bribes. A village accountant, Chen Wanshou, was found to have embezzled some 119 million yuan, about US$17 million. His case is known as a "little official, big graft" case.[3]

Few remember that the early 1980s was a period of soul-searching and profound reflection in Chinese society about the problems of unfettered power and an unconstrained state.[4] The calamities of the Great Leap Forward and the Cultural Revolution were thought to have been caused not only by the idiosyncratic actions of Mao Zedong, but also by the nature of the one-party state that had placed no constraints on the supreme leader. This is a systemic perspective so rare in the Chinese world of ideas.

The Chinese Communist Party has never undertaken a thorough diagnosis of itself, but the 1981 postmortem of the conduct and performance of the CCP since 1949 came closest to such an analysis. The CCP concluded that Mao Zedong had made serious errors of judgment and his personal arbitrariness had undermined the principle of "democratic centralism," causing the "personality cult of Comrade Mao Zedong to be frenziedly pushed to an extreme." The document, entitled "The Resolution on Party History," assigns major blame to Mao for his "erroneous appraisal of the prevailing class relations," but also to the CCP for being "not fully prepared . . . for socialist construction on a national scale" and to China's long tradition of feudalism. The document refers to the "lack of authority of relevant laws" and resolves to "prohibit the personality cult in any form." Yet although it is long on diagnostics, the document is short on institutional solutions. The comeback of the personality cult under Xi Jinping is evidence of the incompleteness of that exercise.

That said, in the 1980s the CCP did move piecemeal and incrementally toward a semblance of intra-party democracy and collective leadership. In the 1980s the formal structure of the state was different than during any other period in the PRC's history. To take just one example: throughout the 1980s, the positions of head of the CCP (general secretary), head of state (president), and head of the military (chairman of the Central Military Commission) were occupied by three different people. Since 1993, one individual has held all three positions.

What if this formal structure had survived the actuarial demise of Deng Xiaoping and other CCP elders? Would Xi Jinping have been able to demolish the constitutional term limit as easily as he did if CCP power had been more restrained and dispersed? We do not know the counterfactual answers to these questions, but it is important to revisit this momentous period in the CCP's history to ponder them. How did the somewhat distributed power structure of the Chinese system metamorphose into the singular structure it is today? How did the autocratic scope conditions of the 1980s collapse?

The simple answer: Tiananmen. The Tiananmen crackdown set off a cascade of dynamics that eventually led to this outcome. First to be toppled was a group of visionary and reformist leaders, among them Zhao Ziyang, general secretary of the CCP, who less than two years before the crackdown had unveiled the most systematic and far-reaching political reform program in the history of the PRC. Others, such as Hu Qili, Wan Li, Tian Jiyun, and Yan Mingfu, were among the most liberal in the Chinese leadership, and they were sidelined as the collateral damage of the leadership reshuffling. In their place arose a group of leaders who hailed from Shanghai, the most statist region of China. Unlike Zhao Ziyang, these "conservative reformers," as Tony Saich calls them, were adamantly opposed to political reforms, while they embraced economic reforms that were radical in some respects but statist in others.[5] The 1980s ideological connections between economic and political liberalism broke down. Politics and economics diverged.

The post-Tiananmen leadership was congenitally weak. Jiang Zemin, in particular, lacked a strong political base as well as the policy credentials and accomplishments of the man whom he had replaced. This created a sense of crisis among China's revolutionary elders and led to a consensus among them—that Jiang Zemin should not be allowed to fail. As part of their attempts to strengthen his position, the CCP elders decimated the fragile and emergent structure that distributed power at the top of Chinese political hierarchy, a structure they themselves had put in place. I will single out one development for emphasis—the demise of the Central Advisory Commission (CAC), an institution that was vested and arguably best positioned to check and balance a future dictator.

The 1980s world of Deng Xiaoping, Hu Yaobang, and Zhao Ziyang is unrecognizable from the vantage point of Xi Jinping's China. The remarkable degree of power-sharing, ideological diversity, and stellar economic performance that characterized the 1980s ended after June 4, 1989, when a new group of leaders promptly reversed the political reforms that had made these achievements possible. The revolutionary elders—in a step designed to buttress the power of the post-Tiananmen leadership—invigorated a single position, the general secretary of the CCP at the expense of other power centers. Xi Jinping became the beneficiary of these cumulative investments. The Tiananmen crackdown paved the way for a future dictator.

## A Most Remarkable Decade

The 1980s was China's most remarkable decade. Its economic performance was stellar. Growth in GDP averaged 9.5 percent in 1980–1990, adjusted for inflation, and growth of personal incomes was also significant, which meant that the economic benefits were distributed broadly. Many associate China's economic reforms with inequality, but this was not the case for the economic reforms of the 1980s. Income equality improved during the first half of the 1980s largely due to a reduction of the income gap between rural and urban China. In a political climate that was still ideologically charged, the reformist leaders implemented new policies that enabled a takeoff of rural private entrepreneurship. Special economic zones were established to attract foreign trade and capital.

In some ways, China's achievements in the political arena at the time are just as impressive. The reformers empowered and institutionalized the M-form economy that fueled income growth and competition. There was a burst of literary creativity and intellectual exploration. The CCP loosened its straitjacket on Chinese society and even began to voluntarily exit from some government agencies, sectors of the society, and areas of economic management. The political power of the CCP became more distributed, more shared, and partially diluted. The autocratic scope was at its maximum. This is all the more notable because at the time the Communist ideologues, hardline military officers, and revolutionary elders still held substantial sway over politics and decision making, and they periodically launched savage and debilitating attacks on reformist leaders.

How do we account for the bursts of both economic and political liberalism during this polarized era in Chinese politics? The question gives away the answer. Political and policy innovations fermented when there was a diversity of ideas and politics. In a top-down system like China's, polarization is the only source of such heterogeneity. It provides a back door for experimentation and opportunities for trial by error. Contrast this situation with the ensuing decades, when these modest openings were closed. The political reforms were reversed, and Chinese high politics was more unified. Yes, China undertook economic reforms in some areas, but it never advanced the reforms far enough to tackle the commanding-height pillars of the Chinese economy, despite the waning of the ideological orthodoxy, greater market-economy knowhow, and far more propitious conditions after the end of the Cold War.

## Fractious High Politics

At the Thirteenth Party Congress in October 1987, Zhao Ziyang announced "the most radical document on political reform ever put forward by the Chinese leadership."[6] Both the timing and the far-reaching nature of the reform program are revelatory. The timing was extraordinarily precarious. Early in 1987, CCP conservatives had launched a fierce assault on the liberal general secretary Hu Yaobang. The trigger was the student demonstrations that first erupted in Hefei of Anhui province in late 1986 and then spread to Beijing, Shanghai, and other cities. The conservatives accused Hu of fomenting "bourgeois liberalization" and "spiritual pollution." In January 1987, Hu was removed and three liberal intellectuals were expelled from the CCP.

The ink of these decisions was barely dry in October 1987 when Zhao unveiled his blueprint for comprehensive reform, a plan that could fundamentally alter the nature and the position of the CCP in the Chinese economy and society. Zhao had devised an ingenious theory to neutralize the CCP ideologues. China, he announced, was at the initial stage of socialism, and this stage, he argued, was not well suited for the prescriptive blueprint envisaged by Karl Marx. Zhao went on to proclaim a vision for the CCP that was more programmatic and actionable than anything the undisciplined Hu Yaobang had ever contemplated: separation of the party from the state, administrative decentralization, a clearer differentiation of the roles and functions of the state, and a more distributed power structure. He unveiled plans to curtail the holding of multiple positions by the same leader, to abolish leading party groups within the administrative units of the state, and to remove the CCP from day-to-day management of enterprises.

How did a such dramatic swing in the political pendulum take place? High politics in the 1980s was famous for its fractiousness. The economic and political reforms unfolded not because there was a solid liberal consensus, but rather because of the space created by the contentious politics at the highest levels. Let us start at the very top. The power structure of the 1980s was described as "two and half," with Deng Xiaoping and Chen Yun at a similar level of status and power and Li Xiannian as a half rung down.[7] Chen Yun and Deng Xiaoping disagreed with each other about the economic reforms and China's open-door policy, but the two agreed on politics—in particular, the imperative to preserve CCP's power. This view set them apart from the frontline policymakers Hu Yaobang and Zhao Ziyang. And in a political system celebrated for the facade of its unity, these differences were laid bare for all to see in a visceral manner. In his book *Prisoner of the State*, Zhao Ziyang writes that Chen Yun got up and walked out of the Thirteenth Party Congress as Zhao was in the middle of delivering his report on political reforms.[8]

The political polarization existed at the operating level of the Chinese state. Of the four vice premiers under Zhao, Yao Yilin and Li Peng were transparent conservatives, and Wan Li and Tian Jiyun were transparent liberals. Today, one is hard-pressed to discern any substantial policy differences between Premier Li Keqiang and his four vice premiers, or any meaningful differences among them. They are bland technocrats who attained their positions by being good at following orders.

The political reforms of the 1980s happened against overwhelming odds. According to Saich, no fewer than three groups of critics, all of whom held powerful positions, were opposed.[9] The first group consisted of ideologues, like CCP theoreticians Deng Liqun and Hu Qiaomu. The second group, led by Chen Yun, the brain trust of China's central planning, consisted of those who were opposed to marketization and the open-door policies. And the third group was comprised of senior officers in the Chinese military. The reformist leaders navigated these treacherous waters tactically and carefully, often taking two steps forward and one step backward.

A trump card in the hands of the reformers was the impressive economic results they delivered. Their political capital was the post–Cultural Revolution consensus on economic growth. The rapid income gains in rural China silenced the ideologues. The reformers leaned on an economic argument to win support from Deng Xiaoping. Deng, a political conservative, was willing to trade off ideology for economic gains, although only up to a point (and an unpredictable point at that). But this strategy had its shortcomings. One is that it required extraordinary economic results to neutralize the vigorous political opposition. The other is that economic missteps had costly political consequences. In the summer of 1988 Deng Xiaoping dictated an unwise combination of policies—a full liberalization of prices and a massive expansion of credit. Zhao was reportedly against these hasty moves by Deng but the conservatives seized on the spiraling inflation to attack Zhao and the entire reform program.[10] A few months later, during the Tiananmen demonstrations, the most serious crisis the CCP had ever faced, Zhao was ousted by Deng and the other elders.

## Reforms by Experimentation

The 1980s were not consistently liberal. There were frequent ideological backlashes against the reforms and the reformers. Retrogressive movements sought to restore China to its pre–Cultural Revolution status quo ante, with "anti-speculation," "anti-spiritual pollution," and "anti-bourgeois liberalization" campaigns. The play *What if I Were Real* was banned after just a few showings. Yet the reforms continued despite these formidable obstacles. The frequency of the prefix "anti" in the various opposition campaigns only underscores the kinetic energy of the liberalizing forces.

The two most prominent political features of the 1980s were "gentle politics"—political rivalries, previously life-and-death affairs, were now decriminalized—and polarization. Left- and right-wing ideologies battled each other at the highest levels of the intellectual and political terrains, and the top leaders were divided between reformers and conservatives. The polarization created space for experimentation and policy innovation.

Rural China accounted for more than 80 percent of the population and it experienced burgeoning entrepreneurship in the real as well as financial sectors of the economy. Despite the barrage of assaults from Maoist ideologues against the private economy, the 1980s gave birth to some of the most prominent private-sector players who still dot the Chinese corporate landscape today. The computer giant Lenovo was founded in 1984. So was Haier, China's largest company in white goods. The Hope Group, once China's largest agri-business company and now split into four different companies (each a giant in their respective domains) was founded in 1983. Huawei, the Chinese 5G company that has been much-maligned in the West, was founded in Shenzhen in 1987.

In Chapter 2, I explained that the M-form economy created room for local leaders to experiment and that reforms proceeded by experimentation rather than by a coordinated central blueprint. But ultimately even if an experiment proved successful, an additional step was required: the central leaders had to approve continuations or extensions of the experiment. Nothing is automatic. A decision is required. This is where the political and policy space matters.

The policy space was created in a number of ways. One is that the CCP ideologues and conservative elders, while powerful in their own right, lacked knowledge of policy and operational details to run a country. They were not in the driver's seat of managing day-to-day affairs of the state. Often the realities on the ground moved much faster than they knew, and they would find themselves in an awkward situation of having to reverse a fait accompli, a hard thing to do compared with preempting a proposed action. The reformers sometimes acted deliberately to keep the conservatives in the dark. In 1983, for instance, CCP theoretician Deng Liqun proposed investigating the employment situation in the private sector, but the reformer Hu Yaobang vetoed the idea out of a concern that the findings might fuel criticisms from the ideologues.

Disagreements among the revolutionary elders contributed to the policy openings. In the early 1980s, the employment size of private businesses was considered ideologically sensitive. The CCP ideologues created a rule restricting private business to no more than seven employees, citing Karl Marx's theory of labor surplus. (In *Das Kapital*, Marx uses a fictional example of a private firm employing eight workers to illustrate his theory of labor exploitation.) The rule was never enforced, and some rural private businesses employed hundreds of workers. We now know why. In his memoir, ideologue Deng Liqun reveals a disagreement between Chen Yun and Deng Xiaoping on this issue.[11] Chen, prompted by a policy memo on widespread private-sector employment, favored some form of restrictions while Deng opposed, but the two men avoided coming to a clash over the issue. Deng argued for a "wait-and-see" stance, while Chen acquiesced on the grounds that it is good to have different opinions within the party. He asked only that the practice not be publicized or promoted.

Such ambivalence gave the reformist leaders the openings they needed. Under Hu Yaobang, the CCP issued Document No. 1 of 1983 on rural work, promulgating the seven-employee rule but urging local officials not to crack down on the violations. The history of the Chinese reforms is one of central leaders acknowledging and approving a fait accompli on the ground, not one of a wise ruler designing and micro-managing each reform measure. Experimentation occurred under a divided central

government rather than under a central government that was united behind one ruler. Therein lies a fundamental difference between the eras of
Deng and Xi.

## Political and Policy Signals

The opening salvo for the Chinese reforms centered on rural interests
and the rural economy. Control rights over land were decentralized and
contracted out to the farmers. Township and village enterprises (TVEs)
boomed. Rural output quadrupled. Poverty declined. The TVEs forced
the urban-based state-owned enterprises (SOEs) to become more disciplined, thereby opening up competition in the Chinese economy.

Descriptions of the reforms in the 1980s typically do not go much beyond this level of detail, but there is much more to the story. For instance,
many believe that the reforms in the 1980s were gradualist and carefully
bounded by state actions and claim that the TVE miracle was a creation
of entrepreneurial local governments.[12] In fact, the TVE phenomenon was
due to the free entry of the private sector rather than government spon-
sorship. In my 2008 book *Capitalism with Chinese Characteristics*, I track
down the original official definition of TVE, which makes it clear that
"township and village" refers to geography, not administration. The TVEs
were enterprises *located* in townships and villages rather than enterprises
administered by township and village governments, as is often asserted.
How much difference does getting this detail right make? In 1985, there
were 12 million TVEs. Of this 12 million, only 500,000 were clearly labeled as "private," giving rise to the impression that TVEs were basically
collective entities. But 10 million out of the 12 million TVEs were household businesses—known as single proprietorships in the West—and the
number of collective TVEs sponsored by townships and villages was only
1.6 million, a tiny fraction of the total number of TVEs. TVEs were an
overwhelmingly private-sector phenomenon.

Aside from the accounting issue, how does one explain the wave of
entrepreneurial activities in the 1980s? This is a perennial puzzle in studies of the Chinese economy: where does the incentive come from? China
then—and now—did not have conventional sources of property-rights
security, such as a constrained government, an independent judiciary, free
media, and political power for the propertied class. Deng's agricultural
reforms touched none of the conventional pillars that supposedly enhance
entrepreneurial incentive. According to standard economic theory, economic agents need to feel confident that their future gains will be safe

before they are willing to expend efforts and capital today. Property-rights security is the purported incentive.

A comment by Liu Chaunzhi, who in 1984 founded the company that would become the global IT giant Lenovo, gives a clue:

> I remember that it was in 1978. There was an article in *People's Daily* about raising cows. I got so excited upon reading it. During the Cultural Revolution, there were only editorials in the newspapers, and every editorial was about revolution and class struggle, non-stop. At that time, raising chickens or growing vegetables was viewed as capitalist tails that were to be cut. Now the *People's Daily* has an article about raising cows. Things have definitely changed.[13]

Liu inferred a change, not from a constitutional revolution embracing a multi-party system and freedom of expression, but from the topic of an editorial in the mouthpiece of the CCP. Liu's mindset was so anchored to the ceaseless "revolution and class struggle" of the Cultural Revolution that a mundane exhortation about raising cows in *People's Daily* signaled a monumental shift in policy. To understand Liu's incentives, we need to understand his psychological anchor and how far the 1978 situation had departed from that baseline of the Cultural Revolution.

The CCP did more than editorialize about cows. It took concrete action to signal that things had changed. In the late 1970s, the CCP released imprisoned capitalists and returned their confiscated assets—bank deposits, bonds, gold, and private homes. There is a distinction between security of a proprietor and security of property. Private property rights have never been secure in China, either then or now. But the restitution measures of the CCP signaled that they were offering more security to private persons. The Cultural Revolution had destroyed Chinese capitalists, but now the post-Mao leadership was reinstating their personhood. Yes, state takings of private property are important, but for potential proprietors of new businesses in the 1980s, the incentive effect of not being arrested must have been massive.

The CCP also elevated the political status of entrepreneurs. Western analysts often hail Jiang Zemin's 2001 theory of "Three Represents," which endorsed the idea of recruiting private entrepreneurs into the party, as an ideological breakthrough. This is adding insult to historical injury. The CCP under Hu Yaobang in 1981 had already endorsed such an idea, but in the ultra-conservative aftermath of the Tiananmen crackdown, Jiang Zemin fiercely attacked and forcefully banned the practice of recruiting party members from the private sector. At best, he should be given some credit for an act of self-correction—rescinding the ban that he himself had instituted eleven years earlier. Getting the timing right is not a minor detail in history; it is about getting the incentive story right: the entrepreneurial incentives were present not after the economic takeoff in 2001, but before the economic takeoff in 1981. This sequence of events sets the record straight about entrepreneurial incentives and it does not require us to strain basic economic logic as do so many of the economic accounts of China.

Finally, there is the sui generis nature of Deng Xiaoping. Much of the writing about Deng describes him as a pragmatic, open-minded statesman who opened China to foreign investment and launched the reforms.[14] All true, but none of this explains the incentive effect of Deng Xiaoping. The single most important fact about Deng is that he had been purged by Mao, twice. The cruelty to him was not just political but personal. During the Cultural Revolution, Red Guards at Peking University pushed his son, Deng Pufang, out of a three-story building, breaking his back—and when he was taken to the hospital, he was refused treatment because of the political status of his father. Deng Pufang was paralyzed from the waist down, and today as a paraplegic, he carries the political scars of that era. Now imagine yourself in 1978 considering entrepreneurship, and seeing Deng take charge of the CCP. That was a very credible signal of policy and political change. Nothing came remotely close to this Deng Xiaoping effect.

In calling Mikhail Gorbachev an idiot, Deng Xiaoping was thinking of Gorbachev's political reforms. But Deng underestimated how the differences in his and Gorbachev's personal backgrounds affected their respective endeavors. Gorbachev was a rising star in the Soviet system, having first ascended from a modest position in a Soviet republic to a prominent national position in charge of agriculture and then, amazingly by any Chinese standard, being put in charge of the entire country. As a beneficiary of the system and an establishment figure, he needed perestroika to signal his determination to depart from the status quo. By dint of his own history, Deng's rise to power itself was sufficient to signal that intention. Gorbachev did not have this luxury; he failed for many reasons, but idiocy is not one of them.

## A Loosening of the Chinese State

In the 1980s, the CCP began to undertake some institutional reforms. Take rural finance.[15] Much of the economic scholarship on China focuses on the

1990s, and it gets quite a few things wrong. One is the idea about the specialness of Zhejiang. Zhejiang, especially its Wenzhou region, is famous for its private entrepreneurship and free-wheeling informal finance.[16] In fact, in the 1980s informal finance was geographically widespread, extending to areas far beyond Wenzhou. Archival research reveals that informal finance was vibrant in regions as far-flung as Guizhou, China's poorest, agricultural, and land-locked province; to Jilin, the bastion of SOEs in the northeast; to Hebei, the province surrounding Beijing. Reports by the regional People's Bank of China (PBoC) in the 1980s describe streets in Guizhou province lined with pawnshops and rotation associations, identical to the scenes documented by Kellee Tsai in the 1990s during her field research on back-alley finance in Wenzhou. In Jilin, a 1987 PBoC report shows that in a survey of rural households, 68.9 percent had borrowed from the informal credit market, and they had used 81 percent of their underground loans for production. Muhammad Yunus won a Nobel Prize for inventing micro-finance, but China was practicing it at scale in the 1980s.

The report by the Jilin branch of the PBoC is revealing in another respect. Then and now, Jilin province has had a reputation for being economically conservative, but the PBoC report is highly laudatory of informal finance in the province. In the 1980s, informal finance was not so informal. It enjoyed sometimes tacit and sometimes explicit endorsements from the highest echelons of Chinese financial policymakers. Consider the following statement:

> Under the banking regulations, individuals are not allowed to engage in financial operations. The emergence of private credit shows that our financial work falls short of what is needed. This requires that our credit cooperatives and agricultural banks improve their services. This is a huge task.

This statement did not come from a random individual in China; it came from Chen Muhua, governor of the PBoC from 1985 to 1988. In this statement, Chen acknowledged something that Chinese leaders today refuse to own up to: the proliferation of informal finance was due to the ownership biases of formal finance. Chen was urging the state-owned banking system to do a better job of alleviating credit constraints on the private sector rather than advocating crackdowns on informal finance.

Informal finance itself is a form of private entrepreneurship, so when private entrepreneurship was legitimized, informal finance flourished too.

The geographic spread of informal finance reflected a confluence of surg-
ing private-sector demand and greater supplies of private credit. Toward
the end of the 1980s, informal finance began to acquire a quasi-official
status. In the 1980s, organizations called rural cooperative foundations
(RCFs) arose organically from the privatization of communes' production
assets, such as plow animals and heavy-duty equipment. These were either
too costly to be acquired by individual households or were indivisible. (A
donkey cannot be cut in two and still remain a viable factor of production.) The villagers securitized these assets and issued shares to subscrib-
ers. They then used the pooled capital to meet the liquidity demands of
rural businesses and households. These were savings and loan institutions
genuinely owned by their members.

The scale of the RCFs was enormous. In 1990, RCFs were present
in 38 percent of Chinese rural townships and in some regions reached
levels comparable to the official credit institution in rural China, the Agricultural Bank of China (ABC). In 1990, the RCFs in Wenzhou pooled
20 million yuan from their members, compared with total outstanding
loans of 26.5 million yuan by the ABC. Most remarkably, after the PBoC
refused to officially recognize the RCFs, the Ministry of Agriculture took
over supervisory responsibilities. This is a salient feature of the 1980s: the
political system did not march to a single tune.

Also in the 1980s, political space opened up. At the elite level, China
entered a period of "gentle politics," when political rivalries were no longer life-and-death affairs. Decision-making powers became more distributed and society was viewed as offering a helping hand for monitoring the
conduct of the state. For instance, in 1980, the CCP publicly sanctioned
the minister of commerce for paying for only a portion of his meals at a
fancy restaurant in Beijing.[17] Yes, the CCP often directs such performative punishments against its own members so the act itself was not unusual. What was unusual was that the sanctioning department, the Central
Commission for Discipline Inspection (CCDI), issued the censure on its
own and did so publicly. Today it is inconceivable that a minister would be
censured without an explicit decision by the PBSC, or more specifically
by Xi Jinping. In the 1980s case, the Chinese media followed up independently on the matter, reporting on subsequent attempts by the minister to
punish the whistle-blower, a chef working at the restaurant.

The Chinese state became a bit humbler, with officials acknowledging their own mistakes and reversing their own policies. The CCP does
reverse its policies, usually long after the policy was enacted, and often

frames the act as a self-congratulating showcase of its infinite wisdom for having delivered the reversal. To the extent that any errors are acknowledged, they belong to one's predecessors, who are probably already languishing in jail, and never those of the incumbent leaders. In the 1980s, by contrast, the state acknowledged mistakes and errors more readily, sometimes accompanied by expressions of contrition and remorse.

In an after-action review of the capsizing of the oil rig in the Bohai Sea described in Chapter 2, for instance, the Ministry of Petroleum made a stark revelation: "Since 1975, the Bureau of Ocean has reported 1,042 accidents of various sizes, of which 33 are extremely serious, but we did not deal with them in a serious manner."[18] At the local levels, officials owned up to their mistakes by issuing public apologies, a rarity in the Chinese officialdom.

In 1982, there was a centrally mandated policy to crack down on "economic speculation"—profiteering from price arbitrage, a common entrepreneurial activity in the 1980s.[19] An early victim of this campaign was Han Qingsheng, an engineer in Wuhan, the capital city of Hubei province. His crime: receiving six hundred yuan for giving technical assistance to a TVE. Like many technicians at SOEs, Han earned extra money by doing consulting work. He and the others were known as "Sunday engineers" because they spent their Sundays working at the TVEs. As part of the 1982 speculation crackdown, Han was sentenced to three hundred days in prison for engaging in "technological speculative activities." As Han later put it, he endured a day in jail for every two yuan he received. (Two yuan was worth about thirty U.S. cents.)

The fate of Han Qingsheng became a cause célèbre. A national newspaper, the *Guangming Daily*, ran a special on the case and aired views on two opposing sides. (This is another lesser-known fact about the 1980s: the Chinese media in the 1980s were extraordinarily free and active. Newspapers often ran two opposing opinion pieces side by side.) Intellectuals and scientists rallied to Han's side, and the government eventually backed down and released him.[20] But it didn't end there. The mayor of Wuhan city apologized. Adding a personal touch, he delivered to Han's home the court verdict as well as the six hundred yuan that the government had confiscated.

Wenzhou, China's bastion of private entrepreneurship, was also heavily impacted by the crackdown on speculation. The government went after the eight richest private entrepreneurs in the city, known as the "eight big kings." Seven were arrested and one fled the city. The economy of

Wenzhou cratered, prompting the Wenzhou government to reverse itself swiftly. It released all the imprisoned entrepreneurs and returned their assets. It even acknowledged its error by publishing its decision in local newspapers.

These are anecdotes and anecdotes are not data, as a common saying goes. But one way to know whether they reveal something meaningful is to ask whether there were similar anecdotes after the 1980s. Under Xi's anti-corruption campaign, many officials have been forced to express remorse and contrition in staged appearances. This sort of contrived accountability points to the state's coercion, not humility. Instead of officials spontaneously apologizing to the public and acknowledging their errors, as in the Wuhan and Wenzhou cases described earlier, these purged officials are paraded on TV as handcuffed criminals. More *1984* the novel than 1984 the country.

## A Great Reversal

In the 1980s, the conservative elders in the CCP behaved in the same way an opposition party behaves in a democracy. They waited on the sidelines, then pounced on every mistake the reformers made. They enjoyed great latitude in the way they leveled their critiques. Removed from the day-to-day administration of the country, none of these conservative elders was intimately involved in actual policymaking or implementation. For all his economic gravitas, Chen Yun had very little engagement with the economic and business dynamics on the ground. Deng Liqun, the CCP theoretician, did some arm-chair quarterbacking, occasionally filing whistle-blowing complaints about the reformers to Chen Yun and Deng Xiaoping. The closest he got to real-world economics was quoting and applying tidbits from *Das Kapital* to business developments that he learned of from the newspapers and government reports.

The precariousness of Chinese politics meant that reformers had zero margin for error. In the summer of 1988, the reformers miscalculated and made some bad moves. Prices were liberalized across the board while there was still a residual shortage of some critical products, and in the context of rapid credit expansions. When inflation surged, conservatives seized the opportunity to mount an attack. By the late summer of 1988, the reformers were on the defensive. Zhao made a self-criticism at a Politburo meeting and his economic decision-making responsibilities were reduced.

From the fall of 1988 to the spring of 1989 a fragile, tense political stalemate held between the reformers and the conservatives, only to be smashed by an uninvited actor—a civil society awakened by socioeconomic flexibilities, emergent intellectual freedoms, and rising expectations. The trigger for the spring 1989 mass demonstrations was the death of liberal reformer Hu Yaobang on April 15, 1989. As a political and economic matter, the 1980s ended one year short of its decadal mark. On June 4, 1989, the Chinese army opened fire on protestors who were occupying Tiananmen Square. In the aftermath, Zhao Ziyang was forced to step down as CCP general secretary. He was replaced by Jiang Zemin, party secretary of Shanghai. China moved in an entirely different direction.

## *Abandoning Political Reforms*

In the 1980s, the reformist leaders made genuine progress in loosening CCP controls over society. Such progress is not well known because the window of implementation was too short: the political reform agenda was laid out at the Thirteenth Party Congress in October 1987, only a year and a half before the Tiananmen crackdown. Yet the CCP had already abolished its branches in several government agencies, and the role of the CCP in Chinese society and the economy was being scaled back.

The surest signs of these directional political reforms, however, were the Tiananmen demonstrations themselves. In the fall of 1988 and the spring of 1989, Chinese university campuses were bubbling over with political activity and intellectual explorations. "Democracy salons" and discussion groups engaged in reappraisals of China's history and culture and contemplated the future of the Chinese political system. At the time, Taiwan had just begun to legalize political opposition, and Chinese intellectuals, many within the CCP, were holding debates about the Taiwan model.

A lead indicator of a revolution, as Alexis de Tocqueville points out in *The Ancien Régime and the Revolution,* is a societal loosening and emergent political flexibility.[21] This is the "Tocqueville paradox": an authoritarian regime is at its most vulnerable when it is least authoritarian. For the CCP, that Tocquevillian moment occurred in 1989. Wang Qishan, China's vice president and one of the seven PBSC members between 2012 and 2017, is a fan of this book by Tocqueville, a preference that is sometimes taken as evidence of Wang's liberalism. The reality is exactly the opposite. The lesson that leaders such as Wang Qishan learned from the Tiananmen events is to never again allow politics to approach that Tocquevillian moment.

The post-Tiananmen leaders rescinded every political reform that Zhao Ziyang had initiated. The 1987 CCP Constitution had stipulated a separation of the state from the CCP and the CCP had accordingly begun to withdraw from some government ministry branches and from the SOEs. The post-Tiananmen leadership reversed this position, revising the CCP Constitution and restoring the CCP branches in the government ministries. In the 1980s, there had been discussions about creating a professional civil service outside of the CCP. That idea was scrapped after Tiananmen.

## Rise of the Shanghai Clique

Since the Tiananmen crackdown, Chinese politics have trended toward the authoritarian and conservative. Intellectual freedom has been curtailed, and suppression of political dissent has intensified. What may be underappreciated is the impact of Tiananmen on the Chinese economy. Since 1989 China has maintained a high GDP growth rate, but a careful analysis of the data reveals that after Tiananmen, China experienced a declining labor share of GDP and, relatedly, a declining household consumption share of GDP. In the 1980s, household income growth outpaced or paralleled the growth of GDP. In many of the years since, GDP growth has outpaced gains in household income.

One startling fact about the post-Tiananmen leadership is that so many of the leaders hailed from the least-reformed region of China—Shanghai. The SOEs in Shanghai remained statically dominant. Measured in percentage shares of fixed-asset investments by ownership, Guangdong (96.6 percent state-sector share) and Zhejiang (100 percent state-sector share) started off in 1977 with a bigger state-sector share than Shanghai (84.6 percent). By 1988, the fixed-asset investment share of SOEs in Guangdong had declined to 71.2 percent, and in Zhejiang, the figure had dipped to 36 percent, but Shanghai remained stubbornly at 81 percent. Jilin, a province known for its bias toward SOEs, also experienced a steeper decline in the state sector's fixed-asset investment share compared with Shanghai, from 78.6 percent in 1977 to 72.9 percent in 1988. The 1980s was a decade of super-charged growth. Between 1977 and 1988, Shanghai's per capita GDP growth averaged 7.7 percent annually, which is not bad compared with today's China, but it paled in comparison to Guandong's 10.3 percent and Zhejiang's 13.4 percent during the same period. Shanghai substantially underperformed against Jilin (9.6 percent per capita GDP growth).

Despite Shanghai's subpar track record, after Tiananmen almost the entire upper echelon of the Shanghai government was transplanted to Beijing, where they took over the central government almost entirely. Between 1989 and 2002, the "Shanghai clique" ruled China in the foreground, and they ruled in the background between 2002 and 2012.[22] Some say that during the one year that Xi was in Shanghai he was so impressed with it that he ignored his much longer experience in the market-driven Zhejiang province. Xi has targeted the Shanghai clique politically, but his economic model hews faithfully to the classic Shanghai statist model.[23]

Who was in the Shanghai clique? Jiang Zemin, party secretary of Shanghai, was elevated to the position of general secretary of the CCP in June 1989. China's economic czar between 1991 and 2002, Zhu Rongji, was the mayor of Shanghai and succeeded Jiang as Shanghai party secretary in 1989. He then assumed the position of vice premier in 1991, executive vice premier in 1993, governor of the central bank between 1993 and 1995, and then premier between 1998 to 2003. Huang Ju, Zhu Rongji's successor in Shanghai, served as China's executive vice premier between 2002 and 2007. Zeng Qinghong, deputy party secretary of Shanghai in 1989, became deputy director of the General Office of the CCP, equivalent to deputy chief of staff in the White House, and then director of the General Office in 1993. Between 1999 and 2002, Zeng controlled CCP's personnel system as head of the Organization Department. He was China's vice president between 2003 and 2008. Wang Huning, a political science professor at Fudan University in Shanghai, was brought to Beijing by Jiang Zemin. Now Wang ranks fourth in the CCP leadership.

The Shanghai technocrats were the beneficiaries of the Tiananmen crackdown. Either ideologically or as a matter of political expediency, they gained from the repudiation of the 1980s approach, which was blamed for the nationwide protests. Economically, the best characterization of the Shanghai method is crony capitalism, a reform approach that fosters private-sector development but in ways that ensure a close nexus between the state and business. Rural entrepreneurship, the most spontaneous and most arm's-length type of capitalism in China, was marginalized. Starved of capital, TVEs took an immediate hit.

The authorities enacted a sweeping crackdown on informal finance. The tacit license granted to the RCFs ended in 1993. In that year, the RCFs were prohibited from taking deposits from villagers, thereby eliminating competition with the state-owned ABC on the deposit side. The Rural Credit Cooperatives (RCCs), run by the local governments and soon to be merged with the ABC, took over the deposit business of the RCFs. Then the authorities cracked down on the lending side of the RCF business, limiting credits to agricultural production only. In 1996, the RCCs took over the entire operation of the RCFs, and in 1998 the State Council criminalized all informal finance activities, including the RCFs. The RCFs, an important funding vehicle of small-scale rural entrepreneurship in the 1980s, came to a crashing end. TVEs, starved of capital, soon faded away.

How do we explain the vibrant informal finance in Wenzhou that researchers have documented? For reasons that are not well understood, Wenzhou did not go along with the rest of country; it avoided cracking down on informal finance. Chinese economists have gone to great lengths to explain the uniqueness of Wenzhou—including its supposed commercial culture and the high level of trust. The explanation, I believe, is more prosaic: Wenzhou continued with the financial policy model of the 1980s whereas the rest of the country did not.

The laws and regulations enacted in the 1990s against informal finance are still reverberating today. The crackdowns on peer-to-peer lending and on fintech can be traced to rules and regulations of that era. Another practice today—imprisoning informal financiers—is also a legacy of that era. In 1991, Zheng Lefang, an illiterate housewife in Wenzhou, paid the ultimate price for engaging in underground finance—she was executed for "financial fraud." Personifying the turning point in China's financial policies, Zheng had committed her alleged crimes in 1986, but she was spared until 1991, when the political climate turned against the private sector.[24]

Since the early 1990s, numerous rural entrepreneurs, who had been forced to tap into underground finance because of the inaccessibility of the formal sources of funds, have been arrested. A famous case is Sun Dawu, a rural entrepreneur who ran an animal feed company in the impoverished province of Hebei. In 2003, Sun was arrested for "illegally absorbing public funds." Sun was not willing to offer bribes to Chinese bankers, often a prerequisite for accessing loans. He turned to his employees instead and pooled capital from them. In the 1980s, this was a routine and widespread practice and a legitimate source of startup capital for many private-sector companies. Huawei raised its initial rounds of capital this way (which is why Huawei is formally an "employee-owned" company). In his prison cell, Sun coined a phrase that was later invoked by many in the media, "Chinese peasantry, your name is misery." Sun was released after an outcry in the media, but in 2020 he was arrested again and in 2021 was sentenced to eighteen years in jail. Among the charges was an illegal funding scheme.

We also have micro evidence of the reversal in financial fortunes in rural China during the 1990s. In papers I published with my coauthor, Meijun Qian, we use two rural household survey datasets, one from 1986 to 1991 and the other from 1995 to 2002, to compare the financial situation in rural China during these two decades.[25] Access to finance collapsed between these two sampling frames. In 1986, about 34 percent of rural households reported receiving either formal or informal loans; by 2002, this ratio had fallen to 10 percent.

In pooled regressions that include data from both periods, a dummy variable for the 1995–2002 period shows up consistently negative and significant when the dependent variable consists of various measures of access to loans. We examined a variety of alternative hypotheses that might explain this reduction of financial access in rural China, such as labor migration and profitability of rural businesses. But none of these explanations could make the negative coefficient of the 1995 to 2002 effect go away, leaving the well-documented policy change in the 1990s as the most likely explanation.

Did this financial reversal matter? Yes, enormously. Consider the growth of personal income in rural China. A conservative estimate is that rural income grew by 7.2 percent annually between 1979 and 1988.[26] Between 1989 and 2001, however, that growth rate was halved, to 3.8 percent. In fact, for a number of years in the late 1990s, nominal rural household income did not grow at all; it only grew in real terms because China was experiencing a bout of deflation in the wake of the Asian Financial Crisis of 1998. By the turn of the twenty-first century, an average Chinese peasant would have been 50 percent richer had the growth rate of the 1980s prevailed into the 1990s. And we cannot blame this slowdown on a base effect. Under Jiang Zemin and Zhu Rongji, the growth rate of urban household income picked up, as did the growth of rural income under the more pro-rural leadership of Hu Jintao and Wen Jiabao. Policy matters.

To understand the macroeconomic imbalances that have plagued the Chinese economy over the past thirty years, we must first get a handle on the contraction of the labor share of income. In the 1990s, rural Chinese still comprised a large proportion of the Chinese population and their declining income growth during the period of rapid GDP growth was an important driver of China's falling labor share of income. Many economists blame China's low consumption to GDP ratios on a high savings rate. This is an incomplete explanation. Falling income share was a more direct catalyst.

## *Crony Capitalism*

Another finding from our research is that in the 1990s, the political status of rural households—that is, whether a household member is a cadre—increased loan access in a significant way. This was a dramatic change from the 1980s, when this status had no effect on access to formal loans. Rural households with an elevated political status could access more loans in the 1990s than otherwise identical households that lacked political status.[27]

Crony capitalism, which bundles politics with business opportunities, had arrived. The state had sanctioned the recruiting of private entrepreneurs into the CCP as early as 1981, as a signal of policy change and stability, rather than as an enticement. There were few takers of the offer. Under the crony capitalism of the 1990s, however, CCP membership was a conduit to valuable resources and business opportunities. Private entrepreneurs began to join in droves.

One long-term effect of the policy reversals enacted by the post-Tiananmen leaders was the rise of rent-seeking and systemic corruption. Ending corruption had been a rallying cry of the student demonstrations in 1989. The demonstrators had insisted on transparency and disclosure of the assets of government officials and their families, demands to which Zhao Ziyang and other reformist leaders had considered acquiescing. Zhao offered to have his own children be investigated first and for the Politburo to launch a formal investigation into corruption.[28] Zhao's stance antagonized other leaders for its cascading effects and hardened the already hardline position of Li Peng, the premier, whose children were active in business. The crackdown after Tiananmen sent an unmistakable message: corruption was politically safe. A taboo was lifted. Political reforms, CCP transparency, and a nascent civil society, the forces that could have dented corruption, all retreated after Tiananmen.

On the economic front, the conservative reformers of the 1990s were selective in their approach, prioritizing those reforms that maximized rent-seeking opportunities. Privatization proceeded on a large scale. According to one estimate, as many as 50 million workers at SOEs were laid off between 1996 and 2003, possibly the single largest shock therapy in history.[29] The technocrats from Shanghai were enamored with urban planning, technology, and globalization. They repressed rural entrepreneurship with one hand and then turned around to liberalize the urban real estate market with the other. They opened China to foreign direct investment and found a kindred ally in Wall Street.

This is the Chinese side of the famous China syndrome—the draining of America's Main Street and the enrichment of Wall Street. The reforms enacted by the Shanghai technocrats led to growth and productivity improvements in China, but they ruined the integrity and the quality of the Chinese political system. The reforms were rife with pricing favoritism, privileged access, insider looting, and regulatory laxity. When combined with political opacity, it was a recipe for large-scale corruption.

Why did the post-Tiananmen leaders aggressively pursue SOE privatization and opening to foreign capital while erecting obstacle after obstacle to rural entrepreneurship? On purely economic grounds, the biased liberalization of the 1990s led to GDP growth rates similar to those of the 1980s. But there was a political calculus: that strategy re-created the vertical capitalism of Chinese history, the kind of capitalism dependent on the state. Foreign capital is subject to a selection effect that makes foreign capital politically safe. Those foreign investors who go to China are least likely to make troubles for the country; the disagreeable ones simply do not show up. You see Ray Dalio in China, but you do not find George Soros there. By contrast, domestic private capital, especially those private entrepreneurs with an arm's-length relationship with the government, are not sorted politically. Some are pro-government; others less so. Sun Dawu, the twice arrested rural entrepreneur, was far more vocal about the rule of law and rights protection than foreign investors.

Under crony capitalism, the power of the CCP was monetized on a global scale rather than being limited to the pool of domestic savings. Crony capitalism also lowers the transaction costs of rent extraction. Extracting rent from millions of small and dispersed rural single proprietorships is costly both in absolute terms and relative to the size of the extracted rent. A single initial public offering on the stock market, however, can yield millions of dollars in benefits to decision makers and their cronies. After the Tiananmen crackdown, both the quantity and the quality of Chinese crony capitalism mutated. The fortune of the former premier, Wen Jiabao, was estimated to be US$2.7 billion, and US$14.5 billion was seized from the family and associates of Zhou Yongkang, the fallen former PBSC member on corruption charges.

The wealth accumulated by Wen's family is eye-opening. Of all the CCP leaders, Wen had the most perceptive diagnostics of what caused corruption. Right before he stepped down, he indicated that the government was considering a limited asset-disclosure requirement, going back to a promise by Zhao Ziyang that was reneged on by the leaders in the 1990s. It was an empty gesture, proffered on the eve of his departure in order to leave a positive impression. He remarked, "Corruption tends to occur frequently in departments that possess great power and in areas where the management of funds is centralized."[30] He was absolutely right about that—and he himself furnished the proof.

Increasing centralization during the 1990s led to a dramatic spike in the monetization of political power. In her book, Yan Sun documents major changes in the type and level of corruption between the 1980s and the 1990s. Before 1992, it was mostly lower-level officials who were found to be corrupt. After 1992, there was "a marked rise" of the bureaucratic rank of corrupt officials, so that "chief and deputy executives of cities, government bureaus, law enforcement, judicial agencies, state banks, and large SOEs" were being caught.[31] The case value escalated dramatically. In her dataset, the highest value from before 1992 was 38,000 yuan, a case in 1990, whereas in her second period after 1992, the lowest value was 64,000 yuan. Case values from the second period include 9.97 million yuan, 18 million yuan, 25 million yuan, and 40 million yuan. These are an order of magnitude larger than the case values in the 1980s. Another change is the nature of the corrupt acts. In the 1980s, the corrupt officials were those who condoned corruption; in the 1990s, the officials actively engaged in corrupt acts themselves. Corruption metastasized.

Sun's study is excellent, but her dataset is small.[32] When there are just a few observations, conclusions can be swayed by outliers. To construct a larger dataset for this era, my research assistants and I identified nine legal terms in Chinese laws that are related to corruption and bribery. We used the Python software to download all the articles in *People's Daily* that were published between 1980 and 2012 that contain one or several of these legal terms. This methodology yielded a total of 568 corruption cases between 1980 and 2012. Some of the articles reported on the case value of corruption, and we used this information to discern the changing values of corruption since 1989 (see Table 4.1).

The data are broken down by three leadership eras as defined by the identity of the CCP general secretary: (1) Hu Yaobang and Zhao Ziyang, from 1980 to 1989, (2) Jiang Zemin, from 1990 to 2002, and (3) Hu Jintao, from 2003 to 2012. The differences among the three leadership eras are stark. During the first era, the mean case value is 121,760 yuan; during the

*Table 4.1.* Corruption case values reported in the *People's Daily*, 1980–2012

|  | 1980–1989 | 1990–2002 (ratios to the previous era) | 2003–2012 (ratios to the previous era) |
|---|---|---|---|
| Mean case value (yuan) | 121,760 | 3,994,009 (32.8) | 30,475,497 (7.6) |
| Median case value (yuan) | 66,167 | 1,353,618 (20.5) | 14,346,648 (10.6) |
| Value of all cases to GDP ratio | 0.042 | 0.161 (3.8) | 0.442 (2.74) |

*Note:* The data are organized by three leadership eras: (1) Hu Yaobang and Zhao Ziyang during 1980–1989, (2) Jiang Zemin during 1990–2002, and (3) Hu Jintao during 2003–2012. The figures in the brackets refer to the ratios of case values to the previous leadership era. The GDP is measured in millions of yuan. The corruption case value is measured in yuan. To obtain the data, we used Python to extract articles from the *People's Daily* from 1980 to 2012 based on the nine legal terms in the Chinese legal codes. The terms are 贪污 (*tanwu*, graft),受贿 (*shouhui*, accepting bribes), 行贿 (*xinghui*, giving bribes), 挪用公款 (*nuoyong gongkuan*, embezzlement), 巨额财产来源不明 (*ju'e caichan laiyuan buming*, unknown sources of significant assets), 渎职 (*duzhi*, malfeasance), 滥用职权 (*lanyong zhiquan*, abuse of power), 玩忽职守 (*wanhu zhishou*, dereliction of duty), and 徇私舞弊 (*xunsi wubi*, malpractice for personal gain).

second era this figure increased to 3,994,009 yuan, and during the third era, to 30,475,497 yuan. During Jiang, the mean case value is 32.8 times of that under Hu and Zhao and under Hu Jintao, it is 7.6 times that of Jiang Zemin. The increase is not driven by a few outliers in the data. The median case value increased substantially between the 1980s and the subsequent periods, as shown in the period ratios in parentheses in the table.

These figures are denominated in nominal terms and one might argue that, given inflation and the rapid GDP growth in China during subsequent decades, the actual value of corruption did not increase to the extent indicated earlier. This is not the case. Table 4.1 presents the ratios of the sum value of all the corruption cases to China's GDP, in order to correct for the GDP growth and inflation, and the pattern is just as clear: 1989 was a turning point. The case value of corruption increased enormously after 1989 under Jiang Zemin and Hu Jintao.[33]

## The Long Shadow of Tiananmen

As of 2018, Xi Jinping had accumulated some twenty-six titles, earning the *Economist* magazine's moniker "Chairman of Everything." Xi acquired power through a series of deft maneuvers, such as the anti-corruption campaign that targeted his political rivals. But there is a chicken-and-egg question. Was his long, extensive campaign proof of his power, or is it what enhanced his power? I tend to believe the first explanation: Xi was powerful even before the anti-corruption campaign began, and this is why he has been able to sustain it for so long.

Anti-corruption campaigns are not rare. Since the days of Jiang Zemin, the newly inaugurated general secretaries of the CCP have all launched anti-corruption campaigns. But prior anti-corruption campaigns tended to be short-lived and surgical. Xi's campaign is wide-ranging and it has aimed at high-value targets. Among the first to fall were Zhou Yongkang, head of the Central Legal and Political Affairs Commission, and Xu Caihou, vice chair of the Central Military Commission. Both were powerful allies of Jiang Zemin. Xi used the anti-corruption campaign to undercut Jiang Zemin, who was already declining in health in 2012.

Personality matters, too. Xi is a more determined and dictatorially inclined leader than either Jiang Zemin or Hu Jintao, and these qualities of Xi manifested themselves only after he rose to the top position. (Jiang and Hu would have been unlikely to promote Xi if they had had any inkling of Xi's intentions.) Amplifying Xi's strong personality was the fact that the CCP in 2012 had lost any capacity to exercise formal or informal restraints on the CCP general secretary. It was a frictionless autocracy. The shadow of Tiananmen loomed long and large, with post-Tiananmen politics more hierarchical and ordered than politics before Tiananmen. Crucially the post-Tiananmen leadership phased out a formal mechanism whereby predecessors could have exercised a degree of power and restraints over successors. That mechanism is the Central Advisory Commission (CAC). These developments together paved the way for Xi Jinping.

## The Path to Xi Jinping

Beginning in 1992, the revolutionary elders moved to consolidate and streamline power. Yang Shangkun was eased out of the presidency and Jiang Zemin took over the office, thus adding to his portfolio as general secretary of the CCP the visibility and the symbolism of the presidency. For the first time since 1982, these two positions were held by a single person, and this has been the case ever since. (The office of the presidency was restored in 1982.) In November 1989, Jiang took over the chairmanship of the CMC from Deng Xiaoping, thereby unifying control over the party, the state, and the military.

On paper, Jiang had more power than Deng Xiaoping, and in some ways he did. Deng exercised enormous power behind the scenes, but also from his formal positions as chairman of the CMC and then chairman and a member of the CAC. There was some formalism to Deng's regency power. By contrast, Jiang Zemin after 2004 held no formal position, and yet in his capacity as a private citizen he constrained and frustrated in more ways than one his successor, Hu Jintao, during Hu's two terms in office. As Joseph Fewsmith noted in the *China Quarterly*, it was the "succession that didn't happen."[34] Hu's PBSC was heavily stacked in favor of Jiang Zemin and, crucially, those who ran China's security and military apparatus on the Politburo hued to Jiang Zemin rather than to Hu Jintao. The result was a persistent policy stalemate and a heavy footprint of Jiang during Hu's tenure. Some characterize Hu's tenure as "collective leadership," but in reality, the situation was thrust upon him without his full consent.

Why has Xi Jinping been so unburdened by his own predecessors? One simple explanation is that the power of his predecessors had faded by the time he took the helm. It is a matter of biology. By 2012, Jiang was eighty-six years old, which limited his capacity to intervene in state affairs; for reasons that are still not clear, Hu Jintao decided to completely abdicate from politics. He stepped down simultaneously from all three positions: general secretary of the CCP, the presidency, and the chairmanship of the CMC. Xi instantaneously acquired all the levers of power that had eluded Jiang between 1989 and 1993 and Hu Jintao between 2002 and 2004. But this begs a question, "What about other former leaders besides Jiang and Hu?" The answer lies at the root of Xi's unimpeded power. The CAC, created in 1982 specifically to give a voice to the retired elders, was abolished after Tiananmen. There was no institutional mechanism for any former leaders to act collectively and to impose regency constraints on Xi. The only suspense in 2012 was whether Xi would use his undiluted power to enact liberal reforms or to strengthen autocracy. By now, we all know the answer to that question.

## A Post-Tiananmen Consensus

Tiananmen—and the fall of the Berlin Wall—produced a consensus among the Chinese ruling elite on both strengthening the power of the CCP, and averting serial failures of the CCP general secretary. Jiang was widely viewed as a transient figure, including by himself. A conservative reformer who hailed from an urban and statist background, the jocular Jiang was a master tactician and power broker, skilled at building coalitions of support and trading favors in a way that his predecessor, Zhao Ziyang, was not inclined. Zhao was a visionary who surrounded himself with young and creative policy wonks and a rare system thinker who viewed political reforms as essential for economic reform. The reign of power from Zhao Ziyang to Jiang represented a sharp rupture in style and substance.

Robert Kuhn's biography of Jiang reveals that Jiang had major misgivings about taking the position.[35] During the 1980s, as I noted earlier, Shanghai had been unexceptional in its economic performance, and in an era when one made a name through one's reform ideas and practices, Jiang did not stand out among Chinese regional leaders. He deserved his own diffidence. He garnered attention only for his politics, not for his economic accomplishments, and mostly from the hardest of the hardline elders. In April 1989 he restructured and then later shut down the liberal newspaper *World Economic Herald* in Shanghai. And on May 25, 1989, he delivered a message to the chair of the NPC, Wan Li, from Deng Xiaoping, demanding Wan's support for martial law. At the time, there was an NPC motion to convene an emergency session to nullify the martial law. The session never occurred because Jiang held up Wan in Shanghai.

These appear to be the sum total of Jiang's accomplishments, all of which took place within two months of being elevated to the leader of China. His two predecessors were far more accomplished before their own ascensions. Zhao Ziyang's pioneering rural reforms in Sichuan solved the hunger problem of 10 percent of the Chinese population and he delivered rapid GDP growth as the premier of the country. Hu Yaobang's accomplishments include rehabilitating officials and intellectuals prosecuted during the Cultural Revolution and solving the thorny, logistical complexities of their cases. If there were Sarah-Palin jitters about Jiang, they were well founded.

The fateful meeting on May 27, 1989, that selected Jiang Zemin lasted a full five hours, maybe evidence that some of the participants needed convincing. Jiang's strongest supporters, Li Xiannian and Bo Yibo, were the ardent hardliners among the revolutionary elders, while Yang Shangkun, at the time president of the PRC and a more liberal leader, stressed that the new leadership team must "maintain the image of reform and opening and win the trust of the people." In the end, Deng told the group: "After long and careful consideration, the Shanghai Party secretary, Comrade Jiang Zemin, does indeed seem a proper choice. I think he's up to the task."[36] Not exactly a ringing endorsement.

The Tiananmen crackdown ousted a pragmatic, experienced, open-minded, and innovative leader, and replaced him with someone short on accomplishments and long on insecurity. To avoid having Jiang's lack of a power base, the main reason for his selection, come back to bite him, the elders felt compelled to take action to buttress Jiang's authority, power, and credentials. Their first move was to get out of his way. At the meeting on May 27, 1989, Bo Yibo remarked, "As long as we stay out of the way and let them [the new leadership team] go, I think they'll do well."[37] This is rich. In 1987, Bo had attacked Hu Yaobang precisely because Hu had called for the elders to "stay out of the way." Now the ultra-conservative Bo was placing his full trust in the inexperienced Jiang.

Deng did his part to stand clear. In November 1989, he resigned from the chairmanship of the CMC, yielding the position to Jiang and giving Jiang command over the Chinese military, an arrangement that had eluded both Hu Yaobang and Zhao Ziyang. The revolutionary elders also agreed that Jiang should be considered the "core" of the Chinese leaders and that power should be centralized in his hands. In 1992, the CAC was abolished, thus removing an institutional base from which the elders could interfere with the frontline management of state affairs. The next move was to edge out Yang Shangkun from the office of the presidency in 1993 and to seat Jiang Zemin in his stead. For the first time since 1982, a single person led both the party and the state.

At the time the office of the presidency was technically a ceremonial post, but the ouster of Yang Shangkun clearly indicates that Deng and his colleagues viewed him as a potential threat to Jiang's power. The real issue with Yang was the Chinese army. Yang had deep ties to the Chinese military and his half-brother was a high-ranking general in the People's Liberation Army (PLA). With operating control over the PLA, the Yang brothers were responsible for carrying out the Tiananmen crackdown.[38] Ousting the Yang brothers cemented Jiang's control over the military and made his leadership position that much more secure.

By 1993, the office of the general secretary of the CCP gained power, responsibility, and visibility, reversing changes that Deng and his colleagues made in 1982. Deng had deliberately "downgraded" the head of the CCP from chairman to general secretary, and stressed the coordination rather than command functions of the role, in an effort to dilute and defuse the power associated with the position. The collective leadership remained the CCP's official mantra but it no longer had an institutional leg to stand on.

*Table 4.2.* Power distribution across leadership positions, 1980s vis-à-vis the 1990s

|                          | 13th Party Congress (1987) | 14th Party Congress (1992) |
| ------------------------ | -------------------------- | -------------------------- |
| General Secretary        | Zhao Ziyang                | Jiang Zemin                |
| President                | Li Xiannian                | Jiang Zemin                |
| Chairman, Central Military Commission | Deng Xiaoping | Jiang Zemin                |
| Premier                  | Li Peng                    | Li Peng                    |
| Chairman, Central Advisory Commission | Chen Yun      | Abolished                  |

*Source*: Various public databases.

The consequences of these decisions are momentous because they removed or weakened built-in obstacles to a future dictatorship. Remarkably, there were no debates, discussions, or deliberations on the long-term impacts of these decisions. No one at the May 27 meeting asked, "What if the Cultural Revolution repeats itself?" The animating purpose of China's reformers of the 1980s was completely forgotten. After a decade of power-sharing, ideological divisions, and internecine jockeying, China was about to embrace a more streamlined, cemented, and ordered autocratic rule. A reversion to the autocratic mean was set in motion and it was only a matter of time before the likes of Xi Jinping would emerge.

Table 4.2 presents five key CCP and government institutions and positions at the time of two CCP congresses—the Thirteenth Party Congress in 1987 and the Fourteenth Party Congress in 1992. The differences are stark. In 1987, there were five power centers, that is, a different individual held each of the five positions. By 1993, only two centers of power remained, with Jiang Zemin simultaneously occupying three positions and Li Peng occupying the fourth position of premier. The CAC was gone.

## The Demise of Regency Rule

The CAC was a fifth pillar of CCP power in the 1980s. Established in 1982 by Deng, its inaugural chairman, it was designed to encourage older cadres to retire so that a younger generation of leaders could take over. (Deng himself, however, undercut that message by heading the CAC and retaining both his seat on the PBSC and his chairmanship of the Military Affairs Commission.) Between 1987 and 1992, Chen Yun, dean of the Chinese conservative elders, was its chairman.

Any organization led by two of China's paramount leaders was destined to be powerful. And in an autocracy, former leaders are the only group of individuals who are not beholden to the incumbent leaders. Through the CAC, the retired revolutionary elders acquired a strong institutional voice and exercised considerable influence. In the 1980s, the CAC had put up roadblock after roadblock to ideas and initiatives proposed by Hu Yaobang and Zhao Ziyang. The CAC also played crucial roles in unseating Hu Yaobang in 1987, adopting a hardline posture toward the student demonstrators in 1989, and sacking Zhao Ziyang.

In September 1989, Deng proposed that the CAC be abolished. His timing suggests that his motive was to shore up support for the weak Jiang Zemin. The other elders, out of fealty to the post-Tiananmen consensus, went along with Deng's proposal, even though it meant a diminution of their voice and influence. An institution that had enabled these predecessors to exercise power and restraints over their successors was gone, breaking up a mechanism for ensuring greater inter-generational consistency of policies and preferences.[39]

During its heyday, the CAC was rightly derided as the bastion of conservatives and CCP ideologues.[40] In the 1980s, the CAC was heavily laden with conservative elders, and it frequently frustrated and undermined the liberal reformers on many issues. But this is a static perspective. Institutions evolve and develop, acquiring new purposes, functions, stakeholders, relationships, and interests. We can imagine a role reversal down the road when a more liberal CAC could check and balance the power of a conservative CCP general secretary. We can also imagine an evolution of the CAC away from the chaotic and disruptive style characteristic of Deng and Chen to one that is rule-based, negotiated, and orderly. It could provide unvarnished advice, a collective voice, and a channel of unfiltered information. The key is to recognize that an autocracy does not suddenly metamorphose into a functional democracy overnight. A better path is to let it evolve, allowing scope conditions, incipient flexibilities, and frictions to emerge over time. A Xi Jinping operating under this setup would certainly be less absolutist than the Xi of today.

In the Western press, the regency rule of the 1980s and the 1990s was known derisively as rule by the "Eight Immortals"—eight revolutionary elders with extraordinarily long political and biological lifespans. And they were powerful—in their time. After Tiananmen, the Eight Immortals shored up support for Jiang Zemin, to avert another catastrophic fail of a CCP general secretary. But their influence waned. After Chen Yun and Deng Xiaoping passed away in 1995 and 1997, respectively, Jiang Zemin, free of their constraints, transformed himself into a more powerful leader than his predecessors.

In terms of both power and stature, the conservatives among the Eight Immortals outnumbered the moderates, but the moderates outlasted the conservatives in life expectancy. Of the four Eight Immortals remaining at the beginning of the twenty-first century, Bo Yibo (1908–2007) was a well-known hardliner; Song Renqiong (1909–2005) had an uncertain political orientation, but Xi Zhongxun (1913–2002, the father of Xi Jinping), and Wan Li (1916–2015) were among the most liberal in their cohort. Xi Zhongxun had stood up against the conservative elders and defended Hu Yaobang at the January 1987 meeting that led to Hu's dismissal. Wan Li had pioneered the rural reforms in Anhui province and was a close colleague of Zhao Ziyang. Given enough time, the ideological orientation of the CAC of the 1990s might have shifted and turned the tables. A more liberal CAC might have erected roadblocks to the conservative incumbents.

An ancient Roman poet once asked, "Who will control the controller?" In the hierarchical system of the CCP, the answer is former leaders. The CAC was a legitimate, powerful channel for these former leaders to air their opinions and to weigh in on issues that concerned them. After 1993, interventions by the elders occurred in a personal capacity, first on the part of Deng and then of Jiang after his own retirement.[41] Personal capacity, however, is subject to biological constraints—death or ill health. By 2012, as compared to 2002 when Hu Jintao took power, Jiang's ability to project regency rule had depreciated substantially and without an institutional base such as the CAC, other former Chinese leaders, including other powerful former living members of the PBSC, could not act as a coherent power bloc. The evisceration of the power of the former leaders is so complete and for the entire world to witness in a sad spectacle of a frail Hu Jintao being forcibly escorted out of the closing meeting of the Twentieth Party Congress, the CCP meeting that sealed Xi's third term.

The Chinese state is strong because it successfully preempts collective action by Chinese society. The CCP system also has an elaborate protocol to limit collective action by its elites. It prohibits unsanctioned peer interactions among Chinese leaders outside of the formal structures of the state, such as Politburo meetings. All state institutions, such as the State Council, the Chinese People's Political Consultative Conference, and the NPC, are under the firm grip of the PBSC. The CAC was the lone institution operating outside this tight orbit of the CCP and enjoyed a degree of de jure and de facto independence.

Chinese liberals bemoan the lack of institutionalization of Chinese politics. They cite interventions by the revolutionary elders to unseat Hu Yaobang and Zhao Ziyang, and these elders' instrumental and extra-constitutional role behind the Tiananmen crackdown.[42] The elders' intervention was particularly egregious during the Tiananmen episode. The PBSC did not vote for the martial law; it was a tie. Martial law was declared only after Deng rallied other elders to take a hardline response to the student demonstration and to sack Zhao Ziyang.

This reading of the CAC, and its role in focusing the power of the elders, is technically correct but flawed in a larger sense. Although in theory the selection and dismissal of a general secretary fell under the purview of the Central Committee of the CCP, not that of the revolutionary elders, the fact is that the Central Committee had no power whatsoever in the real life of Chinese politics. Deng Xiaoping, Chen Yun, and the other revolutionary elders constituted the de facto ruling elites with ultimate decision-making rights and power. They had power because they were perceived to have power, and in that sense, their exercise of power was entirely legitimate. In fact, one can argue, the real problem is the Chinese Constitution. It is written in a way that is at fundamental odds with the reality of Chinese power distribution and political practices.

Also, the Chinese liberals are wildly inconsistent in their complaints and praise. Consider Deng Xiaoping's famous "Southern Tour" in 1992, an intervention that rescued the economic reforms from ruin and launched China on a path to globalization. Chinese liberals hailed Deng's intervention, along with his threat "Whoever does not reform should step down," but this time Deng intervened entirely outside of the formal Chinese system and without even a veneer of formalism. At the time of his Southern Tour, Deng's only position was as honorary chairman of the Chinese Bridge Association.[43] And bridge here refers to a card game, not a component of Chinese infrastructure.

As long as there are leaders, there will be former leaders, and thus the CAC would have an automatic, perpetual life. The only people who had the necessary authority to shut it down were its two most powerful creators, Deng Xiaoping and Chen Yun. They acted to dismantle it before their own demise; otherwise, the CAC could have been a roadblock to an ambitious Xi Jinping, who, by all known indications, is poised to be president for life.[44]

————

We cannot choose our parents. An analogous situation here is that current leaders do not choose the former leaders. In an autocracy, the former leaders are the only ones unbeholden to the incumbent leaders. They command unique legitimacy and standing, and in theory they can pose as a check on the power of the current leaders. The question is whether they have an institutional base to organize collective actions, to act on their legitimacy and standing, and to exercise their power and influence. The CAC came closest to that mechanism, and it could solve the perennial "who is going to control the controller" problem. But Tiananmen dissolved it.

We know the history that happened, but not the history that could have happened. My own view is that the demise of the CAC foreclosed a realistic reform option for Chinese politics, or at least an option for the country to slow down a future dictator. If there is one single counterfactual consequence of Tiananmen, this is it. Democracy is more likely to emerge from negotiated, peer-to-peer politics, and the CAC could have been the CCP version of peerage politics similar to the constraining forces of nobility in the early days of democratic politics of Britain. In some ways, a Communist system is more amenable to this particular path of political evolution than is an authoritarian presidential system. The Communist state functions by a committee system, the Politburo. The twenty to thirty members of the Politburo are more generalists than are the ministers serving in a presidential cabinet. They possess considerable political capital and have accumulated network ties and have the numbers to match the size of their former power.

The demise of the CAC left a gaping vacuum for a determined, dictatorially inclined future autocrat, and given China's autocratic gravity, the arrival of such an autocrat is a mathematical certainty. The only remaining question is whether he will face some obstacles or none. The fateful decision by the post-Tiananmen leaders to centralize power undermined one of their own unheralded achievements—a more diffused and open-ended power structure. These elders had suffered terribly during the Cultural Revolution, and they had agreed on the dangers of excessive concentration of power. Deng Xiaoping and Chen Yun ruled out constitutional democracy, but they at least took meaningful and sensible steps to distribute power among three governing institutions, the PBSC, the CMC, and the presidency, and they created a CAC that could potentially insert some checks-and-balances dynamics into the Chinese system. In other words, they created a frictional autocracy—until they undid it after 1989.

Today, the personality cult has been resurrected, and the specter of the "nasty, brutish and short" politics of the Cultural Revolution is again haunting China. At the Twentieth Party Congress in October 2022, Xi Jinping broke the precedent established by his two predecessors and assumed a third term. China will have come full circle by returning to the disastrous lifelong tenure arrangement under Mao Zedong. The era of Mao was not only autocratic and economically ruinous; it was also perpetually inclined toward destabilizing power struggles and succession conflicts, an unsavory prospect that may await China in the future.

# PART III

# Stability

CHAPTER FIVE

# What Makes Chinese
# Autocracy So Stable?

It may seem a very strange, and a very paradoxical assertion
that the next uprising of the people of Europe, and their next
movement for republican freedom and economy of Government, may depend more probably on what is now passing in
the Celestial Empire.

—KARL MARX, June 14, 1853

As WANLI AND HIS Confucian Mandarins were tussling over affairs of the
heart and succession politics, the wayward emperor never risked losing his
position.[1] Although the Confucian Mandarins feared that Wanli's proposed
anointment of the third son posed an existential threat to the legitimacy of
imperial rule, they never reached out to the generals to plot a coup against
him. Even Wanli's complete abdication of sovereign duties did not cause
them to question his right to rule. Wanli remained "constitutionally" secure on the Dragon Throne. Indeed, throughout Chinese history very few
emperors were toppled by their generals or senior functionaries.

Things were different in the Roman Empire. Praetorian guards
roamed free in the Roman polity and seemed to assassinate at will any
emperor standing in their way. The year 69 is known as a year of four

emperors: in that year, Galba, Otho, Vitellius, and Vespasian ruled in succession. According to one account, between 27 BCE and 395 CE, 70 percent of Roman emperors died of unnatural causes. These include assassinations (37 percent), battle wounds (12 percent), executions (11 percent), suicides (8 percent), and poisoning (3 percent). Roman emperors ruled for only 5.6 years on average, a fraction of the length of the Chinese emperors. No wonder an article analyzing the empire has the title "The Roman Emperor—the Most Dangerous Occupation in Ancient Rome."[2] Reading Nanami Shiono's multi-volume history of the Roman Empire is like reading a chronology of assassinations.[3]

In 1853, Karl Marx boldly predicted the imminent collapse of the Qing dynasty, speculating that the demise of the "Celestial Empire" could spark a revolution in Europe, which in his view had long been poised for a major disruption. But the Qing outlived Marx. The longevity of Chinese autocracy is a source of marvel for some and bemoaned by others. And there are many explanations for it, ranging from political culture to geography.

In this chapter, I build on other scholars' rich insights to offer my own explanation. A key factor for China's imperial longevity is that imperial China figured out how to achieve peace and stability among ruling elites, something that eluded the Roman Empire, through talent recruitment and political control. The recruitment function is meritocracy, a topic I have covered previously; the control function means using the same meritocratic platform to preserve the political monopoly of the throne without dilution of power to independent rival groups, such as the wealthy aristocracy and the landed gentry. I will rely on a database on emperors and senior imperial officials to illustrate this argument.

## A Longevity Puzzle

In his book *Autocratic Tradition and Chinese Politics*, Zhengyuan Fu characterizes the Chinese political system as having five features: "(1) state imposition of an official ideology; (2) concentration of political power in the hands of a few persons, often an individual, without institutional constraints on the exercise of that power; (3) wide-ranging scope of state power over all aspects of social life, including the economy; (4) law as a tool of governance wielded by the ruler, who acts above legal constraints; (5) state domination over all social organization, with private individuals as subjects and possessions of the state."[4]

One would be forgiven for thinking that this is a fitting description of President Xi Jinping's China, but Fu's book was published in 1993, two decades before Xi's ascension. At the time of its publication, Xi was a local official in Fujian province.

Actually, much of Fu's book is about the imperial era from 220 BCE to 1911. That a description of a system founded in 220 BCE still resonates as an approximation of Chinese politics today is a testimony of the remarkable longevity and immutability of Chinese absolutism. I use "political longevity" to refer to the immutability of the fundamental attributes of the Chinese political system as well as the durability of specific regimes. The self-replicative attributes of the Chinese regimes make China different from, say, the British monarchy, which draws its endurance from a bloodline, not from the power it wields. King Charles's bloodline spans thirty-seven generations and over a thousand years: "all of the monarchs are descendants of King Alfred the Great, who reigned in 871."[5] By contrast, the House of Ying, the family that united China and founded Qin dynasty, was completely wiped out after the fall of the Qin.[6] Ying, once a common name and a family that thrived for six centuries before the Qin dynasty, has few descendants in China today. The Chinese political longevity is institutional, not genetic.

## Existing Explanations

Much of the research on the longevity of Chinese autocracy consists of rich and broad articulations about political culture, idiosyncratic decisions by particular emperors (such as the banning of overseas voyages), or structural factors such as the weaknesses of aristocracy and the bourgeoisie.[7] The dominant idea in this large literature stresses the role of political culture. As Fu sums up this view of Chinese history: "The relative stability of the Chinese imperial system was to a large extent due to the stability of its political culture exemplified by official orthodox Confucianism."[8]

There are various strands in this cultural framework. One school of thought places the emphasis on the universal and primordial appeal of Chinese ideology. Yuri Pines argues that the "Chinese empire was an extraordinarily powerful ideological construct, the appeal of which to a variety of political actors enabled its survival even during periods of severe military, economic, and administrative malfunctioning."[9] Pines uncovered textual evidence that Chinese elites expressed a preference for unitary rule even during the fractious era of the Warring-States period

(475–221 BCE). The early dating means that this cultural inclination toward unitary rule predated the Qin dynasty, which created the territorially unified empire. The causal direction ran from culture to politics, not the other way around.

The innate conservatism of Confucianism is another commonly cited factor. According to this view, the imperial Chinese viewed time not as a progression, but as cycled occurrences. Human events and activities unfold at fixed intervals, peaking and declining according to pre-determined and pre-established patterns. History is "a recurrence of fixed patterns and types, variations on the theme of the 'eternal return,' an established inventory, mutatis mutandis, of familiar historical sequences . . . and semi-legendary archetypes."[10] In this formulation, progress was considered an unwelcome intruder and something that should be resisted at all costs. Ruling elites acted on this belief and took action to block advancement.

Others have stressed more tangible forces. In "The Chinese Civilization: A Search for the Roots of Its Longevity," Ping-Ti Ho argued that Chinese stability rested on an economic pillar. The productivity of Chinese agriculture "contributed significantly to making the Chinese civilization the most enduring in the annals of man." He had a demographic explanation: a supposed Chinese "preoccupation with biological and social perpetuation" and the ability of "royal and noble lineages to maintain their status."[11]

Other explanations are grounded more in social science reasoning.[12] One of these is called path dependency—with China's current path created at the dawn of China's political development. For Dingxin Zhao, it was "the dialectic interactions between competition and institutionalization" during the Warring-States period that gave rise to a "Confucian-Legalist state" of the Qin dynasty. This undifferentiated "system of government that merged political and ideological power, harnessed military power and marginalized economic power"—a system that characterized the Wanli era and blended Confucianism and Legalism—contrasts sharply with, say, that of Tudor England.[13] Fukuyama has a similar view about this long shadow of the ancient past. Inspired by Charles Tilly, Fukuyama argues that the intensity of warfare during the Warring-States period led to the rise of a rational bureaucratic state in China.[14]

Still other explanations stress factors such as geography.[15] Social scientists favor this type of explanation because geography is exogenous and it places objective constraints on human agency. China's geographic insulation is sometimes blamed as an enabling condition of Chinese autocracy, in contrast to the more open and more accessible European terrain.

Another often-discussed influence is the Chinese language. Ho pointed to the Chinese script as "a main agent in the prolonged process of sinicizing the various non-Han ethnic groups and as a culturally unifying force, even during periods of alien conquest and political division."[16] Dingxin Zhao reaches a similar conclusion. He argues that it is easier to unify China than it is to unify Europe because of a fundamental difference in language. In European languages, symbols represent specific sounds and over time the variations in the pronunciations led to different spellings and writings. Zhao asserts, "An alphabetic writing system tends to fragment cultures and identities."[17] Even though the Chinese language is pronounced differently in various regions, the written Chinese language connotes the same meaning to whomever is reading it. "This allows people of quite different regional dialects to read a text and understand it in the same way, something that greatly facilitated communication in premodern China."

## *The Search Continues*

In 1984 the German historian Alexander Demandt published a survey of all the causes cited in the scholarly literature for the demise of the Roman Empire, enumerating 210 of them.[18] And Edward Gibbon's magnum opus, *The History of the Rise and Fall of the Roman Empire*, runs thousands of pages long.[19] By contrast, the persistence of Chinese absolutism has generated fewer conjectures, and a number of them are variations on similar themes. In particular, most scholars start with the assumption that China's political formation and its political development are equivalent, that the die was cast by the Qin dynasty and for the next two millennia China pretty much followed this Qin blueprint. This "2Q" perspective looms large.

It is impossible to falsify such a perspective. Neither the dependent nor independent variables have any variances. Also it is not clear what is the cause and what is the symptom. For example, the conservativeness of Confucianism could be an epiphenomenal manifestation of imperial longevity rather than its cause. A ruler is unlikely to revise or give up his ideology if he is successful with it. Some of the proposed variables are not unique to China. Take ideological monopoly. Many European states embraced Christianity as their ruling ideology, but over time the monopolistic grip of Christianity loosened and gave way to other competing ideas and values, such as individualism, secularism, and liberalism. The real question is why ideological monopoly persisted in China rather than that it had started with such a monopoly. Path dependency does not settle the issue. China itself offers a dramatic example of breaking with path dependency: its founding dynasty, the Qin, was Legalistic in its ideological orientation but its successor state pivoted to Confucianism, the arch rival to Legalism. Path dependency implies that human choices are constrained because it makes sense to stay on the current path rather than adopting an alternative path. The question is how available were China's alternative paths in the first place?

Ho's point about agricultural productivity lacks precision. It may explain the longevity of Chinese civilization, rather than the longevity of the Chinese political system. Geography and language are interesting ideas, but they require more detailed specifications. China's geography has accommodated different forms of politics, from the Han-Sui Interregnum that rivaled the polycentric post-Roman Europe to unitary empires such as Tang and Ming. One can go further and argue that geographic constraints are not fixed but are subject to human agency. Europe's easy access to the sea is lauded as a factor for its navigational prowess and its trading proclivity, but let's not forget that China once ruled the sea.[20] Ming and Qing emperors made a deliberate decision to ban ocean voyages, to give up their navigational prowess, and to insulate China from the rest of the world. While geography is exogenous, geographical insulation is not. The logic applies to the inland geography of China. The Sui dynasty constructed the Grand Canal, reducing the geographic insulation within China. Shouldn't we witness new ideas being generated and more ideas being exchanged? Not if the *Keju* system stamped out all the new ideas to be exchanged. The exogeneity of geography is attractive to social scientists, but upon a closer inspection, its explanatory power leaves much to be desired.

Ho's and Zhao's musings about the Chinese language are insightful, but left unsaid in their theory is a propagation mechanism. It is not language per se but written language that has this unification effect. It would require literacy, widespread literacy, for the written language to have produced the unifying effect posited by these two scholars. To make the same argument that Ho and Zhao made requires spelling out what the mechanism is that propagates literacy.

Cultural arguments are often couched in vague terms. For the sake of argument, let's presume that the conservativeness of the Confucian norms stunted China's political development. But exactly how? Was it through brainwashing, perhaps, or the stifling of competition? And what kind of competition—a competition of ideas, or a competition of political and economic forces? And why did Legalism, an ideology as friendly to autocracy as Confucianism, fail to prevail in imperial China? The validity of a cultural argument requires demonstrating that there is a tangible mechanism to put the touted ideas into practice.

My argument earlier that Confucianism was a superior instrument to operationalize *Keju* is a mechanism-based explanation. It spells out the "how" rather than the "what." One way to demonstrate the effect of this mechanism is mapping China's political evolution over time. A thesis known as the "Great Tang-Song transition" is the most famous idea in this genre of the literature. Proposed by Naitō Konan, Japan's foremost China scholar, it asserts that China experienced a milestone transformation during the two great Chinese dynasties, the Tang and the Song. Joshua Fogel sums up Naitō Konan's idea this way: "The major change Naito pointed to with the fall of Tang dynasty was the collapse of aristocratic government in China, and the rise of monarchical autocracy and populism."[21]

This is a promising direction but we can inquire further what instigated the collapse of aristocratic government and its replacement by the "monarchical autocracy." Some have been tempted to blame specific historical events, such as the An Lushan Rebellion that devasted China between 755 and 763. The rebellion shrank the population from 53 million to 16 million, prompting Steven Pinker to call it history's greatest recorded atrocity.[22] These population figures, however, are disputed. Since the rebellion aimed at the elites, maybe the rebellion degraded the capacity of the Chinese state to collect accurate census data.

Whatever the real toll, the rebellion was undoubtedly catastrophic. Nonetheless, the Tang dynasty bounced back and endured for another 144 years. The state also quickly recovered much of the revenue it had lost during the rebellion.[23] This is somewhat incongruous with the claim that the An Lushan Rebellion supposedly wiped out the entire Chinese aristocracy.[24] Even if it did, it remains a mystery why the Chinese aristocrats were unable to reassemble after the fighting stopped. Physical destruction can be temporary in its effect rather than causing a permanent displacement.

There are many examples. A study of the Allied bombing of Japanese cities during World War II found that these devastating attacks did not substantially alter the relative size of cities or urban densities in Japan.[25] A country's urban characteristics are rooted in long-standing economic fundamentals, and they will revert back to their original patterns over time. During the land reforms of the 1950s, the CCP destroyed landlords as a class but some of the Chinese entrepreneurs in the later reform era hailed from this landlord lineage. Destroying a cohort of aristocrats is not the same as destroying aristocracy as an institution. A permanent aristocratic demise requires a sustained institutionalized force suppressing its reemergence. Moreover, a destruction of the aristocracy does not explain why the power flowed exclusively to the emperors rather than to other centers of power such as priests, generals, eunuchs, or merchants. Why was a "monarchical autocracy" the only replacement option? To delve into these and related questions, we revert our attention back to the *Keju* system.

## Unpacking China's Political Longevity

Historians argue that changes in human capital were behind the rise of China's enduring "monarchical autocracy." During the Song, new elites emerged who had obtained their elite status through talent and education, rather than because of family connections.[26] As Robert Hartwell has argued forcefully, *Keju* drove this development.[27]

We can unpack the longevity question in three ways. One is to make comparisons over time. One set of data puts these time variations in sharp relief. The ratio of the period when China was disunited relative to the period when it was united fell from 0.81 to 0.29 after the Sui dynasty.[28] A second method is to consider discrete components of the political system. Each dynasty was comprised of regimes ruled by particular emperors and each emperor in turn ruled over his subordinates. Is it possible that the duration of Chinese dynasties increased because each emperor ruled longer? The number of years that a ruler stayed in power is often used by political scientists to measure political stability.[29] The third method is to identify a milestone, a pivotal moment for Chinese imperial longevity. The "Great Tang-Song Transition" straddles some 661 years in Chinese history. Is it possible to narrow down that transitional window by a notch?

Recall the finding presented in the Introduction that the longevity of Chinese dynasties increased over time. If we count the Han dynasty as two distinct dynasties, the later dynasties lasted longer. Before Sui (581–618), the Western Han dynasty (202 BCE–9 CE) was the longest, lasting 193 years; by contrast, the Tang (618–907) lasted 289 years; the Ming (1368 to 1644) endured for 276 years, and the Qing (1644–1911), 267 years. (The Song from 960 to 1279 lasted 319 years, but it was divided into a northern and southern half.)

The Chinese rulers stayed in power longer as time passed. The average years that an emperor stayed in power was 24 years for the Han dynasty, 17 years for Sui, and 19 years for the Tang. For the Qin, it was only 7 years. By contrast, the ruler duration of China's final dynasties was 28 years for both the Song and the Yuan (1280–1368), 22 years for the Ming, and 36 years for the Qing. The two-way correlation coefficient between emperor duration and dynastic duration is 0.63.

## Rise of the Symbiotic Relationship

How did emperors manage to hold on to their reigns longer over time? Let's investigate one level below the emperor and see if certain characteristics of an emperor's high-ranking officials may have played a part. Milan Svolik observed that the stability of authoritarian regimes depends on the consent of the political elites.[30] If the autocrats can secure explicit or tacit cooperation from the political elites, their rule will be safer. (Roman emperors failed spectacularly in this area.)

Our imperial court database has records of 2,225 unique premiers who served in the imperial dynasties from the Qin to the Qing. Premiers, the most senior bureaucrats, were the "chief operating officers" of the Chinese dynasties, carrying out the day-to-day duties of the court. We collected information on how they exited from their positions and found that in ancient times, the manner was not pretty. Of those premiers for whom we have records, 14 percent were executed, and another 13 percent were exiled. About 19 percent of premiers left their positions through a voluntary route—they resigned.

Figure 5.1 presents a scatterplot with premier resignations on the horizontal axis and the emperor duration on the vertical axis. The resignation measure is given by the premier resignations as a proportion of the total number of premiers of a dynasty. (Other than resignations, the Chinese dynastic premiers also exited by natural death, execution, exile, demotion, and suicide.) Emperor duration is the dynastic mean length of an emperor in power measured in years. The bubbles are sized to the emperor duration.

A strong positive relationship between these two variables is shown in the graph. The two-way correlation coefficient between these two variables is 0.74, a high value. Although these correlations do not prove that voluntary exits of premiers caused the longevity of emperor rule, we can use social science theories to construct a causal connection

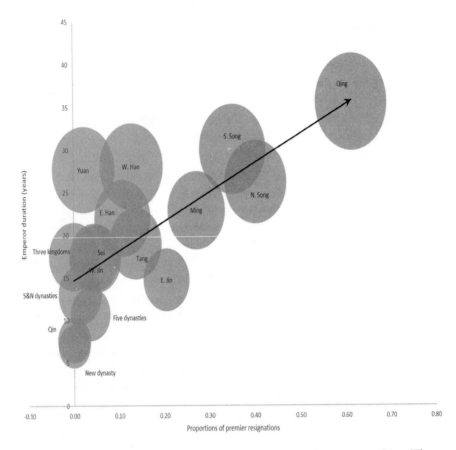

Figure 5.1. Emperor duration and premier resignation, from Qin to Qing. The vertical axis shows emperor duration, measured in the average number of years an emperor stayed in power. The horizontal axis denotes the proportions of premiers who exited their positions through resignations. (Other exit options include exile or death by illness, execution, or suicide.) The calculations do not include cases in which premiers exited because the dynasties they served collapsed. The bubble is scaled to the emperor duration. Calculations are based on the data in the imperial court database. For details of the database construction and sources, see Huang, Zheng, Hong, Liao, and Sun, *Needham Question.*

between the two variables. In his classic book *Exit, Voice, and Loyalty,* Albert Hirschman theorizes how three types of responses by members of an organization—exit, voice, and loyalty—can supply information to an organization.[31] Resignation is similar to the exit option in Hirschman's framework, although the analogy is not perfect. Chinese emperors decapitated quite a few of their premiers, an exit option not available to modern organizations.

Hirschman likely would frown upon decapitation as a poor organizational device, not just because of its ghastly human toll but also because decapitation kills the information along with the person. Organizations that silence information are more prone to decline. Dynasties that allowed bureaucrats to quietly resign their posts were better run and more resilient. In this telling, exits are an informational device that serve to alert the emperors about problems in their dominions. Regimes with this informational feature endured longer.

We can use another theory to explain the relationship between these two variables. Historians use "symbiosis" to describe the relationship between the emperor and his bureaucracy that emerged after the Han dynasty.[32] A symbiotic relationship implies a loyalty based on mutual obligations and dependency and the emperors ruled collaboratively with their bureaucrats. Voluntary exits are a form of symbiosis and they improved incentives and elicited trust and hard work from the premiers, not unlike the regional officials operating under the CCP's M-form economy. In lieu of violence, emperors offered their premiers a safe exit option in exchange for their loyalty. Governance and administrative quality improved; stability ensued as a result.

## A Pivotal Moment

In Figure 5.1, we present evidence compatible with the claim that the symbiotic relationship between the emperor and his bureaucrats arose after Han.[33] The model shown there has the highest predictive values for nine dynasties: Three Kingdoms, Western Jin, Sui, Tang, Five Dynasties, Northern Song, Southern Song, Ming, and Qing. The only post-Sui dynasty with a poor fit is Yuan. The Sui dynasty appears to be a sharp dividing line in the formation and the cementing of this symbiotic relationship between the emperor and his officials.[34]

What was the nature of the relationship between emperors and their officials before it became symbiotic? The antithesis to a "symbiotic relationship" is antagonism and violence. In Chinese history, emperors routinely executed their officials when disagreements or conflicts arose between them. (Other unpleasant treatments include dismissal, exile, demotion, etc.) Figure 5.2 presents proportions of premier resignation on the left axis and of premier execution on the right axis. A clear pattern stands out: the two exit options are inversely related with each other. The

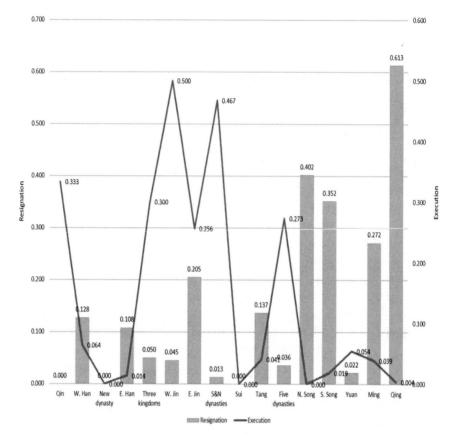

Figure 5.2. Proportions of premier exits through resignations and executions across Chinese dynasties. The left vertical axis denotes proportions of premier exits through resignations and the right vertical axis denotes proportions of premier exits through executions. The resignations are represented by the bars, and the executions are represented by the line. The calculations are based on data in the imperial court database. For details of the database construction and sources, see Huang, Zheng, Hong, Liao, and Sun, *Needham Question.*

dynasties that executed more of their premiers are also those that had fewer resignations and vice versa. (Their two-way correlation coefficient is –0.44.) Dynasties during the Han-Sui Interregnum, Three Kingdoms, Western Jin, and Southern and Northern dynasties were particularly macabre. The Western Jin dynasty executed more than 50 percent of its premiers. During the Southern and Northern dynasties period, 46.7 percent left their positions via execution. Qin is widely believed to be a grim period in Chinese history, but compared with the Han-Sui Interregnum, it was a breeze. Only 33 percent of Qin premiers were executed.

Significantly, the use of these two exit options changed over time. The pivotal moment, as in so much else in Chinese political history, was the Sui dynasty. Before the Sui, an antagonistic relationship prevailed between the emperors and their bureaucrats. After the Sui, the symbiotic relationship, as indicated by resignations, asserted itself. We can support this point more formally by performing a t-test on the mean values of a number of variables before and after the Sui dynasty (see Table 5.1).

The table divides the Chinese history into two periods, with the time around the Sui as the pivotal dynasty. Because the precise pivotal moment is unknown, we define pivot in two ways. If different definitions generate similar results, we can have more confidence in our theory. Panel (1) defines the first period as including the dynasties from Qin to Sui (including the Sui), and the second period as including dynasties from the Tang to Qing. Panel (2) defines the first period as from the Qin to the Han-Sui Interregnum and the second period as the same as under the first definition, Tang to Qing. In the second definition, we exclude the Sui from the calculations.[35]

Under both definitions, the dynastic duration is much longer during the second period (i.e., after the Sui) than during the first period (i.e., before the Sui), almost doubling in length: 184 years on average compared with 95 years on average under the definition including the Sui in the calculation, and 102 years under the definition without the Sui in the calculation. The length of an emperor's rule increased as well, from sixteen years in the first period to twenty-five years in the second period (under both definitions). The t-tests show that the differences are statistically significant at the conventional levels (5 percent or 10 percent).

Emperors served increasingly longer, but not their premiers. In both periods, the premier duration was four years on average. (This finding allays the concern that the increasing emperor duration was driven by a rise in life expectancy.) But the manner of their exits changed dramatically. During the first period before the Sui, 6 to 7 percent of premiers exited their offices through resignation, compared with 26 percent during the second period after the Sui, while exits through executions fell from 22 to 24 percent during the first period to 6 percent. Table 5.1 shows that after the Sui dynasty the regime and ruler durability increased, and that the symbiotic relationship prevailed over the antagonistic relationship by a statistically and politically meaningful margin.

Table 5.1. Leadership turnover during two eras: a comparison

| | Dynasty duration (years) | Emperor duration (years) | Premier resignation (proportions) | Premier execution (proportions) | Premier duration (years) |
|---|---|---|---|---|---|
| Panel 1: Qin to Sui period compared with Tang to Qing period | | | | | |
| Mean values (Qin to Sui) | 95 | 16 | 0.06 | 0.22 | 4.4 |
| Mean values (Tang to Qing) | 184 | 25 | 0.26 | 0.06 | 4.1 |
| p-values | 0.061* | 0.043** | 0.0486** | 0.0666* | 0.761 |
| Panel 2: Qin to Han-Sui period compared with Tang to Qing period | | | | | |
| Mean values (Qin to Han-Sui) | 102 | 16 | 0.07 | 0.24 | 4.0 |
| Mean values (Tang to Qing) | 184 | 25 | 0.26 | 0.06 | 4.1 |
| p-values | 0.089* | 0.046** | 0.056* | 0.043** | 0.895 |

Notes: The variables in this table are calculated from the data in the imperial court database. For details of the database, see Huang, Yang, Hong, and Liao, "Great Tang-Song Transition." The Chinese dynasties are based on the granular definition. For example, Han dynasty is divided into Western Han and Eastern Han. Panel 1 compares the period comprised of Qin (221 BCE–207 BCE), Western Han (202 BCE–9 CE), New dynasty (9–25), Eastern Han (25–220), the Han-Sui Interregnum (220–581), and Sui (581–618) with the period comprised of Tang (618–907), Five Dynasties (907–979), Northern Song (960–1127), Southern Song (1127–1279), Yuan (1271–1368), Ming (1368–1644), and Qing (1644–1911). Panel 2 drops the Sui dynasty in the calculations. Premier resignation and execution refer to the proportions of premiers who resigned or who were executed out of total number of premiers in a given dynasty. Duration refers to the number of years of a dynasty in existence or the number of years an emperor/premier served in the position. T-tests are performed to generate the p-values; ** indicates p-value <0.05, and * p-value <0.1.

## *Keju:* A Longevity Mechanism

We come back to the Sui time after time when explaining China's political evolution. Although the Sui is known for many accomplishments, including construction of the Grand Canal, it is the emergence of the *Keju* examination that exerted the lasting influence on the relationship between the rulers and their officials.[36] *Keju* relied on voluntary participation, incubated values of loyalty, and converged ideas, mores, and values. Compliance became ever more volitional and self-enforcing, thereby alleviating the intra-elite tensions that doomed so many Roman emperors and modern autocracies. It was a two-way street. As the bureaucrats became more compliant and loyal, the rulers sitting on the Dragon Thrones became less violent in their methods. A new social contract of mutuality and reciprocity emerged, and intra-elite peace reigned. The safety of the emperors was assured and so were the dynasties they led. This win-win arrangement then forestalled all other alternative arrangements, an immaculate and static stability par excellence.

## *An Emperor's Dilemma*

Niccolò Machiavelli, the great Italian thinker on strategy and statecraft, wrote about two scenarios that can help us think about how imperial China attained its equilibrium of peace and stability. In one, "the King of France" was unable to remove the privileges of his barons without putting his own reign at risk; in the other, the "sovereign of the Turk" dominated his ministers as his "slaves."[37] The Chinese situation appears to be somewhere between these two scenarios. The emperor preempted the power of his barons, and he gave a lot of autonomy to the ones he successfully co-opted. In other words, the Chinese system exceled at including the right people and at excluding the wrong people. What was that system that gave him a talented staff and yet avoided challenges to his rule?

That system calibrated human capital. If a rational autocrat were to devise such a system, it would look a lot like *Keju*. *Keju*'s recruitment function can be conceptualized as a broader version of what Bruce Bueno de Mesquita and colleagues call the "selectorate."[38] The selectorate theory argues that a rational autocrat is motivated to increase the size of the pipeline to the political system. The easier it is to enter the selectorate, the more costly it is for existing members of the selectorate to challenge the authoritarian ruler. In economics terminology, low entry barriers to the bureaucracy lead to perfect competition among bureaucrats, with each bureaucrat becoming easily replaceable and more vulnerable. The result is greater loyalty to the ruler.

*Keju* lowered the socioeconomic barriers to entering the imperial bureaucracy. This open recruitment feature, in turn, altered the incentives for the political elites so that they were less likely to challenge and defect from the emperor. The elites became more loyal and more compliant due to these selectorate dynamics, and the symbiotic relationship described earlier began to take shape.[39] The beauty of this system is that the discipline effect was in everybody's interest and it was thus self-reinforcing.

Incentive alignment alone may not be sufficient, however. In theory, the meritocratic competition widened the pipeline for everyone, but it could still disproportionally favor the wealthy. Family background, including wealth and parents' educational attainment, usually affects test performance.[40] A Chinese emperor would want to avoid ending up with a court overwhelmingly populated by aristocratic and commercial elites with their own legitimacy and stature. The answer was to add design features to *Keju* in order to optimize the chances that the emperor's preferred candidates would make it through the pipeline.

I have already described *Keju*'s infrastructure, its tiered structure, and its anonymization. Here let me reframe these three features in terms of the selectorate functions they served. *Keju* infrastructure is easy to explain: it alleviated the costs of *Keju* preparations for the commoners and partially leveled the playing field with the wealthy. Recruiting the commoners infused the bureaucracy with their talent but also injected a shift in power balance in favor of the emperor. The emperor exerted more leverage over commoners than aristocrats and he could use that leverage to crowd out or to thwart the elites. (Recall the rule against recruiting imperial consorts from elite backgrounds, which achieved the same effect.) As for the tiered structure, the first two anonymized tiers selected candidates for entry and lower-level positions in the imperial bureaucracy; these were selectorate functions, not the ones of supplying personnel to the highest echelons of the imperial court.

The palace examination did that. It opened the door to the inner sanctum of the imperial court. The high-ranking graduates could communicate directly with the emperor.[41] They were decision makers and policy advisers, not mere cogs in the imperial bureaucracy. Take the example of the grand secretaries during the Ming dynasty. (Grand secretaries served similar functions during the Ming as premiers during other dynasties.

The Ming distributed premier power among several officials.) Of the ninety-two grand secretaries of the Ming dynasty, only six did not come through the *Keju* process. (One hailed from a secret police background.) Of the remaining eighty-six, eighty-five passed the palace examination and held *Jinshi* degrees; the lone exception held a *Juren* degree, having merely passed the provincial examination. (Keep in mind that the odds at that level were already comparable to getting into Harvard.) Of these eighty-five *Jinshi* degree holders, fifteen had placed first among their respective palace examination cohorts and three had come in second place. This was a formidable group of academic achievers.[42]

We are inching closer toward a solution to the emperor's dilemma. The emperor needs *Keju* to provide an initial meritocratic pipeline, but also to allow political loyalty to be considered in the final selection of decision makers. The ingenious third design feature of *Keju*, selective anonymization, did just that.

### Political Control Features of Keju

I previously compared the palace examination to a faculty job talk, whose purpose is to assess those intangible qualities of a candidate not easily discernible in the written materials. At the palace examination, an emperor would inquire candidates about their character and inclinations. Candidates were also required to write policy essays on more open-ended topics. For example, Emperor Wanli came up with the following policy question at one palace examination that read like his cry for help, "Why have I worked so hard but achieved so little?" Another question of his was, "How can one govern without actually ruling?"[43] To ace Wanli's essay questions required a palace exam candidate to be well read and brilliant, of course, but also to have intimate knowledge of Wanli—including his diffidence and insecurity. The policy essays favored insiders—those with some knowledge of Wanli's tussles with his scholar-officials and his infatuation with Lady Zheng.

The evaluations are also based on a set of subjective criteria. Calligraphy, for example, was weighted heavily in the final ranking of the palace examinees.[44] Those deemed the most erudite—that is, those entering into the Hanlin Academy—mastered the highest forms of script, such as "cursive" and the ancient "seal." To evaluate candidates' calligraphy, examiners needed to read the original writings (copyists were not deployed in this stage of *Keju*). This step gave the examiners more leeway and discretion.

The palace examination was set up for a specific political purpose—to tame the economically privileged class. In a royal decree, Emperor Taizong (939–997), the second emperor of the Song dynasty, made the following statement, "In the past, most of the people who passed the Imperial Examinations were descendants of those aristocratic families. This blocked the path towards serving the court for those people with humble backgrounds. [The old imperial examination system] is thus meaningless and worthless. Nowadays, I personally preside over the examination, and decide who can pass the examination. This can eliminate the ills of the old system."[45] Taizong's statement is consistent with the assessment by historians. According to Elman, the emperors viewed the palace examination as "a personal litmus test to ensure political loyalty."[46] In other words, meritocracy demands objectivity and so requires anonymization, while political control demands judgment calls and an element of subjectivity and discretion. It requires knowing who the candidate is and what backgrounds he represents.

The discriminating evidence we are looking for concerns how the family backgrounds and wealth status of the candidates affected performance during the anonymized versus the non-anonymized stages of *Keju*. For the meritocratic elements of *Keju* to function successfully, family background and wealth status should not affect the examination rankings during the anonymized stage of the exam. Indeed, this is the case as I have discussed previously. For the purposes of political control, however, they should have an effect during the non-anonymized stage. But here is the crunch of our idea: a variable such as household wealth should be *negatively correlated* with rankings on the palace examination. This is a demanding hypothesis. It is diametrically opposite of what the established literature on education says. It is much easier to prove the default hypothesis that the wealth variable has a positive effect than proving the alternative hypothesis that it has a negative effect. The political control effect would have to be so large that it shows up as a negative coefficient in our regressions.

### Effects of Family Background

Table 5.2 summarizes the key regression results in the paper I coauthored with Clair Yang.[47] The dependent variable is rankings on the provincial, metropolitan, and palace examinations. Higher rankings denote stronger performances. Our two main independent variables are related to family background, with one indicating the *Keju* candidate's family wealth and the other, his father's governmental rank.

*Table 5.2.* Family backgrounds and *Keju* rankings: main regression results

|  | Anonymized exam stage | | Non-anonymized exam stage |
|---|---|---|---|
|  | Provincial examination | Metropolitan examination | Palace examination |
| Family economic background: | 0.334 | 0.234 | –6.213** |
| wealth | (0.765) | (3.08) | (2.464) |
| Family political background: | 0.943*** | 1.493 | 5.099*** |
| father's rank | (0.280) | (1.05) | (1.017) |
| Other controls | Yes | Yes | Yes |
| Fixed effect | County-year | County-year | County-year |
| Error term | Province-clustered | Province-clustered | Province-clustered |
| Observations | 9,534 | 9,604 | 9,676 |
| R-squared | 0.627 | 0.25 | 0.25 |

*Notes:* For the regression results with a full list of controls, detailed variable explanations, and database, see Huang and Yang, "Longevity Mechanism." Other controls include age, family registration type (official, military, artisan, or commoner), dummy for imperial academy, dummy for prefecture school, and four exam subjects (Rites, Poetry, *Book of Documents,* and *Book of Changes*). Robust standard errors are in parentheses. *** indicates p-value <0.01, ** p-value <0.05.

For the wealth variable we used information on a candidate's number of wives. In imperial China, more wives meant more wealth. For the bureaucratic rank of a *Keju* candidate's father, we used the nine tiers of the Ming dynasty's imperial bureaucracy and assigned a value of 5 to the top officials (tiers 1–3), a value of 4 to mid-level officials (tiers 4 to 7), and a value of 3 to those between tiers 8 and 9. (We also assigned a value of 2 to minor officials and 1 to commoners.)

During the anonymized stage, none of the wealth variables are statistically significant, and the effect of a father's rank is positive and statistically significant, though modestly so, in the provincial examination, and not significant in the metropolitan examination. As a whole, our regressions showed that during the anonymized *Keju* stage, the family background variables either had no impact or only a modest impact on *Keju* rankings.

During the non-anonymized stage, however, two noteworthy differences emerge. First, the father's rank is positive and statistically significant, and the political effects of the father's rank increase substantially, creating a fivefold difference in the candidate's exam ranking compared to its influence on the provincial examination ranking. Second, the wealth variable is negative and statistically significant. Its effect is large. A one-unit increase in the number of wives, our wealth measure, is associated with a decrease by 6.2 positions in the candidate's exam ranking on the palace examination.

It is worth emphasizing just how counterintuitive it is to see wealth having a negative effect on the exam rankings. It is well established that, on average, children from richer families attain better educational outcomes than those from less well-off families.[48] One would expect this positive wealth effect to hold in a *Keju* setting. Preparing for *Keju* was a lifelong affair and was costly in terms of time, attention, and both expended and foregone financial resources. All else being equal, wealthy families should command an advantage on *Keju*. And it happens to be a consensus view among China historians that being wealthy did give that advantage.[49] But our findings contradict this consensus.

That household wealth should reduce one's *Keju* ranking is an extremely demanding statistical result. The countervailing effect of wealth had to be large enough to more than offset the positive effect of wealth on a candidate's individual capabilities. Such a large negative effect is unlikely to have occurred by accident. It would have to be by design.

In all our regressions, we include a series of controls, including the candidate's age, family registration type, subjects tested on the examination, the level of the candidates' preparatory schools, and a year-province (or county-year) two-way fixed effect. Our findings hold across the many robustness checks we performed. For example, we explored the interactions between father's rank and wealth. The usual assumption is that power and wealth should reinforce each other; wealth begets power and power begets wealth. This logic predicts that wealthy political insiders should command an advantage over those less well-off candidates but with a similar lineage of political insiders. Our regression results found the opposite to be true. It seems that *Keju* was especially biased against candidates endowed with both a political-insider status and wealth.

Wealth has a central position in many polities and societies. Often political and social arrangements are created to advantage the wealth-holders, and wealth leads to social, political, and economic change. Barrington Moore famously asserted, "No bourgeoisie, no democracy." Not in China. In China politics controls wealth, not the other way around. In this sense, the Chinese imperial system was quite unusual, and so is the CCP system today, an assessment with which Jack Ma would surely concur.

The Chinese system is not anti-wealth. Since ancient times, China has experienced periods of robust commercial development and widespread crony capitalism. And at lower levels of imperial officialdom, there was no systematic discrimination against wealth holders. The discrimination occurs only to exclude wealth at the highest echelons of power. This careful calibration of inclusion and exclusion has offered protection to the wealth holders while curbing their chances of disrupting the system from within.

## High-Level Equilibrium Trap: Political Edition

In his 1973 book, historian Mark Elvin proposed a seminal conceptualization of the economy of pre-modern China—a high-level equilibrium trap.[50] Elvin argued that by the fourteenth century the Chinese economy had settled into a comfortable steady-state balance between a cheap labor supply and stagnant demand due to China's isolation from international contacts. No further improvement was felt to be necessary.

A political version of this high-level equilibrium trap arose long before the fourteenth century. Around the sixth century, a symbiotic relationship between emperors and scholar-officials prevailed, a relationship that was reinforced by a careful calibration of the pipeline to, and the placement of human capital in, the imperial system. This political equilibrium preceded economic equilibrium and might have been its underlying cause. In this sense, Chinese history turns Karl Marx on his head. The superstructure of politics laid down the foundation and locked in the path of subsequent economic and technological developments. The imperial regime reaped the Smithian growth dividends without ever diluting any of its power. In the very long arc of history, this was a rotten deal for China because it conceivably forfeited China's own Industrial Revolution. But the rulers and subjects in the Ming and Qing dynasties could not possibly have imagined an Industrial Revolution on the horizon. It was a trap, but the Chinese felt that they were sustaining a state of splendid excellence and that their meritocracy was standing at the apex of human civilization.

### Organizational Culture

Worldwide, power transitions from one ruler to another in authoritarian societies are frequently triggered by intra-elite conflicts (such as coups).

Of 316 leaders in modern authoritarian regimes who lost power by non-constitutional means, Svolik found that 68 percent of them were ousted by coups.[51] Another study has also noted that in European and Islamic countries, rulers were quite frequently deposed by coups.[52] The high assassination rates of Roman emperors fit with this pattern.

Imperial China had a different tradition. Between 220 BCE and 1911, of the 233 cases of power transitions, only 38 percent were triggered by intra-elite conflicts. Fu documented many cases of court officials unseating emperors before the Song dynasty, but only one case since the Song. He noted that after the Song, "there was no case of a powerful minister or general usurping the imperial throne, no case of an assassination or deposition of an emperor, engineered by a palace eunuch, and only one case of usurpation of imperial authority by an empress dowager, that involving Empress Cixi in 1861, which might have contributed to the ultimate fall of the last imperial dynasty."[53] Recall that Emperor Wanli was never in danger of being dethroned. The personal safety of Chinese emperors was a sine qua non of the safety of the system they led.

Everything about the *Keju* exams promoted passivity, obedience, and docility, rather than martial bellicosity. The scarcity of coups stemmed from this dominance of civilian values. This is shown in the symbols used by the imperial functionaries to express the dynasty's culture, values, and priorities to the outside world.[54] When imperial court officials attended court ceremonies, they wore "service robes" that featured special embroidered rank badges, known as "Mandarin squares."[55] The top rank was symbolized by "two stately cranes soaring above clouds," whereas the lowest rank was represented by "a couple of earthbound quail pecking the grass." Think of the symbolism of an American bald eagle—strength, individualism, and bravery. What do quails and cranes symbolize? Quails have a feisty spirit whereas cranes, with their delicate and thin necks, convey submissiveness, grace, and serenity. The Mandarin squares expressed a hierarchy of values—with submissiveness and docility taking precedence over martial values.

Army officers did not even have the axiomatic right to represent imperial values; they were only occasionally allowed to wear service robes during ceremonies designated for them. The message was loud and clear: the army officers did not enjoy automatic privilege and they were at the mercy of the civilian officials. There were many ways the Chinese imperial system chose to showcase civilian dominance over the military and it was not shy to advertise that hierarchy.

Even an emperor was not spared the stigma of being connected to the "hard power" of the military. Zheng De, known as the "merry monarch," was a rebellious emperor who pushed back against Confucianist orthodoxy during his rule from 1505 to 1521.[56] He reveled in those activities that Roman emperors found pleasurable—wine, entertainment, music, archery. One of his delights mirrored a hobby of Caligula's: visiting brothels in disguise. Above all he had a passion for the military, a posture that horrified the Confucian bookworms who disdained physical and manual endeavors. Defying his culture, Zheng De wore a military uniform and ordered his civilian officials to wear yellow armor over their silk clothing. He also commanded troops in battle.

From the Confucian Mandarins' point of view, this valorization of martial activities demeaned the Dragon Throne—the ruler was doing something that could have been "relegated to any illiterate." He was threatening their "brand of statecraft, based upon the Mandarin squares, the kowtow, and the quoted verses from the *Four Books*." They strenuously protested against Zheng De's decision to command a military campaign against the Tartar invaders, going so far as to instruct a garrison officer at the Great Wall to stop Zheng De's troops—but to no avail. Then they blatantly refused to certify Zheng De's defeat of Tartar as a victory. They insisted that the Chinese side had lost six hundred soldiers and the Tartar side had lost only sixteen. Fortunately for the Confucian Mandarins and for the imperial system they defended, Zheng De died at the young age of thirty. Upon his death, the Mandarins got their revenge: they arrested Zheng De's top adviser and had him executed by dismemberment.

### Civilian Dominance

In China, the pen was rendered mightier than the sword by the *Keju* system. In the reigning hierarchy, Chinese generals were considered uneducated brutes. One officer who rose to prominence in crushing the White Lotus rebellions in 1796 and 1802 was a jailbreaker and a one-time cannibal, not exactly the qualities that impressed scholar-officials.[57] Confucian antagonism toward the military brass also arose from the fact that many army commanders were eunuchs, the eternal rivals of the Confucian scholar-officials in the power struggles that took place behind the palace walls.

Prejudices aside, these so-called uneducated brutes served a useful function in imperial China. During the Ming, eunuchs were the "doers." They ran the police, the military, and the SOEs of porcelains and shipbuilding, the kind of functions orthogonal to the capabilities of those who aced *Keju* exams. The army officers put down rebellions and repelled invaders, a non-trivial task at a time when China's northern steppe regions were restive.

Qing emperors seemed to be more attuned to this mismatch between the problems they faced and the kinds of leaders they were cultivating. The Qing leadership was more militaristically expansionist, and it implemented *Keju* exams on military subject matters. But the Manchus often lost badly to the Chinese at *Keju*. Emperor Kangxi, who ruled from 1661 to 1722, bitterly complained that successful *Keju* candidates could only "memorize old examination answer books" rather than being good at "riding and archery." He expressed his displeasure that *Keju* passed more *Jinshi* graduates from southern China, a traditional stronghold of *Keju*, than from the western provinces. The western provinces had the strongest and the most eager soldiers, whereas the soldiers from the south were "among the weakest," and they passed on "their posts to their relatives who are also weak."[58]

An intriguing fact is that the Chinese dynasties lost battles not just against the powerful military of the West, but also against less developed nomadic civilizations. The weakness of its military ensured peace in the imperial court, but at the expense of China's external defense. The Roman Empire, which granted the hard power of the military higher status and prestige, had the opposite problem: it scored victories in its military conquests but at the expense of its inner peace.[59] The two empires diverged in their values and the decisions they made, and they reaped the results of their choices accordingly.

The subordination of the Chinese military was a long-standing tradition. The Han dynasty often left many military posts vacant and two generals were appointed to the same posting so that they could monitor each other, an arrangement unlikely to be good for military cohesiveness. Over time, this bias worsened. Naitō Konan, the Japanese scholar who proposed the "Great Tang-Song Transition" thesis, drew the line at the Song dynasty. The higher assassination rate of emperors in the pre-Song era was because the assassins—eunuchs and generals—considered themselves to be more or less equal members of the ruling class. After the Song, the act was considered one of rebellion—a subordinate overthrowing a superior.[60] Killing equals is okay; killing your superior is heinous. *Keju*, by further accentuating distance in status between the emperors and the generals, raised the morality toll of intramural conflicts.

## Reverse Takeovers

Imagine if, after signing the "Japanese Instrument of Surrender" on the battleship USS *Missouri*, General Douglas MacArthur proceeded to implement the Japanese royal system in the United States. An equivalent of this scenario happened several times in Chinese history. The Yuan dynasty, ruled by Mongols, replicated the political and administrative structures of the previous Tang and Song dynasties. After an initial suspension, the Mongols retained—and reconfigured in important ways—the *Keju* system, which had no counterpart in the Mongol empire.

The Chinese system managed to resurrect itself even when China was taken over and overrun by alien powers. The imperial system faced multiple and mortal threats from "barbarian nomads" in its northern steppes, who at one point overtook the imperial capital and kidnapped the Chinese emperor. These invasions destroyed specific dynasties but not the essence of Chinese dynastic rule. In fact, in each case, a reverse takeover occurred, with the interlopers adopting the Chinese ways. To paraphrase Horace, the conquered Chinese conquered their barbarian conquerors.

The Mongols named their dynasty after a quintessentially Confucian concept. The name Yuan was inspired by a quotation in *Yi Jing*, the Confucian classic.[61] The Yuan rulers also famously adopted the most restrictive version of Confucianism, Neo-Confucianism, as the *Keju* curriculum. The later Qing dynasty was established by the Jurchen Aisin Gioro clan of Manchuria, a vassal of the Ming court. The Chinese Confucian literati initially resisted and despised the Manchu rulers, and the Manchu rulers fought back by transforming themselves into ardent Confucianists. The Qing court faithfully subscribed to an unadulterated version of Neo-Confucianism and became its fiercest adherent. The Qing emperors built local Confucian temples and paid yearly homage to the Sage. Qianlong (1711–1799) famously demanded that Lord George Macartney bow to him with both knees and forehead touching the ground. The Qing emperors performed this same ritual to the memory of Confucius: "three kneelings and nine prostrations at Confucius' birthplace, Qufu."[62]

Kangxi, the Qing emperor, made references to the founding emperor of the Confucian dynasty, Han, in the most intimate, personal, and ancestral terms. He remarked, "We venerate Confucius because of his doctrine of respect for virtue, his system of education, his inculcation of love for superiors and ancestors."[63] In statements like these, one cannot tell that Kangxi harbored an awareness of his own Manchu ethnic identity as distinct from that of the Chinese. He was thoroughly sinified.

Confucianism is an autocrat's ideology, both in substance and as a ruling instrument. The Mongol rulers initially suspended the *Keju* exam, but then reinstated it in 1315 with a crucial process improvement that would have monumental consequences for the scaling up of *Keju*. The Qing court did not suspend *Keju*, even though the exam outcome was often lopsided in favor of the Chinese candidates. Just one year after the founding of the Qing dynasty, in 1645, the Qing convened the regularly scheduled *Keju* "in order to eliminate the thought of rebellion" among scholars.[64] The Qing valued *Keju* precisely because early in its reign the Manchus sensed resistance from the ethnically Chinese literati. It needed this control instrument even more.

That alien rulers continued with *Keju* points to the tremendous soft power of the exam system. Institutional memory is required to transmit knowledge and operational knowhow from one generation of leaders to the next and from one cohort of functionaries to subsequent cohorts. With *Keju*, even if the imperial rule was disrupted, its method was not. The periodic alien interregnums in Chinese history did not cause a loss of that memory and a loss of operating knowhow. The reverse takeovers, instrumentalized by *Keju*, ensured the transmission and an uninterrupted lineage of autocratic values and ideas.

## The Final Unraveling

Given its ability to perpetuate itself through *Keju*, why did the imperial system come to an end in 1911? There were significant blows to the system along the way. Emperor Wanli's complete abdication and internecine squabbles, for example, contributed to the decay of the Ming dynasty. He let the once powerful Ming army go into decline and neglected to address a gathering threat brewing at China's northeast border and elsewhere. Twenty-four years after Wanli's death, a massive peasant rebellion erupted and the Manchus were able to topple the Ming.

The Chinese imperial system would endure for another 267 years as the Manchus' Qing dynasty turned itself into a carbon copy of the Ming, but the system began to decay when the Qing weakened the *Keju* system. Qing inherited *Keju* and adjointly used it to advance both its meritocratic and political control purposes, but its stance toward *Keju* was always tinged with ambivalence. Recall that *Keju* provoked wrath from Kangxi, who complained about the weak military capabilities of high *Keju* performers. The later Qing emperors increasingly denigrated *Keju*, in part because it benefited the Chinese at the expense of the Manchus, and eventually started curbing its influence by tightening the admission quotas. The late Qing eroded a pillar operating principle of *Keju*. Purchases of government positions, and even degrees, became widespread. Venality rose.

During the reign of Kangxi, the number of *Jinshi* degrees fell drastically. Between 1662 and 1678, the number of *Jinshi* degrees per *Keju* round averaged 205.8, falling from 370.5 in the 1644–1661 period. During the 1679–1699 era, it further declined to 159.3. The average number of *Jinshi* degrees per *Keju* round fell from 289.3 during the Ming to 238.8 even though the population had expanded substantially.[65] *Keju* was still important during the Qing, with 70 percent of Qing's premiers holding *Keju* degrees. But this figure represents a dramatic decline from the 93 percent who held such degrees during the Ming. Also, the crème de la crème of *Keju* were less dominant during the Qing. *Jinshi* degree holders accounted for just 57 percent of the Qing premiers, as compared to 98 percent during the Ming. The Qing as a whole was less meritocratic than the Ming.

The Qing rulers' actions undercut their own longevity. Social mobility contracted when the only upward pipeline was narrowed. Resentment spread wide and deep. Even if passing *Keju* was a statistical long shot, anecdotal accounts of commoners heroically triumphing at various points of the *Keju* events functioned as an "opium of the masses." When those stories stopped coming, the myth was pierced and frustration began to set in.

One person the Qing's *Keju* should not have failed was a Hakka peasant known as Hong Xiuquan.[66] Hong took *Keju* four times, the first time at age fifteen, and failed every time. He then turned to Christianity and came to believe that God wanted him to launch the Taiping Rebellion. The bloody uprising that followed from 1851 to 1872 caused great losses for the Qing army, and wiped out 35 percent of the populations of the rebellious areas.[67] The Taiping Rebellion so weakened the Qing court that it never fully recovered. The timing was extraordinarily bad. Then the Qing faced the gunboats of Western imperialism and an ideology so powerful that *Keju* was unable to match. A massive tree trunk—not a straw—broke the camel's back. Long before its abolition in 1905, the *Keju* system that sustained the Chinese empire for so long was rotten from within and under bombardment from without. In 1911, the imperial system launched by the Qin, systematized by the Sui, intellectualized by the Song, and brought to a full fruition by the Ming, collapsed in a spectacular fashion.

After the regime collapse of 1911, Vladimir Lenin hailed that "a quarter of the earth's population was moving forward, that hundreds of millions of men were awakening to life, to light, and to freedom."[68] Historians echoed this sentiment. Jerome Grieder wrote that "change is the great theme of modern Chinese history. Not change merely, but a vast, imponderable transformation that overwhelms any defense erected against it."[69] But Lenin and the historians spoke too soon. China's imperial system was indeed gone for good, but after an interregnum of tenuous rule by the Nationalists, a foreign invasion, and a civil war, a Republican system was erected that faithfully adhered to Fu's five autocratic features. In 2021, the CCP lavishly congratulated itself on its centennial, having proudly withstood many shocks that would have toppled lesser regimes. I take up this topic next—the extraordinary stability of the CCP, and its vulnerability.

# CHAPTER SIX

# Tullock's Curse

With you in charge, I am at ease.

—MAO ZEDONG TO HUA GUOFENG, April 30, 1976

If you have questions, go and ask Jiang Qing.

—A rumored addendum to Mao's above compliment to Hua

HUA GUOFENG MAY HAVE been one of the most hapless leaders in the history of the Chinese Communist Party. Mao Zedong plucked Hua out of obscurity as his successor during the waning months of his life. His view of Hua was positive but hardly a full-throttled endorsement for someone about to lead the most populous nation on earth. According to Marshal Ye Jianying, Mao said that Hua was a "fair and not stupid" person.[1]

After Mao died in 1976, Hua started his job in a rather spectacular fashion: he had Mao's wife, Jiang Qing, and the three other members of her Gang of Four arrested. That unexpected decisiveness earned him a confidence that had previously eluded him. He began to accumulate several titles, even overshadowing the number that had been accorded to Mao. He was premier of the State Council and chairman of both the CCP and the Military Affairs Commission (MAC).

All of a sudden, however, he lost them all, first the premiership to Zhao Ziyang in 1980 and then the chairmanship of the CCP and the

MAC in 1981 to Hu Yaobang and Deng Xiaoping, respectively. The fall was unceremonious. Chen Yun, junior to Hua as a vice chairman of the CCP but far more confident as a revolutionary elder, was condescending when he called for Hua to step down at a November 1980 Politburo meeting: "Comrade Guofeng should really know his own limitations and know the pluses and minuses he has collected in his life. The pluses are the correct things that he has done and the minuses are the incorrect things he has done. Comrade Guofeng should cherish what he has done and not casually throw away the contributions he has made."[2] The "pluses" for Chen boiled down to just one plus—the arrest of the Gang of Four. Other Politburo members chimed in. The criticisms were wide-ranging, though one stood out for its seeming triviality: Hua had too many of his calligraphic inscriptions put on public buildings. The unstated premise is that public calligraphy is reserved only for deserving leaders. Mao left behind many public inscriptions.

The attack on Hua's calligraphy is a surviving connection between imperial China and the PRC. *Keju* elevated calligraphy as a symbol of the ultimate status of Chinese scholarly officialdom—it was an achievement evaluated during the palace examination, and an honor conferred on the most erudite of the Confucian literati. Hua, a descendant of peasants, hailed from one of the most rustic provinces of China, Shanxi, and he spoke with a heavily accented dialect commonly associated with low cultural and educational attainments. Deriding Hua's calligraphy was a not-so-subtle jab at Hua's humble background.

Cleaning crews went to work and removed all of Hua's calligraphic inscriptions on public buildings, except one. Today, the Mao Zedong Mausoleum in Tiananmen Square still bears Hua's inscription, a visible symbol that forever links the two men. Hua died in 2008 in quiet obscurity and, maybe still stung by the criticism that his calligraphy was subpar, spent much of his spare time in his final years practicing his calligraphic skills.

Hua Guofeng's experience illustrates the intensity of succession politics in China, but there is a gentler aspect to this episode. However unceremonious his fall was, Hua landed softly. He was not investigated for corruption and he retained nominal positions in the CCP and the associated perks. Also during the reformist era, the CCP accomplished peaceful power transitions twice in a row, in 2002 and in 2012, under a succession framework that Deng Xiaoping devised.

In this chapter, I will discuss the contemporary stability component of my EAST framework. I will address two kinds of stability. One is stability in institutional terms, that is, the ability of the system to preserve itself. The CCP has survived multiple calamities that upended regimes elsewhere. Until the era of Xi Jinping, the record of the reformist CCP was especially impressive: its stability was accompanied by economic growth. For a long stretch of time before the Sui dynasty, China was technologically dynamic but fragmented, violent, and chaotic. Mao Zedong preserved CCP rule, but without growth.

The CCP attributes this stability to its immaculate rule. I beg to disagree and there is a simple way to falsify that claim: China is not short of protests and demonstrations, an indicator of social instability. But it is true that so far these protests have not posed an existential threat to CCP rule. The episode that came closest to undermining CCP rule was 1989's Tiananmen and the CCP survived that threat. At this writing, protests in multiple cities are breaking out against the government's lockdown orders, but like others since 1989, these protests are driven by specific grievances—lockdowns or low wages—instead of taking aim at the overall legitimacy of the CCP rule. (Another factor contributing to CCP stability is the ability of the CCP to address these specific grievances, an issue I will return to in Chapter 10.)

The stability record of the CCP is due to its tenacity to withstand shocks, not to its immaculate rule. That tenacity is in part based on surveillance and suppression, but as the history of the Qin tells us, coercion alone is no guarantee for long-term stability. That tenacity is also rooted in the psychology of the citizens—in norms that axiomatically defer to authority and in an epistemology that views the world in terms of issues, events, and people rather than in terms of a system of incentives and constraints.

There is another type of stability having to do with a vulnerability that afflicts the CCP and other autocracies—the risk that accompanies the transition of power from one leader to another. Here the CCP's record is incorrigibly blemished. Hua Guofeng is but one of the serial succession failures in the PRC. On this issue, in contrast to the stability rooted in Chinese norms, the CCP is completely on its own. History does not offer a useful roadmap for what to do and what not to do. The lessons and precedents of male primogeniture of imperial China do not readily apply. In a narrow sense, the succession politics of the CCP resembles Tudor England more than the era of Wanli: the field of contention is more open-ended. In other ways, CCP succession is afflicted with a dysfunctional fluidity characteristic of all other non-hereditary autocracies: the rules of the game are built and destroyed as things go. It is an invitation to intrigues, power struggles, and betrayals.

I call succession problems in an autocracy a "Tullock's curse," so named after Gordon Tullock who developed a systematic theory about the bad and misaligned incentives in autocratic successions.[3] It is a sobering picture and the history of the CCP makes it quite clear that succession failures are a feature, not a bug, of that system. I use this framework to narrate a number of well-known succession episodes in the history of the PRC. In Chapter 9, I will revisit Tullock's curse in the context of Xi Jinping, who solved Tullock's curse in 2022 in a classic fashion befitting an autocrat—by postponing the succession decision.

## Authoritarian Resilience

During the early 1990s, many in the China-watching community believed that Tiananmen had dealt a fatal blow to the legitimacy of the CCP, an idea that gained traction as Deng's health deteriorated. Chinese political stability was viewed by many as being rooted in strong personalities, such as Mao and Deng. But the CCP failed to crumble—instead it became stronger. After Deng passed away in 1997, the CCP transitioned to the eras of Jiang Zemin, then Hu Jintao, and now Xi Jinping. This tenacity of the CCP is sometimes referred to as "authoritarian resilience."[4] The reasons for this resilience, and whether or not the CCP is resilient, however, have been a matter of some dispute.

In 2001, in his book *The Coming Collapse of China*, Gordon Chang lists a host of China's frailties: popular protests, bad debt, unemployment, loss of ideological legitimacy, the worldwide failure of Communism, inefficiencies of state-owned enterprises (SOEs), a primitive agriculture, splits in the ruling party, out-of-control pollution, corruption, government interference, and fraying relations between the central government and the regions.[5] Although he wasn't wrong about these facts, he missed his target prediction by a wide margin.

An opposite view is "performative legitimacy:" the idea that the CCP derives consent from society by delivering growth and prosperity.[6] This idea does not pass a basic plausibility test. Since 1949, the CCP's rule has survived both calamities and prosperity. It has endured the terrible outcomes of the Great Leap Forward and the Cultural Revolution as well as the supposedly liberalizing effects of growth and globalization. Since

1949, the CCP has been all over the place in terms of its performance, but the CCP's rule has stayed constant. Performative legitimacy may be a part of the explanation, but it can't be a major component.

After these failed prognostications, it is high time to rethink and adjust our basic approach. The correction is not to go to the infallibility narrative that the CCP has constructed about itself.[7] The fallibility of the CCP is too evident to ignore, but it is true that its fallibility has not injured its overall stability and legitimacy, at least not fatally. Let me propose the following way to think about the stability of the CCP. There exist powerful pillars of stability in the CCP system that insulate the CCP from its performance mishaps. These stability pillars are rooted in Chinese norms, an ethos and mindset formed over a long stretch of history. One such norm is an entrenched belief among the Chinese people that can be described as "axiomatic legitimacy"—an upfront grant of trust to the state that is unearned and is often decoupled from state actions. Axiomatic legitimacy offers potent protection to the Chinese state and enables it to withstand many shocks.

## Shocks and Tenacity

So far, the overall stability record of the CCP—its institutional immutability—has been stellar, despite the trauma the country has experienced. Consider the Great Leap Forward and the Cultural Revolution, the mass layoffs of SOE workers in the 1990s, and the lockdowns of Wuhan and Hubei in 2020 and of Xian and Shanghai in 2022 during the COVID-19 pandemic. The CCP has not only ridden out the storm, but has expanded and prospered, now boasting more than 96 million members. If the CCP were a country, it would rank sixteenth globally in terms of population, the same as Vietnam (96 million) and above Republic of the Congo (87 million).

There are varying estimates of the number of civilian deaths during the Great Leap Forward. According to official Chinese government estimates, 16.5 million lives were lost between 1958 and 1962. Independent researchers and scholars put the toll much higher. The highest estimate I have seen is 45 million; others include 30 million.[8] The Cultural Revolution from 1966 to 1976 led to the deaths of an estimated 750,000 to 1.5 million civilians.[9] These were self-inflicted wounds, but there have also been shocks emanating from outside of the system. When the Asian Financial Crisis of 1997–1998 crippled the Suharto regime in Indonesia, the Chinese system remained intact. The CCP has even benefited from some of the external crises that weakened other countries. The Great Recession of 2008 supposedly validated the superiority of the China Model.

The CCP has implemented epic shock therapies and survived to tell the world about them. In the 1990s, the number of layoffs in the state sector was estimated at 30 to 50 million workers.[10] Remarkably, the COVID-19 outbreak that originated in China due in part to the opacity of the Chinese state boomeranged to confer strength on Xi Jinping. The lockdowns of Wuhan, Hubei, and Shanghai are unprecedented in the history of human civilization. Xi Jinping's massive anti-corruption campaign has targeted both flies and tigers. Politicians once viewed as untouchable have wilted like shrinking violets. Among the tigers caught in Xi's dragnet are Zhou Yongkang, a former member of the PBSC and the man who once controlled China's entire security apparatus. Bo Xilai was a Politburo member, the charismatic party secretary of Chongqing, and a princeling. And Ling Jihua was the chief of staff to the former general secretary of the CCP, Hu Jintao. According to one estimate, Xi's anti-corruption campaign has taken down 440 officials at the vice-provincial or vice-ministerial level and some eighty generals in the PLA.[11] Vested interests have been cast aside with seeming ease, and so far Xi has not paid any price for destroying the careers and fortunes of so many powerful people in the system. There is a mystical quality to the tenacity of the CCP.

## *Axiomatic Legitimacy*

The "performative legitimacy" is strangely asymmetrical—there is legitimacy when the CCP performs but no illegitimacy when it does not. We need another way to think about the CCP's legitimacy, and here is my proposal—axiomatic legitimacy. Axiomatic legitimacy in the sense that the legitimacy of the state is unearned, unquestioned, unconditionally accepted as the default condition of the world as we know it. No exchange is stipulated, and no reciprocity is anticipated or demanded. Heads, the CCP wins; tails, Chinese society loses. Bad performance does not necessarily reduce this effect, and economic growth only adds to it. It is an extreme version of what Timothy Snyder calls "anticipatory obedience."[12] It is also the polar opposite of the so-called "Tacitus trap," a situation that Xi himself warned about in which an unpopular government is unpopular no matter what it does.[13] Now we have a framework that can accommodate the eras of both Mao Zedong and Deng Xiaoping.

We go to history for answers. History is a repository of knowledge, capabilities, cognitions, methods, and habits. It creates unquestioned assumptions and presumptive answers. We know that the *Keju*-incubated capabilities have had an extraordinarily long shelf life; it is not a stretch to claim that the attitudinal features of *Keju*—deference to autocrats, credulity, statist legitimacy, the preemption of individual agency—have persisted to the present day, all the more because the CCP has reinforced and amplified them.[14] The seeming objectivity of the meritocracy insulates the Chinese state from the political costs of high unemployment and underemployment, as Elizabeth Perry noted. Employment conditions are viewed in purely individualistic terms rather than as a function of government policy. In China, those seeking civil service positions take qualifying exams; so do hairstylists.[15] It breeds an attitude eerily reminiscent of the "personal responsibility" mantra that the libertarian Republicans in America cherish: if you do not have a job, it is your fault, not that of the system.

The analytical approach based on the *Keju* epistemology looms large. It is a view that diagnoses the world around us in terms of persons or specific grievances, not systems. Chinese historiography celebrates dynastic prosperity as a deed of a heroic emperor and dynastic decline as a deed of a villainous emperor. A "system dynamic" point of view, which portrays a leader as enabled or constrained by the system, is conspicuously missing. Now transpose this approach to how Chinese citizens assign credit and blame to the CCP. The Great Leap Forward and the Cultural Revolution were acts of Chairman Mao. Since he is now dead, the problem is solved. COVID lockdowns are deeply resented; ending that lockdown makes the resentment go away. Corruption is pervasive and thus the person who took down four million corrupt officials is a hero.

There is a surface plausibility to this way of viewing the world, but it conveniently glosses over the deeper forces at work: the twin disasters of the Great Leap Forward and the Cultural Revolution, the policy hubris, and the corruption at a metastasized scale have stemmed from the very nature of the one-party system. Let me use China's anti-corruption campaign to illustrate this mindset. One potential downside of a far-reaching anti-corruption campaign is that it may damage the legitimacy of the CCP. An autocrat justifies the severity and showcases the benefits of the anti-corruption campaign by publicizing the "shock and awe" details of the officials caught in the dragnet. But if so much dirty laundry is revealed, the public may wonder whether the whole system is corrupt beyond the pale. Previous Chinese rulers were probably aware—and wary—of this dynamic. Both Jiang Zemin and Hu Jintao launched corruption investigations, but only early in their tenure, and campaigns were targeted and short-lived.

How far do you go in a campaign that will risk throwing out the baby along with the bathwater? It's a dangerous line to cross, but Xi is apparently willing to risk the baby. His anti-corruption campaign not only jailed a huge number of people but also publicized some eye-popping, sordid details about the corrupt officials. Take as an example the following factoids that have emerged from the anti-corruption campaign: the government seized US$14.5 billion in assets from family members and the associates of Zhou Yongkang, the ex–security chief. (This worked out to be roughly equivalent to 10 percent of the profits of a company Zhou once led, China National Petroleum Corporation.)[16] And in one account on the Chinese internet, when Chinese investigators tallied the amount of cash stored in the basement of Xu Caihou, the Politburo member and the vice chair of the MAC, their bill-counting machines burned out, a claim that prompted some companies to advertise that their machines have made China clean.[17] (They omitted that corrupt officials used bill-counting machines too.)

The exposure effect turned out to benefit the CCP; that is, the anti-corruption campaign is associated with a large increase in satisfaction with the government at all levels, especially local government.[18] In 2011, just before Xi's anti-corruption campaign, 55.2 percent of the respondents rated local government officials as "totally unclean" and 35.4 percent rated them as "totally clean." By 2016, these two metrics had switched, so that only 29.3 percent of the respondents rated local government officials as "totally unclean," whereas 65.3 percent rated them as "totally clean." (Other researchers found a damaging effect on CCP legitimacy, but the size of the effect is modest.[19])

This finding is striking considering the scale and the character of the anti-corruption campaign. Consider the caliber of the fallen leaders. They were Politburo members and individuals at the very apex of the Chinese political system. Zhou Yongkang, Bo Xilai, Xu Caihou, and Ling Jihua were not low-level technocratic functionaries, but top decision makers in the system. And each of these fallen tigers was intimately connected with Xi's predecessors, Jiang Zemin and Hu Jintao. In other words, they are the very embodiment of the CCP system. It is difficult to argue with a straight face that corruption so endemic, and so high up in the system, is merely the doing of a few idiosyncratic bad apples.

What may have saved the CCP is viewing the "system" as a collection of people rather than as, in the language of organizational economics, "a nexus of contracts," a collection and configuration of incentives, rules, and constraints. In this conception, changing the system is akin to doing math. If the campaign purges 100,000 corrupt officials, then the country becomes cleaner by subtracting 100,000 corrupt officials from the roster. If one million officials are purged, then the country is cleaner by one million. It buttresses a case for the strongman rule: only a strongman can drain the swamp on such a massive scale.

"System" is an abstract concept. If you cannot touch it and feel it, it must not be there.[20] The lack of system thinking insulates the CCP in another way—only the local leaders, whom citizens have some direct interactions with, get the blame. Consider a well-known finding about public opinions in China: Chinese citizens are uniformly negative about local officials, but they hold the central government in high regard, the opposite of what researchers have documented in advanced democracies.[21] In a 2003 survey conducted by Edward Cunningham, Tony Saich, and Jessie Turiel, among those characteristics of local officials that received ratings at or close to 50 percent of the respondents were the following: (1) "aloof and conceited" (48.2 percent), (2) "knowledgeable" (50.8 percent), (3) "rhetoric (talk) only" (51.2 percent), (4) "beholden to the interests of the wealthy" (50.1 percent), (5) "only concerned with pleasing supervisors" (54 percent), and (6) "only concerned about own interests" (49.8 percent). By any reasonable yardstick, this is a devastating verdict.[22]

How did this dismal view of local officials translate into an overall view of the political system? A resounding endorsement! In 2003, 86.1 percent of the respondents expressed satisfaction with the central government, and 75 percent expressed satisfaction with the provincial governments. It is a form of cognitive dissonance. Chinese citizens somehow ignore that in a top-down system, local officials are appointed by the central government. Even though 54 percent of the respondents were dissatisfied with local officials being "only concerned with pleasing supervisors," the vast majority of the same respondents were paradoxically satisfied with the very supervisors whom local officials wanted to please. The glaring logical inconsistency is a vivid illustration of an inability to perceive and analyze human affairs in systemic terms.[23]

The CCP has exploited this mindset to its advantage. In the aftermath of COVID protests in November 2022, the central government blamed local authorities for their poor implementation of the control measures and instructed them to make corrections, a stance likely to find some receptivity among the population. That mindset is a friend to the CCP. The central government is the rightful embodiment of a political system but the low esteem held by the citizens accrues only to local officials rather than spilling over into the political system as a whole. The Chinese citizens have more knowledge and information about local officials, and the local officials become the de facto objects of causal diagnostics. Very few Chinese ever interact with and personally experience the central government in their lifetime and it falls out of their analytical horizon.

### Traditional Values and the Status Quo Bias

On October 3, 1959, in the middle of the disastrous Great Leap Forward, a man made his way to the Dragon Throne—the emperor's chair—in the Forbidden City. He declared himself the emperor of China. He was arrested and summarily executed.[24] He was not alone. Fuyang county in Anhui province was one of the hardest-hit regions during the Great Leap Forward. In 1957, thirty-one self-proclaimed emperors were arrested in that county. In Gansu province, police arrested twenty self-proclaimed emperors. In 1985, peasant Zeng Yinlong in Sichuan province launched a resistance movement to China's one-child policy. Thousands rallied to support his cause and his proclamation that he was the new emperor of China.

Traditional values have a strong hold over Chinese society. During this period of chaos and mayhem, nostalgia and reverence for imperial rule surged. This is China's leader-centric framework at work. Zeng Yinlong did not challenge China's population controls based on a notion of individual rights and limited government—he likely was completely unaware of such notions. The solution that he advocated was to change the ruler, not the rules of the game.

Previously I linked the stability pillar of the CCP to the autocratic norms formed over the centuries. There is more direct evidence that traditional values boost autocracy. One piece of evidence shows up as a cohort effect: Chinese citizens born before 1970, and those born after 1990, are less liberal than those born in the 1970s and the 1980s.[25] Political science and psychological research shows that liberalism is inversely correlated with age, which explains the attitude of those born before 1970. It is harder to explain the illiberal attitudes of those born after 1990. The answer is the Chinese educational curriculum. After the Tiananmen crackdown, the Chinese educational curriculum became more nationalistic and more oriented toward traditional values. The cohort born after 1990 had greater exposure to traditional values in school. They are the cohort fueling the wolf-warrior ultra-nationalism of the Xi Jinping era.

Research has linked traditional values directly with support for autocracy and a planned economy. Jennifer Pan and Yiqing Xu report that those who support hierarchy and endorse teaching Confucian classics in schools tend to oppose such ideas as individual rights, globalization, universality of human rights, market determination of prices, and sexual freedom.[26] For example, respondents who agree with the statement, "The process of capital accumulation is always accompanied by harm to the working class," are more likely to agree that "the Eight Diagrams (*Bagua*) in The Book of Changes (*Zhouyi*) can explain many things well." Their paper also describes an inverted U shape of liberal values across age cohorts. Their surveys, conducted between 2012 and 2014, showed that liberal political and economic values were highest among those between the ages of thirty-five and forty. The most liberal Chinese today were born in the late 1970s.

## CCP's Tullock's Curse

Because of these strong norms, the Chinese system is stable—until it is not. What is that "until not" moment? A major vulnerability of the Chinese system is leadership succession. In this area, history does not play an anchoring role. Traditional wisdom from the hereditary successions of imperial China does not apply. The CCP successions are open-ended, and less rule-bound. More contingencies; more surprises.

The ignominious fall of Hua Guofeng, described earlier, is just one of five succession arrangements that went horribly wrong. To understand what happened, let us look to the author who inspired this chapter, Gordon Tullock. His basic claim is that authoritarian regimes are short-lived because of their embedded succession conflicts.[27] He argues that autocracies lack well-regulated and institutionalized succession arrangements, so they decay and degenerate into personalistic rule and chaos. I call this congenital flaw of an autocracy "Tullock's curse," a curse in the sense that it is embedded in the nature of autocracies.

One solution to the Tullock's curse is hereditary rule. North Korea, for example, successfully transitioned power twice within the Kim family. Hereditary successions are more stable because they are more prescribed—successors must be family members.[28] By contrast, the field of CCP's successions is more open and prone to conflicts and as a result there have been many failures. That said, succession struggles do not always translate into open conflicts and a systemic breakdown. A combination of two factors has produced a moderating effect. One is the charisma of the paramount leaders. The strong personalities of Mao and Deng contained the fallout of their actions and missteps. The other is the existence of constraints on the ruler himself: a two-term limit and the norm of a mandatory retirement age. These introduced a measure of automaticity into a system that is long on discretion and short on boundaries. Other norms introduced by Deng also made Chinese politics more stable, such as lowering the ideological temperature and decriminalizing political rivalries. Collectively, these reforms injected discipline and certainty into a process that was otherwise chaotic and plagued by the misaligned incentives and whims of autocrats. They do not solve Tullock's curse, but they ameliorate it.

The overall track record of CCP successions is dismal. Since 1976, just two men, Mao and Deng, have been responsible for installing five out of the six general secretaries of the CCP. The lone exception is Xi Jinping. Xi was a product of a rare peer-based, consensus-driven selection process that has made it easier for Xi to disrupt the status quo—since the people he is beholden to are less powerful than Mao and Deng were. Another set of indicators is equally revealing. Of the seven individuals who have led the CCP since 1949, three were forced out of power under duress, Hua Guofeng, Hu Yaobang, and Zhao Ziyang. Meanwhile, two of Mao's anointed successors never made it to the finish line. Both died on the job. Under Xi, Sun Zhengcai, a man at one time under consideration for heir apparent, is now languishing in a Chinese prison; another man, Hu Chunhua, also once groomed as a successor, failed to make it into the Politburo at the Twentieth Party Congress. These are some ominous signs of instabilities to come.

Why has the CCP experienced so many failed or aborted successions? Historians emphasize specific factors, such as policy disagreements between Mao and his anointed successors. No doubt these disagreements played a role, but problematic successions plagued both Mao and Deng, and I predict that they will likewise plague Xi Jinping down the road. Problematic successions are a feature, not a bug, of non-hereditary autocracies.

Tullock's argument is that an autocracy gets the basic incentives wrong when dealing with successions. Unlike a democracy, an autocracy does not have an external legitimating and validating mechanism—such as an election—to transfer power from one ruler to another. Instead, political insiders fight it out and define the rules of the game as they go. We can use this insight to unlock some of the well-known cases of succession struggles in the PRC.

## The CCP's Serial Succession Failures

The CCP is littered with succession failures. I will focus on three of them, about which we have more information: Liu Shaoqi, Lin Biao, and Hu Yaobang. In each of these cases, the specific precipitating conflicts were different, but the anointment decision itself was a source of instability, by instigating mismatched expectations and mutual suspicions.

The first anointed successor to Mao was Liu Shaoqi. Liu was a fellow Hunanese with a revolutionary background that was as lengthy and storied as Mao's. His successor status was solidified in two steps. The first occurred in 1956 at the Eighth Party Congress, when the CCP devised and formalized a "two line" leadership arrangement whereby Mao would retreat to the background, to focus on setting the strategic and ideological directions of the country, while Liu Shaoqi and Deng Xiaoping would take over the day-to-day operations of the state. The second step was more formal and required Mao to step down from his position as chairman of the state and yield the position to Liu. In December 1959, Liu assumed the chairmanship, thus transitioning from heir natural to heir apparent. (In the 1980s the positions of head of party and head of state were split, in keeping with the prototype established in this 1959 CCP arrangement.)

There was already a rift between Mao and Liu at the time of the 1956 Eighth Party Congress when the two-line leadership arrangement was devised. The congress took the phrase "Mao Zedong Thought" out of the CCP Constitution, signaling a shift in policy priorities away from ideology and toward economic development. The timing and symbolism of the CCP's decision to deemphasize the personality cult are unmistakable. The congress took place after Khrushchev's secret speech denouncing the crimes committed by Stalin and his personality cult. To Mao, maybe with some justice, Liu was emerging as a Chinese Khrushchev.

It is unlikely that Liu Shaoqi and Deng Xiaoping could have pushed their policy agenda as far as they did without approval from Mao, but if he approved, his approval was insincere. In private, he seethed with anger. Liu was in charge of delivering the congress political report, the most important speech of a party congress, and usually delivered by the paramount leader. Mao fumed to his private doctor that Liu had not given him an advance copy: "I am going to resign the chairmanship of the republic," Mao said, "but I am still the chairman of the party. Why didn't they consult me about the Party Congress?"[29] Mao complained that he was being treated like a dead ancestor.

Mao's catastrophic mistakes during the Great Leap Forward intensified his siege mentality. The straw that broke the camel's back was the "Seven Thousand Cadres Conference," chaired by Liu Shaoqi and convened in 1962 in order to evaluate the grave consequences of the Great Leap Forward and to adopt corrective measures. Soon after this conference, Mao began to plot against Liu. The result was the Cultural Revolution that purged the entire political establishment of China, an expensive way for Mao to renege on his anointment decision on Liu. In 1968, Liu was formally stripped of all his positions, and in 1969, he died of pneumonia while in solitary confinement. His wife and family were not informed of his death until three years later.

The demise of Liu vacated the successor position, which Lin Biao formally acquired in April 1969, setting up yet another epic fail. Lin's ascent took place between the two famous conferences at Lushan, a summer resort favored by generations of Chinese political elites—both Chiang Kai-shek and Mao Zedong maintained a villa there. At the first Lushan Conference in 1959, Peng Dehuai, the defense minister, clashed with Mao. He had composed a "ten-thousand-character" statement criticizing the Great Leap Forward for having caused large-scale famine. Mao lashed back against Peng, forcing other leaders to fall in line with him.

Lin Biao did not show up at the conference until the tide was already turning against Peng, and he was particularly vicious once he joined in the chorus attacking Peng. Unlike Liu Shaoqi and Zhou Enlai who limited their critiques to Peng's specific statements and his factual accounting, Lin escalated the rhetoric: Peng was a conspirator, a bourgeoisie, a traitor, an individualist, and "a counter-revolutionary personality." He cleverly bundled his attack on Peng with hagiographic praise of Mao, Lin's specialty. Using lingo more common in the world of banditry, Lin said, "Only Chairman Mao can be a great hero. No one else should want to be a hero. You [Peng] and I are so far away [from being a hero]. Don't even think of it."[30] The implication was clear: you challenged Mao's position, but I will never do so. Lin was angling for successor status by signaling to the incumbent ruler his unwavering support.

He was on his way. Only one month later, Lin replaced Peng as defense minister, and from that perch he mobilized the army to advance his political ambitions. He came up with an ingenious way to ingratiate himself to Mao: the "little red book," or *Quotations from Chairman Mao*, which was first distributed within the military and then to Chinese society at large. At the "Seven Thousand Cadres Conference" of 1962, Lin broke away from the reflective and corrective stance of the rest of the leadership, announcing that the mistakes of the Great Leap Forward had stemmed from a failure to adhere to Mao's instructions.

The Cultural Revolution transformed Lin Biao from an heir natural to an heir apparent. He shed his chronic fatigue and worked tirelessly to topple Liu Shaoqi and Deng Xiaoping. At the Eleventh Plenum of the Eighth Party Congress convened in August 1966, Lin was promoted to vice chair of the CCP, just below Mao and ahead of Zhou Enlai. Liu Shaoqi was demoted to the eighth position in the CCP hierarchy. At the Ninth Party Congress in April 1969, Lin Biao delivered the official report that denounced Liu Shaoqi, and his status as Mao's successor was written into the CCP Constitution, a standing that has never before or since been conferred on any other heir apparent.

In an autocracy, successor status comes with its own perils. At the 1970 Lushan Conference, Lin Biao demanded Mao reinstate the position of chairman of the state, which had been abolished when Liu Shaoqi fell from power. Lin's scheme was to take the position once Mao had exercised his first right of refusal. Aided by CCP theoretician Chen Boda, Lin had pleaded with Mao on several occasions to take the position, with Mao becoming progressively annoyed with Lin's insistence. He had earlier dismissed Lin's trial balloon of the same proposal and he thought the issue had been settled.

Mao had had enough. At the second Lushan Conference, he purged Chen Boda, Lin's collaborator. Lin knew that he would be next on the list. As the delegates were departing from Lushan, Lin told one of his supporters in the PLA, "Doing things in the civilian manner didn't work; using armed force will work."[31] Unlike his predecessor, Lin did not want to go down without a fight.

What happened next is well known, although contested. Lin Biao and his son, a senior officer in the air force, plotted to kill Mao. The plot was code-named "571," which in Chinese is a homophone with "armed rebellion." Mao was given the code name B-52, relevant here because the "571" plot envisaged dropping a bomb on Mao from an airplane. But the plot was amateurish and, despite his formidable power in the military and as Mao's designated successor, Lin could trust only his son to help him. He dared not turn to the heads of the army and the navy, both his supporters, to carry out his plan. The plot was exposed and on September 13, 1971, Lin, his wife, and his son died when their plane crashed in Mongolia during an apparent attempt to defect to the Soviet Union.

In 1982, Hu Yaobang found himself in a situation similar to that of Liu Shaoqi in 1956—being chosen as heir apparent. In that year, the political elders appointed him general secretary of the CCP, nominally the highest-ranking position in the government. Real power, however, still resided with Deng Xiaoping and other elders such as Chen Yun and Li Xiannian. Deng and Chen were first among equals, with Li Xiannian and other revolutionary elders angling for their approval, support, and favors.

Such a setup was awkward. The de jure power did not match with the de facto power. The political elders were constantly intervening with the frontline management team of Hu Yaobang and Zhao Ziyang. Hu grew frustrated, and he called for the senior leaders to retire. His grievances were legitimate: Hu was already the titular head of the CCP and he felt entitled to exercising the power formally vested in him. But this is not how the CCP octogenarians, many active only in retirement, saw things. They perceived that Hu was usurping power from them! In other words, both Hu and the octogenarians felt a sense of entitlement, but their sense of entitlement was based on fundamentally different grounds: Hu, from the formal positions he occupied; the octogenarians, a sense of ownership from the blood, sweat, and tears they had given to the Communist revolution.

The tinder for trouble had been laid for a while and was only waiting for a spark. In December 1986 and January 1987, that spark came in the form of student demonstrations demanding political reforms. In January 1987, at a series of meetings convened under the auspices of the Central Advisory Commission (CAC), Deng and other CCP elders charged that Hu was too soft on liberal ideology and on liberal intellectuals. Their tone was harsh, betraying a sentiment that the elders felt toward Hu—he disrespected them.

By the time of these CAC meetings, Hu's ouster was a fait accompli. Hu had already submitted his resignation to Deng. This was highly irregular. According to CCP procedures, the removal of a general secretary required a decision by the Politburo, a vote by the Central Committee, and final approval by a party congress. As far as we know, only Xi Zhongxun, the father of Xi Jinping, raised questions about procedure and process; no one else seems to have cared. Deng, like Mao, dismantled two

succession arrangements—including the one for Zhao Ziyang in 1989—
of his own making.

## The Achilles' Heel of Autocracy

All three men—Liu, Lin, and Hu—were victims of Tullock's curse, an
Achilles' heel of any autocracy, or as Susan Shirk explains, "a weak point
that threatens regime stability by breeding power struggles and sclerotic
leadership."[32] Numerous scholars have noted the instabilities and power
struggles associated with autocratic successions, but Tullock's insights go
to the very heart of the problem—autocracies get succession incentives
wrong. These wrong incentives can derail even the best-laid succession
plans.

The Tullock of the curse is Gordon Tullock, better known as a founder
of public choice theory, a field that applies economic methodology to politics. His book *The Calculus of Consent*, coauthored with James Buchanan
and first published in 1962, is a seminal work in that field.[33] In 1987, Tullock wrote a far less known book, *Autocracy*, his only foray into the politics
of autocracies and a book he calls his first "scientific" treatment of politics. Some of his predictions were remarkably prescient. He anticipated,
as early as 1987, that both North Korea and Singapore were heading toward a hereditary path of authoritarianism. This was seven years before
the death of Kim Il-sung. Since then, North Korea has lived up to Tullock
twice, with the father and son pair of Kim Jong-il and Kim Jong-un.

Putting Singapore in the same category as North Korea is too harsh.
There is a vast gulf between the two countries in terms of economic and
political development. In 2021, Freedom House rated Singapore as "partly
free," scoring 48 on a 100-point scale. North Korea, by contrast, scored
a dismal 3 out of 100. (China is not far off from North Korea, at 9 out of
100.) And although Singapore eventually did take a hereditary path, it got
there via a detour. After Lee Kuan Yew stepped down, Goh Chok Tong,
unrelated to Lee, stepped in. Then in 2004 Lee Hsien Loong, son of Lee
Kuan Yew, took over. There is no evidence that this was a calculated and
designed move, but the arrangement is ingenious. Lee Kuan Yew was in
full vigor when power was passed on to Goh, so he could have imposed supervision if it was needed. Then when Lee Kuan Yew was more advanced
in age, and less able to exert influence, his son, as family and thus more
trustworthy, took over. The arrangement worked. Singapore enjoyed
uninterrupted peace, stability, and prosperity and is now in a position to

discard hereditary succession. As of 2021, the four candidates in contention to succeed Lee Hsien Loong are not connected to Lee's family.

Tullock's curse has a China connection. Tullock acquired some first-
hand experience of China when he was stationed in the U.S. Consulate
General in Tianjin as Communist troops were gaining control of the
country. During the final chaotic days of the Nationalist government, he
had much unwanted leisure time to read political science and to observe
the unfolding political dynamics in China. Unlike some of the sinologists
at that time who became enamored with the newly established Communist regime, Tullock saw the cracks and dysfunctions in this one-party system. His book captures these insights.

Tullock's curse has two major components. One concerns the incentives of central players in a succession process; the other relates to information, or more accurately, the lack of trustworthy information about the
character, preferences, and capabilities of the heir apparent. The combination of incentive and informational complications renders succession in
an autocracy a messy affair.

Consider the incentives of the autocrat and his chosen successor once
the succession decision has been made. From the perspective of a chosen
successor, the sooner he becomes "dictator in his own right, the better
from his standpoint and shortening the life of the current dictator is an
obvious way of speeding up the succession."[34] The dictator knows that this
is the thinking of his successor and, as a result, he becomes desperately
worried about this threat. Things become further complicated because the
chosen successor suspects that the incumbent dictator may impute that
motivation to him. This game-theoretic dynamic can unravel quickly even
with a well-designed succession arrangement in place.

Many of the dysfunctions of autocratic successions stem from these
dyadic misconceptions and feedback loops. Political scientist John Herz
calls this perilous situation a "crown-prince problem."[35] For a crown
prince, the choice is between acting quickly to further consolidate his
crown-prince status or biding his time in hopes that the incumbent ruler
will deliver his end of the promise. In the history of the CCP, acquiring
titles that denote real power, such as state chairman, and/or calling on the
elders to yield power has triggered conflicts that then unraveled the whole
deal. A safer option is to feign indifference and wait out the observation
window. There is, however, a casualty with this strategy: the veracity of
information about the designated successor is compromised. That autocracies churn out sparse and distorted information about successors is the
second endemic problem identified by Tullock.

An autocrat wants obedience and wants a faithful reproduction of himself, but alas, he can only make such a projection based on information when he is still in power and alive. Mao chose Hua Guofeng in large part because he thought that Hua would not negate the Cultural Revolution. On this specific issue, Mao made the right call, but he was completely wrong on the far more consequential issue of the viability of Hua as a leader—and the unraveling of Hua automatically settled the question on the Cultural Revolution. There are always surprises. When selecting Mikhail Gorbachev to succeed Konstantin Chernenko, the Soviet Politburo probably had little inkling that he would go so far in glasnost and perestroika.

Gorbachev was a dark horse: few expected him to be chosen and few knew who he was. Xi was a dark horse in a different way. His ascension was more certain, but many were in the dark about him before his ascension in 2012. Netizens raved about his ability to speak standard Mandarin, suggesting that many had never before heard him speak.[36] A Chinese energy executive tweeted, "self-confident, young, active, [speaks] Putonghua [that is, standard Chinese]." This is telling. He had been in politics since the early 1980s and was China's vice president, yet his reticence was deafening. China analysts tried to gauge him from a few morsels of information, and some felt that Xi would be a reformer because he had personally suffered during the era of Mao.

In a profile of Xi, Evan Osnos of the *New Yorker* observed that Xi had "endured flea bites, carried manure, built dams and repaired roads."[37] But these factoids are as useful as trying to make a prediction based on the fact that Xi is an adult male. Nearly every member of Xi's urban cohort suffered similar experiences. During the Cultural Revolution, the entire generation participated in Mao's rustication campaign, and that generation has some of China's most liberal thinkers, such as Yang Xiaokai and Ai Weiwei, as well as some of its most conservative defenders. Sima Nan, one of the most vocal Maoist public intellectuals in China today, comes to mind.

The larger point is that reliable information is a precious commodity in an autocracy. Judging from the actions that Xi has undertaken against his predecessors since he assumed power, even the Chinese political elites had little inkling of his inclinations and policy preferences. It never occurred to Hu Jintao, the man who agreed to have Xi as his successor, that one day Xi would have him yanked out from a government meeting in front of all the world to see. Jiang Zemin, who championed Xi to be Hu's successor, probably developed second thoughts about his decision.

The opacity of information is a feature of autocratic successions and it complicates the transition process. The crown prince has an incentive to act in a way that will shape the perceptions of the incumbent in his favor. One way to ensure this is to maintain a low profile. A key lesson from the cases of Liu, Lin, and Hu is that opacity, whether genuine or feigned, is a time-tested technique. Consider the contrast between Xi Jinping and Bo Xilai. Bo was a statist who launched a red-song campaign reminiscent of the Cultural Revolution. He rolled back the private sector and cracked down on crime and corruption. He put in place many populist policies. Bo, however, had a congenital weakness: he was a showman. He reveled at lengthy interviews with journalists, TV appearances, and audiences with international celebrities such as Henry Kissinger. In conduct, not in ideology, Bo resembled a camera-loving Western politician. From a policy perspective, one is hard pressed to tell Xi Jinping apart from Bo, but today Xi is beginning his third term, whereas Bo is languishing in a Chinese jail. Xi made it to the finish line because very few people, including those who selected him, knew him well.

## *The CCP's "Crown-Prince" Problem*

The crown-prince problem plagued the succession arrangements of Liu Shaoqi, Lin Biao, and Hu Yaobang. For all three men, their successor status may have lured them into a sense of invincibility and urgency, while the incumbents, on the other side of the aisle, were put on high alert. Mao and Deng were always on the lookout for any signs, however faint, of disloyalty and ambition among their chosen successors. For an incumbent autocrat, who harbors a mixture of misgivings and hope, the sweet spot is to have a successor lined up, yet one who is not too eager. But how do you know whether someone is eager or disinterested? Only after you have conferred a successor status on him, but this action will initiate the dynamic that emboldens the successor and threatens the incumbent. The succession plans can then go awry in a combustion of the successor's ambitions and the incumbent's suspicions.

In 1986, Hu Yaobang faced just such a situation. In May of that year, Deng had told Hu privately that he planned to retire at the Thirteenth Party Congress, scheduled for late 1987, and that Hu would succeed him as chairman of the CAC. Deng's intention was probably to remove Hu from the position of party general secretary. According to Zhao Ziyang, by 1986 Deng had grown disenchanted with Hu.[38] But Hu interpreted

Deng's offer as a way to ease out all the elders from their frontline management responsibilities. Given his stature, Deng's retirement was guaranteed to lead to a cascade of other elders yielding their power.[39]

Hu jumped on Deng's proposal and expressed his heartfelt support, which antagonized both Deng and the other elders. He then compounded his error by publicizing the issue within the CCP. At a party conference in Sichuan, Hu called for all senior CCP leaders over the age of eighty to resign. (Deng was eighty-two at the time.) The elders felt threatened. This was not a matter of ideology: it was personal. Even those elders on friendly terms with Hu turned against him at the January 1987 CAC meetings. Zhao Ziyang, for one, was struck by the harsh tone and the length of the accusations leveled by Yu Qiuli, a man who had worked closely with Hu Yaobang and whom Hu trusted.[40] Zhao remembers Li Xiannian saying, "I've known all along that this guy was no good."[41]

Hu was rare among Chinese politicians, better at speaking his mind than hedging risks, and he earned vitriol from the conservative elders for it. Contrast him with a man with a higher political IQ, Zhou Enlai. In 1973, as his health began to fail, Mao Zedong proposed the establishment of a CAC with himself as its head, and so signaled, or feigned, his intention to yield the chairmanship of the CCP.[42] Zhou, as second in command, stood the best chance of taking over that position, but he didn't take the bait. Instead, though he had never before opposed Mao, he strenuously objected. Unlike Hu, Zhou Enlai understood a cardinal rule of an autocracy: you can defy an autocrat, but only if that defiance increases the power of the autocrat. Mao responded to the protest, saying, "Since you all disagree with me, I will have to stay on as chairman of the CCP." Then he invoked the Chinese saying "I will remain dedicated to the very end" (鞠躬尽瘁, *jugong jincui*). Mao's lifelong tenure was assured. Zhou had passed the crown-prince test in telegraphing that he harbored no crown-prince ambitions. Not coincidentally, Zhou, who was never fully trusted by Mao, was the lone survivor in a succession field littered with those discarded by Mao. (The relationship between Mao and Zhou provides fascinating insights into Chinese high politics, a topic best addressed elsewhere.)[43]

One feature of CCP politics amplifies the crown-prince problem—the inordinately long grooming process. In the CCP, succession is similar to grooming the next CEO of a company. One must learn the ropes of the position by performing well, over a long time, and in front of a watchful incumbent CEO. The two-front leadership arrangement in China was created in 1956, some twenty years before Mao's death in 1976. Deng began his succession planning in the early 1980s, almost two decades before his death in 1997.

A long gestation period leaves plenty of time for things to go wrong. One risk is that the "lame duck" may not choose to go lame. In an autocracy, the "lameness" is not stipulated and legislated; it is up to the incumbent to decide whether to be lame or active. The incumbent ruler has every incentive to prolong the waiting period and use it as a test of the aspiring candidate's patience. There is an extra twist to this dynamic. The crown and the prince are sometimes not that far apart in age. Imagine the calculus of a crown prince who is inches away from the throne but can get there only when his own mental and physical capacity is waning. (This is a situation to which King Charles could perhaps relate.)

In 1986, Hu Yaobang was seventy-one years old, with only nine years left before the octogenarian threshold for retirement that he himself had stipulated. And in 1956, Liu Shaoqi was fifty-eight, only five years younger than Mao, who was sixty-three. The age gap was not large enough to assure patience in Liu. Liu's sharp critique of Mao at the 1962 "Seven Thousand Cadres Conference" might have struck a nervous Mao as Liu acting out his impatience. The seeds of the Cultural Revolution were planted. Whether the threat to Mao was material or not is irrelevant. So much of Tullock's curse is about perceptions and misperceptions, ego that is fragile and psychology that is insecure. In other words, so many things can go wrong.

The choice of Lin Biao was even more problematic. Both physically and psychologically, Lin was manifestly unfit for office. In 1969, Mao was seventy-six years old, but he was still in vigorous health. In July 1966, he swam across the Yangzi River to showcase his physical prowess. While Lin was young by comparison, at sixty-two, he was a bundle of ill health. He had a condition diagnosed by Dr. Li Zhisui as "neurasthenia." He harbored a variety of phobias, including to water, wind, light, and cold. Even the sound of running water could trigger bodily malfunctions, according to one account.[44] For years, Lin had remained on the sidelines in the care of his doctors. According to Harrison Salisbury, Lin also had a drug addiction, which Mao knew about (but amazingly he still chose him as successor). Mao copied a classical poem and sent it to Lin Biao:

It does not depend upon heaven
A man can live forever if he knows
How to take care of himself.[45]

Inadvertently or not, Mao aggravated Lin's insecurity about his health span. Once, Mao suggested that Lin should anoint his own successor—perhaps Zhang Chunqiao, a member of the Gang of Four.[46] That surely unnerved Lin. A crown prince already has plenty of angst of his own, and now he was being asked to name his own crown prince. Not a comforting thought.

In the wake of the failed coup by Lin, Mao's health deteriorated visibly. He felt a profound sense of betrayal from a man whom he had trusted so thoroughly. And it was not only the matter of the attempted coup. Lin, a devotee of Mao and an unashamed sycophant, was utterly contemptuous of Mao in private. In his diary, Lin wrote that the Great Leap Forward was "based on fantasy, and a total mess," a view not that different from Peng Dehua, the man Lin helped Mao take down.[47] In another entry, Lin wrote, "Today [Mao] uses sweet words and honeyed talk to those whom he entices, and tomorrow puts them to death for fabricated crimes."[48] Lin's own fate proved his prescience about Mao, but Lin was also the proof of another dynamic rooted in Tullock's curse: CCP succession politics has a very high noise to information ratio. Lin was not what Mao thought he was.

The history of the CCP is replete with misplaced trust and betrayed promises. In 1976, as Mao's demise was drawing near, he engineered Deng Xiaoping's fall from power. He feared that Deng would not continue to uphold the Cultural Revolution and he trusted Hua on the issue, leaving the famous parting words I quoted at the opening of this chapter. But Mao mistook a tree for a forest. As mentioned earlier, Hua had Jiang Qing, Mao's wife, arrested, along with the three other members of the Gang of Four. That opened the door for a comeback of Deng Xiaoping, who then proceeded to negate the Cultural Revolution in its entirety.

When choosing Xi Jinping, Jiang Zemin and Hu Jintao probably believed that they had chosen a status-quo leader, not a disruptor. Within several years after assuming office, however, Xi completely upended the power balance within the CCP and substantially degraded the influence of both Jiang and Hu. Autocrats trust their successors at their own peril.

## Overcoming Tullock's Curse

Dysfunctional successions led Tullock to conclude that authoritarian regimes tend to be short-lived, and that they easily degenerate into personalistic rule or chaos. The CCP has so far defied this prediction. The serial succession failures have not led to a systemic crisis. Even more impressively, the CCP has learned the lessons of the past. Under Deng, the CCP made meaningful progress in taming Tullock's curse. The three most recent succession events, Jiang in 1989, Hu in 2002, and Xi in 2012, were by and large orderly, with Jiang's and Hu's terms ending on schedule. Most China observers would agree with Susan Shirk's assessment that "Peaceful and regular premortem leadership succession has been a remarkable political achievement and the most important source of what Andrew Nathan has called China's 'authoritarian resilience.'"[49]

Four factors have been important in containing the fallout of Tullock's curse as well as taming the curse itself. One is that the outsized personalities of Mao and Deng and other idiosyncratic factors curbed the spillover effects of succession difficulties. Second, the Chinese military has not been a main instigator of succession conflicts. Third, in the 1980s Chinese politics entered into an era of gentle politics that lessened the stakes involved in some of the successions. And fourth, Deng Xiaoping initiated reforms that made successions more rule-based. Under Xi Jinping, however, some of these conditions have been weakened substantially. It is conceivable that Tullock's curse may haunt Chinese politics once again in the future.

## Idiosyncrasies

There is a sort of reverse Tolstoy dynamic to the CCP successions: those that failed shared some commonalities and those that succeeded had idiosyncratic factors behind them. One reason that the dysfunctional CCP succession dynamics have not been as destabilizing as they could have been is because all the successions but one—that of Xi Jinping—have taken place under the watchful eyes and with the blessing of China's towering paramount leaders, Mao and Deng. Tullock's curse was clear and present, but the prestige and credibility of Mao and Deng contained the broader damage of the succession failures.

The timing of a succession decision also matters. Hua Guofeng had one advantage over Liu Shaoqi, Lin Biao, and Hu Yaobang—time was on his side. He was chosen during the waning months of Mao's life and his political life outlasted Mao's biological life. That was the only race that mattered. In the case of Jiang Zemin, he was helped by the accidental nature of his elevation. There was no lengthy grooming process like that which had bedeviled so many earlier succession plans. By Jiang's own account, it never crossed his mind that he would one day be appointed the CCP general secretary. In early 1989, at the age of sixty-three, he was already contemplating a post-retirement career in academia. He had presented a paper on "development of energy and a few key energy-saving measures" at Shanghai Jiaotong University, as something of a job talk.[50]

Jiang's plans changed in 1989 because of the Tiananmen events. He was voted in as general secretary by the elders on May 27, 1989, and unveiled to the Chinese public as their new leader on June 24, 1989. This was lightning speed. Jiang's effective rule commenced in 1992, when most of the elders stepped out of the way, a very short wait compared to that of the other chosen successors. The crown-prince dynamics were absent.

I will come back to some of these issues in Chapter 9, but a question about a future succession under Xi is whether there will be enough favorable idiosyncratic factors to offset the structural instabilities that Xi has injected into Chinese politics. This is unknown and probably unknowable, but one thing is certain: successful successions depend on a combination of favorable conditions and structural stabilizers. By rescinding guardrails such as term limits and mandatory age retirements, Xi will need more favorable conditions to ensure that his own succession goes smoothly.

## Subjugation of the Military

In Chapter 5, I contrasted China's civilian rule with the organizational culture of the Roman Empire, which valorized war and a martial ethos. Coliseums and gladiators were representative symbols of the Roman Empire, not the delicate cranes sewn into the Mandarin squares worn by civil servants of the Ming dynasty. Pompey the Great and Julius Caesar made bids for political power, whereas Chinese military strongmen stood on the sidelines. In a famous legend, at a drinking party, the founding emperor of the Song dynasty persuaded his generals to relinquish their power and retire. The generals obliged, launching a period of civilian rule that would last for centuries.[51] A cup of wine was all it took.

In 2003, Slate.com ran an article titled "Why Is Qaddafi Still a Colonel?" According to the author, Qaddafi had envisaged his country as a utopian, egalitarian society in which grandiose titles did not matter. It did not matter in 1969 that Qaddafi was only a captain and all of twenty-seven years old—he still was able to launch a successful coup. In some developing countries, it is not infrequent that an army officer of modest rank can rise up and seize power. To a political theorist such as Samuel Huntington, this is a telltale sign that the Libyan system lacked institutionalization.[52]

Consider by contrast the case of Marshal Lin Biao, whose audacious plot was superseded only by the ineptness of its execution. At the time of the plot, Lin was the defense minister, vice chairman of the Communist Party, and first vice premier of the State Council. He was a marshal in the PLA and was Mao's anointed successor, a status enshrined in the 1969 CCP Constitution. But when it came to plotting and carrying out a coup, Lin had only his wife and his elder son as co-conspirators; he failed to mobilize even a single foot soldier in the Chinese army. Peng Dehuai, Lin's predecessor in the Ministry of Defense, had met a similar fate. He was easily dispensed with by Mao at the 1959 Lushan Conference. In a fiery exchange with Mao, it was not the defense minister but Mao who threatened to pull off a revolt.

During the PRC era, the Chinese military has not been a frontline player in the many and frequent power struggles and succession conflicts. The civilian primacy norm and the institutionalization of military subordination have contributed to the basic integrity of CCP rule, even as it has faced momentous shocks and calamities. The fall of the Gang of Four in 1976, in which Marshal Ye Jianying played a central role, came closest to a military intervention in politics, but it was not a coup at all in a conventional sense. At the time, Hua Guofeng was the chairman of the CCP and of the MAC. The members of the Gang of Four were Hua's subordinates per CCP's organizational chart. If not for the fact that Jiang Qing was the wife of Mao—who was deceased when Jiang was arrested—this would be viewed as a straightforward purge. The ousters of Hu Yaobang and Zhao Ziyang were also more of a purge than a coup. Yes, Deng was the chairman of the MAC, but he did not deploy tanks to take down the two titular heads of the CCP. Deng and other revolutionary elders commanded de facto power regardless of their military pedigree.

The Chinese system has many "coup-proofing" elements. Institutional controls surrounding civilian primacy over the military are strong, and the institutionalization of the Chinese military itself increased during the reform era.[53] One example is Jiang Zemin's successful effort in the 1990s to decouple military ties to business and commerce. In the 1980s, the Chinese military had made up for its budgetary shortfalls by engaging in business on the side, a stance approved by Deng. Jiang reversed this practice, formalizing the resource controls of the military by increasing its budget and improving the living standards of rank-and-file officers.

The military dutifully agreed to exit from commerce.[54] Outside of some extraordinary circumstances, the Chinese military has been a stabilizing, rather than disruptive, force in Chinese politics.

## An Interlude of Gentler Politics

Although Deng is mainly remembered for his economic reforms, his contributions go well beyond economics. He restored a sense of normalcy to Chinese politics and society, and he created a succession framework that alleviated a crippling flaw of the Chinese system.

During the Mao era, the Chinese people had been subjected to unceasing and disruptive campaigns. Within the first five years of the PRC, Mao launched six distinct campaigns, averaging more than one each year. There were also campaigns during Deng's era, but they were abbreviated and targeted. In 1983, the "Anti-Spiritual Pollution" campaign lasted for a mere twenty-eight days, and many officials declared that it didn't apply to their areas of responsibility.

In the 1980s, there was a tolerant intellectual climate. Although Deng harshly criticized the film *Unrequited Love* in 1981 for its anti-CCP insinuations and tones, and the film was banned, its creator, Bai Hua, continued to write with impunity. Three prominent liberal intellectuals—Fang Lizhi, Liu Binyan, and Wang Ruowang—criticized Deng by name, and eventually the trio were stripped of their party membership, but they were permitted to leave for the United States. Contrast this treatment with that of intellectual dissident Liu Xiaobo, who was awarded the Nobel Peace Prize in 2010 but was not allowed to receive it, nor to have his wife receive it on his behalf. He died in prison in 2017. (In 1975, when Andrei Sakharov was awarded the Nobel Peace Prize, the Soviet authorities allowed his wife to travel to Oslo, Norway, to collect the award.)[55] In 2020, Ren Zhiqiang was thrown into jail for his criticism of Xi.

Deng made Chinese politics gentler. He defused political tensions by focusing on economic performance and by decriminalizing political conduct. With the prominent exceptions of the ousters of Hu Yaobang and Zhao Ziyang, Chinese leaders during this era resolved many of their disagreements through compromise and negotiation. Unlike Liu Shaoqi and Peng Dehuai who died under horrendous circumstances, Hu Yaobang and Hua Guofeng landed softly, retaining high-level positions and personal freedom. Political rivals were no longer considered enemies, and a nascent form of politics by consensus softened the edge of power struggles.

We can gain an appreciation of Deng's gentler politics by contrasting it with what happened in China later. Chinese politics hardened noticeably after Tiananmen. Zhao Ziyang was put under house arrest, and to this day, the CCP has not released the investigative report on his role in the Tiananmen demonstration, an acknowledgment that the CCP has trouble reconciling its treatment of Zhao with its own principles, rules, and factual findings. He was deprived of personal freedom for sixteen years without cause.

Jiang Zemin pioneered a tactic that was later passed down to Hu Jintao and then weaponized by Xi Jinping—using charges of corruption to frame political rivals. In 1995, Chen Xitong, party secretary of Beijing, was removed from office on charges of corruption. He had served as mayor of Beijing during the Tiananmen events and had played an instrumental role in the crackdown, an act that positioned him as a powerful rival to Jiang Zemin. There are mysteries surrounding his case, including the alleged suicide of his deputy, Wang Baosen. According to a rumor, Wang was so skilled at committing suicide that he shot himself in the back.[56] In 2006, Hu Jintao toppled a close ally of Jiang Zemin, Chen Liangyu, party secretary of Shanghai, on corruption charges.[57] Xi, as is well known, weaponized the anti-corruption campaign. This tactic of politicizing corruption, used widely in many developing countries, acquired its Chinese cadence.[58]

## Term Limits

In his book, Tullock is puzzled by why successions in Mexico and Brazil, both authoritarian countries at the time, proceeded relatively smoothly. He notes in passing that these two countries had term limits. Although Tullock didn't connect the dots, I believe that term limits are a stabilizing factor. Similar to hereditary successions, term limits proscribe scope for choices and actions. They legislate some certainty into the gestation period for a new ruler, and such certainty stabilizes the incentives of both the incumbent and the heir apparent.

Autocrats hesitate to anoint a successor because the act of anointment may lead to a loss of power. As soon as a successor is appointed, political elites "begin planning their own maneuvers on the theory that they will spend more of their life under the rule of the successor than under the rule of the current dictator," writes Tullock.[59] To forestall this loss of power, an autocrat delays making a decision on succession. A last-minute decision may shorten the incubation period and increase the probability that the succession will eventually go forward for the obvious reason that an autocrat has less time to change his mind.

But there is a downside. The quality of the last-minute succession plans can be subpar. Hua Guofeng, "fair and not stupid," fell into this category; so did Jiang. We know what happened to Hua; less known is the fact that Jiang almost lost his job. During his 1992 Southern Tour, Deng, frustrated by Jiang's economic conservatism, ominously remarked, "Whoever doesn't reform will have to step down," and he brought two senior military officials to underscore that message. In the end, Deng relented; sacking three general secretaries in a row would have been too disruptive.[60]

Term limits solve some of these problems. They are a forcing mechanism that removes discretion from the decision timetables. The succession timetable is now calendric rather than biological. China's term limit for presidency was ten years, which warranted a reasonable age gap between the incumbent autocrat and his successor. For these and other reasons, China managed to limit Tullock's curse when the term limits were in place.

Between 1989 and 2012, under term limits, the CCP worked out nearly all the details of the succession long before the term of the incumbent leader expired. Xi's assumption of power is a good illustration of the stabilizing effect of the term limits. In 2012 Chinese politics was fraught with tensions, caused by an explosive exposé of Premier Wen Jiabao's family wealth, the defection of a high-level Chongqing official to the U.S. Consulate in Chengdu, and the very public removal of Bo Xilai.[61] That Xi assumed power on schedule, despite these debilitating events, is testimony to the steadfastness and resilience of the succession plan devised under China's term limit.

But that reformist era is long gone. Xi Jinping has escalated the stakes of political rivalries, and he has rescinded term limits and weakened many other norms. There are no longer any guardrails in place to circumscribe the selectorate dynamics that the reformist CCP relied on to ameliorate Tullock's curse. Sooner or later, the CCP will feel the damage of Xi Jinping's actions and will appreciate the impact of the term limits in their absence.

———

Autocrats hate to relinquish power because they know loyalty is fungible. As Hua Guofeng's power began to wane, his subordinates started shifting their allegiance. In January 1980, when Hua was speaking with a visiting American official at a meeting, the attending Chinese officials carried on side conversations among themselves, ignoring the titular head of the CCP.[62] They sensed that power had already begun slipping away from Hua, maybe imperceptibly at first but cascading rapidly in due course. A new order was dawning on the horizon.

Few foresaw then the transformative and consequential impact of the transition that lay ahead. The era of Deng Xiaoping turned out to be one of explosive growth, political flexibility, and overall stability—as well as rapid developments in technology, the last component in our EAST framework, a topic I will take up next.

# PART IV

# Technology

# CHAPTER SEVEN

# Reframing the Needham Question

Printing, gunpowder, and the nautical compass . . . have altered the face and state of the world: first, in literary matters; second, in warfare; third, in navigation.

—FRANCIS BACON, 1620

IN 1405, THE THIRD year of Emperor Yongle of the Ming dynasty, a flotilla of sixty-two large ships set sail from the port of Wuhumen in Fujian province to the distant seas. The commander of the expedition was Zheng He, a eunuch of the Ming court and a Muslim, who was also known as the "Three-Jewel Eunuch," an apparent reference to the Buddhist faith of the Ming emperors. Between 1405 and 1433 there were seven such expeditions—all of a similar grand scale as the first—which sent ships as far as the South China Sea and the Indian Ocean, from Taiwan to the Persian Gulf, all the way to the Eldorado, the land of Africa in the imagination of the Chinese.

The 1433 expedition was to be Zheng He's last; he died that year. And after that seventh expedition, Emperor Xuande of the Ming imposed a complete and strict "voyage ban." Construction and repair of seafaring ships were prohibited, and some 3,500 ships were burned. Records of the voyage were expunged from archives. Private citizens who violated the voyage ban were punished. For the four hundred years that the ban was in place, China turned inward. Its voluntary withdrawal from global affairs at the peak of its naval power shaped and rearranged the geopolitical and economic order for the five hundred years that followed. China's absence paved the way for the rise of a Pax Britannica, then a Pax Americana. In the nineteenth century, when the West waged "gunboat diplomacy" against China, rather than the other way around, few in the West were aware of a time that China had ever, as Louise Levathes documents, "ruled the seas."[1]

Did the "bungling idiots" of the Ming dynasty singlehandedly stop an emergent Pax Sinica in its tracks?[2] A counterfactual scenario of a world order molded in the image of Confucianism and powered by the Ming's advanced navigational technologies has fascinated generations of historically minded scholars and observers. At the time, China was, according to Jones, within "a hair's breadth" of its own Industrial Revolution.[3] In this narrative, the Ming shouldered much of the blame for why China stagnated when the West was just beginning to take off.

This is an understandable sentiment. The Ming's voyage ban froze China's technological development. During the thirty years of Zheng He's voyages, China had imported a large amount of foreign goods, medicine, and geographical knowledge. Although Zheng He himself was not the agent of these technological exchanges (his voyages were not commercial operations), the voyage bans were a part of China's wholesale retreat from the world market, which brought the technological exchanges to a sudden stop. The first emperor of the Ming, Zhu Yuanzhang, who micromanaged *Keju*, suffocated the intellectual climate. The succeeding emperors, however, were less tyrannical, and had there not been the voyage ban, the Ming could very well have restored the pace of invention to the levels that had prevailed during the Tang or Song dynasties.

The Ming voyage ban features frequently in debates and discussions on why Chinese technology collapsed. A British biochemist by training, Joseph Needham, who inspired the coinage of the term "Needham question," is most well known for having created the field of the history of Chinese science and technology.[4] In his 1969 book *The Grand Titration: Science and Society in East and West*, Needham asks: Why did imperial China fail to capitalize on its earlier advantage in technology and to launch its own Industrial Revolution?[5]

Throughout his long and distinguished career, Needham offered myriad explanations, ranging from China's putative absence of scientific thinking to feudal bureaucracy and the underdevelopment of commerce. He contrasted China with Western city-state empires, and he sometimes credited democracy for the West's rise.[6] He blames bureaucratic control for blocking the absorption of foreign knowledge after the 1430s. Time after time, he traces the start of the Chinese decline to the seventeenth century, when science rose in the West and the long and oppressive Ming dynasty ended.

Joseph Needham spawned a large literature answering the question he posed. This literature is massive in one particular dimension—an abundance of speculative conjectures and rich narratives relative to the detailed empirics that could have been marshalled to support these speculations. One major point of departure is that I rely on a detailed database of over ten thousand Chinese inventions over the course of history to frame my argument and to provide an empirical grounding. To the best of my knowledge, this is the largest database assembled to analyze the Needham question.

A salient finding from the data we have assembled is that the Ming dynasty was not a point of discontinuity in Chinese technological development. Such a discontinuity took place much earlier, in the sixth century rather than during the Ming as many have thought. The voyage bans compounded China's decline, but they were not the original instigator of China's decline. The Ming rulers still bungled, badly, but they bungled by accelerating a trend that had already been set in motion more than seven hundred years earlier. By the seventeenth or eighteenth century, China was nowhere near industrialization.

Many explanations in the literature are cross-sectional in orientation—explaining why Europe and China differed. By construction, this is a difficult research question. China and Europe differed in many dimensions other than the ones featured under the spotlight—such as the presence or absence of scientific thinking. Some of these factors might be correlates, rather than underlying causes. Or technology and the pinpointed variables shared a common causal origin, something that lies completely outside of a proposed explanation. The Needham question can be more productively pursued by asking, "Why was China inventive at certain times but uninventive at others?" Repositioning the Needham question as one about dynamics over time yields a methodological advantage: we hold some variables constant while zeroing in on those variables that have covaried with the Chinese inventiveness. This is not a guarantee of a definitive causal account, but it is a more tractable approach than one that compares two continental geographies, each of which has its own idiosyncratic features and conditions.

We get history right to get causal dynamics right. To answer the Needham question, I compare China before and after the sixth century. We do know about a momentous event in the sixth century—the Sui reunified China and invented *Keju*, which perpetuated China's absolutism. The introduction of *Keju* produced a host of political, social, and cognitive effects. The question here is whether these *Keju*-induced effects set off China's technological decline and stagnation after the sixth century. I answer in the affirmative. I use the framework about scale and scope to narrate the rise and fall of Chinese technology. The narration draws from data but also from invocations of the established social science theories on innovations and on the Industrial Revolution.

Let me close this summary of my argument by returning to a question often lost and forgotten in the search for answers to the Needham question: how did China establish its early lead in technology in the first place? The Needham question pivots our analytics toward China's failings: the staggering achievements of the ancient Chinese are often affirmed in their negative—that Chinese technological supremacy completely collapsed in later dynasties. The problem with this approach is both substantive and methodological. Substantively, it is not a complete explanation if Chinese accomplishments are left unaccounted for. Methodologically, a good explanation should be parsimonious, that is, capable of explaining, or at least accommodating, China's stagnation as well as its real accomplishments. Parsimony also requires that we evaluate an argument from opposing sides. For example, a prevalent explanation blames Chinese stagnation on Confucian ethics—for being antiscience and conservative—but how does one reconcile Confucianism with China's early successes in technology? An explanation predicated on innate Chinese ingenuity has the same problem but in an opposite orientation. How can it explain China's later decline? A fixed effect does not explain a variance. To unlock the Needham question requires an explanation of Chinese technological accomplishments in the first place, a topic I discuss next.

## Imperial Science and Technology

The ancient Chinese were highly inventive and made substantial advances in technology, often far ahead of the rest of the world. For example, the Chinese knew how to cast iron by 200 BCE, whereas the technology didn't arrive in Europe until at least the late fourteenth century.[7] Chinese achievements in maritime technology are no less impressive; the Chinese were much more advanced than Europe in ship construction, as well as maneuverability and navigation techniques. Other Chinese technological achievements include paper, the water clock, and the moveable-type printing press.[8] The Chinese were also pioneers in hydraulic engineering, rice cultivation, irrigation, textile spinning, porcelain, wheelbarrow design, and numerous other fields.[9]

The most famous Chinese inventions are the "Big Four"—paper, printing, gunpowder, and the compass. But the ancient Chinese invented far more than these well-known technologies. Robert Temple, a student of Needham and author of *The Genius of China*, observes:

> The biggest secret in history that has not yet been disclosed is that the "modern world" we live in is an excellent synthesis of Eastern and Western elements, and the basic inventions and discoveries on which it is based. Perhaps more than half of them are from China.[10]

Temple lists a hundred ancient Chinese inventions that ranked as the most advanced at the time of their creation, including—surprise—brandy and whiskey.

There have been surprisingly few detailed attempts to explain China's precocious inventiveness. The default explanation, more inferred than explicated, more asserted than demonstrated, is that innate Chinese ingenuity gave rise to its early technological lead. This premise then leads to a focus on what supposedly impeded Chinese ingenuity. Often the state is singled out for the blame. If the state had not been so stifling, China would have successfully emerged as an industrialized nation. "It is the State," David Landes writes, "that kills technological progress in China."[11]

Although never intended by its proponents, this interpretation of history can come off as a remote cousin to a better known—and far more pernicious—claim that European prosperity and industrialization were due to the superiority of the Europeans as a people. Morris calls this idea "the long-term lock-in theory of Western superiority."[12] The idea that some civilizations were intrinsically more creative than others is not just problematic in its connotations; it is simply a bad theory without falsifiability and external validation. Whether its Western or Eastern rendition, the claim is made based on observed outcome, and often on the observed outcome alone. Selection on the dependent variable looms large.

I propose here an alternative explanation: inventiveness varies because conditions that permit and enable inventiveness vary. My conjecture is that China's early lead in technology was derived critically—and possibly exclusively—from the role of the state.

Douglass North points out, "If you want to realize the potential of modern technology you cannot do it with the state, but you cannot do without it either."[13] This is equally true in pre-modern times. The Chinese imperial state supported technology both directly and indirectly. It compiled and disseminated technical standards and registries of medical and agricultural knowledge on a large scale. The emperors also rewarded inventors directly through financial compensation and promotion. Zhang Heng, inventor of the seismograph, became president of the Imperial Chancellery. Many provincial officials achieved their positions as a reward for their inventions; for others the reverse was sometimes true: the promotion preceded the invention. For example, Cai Lun, widely credited for having invented paper, one of the most celebrated technological achievements in human history, was promoted to be director of the Imperial Workshops in 97, and announced the invention of paper in the year 105.[14]

Direct support from the state was unlikely significant enough to explain China's early edge. Ex post support may explain a few high-impact inventions, such as paper and the seismograph, but not mass inventions. Some emperors fancied technologies; others did not. The rewards were not institutionalized, and they tended to go to discoveries that advanced divinations valued by emperors. The Song dynasty, for instance, created an entire government department devoted to astronomy called the Hanlin Astronomical Bureau. Direct support contributed to Chinese advances in astronomy and related fields, but not necessarily to breakthroughs in other fields.

The far more consequential role of the state in seeding early Chinese inventions was indirect: the Chinese imperial state rewarded government service, and it did so at scale. One way it did this was to keep inventors on the government payroll. Compared with an ex post reward, lowering the costs of inventive activities contributed to technological advances across the board. This ex ante support function of the state was most likely unique among ancient civilizations, and a true source of the Chinese edge.

Needham notes "the relatively 'official' character of science, pure and applied."[15] "The astronomer," he remarks, "was not a citizen on the outskirts of the conventions of his society, as perhaps in the Greek city-states, but a civil servant lodged at times in part of the imperial palace and belonging to a bureau that was an integral part of the civil service." Needham, however, does not connect the role of the government with the record of the Chinese technological accomplishments he compiled. In fact, he is dismissive and harshly critical of governmental science. He remarks: "We may conclude that something like 'Parkinson's Law' was already manifesting itself in ancient China." (Parkinson's Law states that work is done to fill up an allotted time rather than for its intrinsic value.) He emphasizes that many inventors were commoners rather than government officials, and he blames the atheoretical orientation of Chinese science partially on heavy government involvement.

We now have data to show how substantial the Chinese government's employment of scientific and technological personnel was in Chinese history. A Chinese historian has analyzed bibliographical data on 249 technologists from 700 BCE to 1900.[16] Of these technologists, 55 percent were directly employed by the state, while another 5 percent were employed as court doctors. Just 26 percent of the 55 percent were born into official families, suggesting that recruitment was involved. Another analysis arrives at a lower figure of 48.5 percent.[17] Although Needham on the whole is negative about governmental science, he also notes that most of the technicians belonged to the category of "minor officials," thus affirming the role of government.

The two papers I have just cited rely on source material that applies an exacting criterion for compilation. The compilers are researchers at the Institute of Natural History of the Chinese Academy of Sciences and they include only entries on those technologists with documented "substantial scientific achievements." In other words, only elite technologists or scientists in Chinese history are included, and the selection is biased toward those who left documented accomplishments. We have corroborating evidence from another source: an encyclopedia of prominent figures in Chinese history, which is organized by field.[18] One field, labeled science and technology, includes 424 individuals. For the entire imperial period, 66 percent of the science and technology personnel were employed by the government, higher than the figures by Chinese historians. Another field in this encyclopedia is the humanities. Interestingly, in this field governmental dominance is even more pronounced: 85 percent of the creative talents in the humanities were employed by the government. For science and technology personnel, the height of government employment was during the Sui-Tang period, 76 percent, while the Qing represented a low point, at 55 percent.

The imperial court did not have a technological agenda.[19] Inventions were an incidental rather than an intended effect of the talent-monopolizing role of the government. The Chinese accomplishments were not a result of a coordinated funding program run by the state but were a result of the state's ability to shape incentives. Needham sees the applied nature of governmental science as a problem, but he never delves into the behavioral side of this issue and considers the positive incentive effect of governmental involvement. This warrants a discussion.

Inventions have high fixed costs and the payoffs are uncertain. Even in modern times, innovations are costly and time-consuming, based as they are on conjectures about how a technology might work in the future. There is no guarantee of a successful outcome. The conjectures may be totally wrong, or the conjectured futures may fail to materialize. In ancient times, this was an even more severe problem. Commoners in a pre-modern society were barely surviving on the minimum caloric intake required to sustain life. Taking on a new activity with uncertain returns was risky, because it would take away from the time and effort needed to satisfy those subsistence needs. The opportunity costs of undertaking inventive and technical pursuits and activities have always been high, but especially when the potential inventors are living on the edge.

By putting inventors on its payroll, the government lowered the costs of inventive activities. The imperial workshops, known today as state-owned factories, employed large numbers of technicians and artisans. Think of the enormous financial security associated with this arrangement in ancient times when meeting subsistence needs was a daily struggle. Contrast it with the situation of a commoner in the Han dynasty, who in the words of Needham himself, faced becoming part of "an inexhaustible supply of obligatory unpaid labour in the form of the corvée."[20]

Chinese inventiveness may well have initially prevailed because the state kept on its staff a retinue of technologists who had the luxury of eschewing the menial, back-bending work of primitive farming and could instead undertake creative activities that offered no immediate material payoff. Some of these people succeeded in inventing. In other ancient civilizations, the size of this leisure class was smaller, possibly because the state was much smaller. The bureaucracies of the Roman Empire and Tudor Court were a fraction of the size of the bureaucracy during the Song.[21] The smaller bureaucratic class in these civilizations was also due to those states' being staffed with functionaries who provided immediate services to the state, such as winning battles or collecting taxes, rather than the literate kind of human capital that populated the Chinese state.

What about private patronage? In Europe, aristocrats provided similar funding functions and they patronized the sciences and arts. Leonardo da Vinci had multiple patrons, such as Lorenzo de' Medici. But this private funding probably did not give Europe a technological edge over China, at least not until the Renaissance. Why not? Perhaps because such aristocratic patronage was unique to Italy and it arose during the time of da Vinci. Chinese inventors had an edge because government employment of creative personnel dated back as far as the Warring-States period, that is, to sometime between 475 and 221 BCE. The other difference is scale. The Chinese imperial state was national in scale, whereas the European aristocrats were regionally based. Also, just like private science in modern times, aristocratic patronage rewarded demonstrated talents and achievements that had already been accomplished. By contrast, the payroll function of the state funded inventors ex ante, which led to more inventions because both actual and potential inventors were funded.

Other than the government employment data on technologists, I do not have data to prove my claim that early inventiveness was a function of the number of non-pecuniary professionals enabled by the state capacity. It is a conjecture; as a conjecture it is appealing because it is so simple. The hypothesis assumes no more than a similar distribution of creativity and talent across different civilizations and that their activation is a function of available time and cognitive freedom. And the idea is in theory falsifiable. Another advantage is its parsimony. It could explain why China was inventive early as well as why the arts and literature flourished as well.

There are downsides to this arrangement, at least according to our modern sensibility. One is the politicization of science. As mentioned earlier, emperors privileged astronomy as a divination technique; not surprisingly, astronomy had the highest share of governmental employment, at 87.5 percent, followed by alchemy (66.7 percent), geography (63.6 percent), and agronomy (60 percent).[22] The heavy premium on celestial knowledge was rooted in the doctrine of the Mandate of Heaven, which viewed natural disasters as a lead indicator of upheavals and mass rebellions. There was a political application of astronomical knowledge and for this reason, the Chinese astronomers fared better with the authorities than their European counterparts. Maybe because their research agenda was political rather than intellectual, Chinese astronomers, despite their many discoveries, failed to make fundamental breakthroughs remotely on par with those of Galileo and Copernicus.

## Getting History, and the Causal Dynamics, Right

There have been many explanations for the well-known collapse of Chinese technology. All of them are plausible, but the problem is that because of a lack of data, scholars do not have any way to test them explicitly. Without quantification, we cannot arrive at a reasonable estimate of when the turning point occurred, and without that estimate nailed down, we cannot even begin to offer a reasoned explanation. The ideas that have been offered are interesting descriptive narratives rather than social scientific explanations.

A volume published in China in 2012 summarized the ideas and perspectives of some of the most luminary scholars and thinkers in China on the Needham question.[23] The scholars included Chen-Ning (Franklin) Yang, a Nobel Prize winner in physics; Fei Xiaotong, the father of Chinese sociology; Qian Mu, an eminent historian; Lin Yutang, a pioneering linguist; and many others. Their consensus: Chinese science suffered because Confucian culture lacks scientific reasoning as well as a spirit of exploration.

This is a prevalent view, especially among the Western-educated intellectual elites in China. It is a plausible idea, but we cannot test or falsify it given the way the argument is formulated. For one thing, Confucianism and the absence of scientific thinking are conceptual cognates. The formulaic and normative assertions that peppered the Confucianist proclamations are the very definition of "not science." Saying that Confucianism lacks scientific reasoning is no more or no less insightful than asserting that astrology is not astronomy or alchemy is not chemistry. The statement is ipso facto true, but it does not constitute an explanation. Confucianism is not science. We know that already.

Confucianism isn't the only ideology in the world that has an anti-science bias. At one point in history, the Catholic Church was violently hostile to science, but despite "the Galileo affair," the Catholic Church did not derail science completely. Why was China different? A reasonable hypothesis is that all civilizations started with random ideas with respect to the degree of their preexisting accommodations to science. Because these ideas predated science, their "stances" on science were incidental rather than designed specifically for that purpose. They were not formulated as contemporaneous rejoinders to scientific ideas. Then deep historical forces propelled the Chinese polity, society, or economy to move in ways that favored an idea that happened to be the least accommodative to science, whereas the same tournament of ideas in Europe played out differently and led to a triumph of an ideology that was more accepting of science. Our inquiry should be directed not to the amorphous idiosyncrasies of an ideology, but to the mechanisms of this tournament process that led some ideologies to survive and others to die.

A social scientific explanation begins with investigating variances, and such an investigation should go beyond the one well-known variance featured heavily in the literature on the Needham question—the Great Divergence between China and Europe.[24] An advantage of studying Chinese history is that there is a lot to study. Chinese history is long, complicated, and, crucially, well documented. Needham and his collaborators relied on the rich Chinese source materials to compile a record of Chinese inventions, but they did so in a format that is not amenable to a quantitative analysis. With digitalization, we can apply a quantitative approach to the Needham question.

## Chinese Historical Inventions Database

Since 2014, I have directed a major database construction project. The database, the Chinese Historical Inventions Database (CHID), has underpinned several research projects I am undertaking with other scholars.[25] The primary source of CHID is *Science and Civilization in China* (*SCC*), a series of books written, compiled, and edited by Joseph Needham and his colleagues and students that present the history of, and explanations for, science and technology in ancient China. The compilation is in free-form texts. To date, twenty-seven volumes, organized under seven themes, have been published. A complementary data source in our project is a series of books by scholars at the Chinese Academy of Science, collectively titled *The History of Chinese Science and Technology* (*HCST*).

In our database construction, we refer to all recorded entries in *SCC* and *HCST* as "inventions." An invention can refer to a scientific theory, a mechanical gadget, a particular production technique, an approach in medicine, or a discovery. There is not enough detailed information in *SCC* and *HCST* to sufficiently differentiate between science and technology or between a mechanical device and a novel method.[26] Throughout this book, I use the term "inventions" in this broad sense and employ "science" and "technology" interchangeably.

CHID contains 10,350 inventions, of which 7,913 can be unambiguously assigned to their dynasties and 2,437 are assigned based on an imputed method that we have developed. In this book, I have analyzed the information based on 7,913 inventions as well as the information based on 10,350 inventions. The same patterns hold in both scenarios.

## *Chinese Inventiveness*

There are several ways to measure a dynasty's inventiveness. The simplest way—the one used in some academic studies—is to count the number of inventions for a given time period, say every one hundred years, or per dynasty. This approach is problematic. If we believe there is a fixed proportion of inventive individuals to the population, the right measure should be inventions scaled by the population. The Chinese dynasties vary tremendously in terms of the size of their populations. A simple count of inventions would exaggerate the inventiveness of more populous dynasties. (It may also overstate the inventiveness of longer dynasties, although to a lesser extent—an issue I will take up later.)

To illustrate the flaw with this method, imagine declaring that Russia is more inventive than Singapore because in 2019 Russia filed 29,711 patents compared with 7,354 patents filed by Singapore—ignoring the obvious fact that the Russian patent filings were generated by 144 million people, whereas those of Singapore were generated by a population of 5.45 million.[27]

My primary measure of inventiveness for a dynasty is the number of inventions in that dynasty divided by its population (in million people). I call this measure Chinese dynasty inventiveness (CDI) index, and to the best of my knowledge, this is the first time such a metric has been applied to a historical analysis of Chinese technology.

One objection to the CDI index is that it can understate the inventiveness of the populous dynasties, leading to an opposite bias from the one based on a count measure. The validity of this criticism matters for our historical judgment. Since the more populous dynasties congregated toward the end of the imperial era, our measure will exhibit a declining pattern of Chinese technology over time. This is a complicated issue but let me note that choices of a correct measurement should not be dictated by a mathematical mechanic, that is, a larger denominator resulting in a lower ratio. They should be based on spelling out how a population increase affects inventiveness. Implicitly, this objection to the CDI measure is based on a Malthusian logic—that more people will lead to fewer inventions and lower productivity. This logic has been shown to be false. A more sensible assumption would be that creative and inventive people represent a fixed proportion of the total population. The population grows and so does the number of inventors. We have a supporting case from Europe. Between 1750 and 1850 the population doubled, but Europe experienced no diminishing returns from agricultural technology.[28]

The opposite, however, is closer to the truth. More people, more ideas. This is a logic that scholars have used to explain why some civilizations produced more inventions than others.[29] One channel is population density. If a population increase is due to the growth of an urban population, then a larger population can raise inventiveness. Urban populations are more inventive than those in the countryside, on average, because of various cluster effects, including the greater probability of creative and inventive minds interacting with one another in a dense setting.[30] But if a population expands through the acquisition of new far-flung or rural territories, it may not be accompanied by an increase in population density. A larger population may or may not raise our CDI index.

Another objection is that the CDI measure fails to take into account the length of the dynasties. Unlike modern economic data that are organized according to the same time unit—annual, quarterly, or monthly—our data are organized by a political unit, dynasties, which varied greatly in duration. The Tang, for example, lasted 288 years, whereas the Sui lasted only thirty-seven years. The Sui generated a CDI index of 1.8, meaning there were 1.8 inventions per million population, whereas the index for the Tang is 17.6. Is this a statistical artifact of compressing the Sui's inventiveness into thirty-eight years?

Misattributions are more likely for short dynasties than for long dynasties because the average life expectancy of an inventor can outlast a short dynasty. The Sui dynasty lasted thirty-seven years and the Qin, only fourteen years. The productivity of an inventor can be impacted by multiple dynasties if they are short enough. The usual treatment in Chinese historical research is to lump short dynasties together with their succeeding longer dynasties, for example, Qin-Han or Sui-Tang. (Because Qin is so short, my CDI index for Qin and Han are combined into a single dynastic CDI index.) If the CDI index is erroneous, in all likelihood it will contain an upward bias for the short dynasties. Sui's index at 1.8 may overstate Sui's inventiveness.

Time compression is not driving our data anyway. Let's look at two dynasties—the Five Dynasties and Ten Kingdoms (FDTK) period (908–979, 72 years in duration) and the Qing (267 years in duration). The Qing lasted 3.7 times as long as the FDTK period, but its CDI index is 2.85, nearly identical to the FDTK's CDI index of 2.8. Dynastic duration is not the only factor driving our measure, and there is no theoretical reason why it should be. To a degree, our population denominator already incorporates a time effect. The longer dynasties tended to be more peaceful, and the more peaceful dynasties tended to have larger populations. Inventions scaled by population are already partially scaled by dynastic duration.

A separate question is the validity of weighting equally all the inventions in the construction of the CDI index. One can counter that this approach compares apples with oranges. For example, the Song invented gunpowder, printing, and the compass, three inventions that changed the world, yet our CDI measure does not make any allowances for the relative economic importance of Chinese inventions. This is a fair point and let me answer this question in two ways. First, apart from a few inventions, we do not have an objective way to differentiate the ten thousand inventions by their economic importance. Second, and more important, the modern economics research that tracks the economic importance of the inventions asks an entirely different question from the one I am asking here. It asks, "Has the research productivity increased or decreased?" This line of research compares the inputs into the production of R&D against the output—the economic impact of that R&D. The inputs are the number of researchers and R&D spending.[31]

In our case, the inputs into Chinese inventions were the payroll costs and the total number of researchers, but there was no "output" as we understand it in a modern sense. Keep in mind the broad context of this research: China failed to launch its own Industrial Revolution, which by definition means that Chinese inventions were not deployed and commercialized at scale and in economically meaningful ways. In theory, all the inventions in CHID have identical economic importance—zero or near zero. Yes, the great Chinese inventions of printing, gunpowder, and the compass did eventually have an enormous economic impact, but in Europe, not in China. It is in this sense that assigning an equal economic weight to all the CHID inventions is the correct procedure. The Song dynasty might have been more consequential to human civilization than other dynasties, but this is a different research question from the one I am concerned with—which dynasties came up with more inventions and why.

My CDI index is a density measure similar to an indicator developed by the World Bank to measure a country's business environment: the annual newly created business entities per working-age population. The operating assumption is that every individual in the working-age population is equally disposed to start a new business if the business environment so permits. This assumption applies in our case.

## Three Eras of Chinese Technology

What are the salient patterns of Chinese technology in our data? What is the historical trajectory of Chinese inventions? Which dynasties were the most inventive, and which were the least inventive? Figure 7.1 presents the CDI index on the vertical axis and across Chinese dynasties from the Warring-States period to the Qing dynasty on the horizontal axis, a span of some 2,400 years. There are three eras of Chinese technology. The first era, from 475 BCE to 581 CE, represents the peak of Chinese technology, with an average CDI index of 24.5. The second era is from 581 to 1279, with an average CDI index of 9.4, and the third era is from 1279 to 1911, with an average CDI index of 5.3. Earlier in the book, I quoted scholars describing the Chinese polity as "precocious." There is a precocious quality to Chinese technology as well: it developed and peaked early.

One striking pattern in Figure 7.1 is that Chinese inventiveness peaked and troughed, as indicated by the cyclicality of the CDI index. Technological development in imperial China was not cumulative. Chinese inventors did not stand on the shoulders of the giants of the previous eras. Earlier inventions did not fuel later inventions, and individual spurts of creativity did not cohere and translate into subsequent waves of creativity and inventiveness. In this sense, Chinese inventions may not even qualify as "technology" in a strict definition of the term. Technology, as Brian Arthur argues in his influential book *The Nature of Technology*, evolves through combinatorial and re-combinatorial dynamics of existing inventions and component blocks of technologies.[32] Why did a non-cumulative pattern occur in China? One reason is that Chinese inventions took place in a vacuum: an environment without science, without commercial developments and a market economy, and without institutionalized knowledge creation and protection (such as patent rights).

But note that before the Industrial Revolution, technological development was not exponential in the West either. An exponential spurt

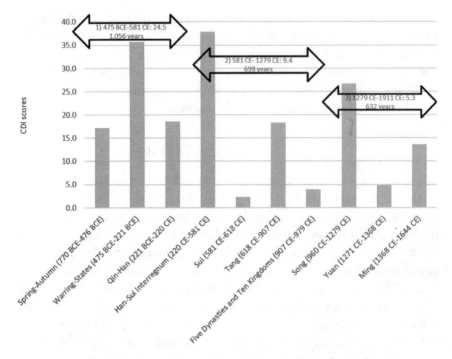

Figure 7.1. Three eras of Chinese technology, 475 BCE–1911 CE. The CDI
scores are calculated from the inventions data in the Chinese Historical
Invention Database, in which the dynastic inventions are divided by the dynastic
population. The population estimates are from Ge Jianxiong, *Zhongguo Renkou
Fazhanshi.*

occurred hundreds of years after steady progress and isolated developments. China could have maintained its dispersed and somewhat random technological advances at their steady and leisurely pace rather than
spiraling downward as shown in Figure 7.1. I wrestle with a more basic
question—why did individual and isolated inventions backslide after the
sixth century?

Figure 7.1 shows two waves of declining CDI index. The first took
place in about the sixth century, and the second occurred in about the
fourteenth century. Between these two waves are the Tang and Song dynasties, widely regarded as the two most prosperous and inventive dynasties in Chinese history. They dented and flattened the declining curve, but
they did not reverse it. The Ming and Qing dynasties show up poorly in
our measure, refuting the view that China's technological progress was

sustained during these two dynasties. The Ming's CDI index is only 8.51, a sharp decline from the index of 14.5 in the Song, while the Qing experienced a further decline, to only 2.85.[33]

One surprise that emerges from this figure: Chinese inventiveness peaked much earlier than is commonly assumed. The highest CDI index was attained between the years 220 and 581 during the "Han-Sui Interregnum," the period between the Han dynasty and the Sui dynasty. The CDI index during the Han-Sui Interregnum is 31.1, more than ten times the CDI index during the Qing and roughly two times the CDI index during the Tang and Song dynasties. This obscure period in Chinese history—its significance is mainly remembered for a novel *The Romance of the Three Kingdoms*—holds the key to unlocking the answer to the Needham question.[34]

I know of at least one quantitative study whose findings are consistent with the pattern shown in Figure 7.1—that Chinese technological development led early, and peaked early. It is based on a smaller-scale database supposedly focused on "breakthrough technologies."[35] The paper lists 1,700 breakthrough technologies from time immemorial to the twentieth century. Of these, seventy-seven originated in China, fifty-seven of which were invented before the end of the Han-Sui Interregnum.

If this finding holds up, it will overturn a number of conventional ideas about Chinese technological history. It is generally believed that the Tang and Song were the most glorious dynasties in Chinese history. In particular, the Song features prominently in the annals of technological history because it was then that three out of China's "Big Four" technologies—the compass, moveable-type printing, and gunpowder—were invented. But this glowing portrait of the Tang and the Song is driven more by the salience of these two dynasties rather than by the scale of their inventions. These two dynasties pale in comparison with the Han-Sui Interregnum and with the earlier Warring-States period. The Tang and the Song may have been inventive eras in their own right, but they were merely an afterglow of the preceding dynastic glories.

## Getting the Causal Dynamics Right

The first step in a causal analysis is to ask, "Are there variances?" Or, for the research question at hand, "Is there a turning point in Chinese technological development, and if so, when did it occur?" Most of the existing accounts assign a much later date to this turning point than that shown in Figure 7.1, and such assignments matter in terms of identifying the correct causal factors.

To date, the most frequently invoked explanation for the decline of Chinese technology is culture—the effects of a Chinese family culture that is supposedly antithetical to industrialization, or the lack of an analytical culture in China due to a deficiency in formal logic and the absence of a scientific mindset, or a failure to apply scientific knowledge to product development.[36] A second category emphasizes the nature of Chinese technology itself. According to one theory recounted by Bray, the preponderance of wet rice agriculture did not lend itself to mechanization.[37] Another theory is that Chinese technology was concentrated in the agricultural sector that had limited inventive potentials.[38]

There's more. Some scholars point to politics, claiming that the imperial state, buttressed by sophisticated bureaucratic controls, dominated the social power hierarchy and dampened inventiveness and commerce.[39] Another category of explanations assigns the blame to the anti-trade voyage bans and the stoppage of foreign knowledge. And still another collection of explanations refutes the idea that China ever stagnated; it is just that the West took off.[40]

Several of these explanations can be set aside given the patterns established in Figure 7.1. Family attitude is a fixed factor, and so can be ruled out as a primary explanatory variable for the wide gyrations in inventiveness over time. The wet-rice and agricultural-concentration arguments are problematic both conceptually and empirically. Chinese inventions were actually widely distributed. Our CHID includes 809 agricultural inventions, out of the ten-thousand-invention total. It is simply not true that Chinese inventions were only agricultural. Also, if inventions in a single sector failed to spill over into other sectors, an additional explanation is required to explain why the single-sector inventions could not expand into other sectors. Sectoral concentration itself is not a convincing explanation.

Trade bans occurred much later than the initial wave of decline shown around the sixth century. (Zheng He's last voyage was in 1433). And although the trade bans compounded and might have accelerated the Chinese decline by contributing to the second wave of declining CDI index, they do not explain the first wave. The Western-takeoff theory is also incongruous with our graph. Its premise is that China did not decline, but we can see that this is not the case.

The two remaining explanations, one based on science and the other based on bureaucracy, may be reconcilable with the pattern presented in Figure 7.1, but only with substantial adaptation and reframing.

## The Evolution of Chinese Contestability

In a remarkable historical confluence, Europe and China crossed their respective political milestones within a hair's breadth of each other. The unraveling of the Western Roman Empire in 476 led to the political and economic fragmentation of Europe and Europe never looked back. Just a hundred years later, the opposite happened in China. The fragmentation of China was brought to an abrupt end by the Sui dynasty. The Sui was itself short-lived, but it devised an instrument, *Keju*, that forestalled China from becoming fractious again. A remarkable homeostasis ensued, one that turned out to be catastrophically detrimental to technological development.

The Sui dynasty holds the key to one of the most enduring enigmas in the history of technology—the collapse of Chinese technological supremacy.[41] Although the Chinese economy continued to grow, it was mostly of the Smithian variety based on an expansion of commercial activities and monetization.[42] As Europe entered into the age of Renaissance and industrialization, China's technological progress languished. By 1600, China's technological inferiority was apparent to most visitors.[43] This technological gap between the Chinese and European civilizations is a defining historical watershed, followed by centuries of the Opium Wars, unequal treaties, and the general instability and chaos in China itself.[44]

The Chinese scientific collapse was total, as we see in Mansel Davies's devastating quantitative portrait.[45] Of the 3,988 notable scientific achievements between 988 and 1988, only 45 of them originated in China, and of these, 38 occurred between 988 and 1600. By this measure, China was already lagging behind Italy, with 81 achievements, and Germany, with its 47, during the same time period. The Chinese decline and its potential stagnation relative to the West long preceded the Ming dynasty.

This is the power of data: it can reveal a pattern that is difficult to discern from qualitative accounts. Many blame the Ming dynasty for ending China's technological supremacy, possibly because of the visibility of the voyage bans and because of their saliency and the fact that voyage bans can be convincingly linked with technological decline. But if our data are to be believed, Chinese technology began to decline some seven centuries before the Ming.

The more critical timing is between the sixth and the eleventh centuries, the focal period of my earlier analysis. During this period, the *Keju* platform was established and perfected; the ideological space contracted; political fragmentation ended; and ruler stability improved. China's entry in the sixth century into a long span of political homeostasis was detrimental to Chinese inventiveness and brought about the first wave of decline in Chinese inventions. After the Song dynasty, the Chinese ideological space narrowed further, seeding a second wave of technological decline.

## Reframing the "Needham Question"

Needham posed his famous question as a thought experiment to perform a "titration." A titration is a chemical experiment to induce a change in a compound by adding a calibrated amount of another compound. Needham, however, did not base his views on a quantitative analysis of the materials he himself meticulously compiled. In "The Roles of Europe and China in the Evolution of Oecumenical Science," he drew a schematic sketch of the development of science in China and Europe between 300 BCE and 2000 CE.[46] In it, China maintained a lead in science over Europe before the seventeenth century, and then a series of developments in the West, specifically the Renaissance and the Scientific Revolution, personified and symbolized by Nicolaus Copernicus, Galileo Galilei, and Johannes Kepler, catapulted the West to a leadership position. Technological breakthroughs came on the heels of these scientific breakthroughs.

The centrality of science in seeding the Industrial Revolution is debated. Joel Mokyr argues that the ancient Greeks had science, but pursued it as an act of curiosity and devoid of experiments and applications.[47] What made Europeans in the seventeenth and eighteenth centuries unique is that they applied science to improve their material welfare. Mere production of knowledge did not lead to the Industrial Revolution. In seventeenth-century England, scientists shared their findings and knowledge across space and time through scientific societies and institutions. Knowledge accumulated rather than being lodged in silos. The Industrial Revolution was a product of broader intellectual, cognitive, societal, and institutional developments.

A deeper and more expansive question is why China failed to develop a similar institutional and intellectual milieu to nourish and to sustain its early lead and why China's individual discoveries and inventions did not accumulate into a system of knowledge. Needham's sketch shows that Chinese science was on a continuously upward curve, until it was surpassed by Europe in the seventeenth century. But this is not supported by CHID data, data that are compiled from Needham's own volumes. Data reported by Davies also contradict that view: between 988 and 1600,

China was already lagging behind Italy and Germany in terms of major scientific breakthroughs.

The seventeenth century might have been convenient timing for Needham because of the confluence of the Scientific Revolution in the West and the end of an intellectually and politically repressive Ming dynasty. There is a hint of dynamism in Needham's thinking here. In a discussion of the evolution of the imperial examination system, he states his belief that early on, *Keju* made allowances in subject areas such as mathematics and astronomy, enabling Chinese inventiveness, but subsequently the focus on the classics crowded out all other subject areas.[48] This reading of *Keju* is consistent with the narrative I present in Chapter 1 that the intellectual scope of *Keju* narrowed over time.

For Needham, *Keju* is compatible with science as long as it had some scientific content.[49] It is true that the Tang and the Song had a more flexible and more open-ended form of *Keju* compared with later dynasties, but the fact is that the Tang and the Song were already on the declining portion of the inventive curve. The populations of the Tang and Song were more inventive than those of the later Yuan, Ming, and Qing dynasties, but they lagged behind those of the Han-Sui Interregnum and the Warring-States period. A more straightforward interpretation of our data is that China was more inventive without *Keju* than with *Keju*. The scaling and the restrictive scope of the *Keju* curriculum during the Yuan, Ming, and Qing dynasties produced an additional knock-on effect, but the initial precipitating factor of Chinese technological decline was brought about by the broader political and cognitive changes that accompanied the establishment and scaling of *Keju*.

## The Sui Era as the Turning Point

As Joel Mokyr explains, the Enlightenment emerged "from a unique concatenation of circumstances: the political fragmentation of Europe, which made the suppression of innovators by the ruling orthodoxy and vested interests more difficult," and "an intellectual coherence that manifested itself in the transnational republic of letters."[50] This is the "contestability" perspective on European economic and technological takeoffs, and it is analogous to the scope side of the scale and scope framework I have used throughout this book.[51] Let me apply this concept to China.

The following is my basic proposition: China before the sixth century was more "contestable" than China after it. It was a more heterogenous society, polity, and system of ideas. To return to the scale and scope dichotomy, China before the sixth century had a more balanced combination of scale and scope. The size of China was akin to that of a kingdom rather than that of an empire, and territories existed as competitive and relatively autonomous entities. Within the polities, different ideas clashed with each other and competed for attention from the educated elites.

The Sui is the turning point in this historical arc of China. In 581, the Sui dynasty reunified China, bringing to an end 361 years of the fractious Han-Sui Interregnum. Not only that, but the Sui put the Chinese political system on a permanent institutional footing. As I explained in Chapter 5, the stability of the rulers and dynasties improved, and conflicts between emperors and their premiers eased. The political and territorial unification of China set off a cascade of other developments—*Keju*, the collapse of ideological contestability, political longevity, and, eventually, technological sclerosis. This political Great Divergence laid down the foundation for the much later and better-known economic Great Divergence of the seventeenth and eighteenth centuries.

Table 7.1 presents six representative historical periods in terms of their contestability conditions and their inventiveness: (1) the Warring-States period, (2) the Han-Sui Interregnum, (3) the Tang, (4) the Song, (5) the Ming, and (6) the Qing. At the top of the ideological and political contestability are two periods in Chinese history when China was not even a single united territory. Seven political entities existed and competed with each other during the Warring-States period and some thirty-one political or territorial entities existed either in parallel with each other or in rapid succession during the Han-Sui Interregnum.

The first wave of technological stagnation in China coincides with the end of China's political fragmentation. As shown in Table 7.1, there was only one political unit in China starting in 581. The second wave of technological stagnation occurred after the Song. The CDI index declined from the levels of the Tang (17.6) and the Song (14.5) to 4.43 in the Yuan, 8.51 in the Ming, and 2.85 in the Qing. In terms of timing, this second wave overlapped with another transformation after the sixth century: a collapse of the contestability of ideas that began during the Song.

We have some fragmentary data that can be used to measure China's ideological development. The database was constructed from biographical profiles of some ten thousand historical figures in imperial China.[52] They are prominent individuals in Chinese history, classified by the fields for which they gained their prominence, such as science, humanities, or

*Table 7.1.* Schematic conception of contestability, by dynastic period

|  | Political/ territorial fragmentation (units) | Ideological diversity (proportions) | Inventiveness (CDI score) |
|---|---|---|---|
| Warring-States period | High (7) | High (0.01)* | High (21.8) |
| Han-Sui Interregnum | High (31) | High (0.05) | High (31.1) |
| Tang dynasty | Low (1) | High (0.06) | Medium (17.6) |
| Song dynasty | Low (1) | Low (0.02) | Medium (14.5) |
| Ming dynasty | Low (1) | Low (0.01) | Low (8.5) |
| Qing dynasty | Low (1) | Low (0.00) | Low (2.9) |

*Notes:* Political/territorial fragmentation refers to the number of independent political and territorial units. Information on territorial units is based on Wilkinson, *Chinese History*. Ideological diversity is indicated by the Buddhist and Daoist figures as proportions of the historical figures of dynasties based on Ouyang and Hu, *Zhongguo Gudai Mingren Fenlei Dacidian.* * Ideological diversity for the Warring-States period is judged to be high despite its low ideological diversity figure, because one of the two components of the index, Buddhism, arrived in China during the Han dynasty, long after the Warring-States period, thus its value is zero. (See Figure 7.2, which presents Buddhist and Daoist developments separately.) The overwhelming consensus among scholars is that the Warring-States period was one of the freest periods in Chinese history. The inventiveness measure is our CDI score and is calculated from the Chinese Historical Invention Database.

the military. For the field of religion, the biographical profiles identified historical figures who adhered to Daoism and Buddhism, the two main religions in Chinese history.[53] From this information, we can calculate the Buddhists or Daoists as a proportion of all the prominent historical figures. The thinking behind this measure is that because the default ideology is Confucianism, the higher proportions of Buddhists and Daoists can denote relatively greater ideological diversity.

The measure is an underestimate of the Buddhist/Daoist prevalence; the denominator treats all non-Buddhists and all non-Daoists, such as Legalists or non-believers, as Confucianists, but this is the best we can do given the constraints of historical data. The caveat is that while proportion figures themselves may be inaccurate, their changing values over time can still indicate meaningful dynamics.

Figure 7.2 presents both the dynastic CDI index shown in Figure 7.1 and the proportions of Chinese historical figures who were Buddhists or

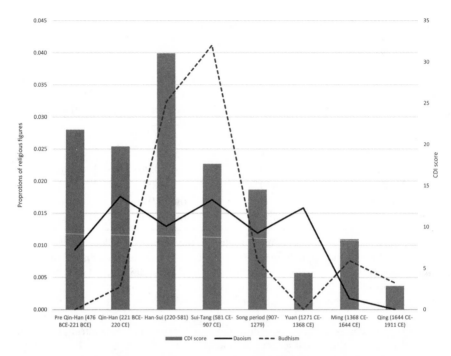

Figure 7.2. Buddhism, Daoism, and CDI scores. The left vertical axis denotes Buddhists and Daoists as proportions to historical figures. The data on historical figures are coded from Ouyang and Hu, *Zhongguo Gudai Mingren Fenlei Dacidian [Encyclopedia of Prominent Figures in Chinese History]*, 4 vols. (Beijing: Huayu jiaoxue chubanshe, 2009). The right vertical axis denotes the CDI scores. The horizontal axis represents the Chinese dynasty. The CDI scores are calculated from the inventions data in the Chinese Historical Invention Database. They are given by the dynastic inventions divided by the dynastic population. The population estimates are from Ge Jianxiong, *Zhongguo Renkou Fazhanshi*.

Daoists. The left vertical axis represents the proportions of figures who were affiliated with each religious belief system, and the right vertical axis represents the CDI index. Buddhism arrived in China in the first century CE. The low proportions of Buddhists before 220 CE is not evidence of ideological homogeneity. As proof, the proportions of Daoism are high during this period. Figure 7.2 shows that China's ideological diversity declined substantially over time. The timing of the decline was stretched over centuries, in contrast to the sudden end of political fragmentation in the sixth century. Buddhism declined in the middle of our second technological era, and Daoism declined during the middle of our third technological era. Our data span hundreds of years and are not precise enough to conclude that ideological contraction "caused" technological decline. Figure 7.2 shows that there is an overlap between ideological contraction and the declining CDI index, but it is not proof of a specific causal direction.

To pin down causation in the type of long-range historical data we have here is extraordinarily difficult, but maybe we can settle for a second-best answer. Let's ask, "Which hypothesis is more plausible given the pattern presented in Figure 7.2—that ideological contraction caused technological decline, or that technological decline caused ideological contraction?" While the causal influence of technological decline cannot be ruled out, as far as I know, no one has ever argued that China's ideological contraction occurred because its technology was in decline. The literature in general treats technology as a dependent variable. Many of the ideas proposed to explain the "Needham question" have this causal direction in them. (That said, some technology scholars argue that technology liberates ideology. Printing, for example, is believed to have contributed to the spread of liberalism and democracy. That clearly did not happen in China. As shown Figure 7.2, the high CDI index of the Han-Sui Interregnum was followed by ideological decline in later centuries.)

Until contradicted by more granular data, it makes sense to default to the well-established general proposition that a more controlling ideological environment is detrimental to inventiveness. To reason from ideology to technology rather than the other way around is also plausible from what we know about history during this period. Recall the evolutionary trajectory of *Keju*. The *Keju* exam system started out as a multi-plex platform and during the Song dynasty was transformed into a rigid single-plex platform. The closing of the Chinese mind occurred as *Keju* scaled. Both Joseph Needham and Justin Lin indicted *Keju* as the culprit for China's technological decline, a view supported by Figure 7.2. But their reasoning—and their placement of this decline in the seventeenth century—is wrong. They emphasized the crowding-out effect of *Keju* on human capital. Maybe crowding out happened, but keep in mind that the first-order effect of *Keju* was an overall increase of human capital. A more pernicious development for China's technological inventiveness was the thwarting of political and ideological competition.

## *Ideological Hegemony*

Now we return to the consensus view among China scholars that Confucianism undermined Chinese inventiveness. Let me differentiate my view from that consensus view as sharply as I can. My emphasis is on the dominance, hegemony, and monopoly of Confucianism, not on its specific tenets. I believe that the hegemony of Confucianism, or of any other ideology for that matter, is bad for science. If *Keju* had scaled Legalism—or Christianity for that matter—at the expense of everything else, history would not have turned out that differently.

Hegemony preempted the emergence of alternative and unconventional ideas and values. The rigidities of rote memorization and its "eight-legged" format deterred candidates from developing a skeptical mindset and inhibited their causal thinking and reasoning skills, as well as their abilities to generate hypotheses, all of which are the bread and butter of doing science.[54] Confucianism is anti-science in that it is more amenable to standardization and formalization, lending its arsenal of 400,000 characters and phrases as the best technical tool to homogenize China.

That said, the specific tenets of Confucianism are probably more antithetical to science than those of other Chinese ideologies. According to Needham, Daoism approaches nature from an intuitive and observational perspective, and facilitated early advances in chemistry and astronomy.[55] Mohism, the most abstract and metaphysical of all Chinese faiths, is grounded in consequentialist reasoning and highly developed in logic and argumentation.[56] One of its most prominent believers was Liu Hui, a third-century Chinese mathematician who supplied independent proof of the Pythagorean theorem. And Buddhism, some modern neuroscientists argue, shares with science an empirical approach to the human mind.[57] These musings may or may not hold true, but I know of no claim that Confucianism contains any scientific predispositions.

The most lethal effect of ideological hegemony is probably the destruction of curiosity. Contrast Zheng He with Marco Polo, not in terms of their navigational technologies, but in terms of their awareness and knowledge of a world external to their existence and being. Marco Polo regaled his European compatriots with his detailed and vivid travelogues to China. He commanded an audience because the European chattering class was genuinely curious about an exotic and mysterious land they could not experience themselves. Adam Smith, Frederick William, Gottfried Wihelm Liebniz, and Samuel von Pufendorf all pontificated about China. By contrast, I know of no evidence that tales of Zheng He's travels elicited excitement or interest among the educated elites of Chinese society.[58]

Modern researchers lament the paucity of knowledge about Zheng He's voyages and blame Ming's destruction of the official documentation related to the voyages. This is itself revealing—how thorough the official monopoly over that knowledge was. There was no unofficial account of this greatest navigational feat of China. Not one of those tens of thousands of sailors who went on the voyages published a travelogue of their encounters. What really happened, I think, is that the Chinese during the Ming dynasty no longer entertained any curiosity about the outside world, and there was very little that could have ignited and nurtured this curiosity.

In the fifteenth century, the Europeans did not command advanced navigational technologies, but they were light years ahead of the Chinese in being aggressively globalizing, thirsty for knowledge, and curious about a new and exotic world beyond their own direct experience. Marco Polo explored China whereas Zheng He dropped by and window-shopped in the lands he reached. Today, modern historians rely on accounts by Marco Polo and Western missionaries to reconstruct Chinese life in Song and Ming, but they do not turn to Zheng He and his fellow travelers for information on Southeast Asia and Africa. The modern mindset—drive for knowledge and for answers—matters far more than a static piece of technology. A far more foundational question than Needham's question about Chinese science is, "What happened to the Chinese curiosity?"

## The Song Anomaly

The Tang and Song eras represent a second peak of Chinese inventiveness after the Warring-States period and the Han-Sui Interregnum. The Tang's high CDI index is easily explainable by our contestability framework. Yes, the Tang dynasty featured political unity, but that political unity was primarily territorial rather than ideological. The Tang was cosmopolitan and open to the outside world. Tens of thousands of foreigners resided in Chang'an, the Tang capital, on a long-term basis.[59]

The Song is a harder nut to crack. Why was the Song inventive at all? Does our contestability framework explain the Song? On the surface, it had none of the contestability conditions that I have discussed so far. It was politically and territorially unified, and it seeded the decimation of imperial China's ideological diversity. Yet the Song has a CDI index comparable to that of the Tang, and it was famously inventive, having been the era when three of China's "Big Four" breakthroughs occurred. Some even described it as a mini Renaissance.[60] Some of the most innovative thinkers lived in that era. Shen Kuo (1031–1095) was widely regarded as one of the greatest polymaths in history, as well as an inventor, a scientist, and an erudite thinker who preceded Leonardo da Vinci by five hundred years.

He explained mineralogy, erosion, sedimentation and uplift, mathematics, astronomy, and meteorology in his 1088 work *Dream Pool Essays*. Yet it was Song rulers who introduced the practice of foot-binding, a physical instrument to enforce the moral subordination of women by the chauvinistic Neo-Confucianism. Neo-Confucianism, of course, was another product of the Song. The status of Buddhism, which is more accepting of gender equality, deteriorated during the Song.

Chinese historians hold diametrically opposite views of the Song. Some argue that the Song was both "weak and poor" (积弱积穷); others argue that although the Song state was weak and poor, Song society was not.[61] According to this line of argument, the Song encouraged commerce and wealth accumulation, and the state was strapped for cash because it practiced a version of supply-side economics. One thing that historians do agree on is that the Chinese imperial market economy reached its apex during the Song. In a meticulous study, William Liu documents just how advanced the Song's market economy was, especially compared to the subsequent dynasties of the Ming and the Qing.[62]

One hypothesis that may explain the Song's high CDI index is that the market economy helped to spark innovation. Among all dynasties, the Song probably stood the best chance of developing a vibrant private sector able to capitalize on technology and to realize material gains. A group of intellectuals during the Song supported an applied orientation of knowledge and learning. Hu Yuan, Bai Juyi, Han Yu, and Liu Zongyuan all advocated that discoveries be applied to more utilitarian purposes. A "culture of growth" might have emerged from this intellectual climate.

Private-sector development in an autocratic context qualifies as a scope condition. Contestable markets have features that affect both the demand side and the supply side of technology. Technology depends on demand, generated either by the government or by the private sector. And on the supply side, technological change can occur through new ideas and innovations, produced exogenously and often in a highly unpredictable fashion.[63] The Song's ideological contraction might have suppressed contestability on the supply side, but its strong private sector might have been a driver of technology on the demand side. One example is navigational technology. The Ming court monopolized demand for navigational technology, but during the Song dynasty, the private sector deployed navigational technologies to assist the sizeable private fleets engaged in foreign trade.[64] Similar to China under the reformist CCP, Song's market economy ameliorated the effects of the ideological rigidities, created a market for commercial applications, and facilitated technological development.

## Kingdoms vis-à-vis Empires

In Europe, political fragmentation, democracy, civil society, and a market economy developed in tandem with science and technology, and they spurred each other on in self-enforcing virtuous cycles. Imperial China offers a sharper illustration of the contestability effect from the other side of the technological divide: it reversed itself technologically. Reversing a development prone to cumulations and subject to the natural path-dependency entrenchments requires a potent countervailing force.

The Ming emperors could enact and enforce voyage bans because no other political entities checked and balanced their power. Under a single hierarchy, there were intramural disputes, such as between the eunuchs who supported voyages and the Confucian scholar-officials who opposed them, but these power struggles lacked legitimacy and sustenance. They provided no outside options to aspirational explorers who might have wanted to launch their own voyages. The imperial court monopolized all the talents and funding channels. Zheng He was backed by the most powerful man in China, Emperor Yongle, but the support of an autocrat was capricious. One day there was a lot of support; the next day there was none. (Some of the high-tech entrepreneurs in China today would surely appreciate this assessment.)

As Mokyr notes, the true difference between Europe and China is that the preferences of the rulers mattered greatly in China but not so much in Europe.[65] There were European rulers who were similarly averse to innovations and trade, but they did not control the entire continent. If the Spanish king had rejected Columbus, another ruler could have come forth to supply the needed funding. The economic gravity might have shifted depending on the preferences of the rulers, but economic growth and technological innovations could still be funded and sustained. Starting in the sixth century, China lost this condition. Instead of imagining a counterfactual Pax Sinica based on Ming's naval prowess, a more productive approach is to ask, "What would have happened to China's technology if China had retained its contestability conditions beyond the sixth century?"

In 476, Germanic King Odoacer deposed Emperor Romulus Augustulus, ending the long reign of the Western Roman Empire. As historian

Walter Scheidel argues in his book *Escape from Rome*, the end of the Roman Empire unleashed the political, economic, and intellectual forces that eventually produced GDP growth, technology, increases in life expectancy, and democracy. The "escape" from Rome gave us the modern world as we know it.[66]

In 581, a mere hundred years later, a reverse development occurred in China: the Sui dynasty ended 361 years of fractious rule and political and military competition among a multitude of territories and political units. Sui Wendi reunified China, not just as a brilliant military commander but also as an institutionalist. The Sui emperor invented a scaling instrument that perpetuated a unified Chinese empire—*Keju*.

The Sui dynasty converted China from a collection of kingdoms to one big empire. Kingdoms compete with each other by necessity; empires compete with other empires by choice. The CDI index is very sensitive to the changes in the state of competition. Between the Warring-States period and the Han-Sui Interregnum was the Qin-Han period. The Qin and the Han were China's first and second empire-sized dynasties, respectively. Other empire-sized dynasties were the Tang, Yuan, Ming, and Qing. The unified, empire-sized dynasties are not nearly as inventive as the fractious kingdom-sized dynasties. When China transitioned to the Qin-Han period from the Warring-States period, its CDI index declined from 21.8 to 19.8, and when China transitioned from the Qin-Han period to the Han-Sui Interregnum, its CDI index rose from 19.8 to 31.1. Empires, which are homogenous and territorially expansive, turned out to be detrimental to technological development. Kingdoms, which are smaller and often compete externally and sometimes internally, exceled in inventiveness.

This pattern holds in general. There is a negative correlation between empire size and CDI index. Figure 7.3 plots the CDI index against the territorial size of the Chinese dynasties, with the CDI index on the vertical axis and the territorial size—measured in million square kilometers—on the horizontal axis. The size of the bubble is scaled to the territorial size. A clear downward sloping pattern is visible in the graph. The Yuan, the largest Chinese dynasty, is at the very bottom, followed by another empire, the Qing. Kingdom-sized dynasties, such as the Warring States, Han-Sui Interregnum, and Spring-Autumn, outperformed medium-sized empires such as the Qin-Han, Tang, and Ming, while medium-sized empires outperformed the giant-sized empires, such as the Qing and the Yuan. Interestingly, the two prominent exceptions to this "small-is-beautiful" pattern are the Sui and the FDTK. Both, although small, were uninventive. These

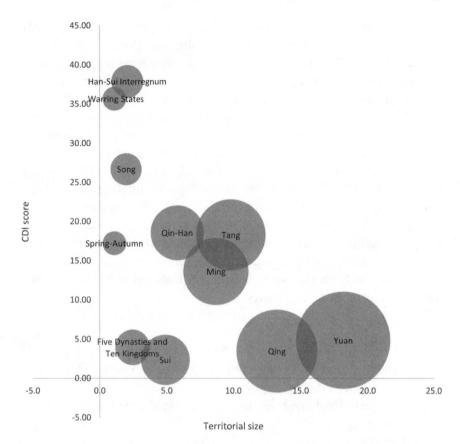

Figure 7.3. Scatterplot of CDI score and territorial size of Chinese dynasties. The CDI score is on the vertical axis and it is given by the invention count divided by the dynastic population. The territorial size is on the horizontal axis and is given in million square kilometers. The bubble is scaled to the territorial size. The CDI scores are calculated from the Chinese Historical Invention Database. The population estimates are from Ge Jianxiong, *Zhongguo Renkou Fazhanshi*.

two dynasties existed under the shadow of China's autocratic transformation. The inventiveness advantage of their smaller size seems to have been completely neutralized by their political and ideological homogeneity.

## China's European Moment

To me, the most fascinating period of Chinese history is from 220 to 581, which I label the Han-Sui Interregnum. That period in Chinese history was chaotic, war-torn, rivalrous, and politically dispersed. In other words very much like the "polycentric" Europe after the Roman Empire collapsed. There is another similarity with Europe: it was the peak of Chinese technology. It had the highest CDI index, 31.1, compared to all other eras of Chinese history. This is China's European moment, and China arrived at that moment before Europe did. The Han-Sui Interregnum commenced in 220, whereas post-Roman Europe commenced in 476.

Like the Sui dynasty, this period of Chinese history is virtually unknown in the West. And like the Sui, it is a consequential era in Chinese history.[67] The official nomenclature for the Han-Sui Interregnum is "Wei, Jin, the Northern and Southern Dynasties." It is mouthful, and for a good reason. It is the most complex and heterogenous period in Chinese history, with multiple regimes and ethnic groups vying for territories and control. My coinage of this period, the Han-Sui Interregnum, reflects its sharp departure from the two dynasties that bookended it. Han and Sui were centralized, unified dynasties.

Some facts about the political arrangements during this era:

- During this span of 361 years, there were altogether thirty-one dynasties or regimes that either coexisted with each other or rapidly succeeded each other;
- The period had one brief stage of unified rule, the Western Jin from 265 to 316;
- China was otherwise divided into independent and often warring kingdoms, the most famous of which was the Three Kingdoms (220–280);
- Between 304 and 439, a number of northern ethnic tribes, such as the Xiongnu, Jie, Xianbei, Di, and Qiang, invaded China proper and established respective footholds of their rule;
- Between 420 and 581, China was effectively divided into two halves, the South and the North. During this period of division, regimes in the South rapidly succeeded each other, whereas several regimes in the North existed in parallel with each other.

This was an "Age of Division," as historian Patricia Ebrey calls it, and an age of an unshackled society, vibrant intellectual dissent, exploration, argumentation, and clashes of ideas and ideologies.[68] If I were to write a book about this period, I would entitle it *Escape from the Han*. The Han had installed Confucianism as the official ideology and had built on and vastly expanded the imperial bureaucracy they had inherited from the Qin. The Han had reigned over an expansive empire under a unitary political architecture.

Politically and intellectually, the Han-Sui Interregnum could not have been more different than the Qin-Han era and the dynasties that followed. In terms of its political system, the period marked a return of patrimonial and aristocratic rule, as Fukuyama notes, but it was far more than that. Many of the rulers during this era came from military backgrounds. They knew how to win battles, but were less skilled in managing government. They sought help and resources from aristocrats, who in return extracted concessions from the rulers. It was give-and-take politics, and neither side was absolutely dominant. An ad hoc equilibrium of checks and balances and a nascent milieu of mutuality and interdependence tentatively held. Recall that Europe had similar political dynamics in later centuries, dynamics credited with planting the seeds for executive constraints and political pluralism.

Another similarity to Europe: some of these aristocrats became patrons of creative talents, although we do not know if private patronage complemented or substituted for payroll support from the state, which was relatively low during this period. A proliferation of new territorial entities and a loosening of control by the state likely added to the value of this patronage. Intellectuals were not well-educated appendages to the state; instead they gained operational autonomy and cognitive freedom, green shoots of intelligentsia in formation.

We have some quantitative measures of intellectual creativity during this era, constructed from the encyclopedia of prominent historical figures.[69] The biographical profiles of the historical figures record both the number of literary works—poetry, fiction, and essays—created by these historical figures, as well as the number of literary productions that have survived to the present day. By the first measure, the Han-Sui Interregnum dominates all other eras. Per million population, the Han-Sui Interregnum produced 347 literary works, followed by 176 in the Sui-Tang era. (The corresponding numbers are 85 for the Song, 52 for the Ming, and 30 for the Qing.) By the second measure, the number of literary productions that have survived to the present, the Han-Sui Interregnum ranks second to the Sui-Tang era, perhaps in part because some documents were destroyed during the wars of this era.

The Song period is sometimes celebrated as China's Renaissance, but the Song invented a stultifying *Keju* ideology and the foot-binding of Chinese women.[70] The little-known Han-Sui Interregnum in fact was China's true Renaissance moment, arguably closer to a Renaissance era than China today. The Han-Sui Interregnum's European moment was not by happenstance but created by a structural condition: China was under a federated rather than a unified political arrangement.

Not only was the quantity of intellectual creativity substantial; so was the diversity of ideas and ideologies. Ebrey points out that the educated elites during this era lost confidence in Confucianism and sought solace in the alternative spiritual traditions of Daoism and Buddhism. We see this in our data. In Figure 7.2, in terms of ideological diversity, the Han-Sui Interregnum ranks second to the Sui-Tang period, but this figure likely underrepresents the popularity of Buddhism. Buddhism was a new arrival to China, arriving in China only one hundred years before the Han-Sui Interregnum, and it rapidly caught on to claim its second highest place in Chinese history. The prominence of Buddhism during the Tang rode on the momentum that surged during the Han-Sui Interregnum.

Ideological diversity engendered clashes of ideas among Confucianists, Buddhists, and Daoists. "Confucian ideals of public service lost much of their hold," Ebrey writes, "as the educated and well-off vied instead in extravagant and often unconventional living."[71] The educated class approximated true and independent intellectuals. They engaged in the "Study of the Mysterious" and debated with each other over metaphysical questions such as the meaning of "non-being" and its relationship to "being." They also engaged in a style of conversation called "pure talk" (清谈) that eschewed applied and practical topics. They were argumentative and often engaged in clever repartee to upstage one another. This was "discussion democracy," Chinese style.[72]

Individuality, rather than collective morality, animated intellectuals of this age. Writers and artists searched for "naturalness" and "spontaneity," and abhorred politics and public morality. A group of gifted poets from this era, later immortalized as the "Seven Sages of the Bamboo Grove," valorized individuality and self-expression, while disparaging forced displays of collective morality. One of them, Ruan Ji, went out of his way to defy and offend Confucian sensibility. He cried when his neighbor, an unmarried girl, died, but he wined and dined when his own mother passed away. In response to a rebuke, he replied: "Surely you do not mean to suggest that the rules of propriety apply to me?" Another one of the Seven Sages, Liu Ling, often greeted his guests in the nude, arguing that he wore his dwelling as his attire.[73] It is not a strained comparison to liken this era to that of the Greek city-states. The origin of the word "hedonism" is Greek. Ruan and Liu, like their Greek counterparts, not only behaved hedonistically; they also developed a rationale for such behavior. Imagine what would have happened in China if this spirit of free exploration had survived and thrived.

Did this burst of exploratory fervor and intellectual freedom spill over into science and technology? We do not know for sure. What we do know is that this era claims the highest CDI index of all Chinese dynasties. Correlation, if not causation, is there. Also consider that both of the most prominent theoretical mathematicians in Chinese history were from this era. Liu Hui independently supplied proof for the Pythagorean theorem, while Zu Chongzhi used an approach similar to that of Archimedes to calculate the value of pi. The Han-Sui Interregnum was the closest to ancient Greek civilization in terms of advances in abstract thinking and reasoning. Its CDI index is 1.8 times that of the Tang (17.6), 2.1 times that of the Song (14.5), and ten times that of the Qing (2.9).

The second highest index, 21.8, belongs to the Warring-States period. This is not by accident. The Warring-States period and the Han-Sui Interregnum share many attributes. It was a part of what is described as the "Axial Age"—when major religious and spiritual ideas emerged simultaneously in various geographic locations. It was an era of "the Hundred Schools of Thought," and Confucianism, Legalism, and other philosophies contended with each other. There was a high mobility of human capital and ideas across kingdoms. Victoria Hui attributes that freedom to regimes' need to motivate "people to fight and die in war."[74] The Legalist reforms enacted by the Qin kingdom provided for "material welfare, legal protection, and freedom of expression." Both eras lacked an overweening central authority, and both experienced a burst of intellectual and creative freedom. The scope conditions thrived.

Did the Han-Sui Interregnum get the scale and scope balance right? Yes, in terms of technology, but remember that during the Han-Sui Interregnum many premiers were executed. It was a violent period. The kingdoms fought each other savagely for territories and human capital. If we look beyond technology, the Han-Sui Interregnum erred on the side of excessive scope. A lot of creation was accompanied by a lot of destruction.

A reasonable compromise was the Tang dynasty era. Its CDI index is not as impressive as the Han-Sui Interregnum, 17.6 compared with 31.1, but it still had some notable technological achievements. The Tang was an empire-sized dynasty, and it both lasted a long time and had stable rule; few premiers were executed. The Tang offers a better model than the Han-Sui Interregnum. A good society values peace and stability and balances these imperatives against an optimal level of "creative destruction."

Is China today in another Tang dynasty era? It has the size and national unity of the Tang, with a reasonably stable rule. It is in the midst of a golden era of technology. It is science-driven, and legions of Chinese entrepreneurs are applying new technologies to real-world problems. But the CCP is also notoriously autocratic, repressive, and stifling of freedom and dissent. Are there any scope conditions under the CCP?

CHAPTER EIGHT

# A Republic of Government

You cannot think different in a nation where you cannot breathe free. You cannot think different in a nation where you aren't able to challenge orthodoxy, because change only comes from challenging orthodoxy.

—Vice President JOE BIDEN, 2013

RAO YI, SHI YIGONG, and Yan Ning, three accomplished life scientists, were born in China and educated in the United States. Rao is a neurobiologist and was on the faculty at Northwestern University until 2007, when he moved back to China to become the dean of the School of Life Sciences at Peking University. Shi was the Warner-Lambert/Parke-Davis Professor in the Department of Molecular Biology at Princeton University until 2008, when he assumed the deanship of Tsinghua University's School of Life Sciences. Yan, a structural biologist, had been a postdoc at Princeton University and was Shi's student. In 2007, at the age of thirty, she returned to China and became the youngest professor at Tsinghua.

Once in China, these three talented scholars encountered a similar situation. Despite their substantial accomplishments, none was elected to the prestigious Chinese Academy of Sciences (CAS). The precise reasons are not clear. One possibility is that they lacked the requisite political connections. Ray Fisman and his coauthors have found that elections into the CAS depend heavily on political capital and connections—and that those scholars who do rely on connections to get into the CAS publish papers with a lower "impact factor" (how frequently the papers are cited by other academics).[1]

In 2017, Yan accepted a faculty position at Princeton University and headed back to the United States. Two years later, in 2019, the scholar who failed to be elected to the CAS was elected to American Academy of Sciences as a foreign associate. You might say that, in leaving China, Professor Yan left behind a "Republic of Government" to rejoin an academic world known as a "Republic of Science."

That Republic of Government has received a lot of attention lately. It is feared by many and envied by some. In 2019, the *MIT Technology Review*, a premier publication on technology topics, devoted an entire issue to China. In it, Editor-in-Chief Gideon Lichfield ponders, "What is China good at? The common prejudice that China doesn't innovate and steals all its intellectual property from abroad has been outdated for a while, but can its companies build world-changing products, and can its scientists win a Nobel? Could its top-down system of government be even better than the world's increasingly fractious democracies at tackling urgent problems like climate change?"[2] The special issue examines China's progress across a broad spectrum of technologies, from autonomous and electric vehicles and microchips to nuclear power, high-voltage grids, space exploration, quantum computing and communications, and gene editing.

China has invested heavily in basic science and breakthrough projects. One of the world's largest single-dish radio observatories, the Aperture Spherical Radio Telescope (FAST), is located in China. Using its five-hundred-meter-diameter dish, the telescope can detect gravitational waves and probe the mysterious fleeting blasts of radiation known as fast radio bursts.[3] In quantum communication, China has emerged as a leader in the field. Professor Pan Jianwei at the University of Science and Technology of China has been dubbed the "Father of Quantum" for his breakthroughs.[4] Quantum communication relies on relays between two ground stations, but the relays were vulnerable to security breaches. Pan and his team made advances in satellite relays and improved the efficiency of the downlinks.[5] The military applications of "unhackable" quantum communication are immediate and immense. Papers written by Chinese scientists and Chinese patents on quantum communication have far surpassed those by American scientists.

*MIT Technology Review* was founded in 1899, near the end of the Qing, China's last dynasty, which was collapsing under the weight of internal rebellions and foreign invasions. Since that time, China has come far, especially over the past forty years. Recently several research reports have converged on the view that the United States continues to lead technologically but it is not leading all by itself. China is a "full-spectrum competitor" in some areas and ahead of the United States in others.[6] The ranking of countries' technological leadership may vary, but their overall message is the same: China is rising to challenge America's technological hegemony.

This chapter examines the second half of the "T" in the EAST formulation, that is, technological developments under the CCP during China's reformist era. The topic is vast and extraordinarily complex. A single chapter cannot conceivably cover it all, so I will zero in on one question: "Without the basic rule of law and rudimentary freedom of ideas, how has an autocracy managed to achieve so much?" It is not enough to cite the precedent of the Soviet Union, which exceled in scientific research but failed in commercialization.[7] China has exceled in both.

Does contemporary China represent an exception to the idea that technological and economic dynamism depends on a balance between scale and scope? How do we reconcile China's achievements with the CCP's entrenched panoply of controls, including over universities and the educational curriculum? Is it possible that scale alone explains it all? The answer is a resounding yes, judging from the reports about Chinese technology produced by prominent technologists, researchers, and institutions. One report describes the state of artificial intelligence as "asymmetric competition," one that has resulted from China's (1) lack of separation between public and private sectors, (2) large population base, (3) substantial capital support from the state, and (4) data-generating surveillance apparatus.[8]

Such reports are better at cataloguing facts than analyzing them. Notice the fourth factor listed in the report, data-generating surveillance apparatus. This factor is used as a metric of China's success as well as being treated as a reason for its success. The report was led by Eric Schmidt, former head of Google. Imagine if someone made the following argument: Google had successfully invented an efficient search engine and the reason for this inventive success of Google was its efficient search engine. There is a bit of tautology and circular reasoning. The other three factors listed in the report are all about scale. China's scale advantage is the most visible feature of that country, and it is an advantage extolled by the CCP. On this point, the official rhetoric of the CCP and the American researchers agree with each other.

Let me be clear: scale matters. China's willingness to spend on R&D is unequalled by any other developing country and comparable to that of developed countries. Its formidable administrative apparatus is used as a dissemination and implementation platform to onboard new technologies. Its ability to collect, collate, and compile data across an array of domains without privacy encumberments is unrivaled in the world. Maybe for this reason, Yan Ning, the Princeton University professor I mentioned, decided to go back to China in 2022. The speculation is that the research institute she will head is funded generously by the Chinese government, far more than what the National Institutes of Health have funded her research at Princeton.

But what about scope? Before I answer this question, let me step back and recall that in the past quite a few influential people were skeptical about China as an innovative power. One of them is the current president of the United States, Joe Biden. In 2013, when he was vice president of the United States, Biden scorned the idea that "China is going to eat our lunch." He listed the advantages of the United States: universities, an open and fair legal system, venture capital, and leadership in innovation and technology. He then cited Steve Jobs to explain why the United States leads: Americans "think different."

As the president of the United States, Joe Biden changed his tune. In his 2021 address to the joint session of the U.S. Congress, Biden urged Congress to increase public spending because China is closing in fast on the United States.[9] What happened to that nation that cannot think different?

In 2013, Biden underestimated China not because his—and Steve Jobs's—logic is wrong, but because he had wrong facts. China does have the conditions necessary to "think different," but China's scope conditions that enable the Chinese to think different are manifested in an unfamiliar format and form. They often go unrecognized.

It's high time to examine these hidden scope conditions created by the reformist CCP. One of them is what I call "academic globalization"—international collaborations in research and education. The story of China's overseas educational and research programs is well known; I will not repeat the facts here but simply supply a conjecture—that China's international collaborations expanded China's de facto academic freedom, but in a highly curated and calibrated fashion. The other scope condition is the access on the part of the capable Chinese entrepreneurs to market-based finance and protection of rights outside of the immediate supervision of the CCP. Hong Kong plays, or used to play, a vitally important role in this regard.

Here is the catch: these scope conditions expanded without the telltale signs of reforms and liberalization and therefore are easily missed in various explanations for why China could have achieved technological and entrepreneurial successes in an autocratic context. What has further clouded our analysis is that China has moved in the opposite direction. Since the early 1990s, the CCP has tightened controls over universities and educational curricula; political reforms have been reversed; rule of law is non-existent; finance remains statist. It is easy to draw the conclusion that Vice President Biden drew in 2013: China cannot think different.

But there is autocratic scope, and during the reformist era China has succeeded under more autocratic scope, similar to when it scored high on the CDI index during the Han-Sui Interregnum and the Tang. The reformist CCP devised a heterodox model, a model that combines openness with domestic illiberalism. That heterodox model has served the reformist CCP well. China has made progress in science and technology and it has attracted and enabled high-tech entrepreneurship at a time when it has steadfastly eschewed reforms of *Gaokao* (China's college exam system), liberalizing educational curricula, or broader institutional and legal reforms. Recall the M-form economy that performed a balancing act between autonomy and control. There is a similar dynamic here.

We are familiar with China's scale advantage, R&D spending, industrial policy, and state-organized implementation. The scope components are less visible, but they have contributed vitally to China's success in the background. Take rule of law. Biden is correct that China does not have an open and fair legal system; what he missed is that many Chinese high-tech entrepreneurs chose to domicile their assets in Hong Kong, a British territory before 1997 and a region with substantial autonomy after 1997 under the "one country, two systems" formula. China also "outsourced" think-different attitudes. Through its overseas educational and research programs, China has placed its students and researchers in an environment that cultivates and encourages creativity, risk taking, and an inclination to question authority. Little wonder that the highest-impact research papers are a product of international collaborations and that U.S.-educated returnees have founded and run the most innovative biotech firms in China.

It is extraordinarily important to get this story right. Recall that Biden underestimated China's scope conditions; let me add another group of individuals who have made the same analytical error—the Chinese leaders themselves. Under Xi Jinping, CCP's heterodox model has been undermined beyond repair. Educational and technological collaborations with the West have come under increasing strains because of China's anti-Western foreign policy postures; the autonomy of Hong Kong has been decimated. The Chinese leaders bought into the narrative many Western researchers pitched—that China's formidable edge is its scale. China's history—and its future—will prove this proposition wrong.

## Scaling Successes

China is an upper-middle-income country. In the area of science and technology, however, we typically put China in the same league of high-income countries such as the United States, European Union nations, and Japan. The country seems to have long had "excess" capabilities relative to its development level. In the eighteenth century, China had a surprising level of numeracy relative to its economic status. In the 1960s, it developed a nuclear weapons program on the foundations of a rural economy, and in 1970, during the chaotic Cultural Revolution, it sent a satellite to space. In the 1990s, China was the only developing country to participate in the Human Genome Project. Today, China's advances in artificial intelligence and quantum communications are well known. Some have hailed these achievements; for me, a deeper question is why the Chinese have not been able to translate these capabilities into comparable economic gains.

Artificial intelligence (AI) is the latest domain in which China has vaulted to the front of the field. Kai-fu Lee, a prominent venture capitalist, dubs China an "AI superpower."[10] One of China's rapidly rising AI companies, iFlytek, is developing a translation tool that rivals the most advanced in the world. Baidu, the country's search giant, is pouring its resources into deep learning and has developed an advanced system of self-driving cars and smart robots. China is an acknowledged leader in fintech and electronic payment—and, of course, facial recognition. Data collection, integration, and analytics are rooted both in China's technical and infrastructural capacity as well as the attitudinal traits of the society. The Chinese population is more accepting of the visible and intrusive hand of the state. In the same way that the seafaring tradition of Great Britain launched a navigational Pax Britannica, this Chinese cultural proclivity has contributed to the rise of Pax Sinica as a data superpower. History matters.

## *A History of Capabilities*

"Doing science" requires imagination, raw intelligence, inspiration, and hard work. It is also a manpower issue. Milton Friedman reportedly said: "The conquest of the technological frontier, like the conquest of the geographical frontier, requires millions of individuals." Inventions and scientific discoveries are becoming more and more demanding in terms of human capital. Today to achieve the same doubling of the density of the computer chips that became famous as "Moore's Law" requires eighteen times the number of researchers as in the early 1970s.[11] Size, in this case the numbers of scientific personnel, matters. And this is an area where China has a decisive advantage.

In 2018, 1.8 million individuals graduated with a bachelor's degree in the United States, while China graduated 7.5 million the same year. As early as 2007, China graduated more Ph.D. students than the United States. One can question the quality of Chinese graduates, but we should bear in mind Milton Friedman's observation here. Even if just a fraction of these Chinese graduates is of high quality, this far larger base of college graduates in China gives the country a competitive edge. Also keep in mind that a scientific enterprise is not run only by superstar scientists, but also by legions of lab technicians and research assistants who work behind the scenes to contribute to the overall production of knowledge.

Most analysts would stop here and proceed to assert China's advantage in human capital. But let's pause and ponder the following: China destroyed its own systems of higher education during the Cultural Revolution. Between 1966 and 1976, Chinese universities stopped functioning in their educational and research capacity. We see this in the numbers: in 1960, there were 960,000 university students in China; in 1970, only a paltry 48,000.[12] Contrast this with India, a country that poured massive and continuous resources into its higher education during the same period. Yet China quickly left India behind as soon as the country emerged out of the Cultural Revolution. China's university enrollment recovered to 1.28 million in 1981, 2.1 million in 1990, 9 million in 2002, and then 19 million in 2007. In 1998, China had 70,000 students enrolled in masters and Ph.D. degree programs; by 2007 it was 365,000.[13]

The speed of recovery is remarkable, and this is where China's long history of literacy looms. History affects current technological development through invocations of norms, methods, and cumulative capabilities in the population. Recall the point by Joseph Henrich that literacy rewires the brain and incubates mental processing and cognitive capabilities. The right way to think about the Cultural Revolution is that it was a temporary, albeit dramatic, detour from a well-entrenched latent store of capabilities and educational inclinations that had been accumulated over a millennium. Once the shock was over, those capabilities quickly bounced back.[14]

A big part of China's cognitive history is the *Keju* system, which the CCP has aggressively adapted and repurposed as the *Gaokao* college entrance examination, one of the world's most rigorous, double-blind standardized tests that millions of college-bound Chinese students take every year. *Keju* operated on Confucianism; *Gaokao* is unabashedly modern, requiring mastery of mathematics, physics, chemistry, English, and other topics. The software has been updated, but the infrastructure has been there all along.

There is another area where history is having a powerful effect on current affairs: artificial intelligence. Chinese society has given the Chinese state a generous dose of "prior consent" or a near blank check for collecting and harnessing behavioral data. True, this consent is implicit or implied, but an inference of its existence should not be too controversial. Discussions about China as an archetype of "digital authoritarianism" often belie the significant degree of support that the Chinese government enjoys from its public for surveillance technologies.[15] I am not justifying digital authoritarianism, but I am making a case that a critique of it needs to take into account the cultural norms of the Chinese population. An intelligent critique of digital authoritarianism should zero in on the constrained nature of the Chinese population's consent, rather than the idea that it is automatically injurious to and repressive of Chinese inclinations and interests.

China has a long history of collecting data from its society, down to the household level, as far back as the Qin and Han dynasties, and *Keju*, as noted earlier, entrenched a deferential culture. This historical context may explain Chinese optimism about emerging intrusive technologies. Survey findings by German sinologist Genia Kostka in 2019 show that 80 percent of respondents in China approve of the social credit system, with just 1 percent reporting either strong or moderate disapproval. Moreover, Kostka shows that socially advantaged citizens—wealthier, better-educated urban residents—along with older people, have the highest levels of approval of these systems.[16]

Contrary to the distrust and political discord that accompany the introduction of disruptive technologies in the United States, the Chinese are generally enthusiastic about them, especially those that promise to help address long-standing governance challenges. In the Kostka survey, 76 percent of respondents consider the trust deficit to be a serious problem in China, and they see social credit as an effective remedy for combating fraud and punishing wrongdoing by firms. Survey results from the 2018 Tsinghua report on AI in China likewise suggest a remarkable level of support from the Chinese public for AI development.[17] This sociocultural basis that evolved over many dynasties and survives today has helped make the intrusive measure of digital surveillance more palatable. The state capacity owes much to this engrained habit of psychological compliance.

A rule of thumb is that in anything that involves "bigness," we should presume a degree of Chinese advantage. In the current state of technology, AI is data intensive.[18] AI is also skill intensive, another axiomatic edge of China. A large amount of reasonably skilled labor is required to hand-label data and perform verifications. Mary L. Gray and Siddharth Suri uncovered a reality of AI that we often do not associate with the glamor of algorithms and computer science.[19] Their book, *Ghost Work*, shows that the AI edifice is built on manual and menial work performed by a massive digital labor force, often underpaid or unpaid, toiling in image labeling. Already "a factory of the world," China has repurposed its skilled labor force to propel itself to the forefront of AI. This is a traditional area of Chinese strength—its disciplined, literate labor force with a formidable work ethic.

## Political Commitments

Data from the World Bank show that Chinese expenditure on R&D rose from 0.563 percent of GDP in 1996 to 2.14 percent of GDP in 2018.[20] For the countries in the same upper-middle-income bracket as China, the average R&D expenditure to GDP is 1.6 percent. The usual strategy for developing countries is to free ride on the R&D fruits of the developed countries. R&D is expensive, and the payoffs are uncertain. India, for example, spends only 0.65 percent of its GDP on R&D. China, however, outspends even Singapore (1.92 percent). China's political commitment to science and technology is unrivaled. This is China's scaling advantage par excellence.

In absolute terms, China now spends the same amount on R&D as the entire European Union and more than Japan. In recent years, "Made in China 2025" has garnered media and policy attention in the West, but it is just the latest of many large-scale initiatives the Chinese government has launched over the past three decades. The Chinese commitment to science and technology is extensive and includes the National High-Tech R&D Program or 863 Program (1986), the Spark Program, the Torch Program, the National Key Technologies Program, Project 211 (1996), Project for Funding World-Class Universities, Project 863 (1998), and Project 111 (2006).

The Chinese government employs a whole government approach. Take the example of the so-called 973 Program, formerly the "National Basic Research Program," which focuses on basic research in "strategic" industries. Basic research funded under the 973 Program received ten to fifteen times the funding normally allocated through the National Natural Science Foundation. The definition and the specification of "strategic" industries and interest rested with the government. The National Steering Group for Science, Technology, and Education was personally chaired by Zhu Rongji, China's premier. All the major producers of scientific research, such as national academies and universities, reported to this group.

As part of its mission, this steering group laid out long-term scientific and technological goals. For example, the Middle and Long-Term Program for Science and Technology Development 2006–2020 outlined a vision for China based on increasing measures of patents and academic citations, raising R&D levels fourfold to RMB900 billion to reach 2.5 percent of GDP in 2020, and increasing to 60 percent science and technology's contribution to the country's development. The plan focused not only on fostering "frontier" and breakthrough technologies in biology, information technology, and nanotechnology, but also on addressing China's energy, water, and human-organ shortages and on developing technologies to explore the seas, oceans, and space. Many of these programs seek out foreign collaborations in the short run, but are designed to reduce long-term dependency on foreign technology.

## *Three Scaling Projects*

We can think of scaling in three ways. One is to scale up. For example, the Chinese state built out the country's high-speed rail system to 37,900 km, the world's longest. Another is to scale over. To roll out a new technology often requires replacing an existing technology, which is costly. In the United States, one difficulty of building out the Acela high-speed railway is that it requires a different kind of track than the one already in use—which means building new tracks, as well as scrapping the existing tracks.

The third is to scale fast. A mega project, such as Boston's Big Dig, took decades to complete. It had the scale but not the speed. I will discuss three technology projects, sensor-enabled infrastructure, the 5G network, and China's health code for COVID-19. Each one of them embodies the three dimensions of scaling—they are big, built over an existing technology, and built out very quickly.

Let's jump into the example of sensor-enabled infrastructure. The backbone of AI is data, and an infrastructure or a system of collecting, collating, and compiling data from a range of domain activities. As a comprehensive report by the National Security Commission on Artificial Intelligence points out, the United States still maintains an overall lead over China in AI, but China is rapidly closing the gap in some areas and is ahead of the United States in others.[21] An undisputed area of Chinese leadership is data. This is a true difference between China and the United States. The Chinese government has a systematic program and approach on data and has built an advanced data infrastructure.

The Western media has focused on the surveillance cameras installed in public spaces in China. And it is true: China has extensive capabilities to collect behavioral data. Some 600 million surveillance cameras have been mounted, according to one estimate, and they amplify the power of the dense police network China already has in place.[22] But it is a mistake to assume that China collects only behavioral data, for there is also an industrial aspect to China's surveillance. The industrial sensors are critical to the development of AI in autonomous vehicles, predictive analytics, environmental monitoring, and other big-data applications. The CCP surveils people for sure, but it also surveils objects, flows of energy, and movements of fluids. And while behavioral data are closely associated with digital authoritarianism, sensor-embedded infrastructure improves energy efficiency, conservation, and safety, and it brings about genuine benefits to society.

Wuxi, a city in Jiangsu province in eastern China, has been a pioneer in building out sensor-embedded infrastructure, with some companies in Wuxi emerging as global leaders in this domain. The wireless sensors developed by Wisen Innovation, for instance, monitor bridge safety, landslides, tunnels, and subway systems in China, Hong Kong, Indonesia, and Great Britain.[23] After Wisen Innovation installed more than twenty sensors on key parts of Wuxi's Changjiang Road First Bridge—to monitor motion, vibration, displacement, fissure, and temperature and humidity—authorities demolished that bridge for safety reasons.

Sensors are also widely deployed in China's underground utility tunnels, which supply water, power and gas, drainage, radio transmission, and telecommunications signals. Real-time data collection by sensors enables more efficient distribution and optimization of these tunnels. Take the example of Nanning in the poor province of Guangxi. The city constructed a sensor-embedded utility tunnel that is 89 meters deep and spans 1.57 kilometers. The tunnel is equipped with carbon dioxide, temperature, and humidity sensors. The fire safety tunnel has a fire-fighting system that can cut power and activate fire extinguishers automatically. In Shanghai, the Chenta Bridge is embedded with 181 sensors of various types and functionalities to detect any distortions in the structure of the bridge. Patrol robots on top of tunnels in Shanghai are equipped with high-precision sensors to detect any warning signs on a real-time basis.

China excels not only at building new infrastructure, but also at setting aside existing infrastructure to make way for the infrastructure of the future. 5G infrastructure is a case in point. 5G is critical to AI development, notably in autonomous driving, vehicle-to-vehicle, and vehicle-to-infrastructure communications, because it can transfer data as much as ten to a hundred times faster than 4G. China leads the rest of the world in 5G base stations and infrastructure. Huawei ranks first in the world in terms of the number of 5G patents it has registered, with 3,325.[24] ZTE, another Chinese firm, ranks fifth in the world with 2,204 patents.

Technological leapfrogging is not always easy because of path dependency and incumbency advantage. A technology can persist because it is "good enough" and because of the conservative biases of business. Doctors write prescriptions on a piece of paper simply because they are used to that method, not because it is the best way to prescribe medicine. (In fact, mistakes in drug dispensing can occur due to the illegibility of handwritten notes.) Technology adoption is also costly. Early adopters can pay a price for adopting a technology that turns out to be a flop. (Remember Segway?) A technology can fail precisely because of a low rate of adoption. The trap can be self-reinforcing.

In this scenario, as Alwyn Young shows in a famous paper on Singapore, a powerful role of the government is to "scrap" capital stock.[25] Young is critical of Singapore for prematurely scrapping too much capital stock, but this disruptive role of the government may have helped Singapore achieve its status today as a technological pioneer in the world. A critical question is whether the potential productivity payoff of the newly installed capital stock substantially exceeds the capital stock that has been set aside. Singapore made the right bet.

Whether China has made the right bet on 5G is still debated. Largely unknown in the West, the rollout of China's 5G network is not without controversy within China. In September 2020, Lou Jiwei, a highly respected economist and a former minister of finance, caused a stir when he criticized the government's plan to spend "hundreds of billions" on 5G infrastructure.[26] He argued that 5G technology is still immature, is costly to operate, and has only limited applications. In addition, the 5G network has to be scaled over existing networks. Network installations lead to more "capital scrapping" than does installing individual technologies. It is an expensive proposition. Criticisms such as this have not stopped China from building its 5G infrastructure.

China's fast rollout of health codes—digital passports for contact tracing and making decisions about individual quarantines—illustrates the third dimension of scaling: speed. In an epidemic, timing is everything. China's COVID-19 management repurposed the country's vast system of digital surveillance and used it for COVID-19 tracking. The *Economist* wrote that this approach has afforded the Chinese authorities a "more tailored approach" by "allowing most people to resume their normal lives while monitoring those who might be infected."[27] It might sound strange to call locking down Hubei, a province of 58 million people, "a more tailored approach." What the *Economist* could have meant is that during the initial phase of the outbreak China did not lock down the entire country of 1.4 billion people. One reason it did not have to is that during the critical first months of the outbreak, the Chinese state scaled the health code to the entire country in record time.

The United States has never developed, and quickly gave up on, an electronic health code for the purpose of contact tracing. The closest thing the United States has is the "exposure notification" app developed jointly by Google and Apple. With complete anonymity and voluntary opt-in, the app uses Bluetooth communications to notify a phone user when they were near someone known to be COVID-positive. The usage is sparse. My own state, Massachusetts, did not activate the app immediately.

The Chinese health codes are far more intrusive, transparent, and verifiable than the app developed by Google and Apple. China is advanced in AI not only because it has a size advantage, but also because it has a scope advantage. Scope here refers to data from multiple domains of activities. Travel information is integrated with information on shopping expenditures, online search patterns, medical records, and so on. Integration involves accessing multiple databases—location, health, behavior, and personal—with user-supplied information cross-referenced with and verified by the behavioral data. The two kinds of scaling advantages, the capacity of the government to build out the data infrastructure and the algorithmic power that comes from data integration, reinforce each other.

Two types of data integration are needed. One, integration of data from different domain activities, brings up a huge difference between Chinese and American digital platform companies. There is a common perception that Chinese firms are juggernauts. In fact, they are much smaller than their American counterparts, in both market valuation (even on a good day) and in operation. In 2018, Alibaba generated sales of $23.2 billion, much smaller than Amazon's $232.9 billion.[28] The reason is that Chinese firms operate in a far more competitive environment. In e-commerce, Amazon has no significant peer rivals, but in China, Alibaba is dogged by competition from companies such as Pinduoduo and JD.com. The other reason is that Chinese firms are conglomerates. Alibaba operates in multiple sectors, such as e-commerce (like Amazon), electronic payment (PayPal), and fintech (Wall Street). Its advantage is its scope, not its scale, and it has the capacity to integrate data in many domains of the everyday life of ordinary Chinese.

The second data integration is between government and business. Alibaba does not own the data stored in its health code supplied by users; the government maintains that database. But it was Alipay, the electronic payment arm of Alibaba, that developed China's first health code. Alipay has data on the transaction activities of the Chinese people. And in the first days of COVID-19, when the focus was on a person's exposure to Wuhan, Alipay, not the government, knew whether a person had traveled there. Alipay verified the information supplied by users against its vast payment database. By harvesting colossal amounts of user data in real time, these firms know more about population movement than the government. Similarly, the amount of data amassed by WeChat does not make it "super," as large as the size of the data is—WeChat has a little over a billion active users and in 2019 they were on WeChat more than double the average time spent on Instagram. Rather, it is the integration of social media, instant messaging, payment, food delivery, ride hailing, healthcare, and other behavioral data into its own platform that enabled the rollout of the health codes.

Alibaba's health code assigned its users into one of three categories based on their COVID-19 risk profiles, which had been calculated using self-reported and collected data: green for unrestricted travel, yellow for a seven-day quarantine, and red for a two-week quarantine. Alibaba wrote the algorithm; the custodian of the data was the government. It is a showcase of the kind of seamless government-business collaboration that is usually frowned on in the West, and a concrete illustration of the fusion between public and private sectors highlighted by the China Strategy Group.

On February 9, 2020, the city of Hangzhou, where Alibaba is based, formally launched the Hangzhou Health Code, more popularly known as Alipay Health Code. The city government required all of its residents to download the app and fill in information such as travel history and body temperature in the health declaration. The information was then cross-referenced and checked against Alipay's huge payment database. Visitors to Hangzhou were also required to use the health code. On the first day of the launch, there were 10 million downloads of the app, matching the size of Hangzhou's population. On February 14, there were 35 million downloads.

On February 16, the national government acted. The State Council instructed Alipay to scale its health code nationwide. From there things moved quickly. By February 20 all eleven cities of Zhejiang province—Hangzhou is its provincial capital—were covered by the Alipay Health Code. As of February 24, the whole Zhejiang province was covered. So were two other provinces, Sichuan (81 million) and Hainan (9 million). At the end of March 2020, there were 900 million users of various versions of health codes.

Multiple health codes then spontaneously sprang up. In addition to the Alipay Health Code, the other biggest one was developed by Tencent. Tencent's WeChat pay is the rival to Alipay in China's electronic payment market. Tencent used its payment data for cross-referencing and verification in its own health code. There were also localized health codes. Beijing and Shanghai had their own local versions; Guangdong province had three. In Jiangsu, many locations named the local health codes after the names of the cities. These local health codes were based on different standards and formats. They lacked interoperability and users were unable to travel outside of their own regions.

The challenge of rolling out a health code is not just technical; instead scalability, speed, and interoperability come into play. Health codes need to exchange and recognize information among themselves. Alibaba and Tencent, two bitter rivals, each ran their health codes on the ElasticSearch system, a technology that handles and stores digital data. Then the government ordered these two firms to make their health codes interoperable.

By the end of February, three provinces (Anhui, Jiangsu, and Zhejiang) and one city in the Yangtze River Delta region (Shanghai) resolved the incompatibility of their health codes. Zhejiang extended the protocol to Henan, Hainan, Shandong, and Guizhou. Within one month of the first rollout, China's health codes were operating in an integrated fashion in several provinces, and by late March, China had achieved "One Code for the Whole Country."

How would COVID-19 have spread in 2020 without the health code? The aggressive lockdowns contributed to early "flattening of the curves" (plateauing of the infection rates), but it is also conceivable that the infection rate would have been higher without the health code. The health code obviated the need for even larger lockdowns than the ones that occurred. There are grumblings about the Chinese health codes, such as inaccuracy and lack of privacy concerns. All valid, but we should be mindful that an authoritarian regime would use other methods to contain COVID-19 if it did not have a health code. China would have resorted to a manual verification approach, which would have also produced errors and privacy violations—but without the redeeming benefits of scale and speed.

## Republic of Government or Republic of Science?

The term "Republic of Science" was coined by Michael Polanyi in his classic 1962 article "The Republic of Science: Its Political and Economic Theory." Polanyi identifies two critical features of the scientific community: freedom, as in "freely making their own choice of problems and pursuing them in the light of their own personal judgment," and collaboration, or "cooperating as members of a closely knit organisation." Polanyi further asks us to imagine a scientific community with freedom but without collaboration:

> Each scientist would go on for a while developing problems derived from the information initially available to all. But these problems would soon be exhausted, and in the absence of further information about the results achieved by others, new problems of any value would cease to arise, and scientific progress would come to a standstill.[29]

Freedom and collaboration require each other. It is not a collaboration if I am forced to write this book with another author. Chinese science during the Han-Sui Interregnum, or primitive science of any civilization, was science performed in isolation. Individual inventions thrived, but these inventions failed to evolve combinatorially into further inventions and into a system of knowledge. Recall my discussion on how *Keju* had individualized Chinese society and suppressed collaborations. After the sixth century, imperial China lost the scope conditions and the freedom to explore and to collaborate. Its considerable technological lead never materialized to make China into a Republic of Science.

Polanyi took the free and independent judgments of scientists for granted, because he wrote about science performed in a democracy. I call the Chinese system a "Republic of Government" because it has a funding advantage often associated with government, but it lacks elemental components of a Republic of Science—such as exploratory freedom and collaboration. Chinese universities are tightly controlled and supervised by the government, often at the minute level of operational details. All Chinese universities are technically a part of the bureaucracy. Each has an administrative rank, much like the Ministry of Finance or Ministry of Foreign Affairs does. Peking University and Tsinghua University, for example, have a vice-ministerial rank, which means they enjoy privileges over lesser universities saddled with a bureau rank. The Chinese government appoints presidents of universities, and within a university a strict hierarchy is enforced. Faculty are an administrative appendage to the leaders of the university, such as deans or presidents. Research funding comes from the government, which is not unusual, but unlike the National Science Foundation and National Institutes of Health in the United States, bureaucrats have more control over the funding decisions, rather than academic peers.

## Republic of Government

Let me begin with a tale of two MITs. The Massachusetts Institute of Technology is located in Cambridge, Massachusetts, but there is also a "Chinese MIT" known as Tsinghua University in Beijing. Both institutions are powerhouses in scientific and engineering research. Both receive a large sum of research funds from their respective governments. Both have exacting standards in their admissions and academic curricula. Both have graduated some of the most well-known high-tech entrepreneurs in their own countries, with a few receiving degrees from both institutions. Charles Zhang, the founder of Sohu.com, one of the earliest search engines in China, has an undergraduate degree from Tsinghua and a graduate degree from MIT. And the four biggest facial recognition firms, SenseTime, Yitu, Megvii, and Cloudwalk, are reportedly split in their connections with the two universities: MIT graduates run SenseTime and Yitu, while Tsinghua graduates run Megvii and Cloudwalk.

This is where the similarity ends. Despite receiving hundreds of millions of dollars in federal research grants, MIT is not only independent from the federal government, but also willing to push back against the federal government on issues of academic freedom. In January 2021, one of its faculty members, Gang Chen in the Department of Mechanical Engineering, was arrested and charged by the U.S. Department of Justice on wire fraud and tax evasion charges. The real target was the joint research that Professor Chen has undertaken with Chinese scientists. Over two hundred MIT faculty members rallied to support Chen while the president of MIT, L. Rafael Reif, issued a public statement defending not only Chen, but also the principles of open science and academic freedom. MIT paid all of Professor Chen's legal expenses.[30]

This is not the first time that MIT has stood up to the federal government. One of the most prominent critics of the U.S. government is Noam Chomsky, professor emeritus in MIT's Department of Linguistics and Philosophy. During the Vietnam War era, the Pentagon asked MIT to fire Professor Chomsky on several occasions, a request MIT steadfastly declined. In response to the question of how he could work for a university that did a lot of war research, Professor Chomsky stated that MIT also embodied "libertarian values" and a long tradition of individual rights and civil disobedience.[31]

Contrast Chomsky's situation with that of Xu Zhangrun, a professor at Tsinghua's law school. In February 2020, Xu published the essay "Viral Alarm: When Fury Overcomes Fear," which was a scathing critique of the Chinese government's handling of the COVID-19 outbreak in Wuhan. That was not the first time that Xu had clashed with the CCP. In 2018, he had issued an open letter decrying the authoritarian reversals under Xi Jinping. In July 2020, the police detained him, and upon his release, Tsinghua University promptly fired him. Not a single faculty member—let alone Tsinghua's president—spoke up openly in defense of Professor Xu.

In the 1980s and the early 1990s, there was a brief period when universities were given more operating autonomy from the state. The 1993 "Program for Education Reform and Development in China" envisioned a transition from state-controlled to state-supervised status, whereby "university presidents would become responsible for their own institutional policies and long-term development plans."[32] Not any longer. In recent years, the secretary of the CCP has increasingly wielded more power than the university president. The Ministry of Education determines which faculty members are eligible to supervise Ph.D. students and decides the degree-granting requirements for the universities. Even curriculum developments require reviews and approvals from the ministry. Micro-management has become numbingly "micro." According to one account—although not widely verified—the Ministry of Education not only requires the teaching of *Das Kapital* in all the political economics classes, but also specifies which Chinese edition should be taught. A few years ago, a prominent professor of economics told me that in his class, students were free to discuss any topics they wanted, except for advocating independence for Taiwan and Tibet. Now he says that he is often instructed what to teach and some students report to university authorities what he says in class. The Chinese universities have moved from negative to positive controls.

In recent years, there was one bottom-up attempt by a visionary Chinese scientist to move a university in the direction of the Republic of Science. That scientist is Zhu Qingshi, the founding president of Southern University of Science and Technology (SUSTech) from 2009 to 2014. The attempt failed completely.[33]

Zhu Qingshi is a reputed descendent of a transformative figure we encountered earlier, Zhu Yuanzhang, the peasant rebel who founded the Ming—and he is as unconventional as his famous forebear. In an interview he gave in 2008, he called for abolishing the government supervision of universities, and criticized *Gaokao*. At the time, he was president of the Chinese University of Science and Technology and his unconventional view, voiced from the perch of an elite university, went viral in China. The next year, he lost his position, but was recruited by SUSTech as its founding president. SUSTech was established by the more liberal Shenzhen government, which was on a mission to create a university with more operating autonomy from the Ministry of Education.

But the Ministry of Education would not let go so easily. For three years, the ministry refused to authorize SUSTech to enroll any students. In 2010, Zhu admitted fifty students on his own and sidestepped the *Gaokao* process altogether. In 2012, the Ministry of Education relented and formally recognized SUSTech, but under Xi Jinping, the Ministry of Education reversed itself. Zhu resigned in 2014. To add extra political insurance, the party secretary appointed to SUSTech was the former head of Shenzhen's Bureau of Public Security. The university is now run by a police officer. SUSTech was squarely folded back into the Republic of Government.

## A Revolution of Quantity

In a Republic of Science, academic controls are managed by universities and researchers.[34] Its reigning principle is "open science," which includes faculty autonomy, academic freedom, disclosure, and peer review, as well as a reward system that promotes and tenures people for their cumulative research contributions.[35] "Publish or perish" is a necessity in academia. Peer reviews are performed on the basis of knowledge in the public domain and often by people who have never met the person under evaluation. You cannot be evaluated if nobody knows who you are. (By the way, this partially answers the question why teaching is not given the same weight as research in evaluations. The ability to teach is often not indicated in the public domain.)

The Republic of Government has entirely different operative principles. It relies on piecemeal assessments and on financially based incentive schemes. Like top-down performance reviews in the CCP system, performance reviews in Chinese academia are scripted and metric-driven. Although less common in recent years, the compensation of a faculty member is often directly linked to his or her number of publications.

The two reward systems reveal some fundamental differences. The Republic of Science relies on peer reviews by intellectual colleagues in an "invisible college," a community of scientists like that described by Polanyi. The judgments reflect the consensus of fellow academics about the aggregate impact of a scholar rather than his or her individual, piecemeal accomplishments. The Republic of Government, by contrast, performs vertical reviews and renders judgments from the top down. The decision makers are government officials who have no expertise other than an ability to count. The piecemeal and incremental accomplishments loom large in bureaucratic decisions and judgment calls.

In a scathing commentary in *Science* magazine, Professors Rao Yi and Shi Yigong decry the top-down and bureaucratic nature of the Chinese scientific funding establishment. They point out that the funding guidelines are narrowly described in ways that leave little doubt who the intended recipients are. They remark, "Committees appointed by bureaucrats in the funding agencies determine these annual guidelines. For obvious reasons, the chairs of the committees often listen to and usually cooperate with the bureaucrats." In that system, bureaucrats wield enormous power. "To obtain major grants in China," the two academics continue, "it is an open secret that doing good research is not as important as schmoozing with powerful bureaucrats and their favorite experts."[36]

Rao and Shi's pointed rebuke of China's Republic of Government is unlikely to see the light of day in today's China. An e-letter published in *Science* in 2016 from Guangchao Charles Feng, professor at Jinan University, and Yu Huang, professor and dean of Hong Kong Baptist University, noted that the two establishment academics were "disqualified from their application for academician, or Yuanshi, of the Chinese Academy of Science, apparently as a sort of punishment for their outspokenness."[37] If true, it only confirmed the essence of the criticisms they leveled at the Chinese system.

Because of the sheer enormity of the Republic of Government, a lot of research projects have been funded and a quantity revolution occurred. The piecemeal incentive program links faculty compensations directly to the number of their publications. The original intention behind this compensation scheme was to reduce the discretion of bureaucratic reviewers by tying their decisions to objective metrics. The bean counting is an explicit deference to academic journals and an implicit deference to peer reviews. The Chinese educational reformers envisioned it as a way to chip away some of the power of the bureaucracy. The compromise solution preserved the decision rights of the bureaucrats but diminished their discretion in making these decisions.

Mention the name of Eugene Garfield at your next faculty meeting, and you will likely draw blank stares. Mention his name to a group of Chinese academics and you will set off an animated discussion on the pros and cons of a particular methodology to evaluate scholarly achievements. Garfield is the founder of the Science Citation Index (SCI). Since the early 1990s, many Chinese universities have devised elaborate systems to reward their faculty to publish in SCI journals. In a way, Chinese academia resembles Wall Street in its compensation scheme: the total compensation includes a relatively modest base pay supplemented by the possibility of earning a high bonus payment. Over time, the financial incentives linked to SCI publications escalated and became calibrated to the rankings of the publications. Some universities have offered to pay hundreds of thousands of RMB to publish in the journals *Nature* or *Science*.

In recent years, the piecemeal incentive program has waned in importance, especially at elite Chinese universities, but it has left a powerful impact on Chinese science. An analysis of the citation data tracked by Web of Science between 2007 and 2017 shows that Chinese knowledge production is overwhelmingly oriented toward quantity, not quality.[38] Chinese scientists published 2.06 million papers during this period, second only to American scientists, who published 3.8 million papers. But the average number of citations of those papers is 9.4, compared with 17.47 for papers published by American scientists. Of the ten countries listed in the analysis, China comes up dead last in terms of the average number of citations.

## A Heterodox Model

The absence of academic freedom at Tsinghua has not kept it from rising in world rankings of universities. In 2015, the *Wall Street Journal* ran an article titled "Chinese University Tops MIT in Engineering Rankings."[39] While that specific observation may or may not be true, it is undisputable that China has made substantial progress in science and technology. On the surface of it, scope seems not to matter at all.

The Republic of Government excels at scale. China has spent aggressively on R&D in a way that only a one-party system, at China's level of per capita GDP, can. This traditional advantage of the Chinese system has been accentuated by the failure of the United States to increase its own investments in science and technology. U.S. federal spending as a proportion of the federal government's budget is now a fraction of what it was during the 1960s.[40] Real spending, adjusted for inflation, has remained stagnant for a period of time. Biden is not wrong that the Republic of Science has an innovative edge, but that edge is being eroded by its loss of scale. China, by contrast, makes up for its scope disadvantage by leaning into its scale edge—spending money on R&D, launching big projects, and proactively seeking out collaborations.

The collaborations with foreign countries are a key enabling factor of Chinese science and technology. Academic globalization is a version of comparative advantage at work. China is relatively better at scale than at scope. The basic economic logic dictates that China will specialize in scaling while tapping into the scope conditions via the global marketplace. But unlike endowment factors such as capital and labor, China's academic scope conditions are due to the deliberate decisions of its policymakers. Intellectuals in China have long called for reforms to reduce administrative interventions in the Chinese universities, coupled with a dire warning that the Chinese system stifles creativity and originality and runs counter to the CCP's innovation policy agenda. The CCP has steadfastly resisted these clarion calls for real reforms. If anything, it has moved in the opposite direction.

The CCP desires one specific outcome of the "think-different" mindset—science and technology—but it abhors the process that produces that outcome. The reason is not complicated. Chinese universities are a control lever in the hands of the CCP. They impart thought controls and reign in freedom of ideas and actions on the part of a critical demographic group—China's young people. Ever since the 1989 Tiananmen protests, the CCP is especially sensitive to the political activities on university campuses. Loosening controls over universities presents an immediate downside to the CCP, a negative externality, if you will. Yes, the CCP will benefit from having more creative scientists and technologists, but it will also have to face the consequences of having more creative lawyers, social scientists, journalists, student activists, and NGO organizers. The CCP may have an intuitive grasp of what Alexander Solzhenitsyn once said: "A great writer is, so to speak, a second government in his country." The CCP is determined to thwart that second government.

Instead of reforming its universities, the reformist CCP devised an ingenious solution: acquiring creative capabilities through collaboration. One way to think about the CCP's academic globalization is that it serves this outsourcing function. It collaborates with a Republic of Science around the globe through study-abroad programs, via research collaborations with foreign scientists, and by targeting and recruiting talent from abroad. Academic globalization is a substitute for, not a complement to, the liberalization of China's own academia. This heterodox model gives the CCP some advantages associated with a Republic of Science by proxy while defraying the costs of a Republic of Government. It enables the CCP to pick and choose. The CCP can fund collaborations in the fields it values while eschewing those that have a political downside. Globalization of China's knowledge enterprise gave the CCP that outside option and until Xi Jinping, it delivered for the CCP both political and intellectual benefits.

## International Collaborations

China sought scientific collaborations with the West even before it opened itself to foreign trade and investment.[41] In 1978, China and France signed an agreement on technological cooperation, the first such agreement with a Western country. The next year, China entered into a similar cooperation agreement with the United States. China also entered into collaboration agreements with Japan and Germany. A little-known fact is that in the 1990s, German scholars and research institutions provided technical support for the establishment of the internet in China.

A very fruitful collaboration was the establishment of the Beijing Electron-Positron Collider (BEPC), which significantly advanced the field of high energy physics in China. As part of the project, hundreds of Chinese scientists went to the United States to study and conduct research on high energy physics. The government-to-government collaborations were followed by programs to fund peer-to-peer collaborations. The first funding program designed to create bottom-up access to the Republic of Science was launched in 2001: the International S&T Cooperation Program (ISTCP) of China, administered by the Ministry of Science and Technology.[42] It is application-based and local governments use ISTCP as a template to provide additional support. The size of the support is substantial.

China's overseas educational program was also launched at the forefront of China's open-door policy. The first wave of officially sponsored students left for America in 1978, even before the two countries formalized their diplomatic relations and before China promulgated its first foreign investment law in 1979. The size of the Chinese overseas educational program is massive and amply documented.[43] In comparing China with India, which is similar in demographic profile and like China still a developing country, a National Science Foundation report finds that China dominates India across the board in terms of advanced degrees in science and engineering granted at U.S. universities.[44]

In 1995, in the United States there were more Indian than Chinese doctoral degree recipients in science and engineering. By 2015, the situation had been reversed. In that year, five thousand Chinese received doctoral degrees in science and engineering, compared with only two thousand from India. (The data include only those recipients on temporary visas and thus exclude Chinese Americans or Indian Americans.) Between 1995 and 2015, there were 63,576 science and engineering doctoral-degree recipients from China compared with 30,251 from India. The two groups are broadly comparable in terms of which fields they receive their degrees in: the top three fields account for 67 percent of Chinese doctoral recipients; 68 percent in the case of India. China dominates India in all fields, even in a field in which India supposedly holds an edge: computer science. Between 1995 and 2015, there were 4,229 doctoral degree recipients in computer science from China compared with 2,477 from India. Most amazingly for a country that is still struggling with hunger and malnutrition, India does not come close to China in the overseas training of agricultural scientists. There were 1,745 Chinese recipients in agricultural science compared with only 823 from India.

The quantitative revolution of Chinese science that I referenced earlier is driven by a long left tail of replicative research powered by the incremental incentives. Yes, the high-impact papers are few and far between, but because Chinese scientists are so productive, even a small proportion of high-impact papers translates into a considerable quantity in absolute terms. This is where international collaborations matter: Chinese scientists are producing high-impact papers, but almost always in collaboration with foreign scientists.

My MIT colleague, Fiona Murray, and I have investigated this phenomenon. We collected data on scientific papers in one publication outlet only—*Nature* and its "derivative" publications such as *Nature Biotech*, *Nature Materials*, *Nature Nanotechnology*, and *Nature Medicine*, each of which has become established as a highly cited field-specific journal with high impact factors. Our research shows that when Chinese scientists publish in *Nature* and its derivative journals, it is overwhelmingly as part of an international collaboration. A full 80 percent of *Nature* and *Nature*-related papers with Chinese authors are joint collaborations with international researchers, with 43 percent of these papers coauthored with scientists in the United States, 23 percent with coauthors based in Europe, and 11 percent with coauthors based in the rest of Asia. Only 20 percent of the publications were written by only Chinese authors.

International collaborations offer access to foreign talents, capabilities, and ideas but also to the "think-different" attitudinal attributes that have been missing and suppressed at home. While we cannot disentangle the multiple factors that drive up the quality of collaborative projects, it is reasonable to speculate that Chinese researchers, once outside of the narrow scope environment of China, produce more impactful research.[45] Scope is a neglected variable in many of the analyses of the state of Chinese science. It escaped our attention because it is outsourced rather than being an elemental feature of Chinese academic system.

## "Startup Nation," Chinese Style

In *Lonely Ideas: Can Russia Compete?* historian Loren Graham documented many technologies pioneered by Russia and the Soviet Union, including weapons, railroads, and lasers—but none of these benefited the economy in a substantial way.[46] Graham attributed this to the country's lack of entrepreneurship. Imperial China also came up with many ideas, but all similarly "lonely." China today, however, is altogether different from both Russia and its own imperial past. It has a large and dynamic entrepreneurial sector, and its entrepreneurs are highly motivated and able to scale technologies. The Chinese ideas now have a lot of company. They are deployed to generate economic growth, health codes, and much to the chagrin of the West, military capabilities.

To use the distinction made by William Baumol, imperial China and the Soviet Union were inventive, not innovative. Inventions alone do not contribute to economic growth. Growth is powered by innovations—entrepreneurship and business development that take inventions to market. Capitalism is an innovation machine in that it has mechanisms to turn inventions into innovations.[47] China under the reformist CCP is also an innovation machine.

This is puzzling. In their best-selling book, *Start-up Nation: The Story of Israel's Economic Miracle*, Dan Senor and Paul Singer show how a culture of informality, risk-free inquiries, and organizational egalitarianism, supported by government policies and programs, makes Israel a leading nation of entrepreneurial successes.[48] The book contains vivid details of how subordinates push back against their superiors, even in the military, an institution that is synonymous with hierarchy. China is the polar opposite of Israel. It is top-down, hierarchical, repressive, and stifling of individual initiatives. It lacks Israel's culture of democracy, as well as its rule of law and property rights protection. China's deficits in some of the most invoked factors behind innovations are so glaring that scholars have understandably discounted China's innovative potential.[49]

The institutional foundation of capitalism is rule of law, while Chinese laws place no meaningful constraints on its leaders. Vice President Biden touted venture capital as an advantage of America, whereas Chinese finance is dominated by the statist banking system. In more recent years venture capital has grown exponentially in China, but companies such as Alibaba, Huawei, and Lenovo were not funded by Chinese venture capital in their startup phases. How did Chinese entrepreneurial capitalism flourish? How is it that China can be a start-up nation in its own right? Let me unlock this puzzle by looking closely at the history of one company, the global computer giant Lenovo.

## One Country, Two Systems

In 2004, Lenovo acquired the manufacturing division of IBM.[50] Richard McGregor, a reporter for the *Financial Times*, captured a widespread sentiment when he wrote that the purchase was "a symbol of a new economic era, of how a fast-rising China had suddenly grown powerful enough to subsume an iconic American brand."[51]

But Lenovo is not a Chinese company in a conventional sense; it is technically a foreign company. Lenovo has succeeded precisely because its legal status offered some distance between the company and the Chinese system. Founded in 1984 under the Chinese Academy of Sciences (CAS), the real corporate control and equity holdings of the production and technology development of Lenovo reside in its Hong Kong office. The two business units, Lenovo (Beijing) and Lenovo (Shanghai), run manufacturing, R&D, software development, and customer service. Both are registered as wholly owned foreign firms; that is, they are 100 percent owned by a legal foreign entity, which is Hong Kong Lenovo.[52] As wholly owned foreign firms, the Beijing and Shanghai divisions of Lenovo are more legalistically foreign than GM's operation in Shanghai, which is a 50–50 equity joint venture.

In 1993 when Lenovo was domiciled in Hong Kong, the city was a British colony. Today, under Chinese law and per international conventions, Hong Kong is still treated economically as a foreign entity, and it operates under "one country, two systems," a formula that enforces Chinese sovereignty over Hong Kong but preserves its legal and operational autonomy. How critical is Lenovo's status as a Hong Kong company? Is there anything more to this status than a legal frivolity? The answers to these questions show how important it is to get the details of the Lenovo story right. It matters for how we explain Lenovo's success and the broader success of Chinese high-tech entrepreneurship.

Hong Kong historically has been a laissez-faire economy based on a market-oriented financial system, rule of law, and property rights security. (Under Xi, these have eroded substantially.) While China itself does not furnish these scope functions, it has made them available to some of its entrepreneurs. A milestone development in Lenovo's history was its ability to tap into Hong Kong's finance. Lenovo raised most of its financing in Hong Kong during its startup phase. Apart from initial financing from the Chinese Academy of Sciences in 1984, it was the market-oriented and conventionally Western Hong Kong capital market that supplied Lenovo with subsequent rounds of capital during the firm's critical growth period.[53] In 1988, Lenovo received HK$900,000 from China Technology, a Hong Kong–based firm, to invest in a joint venture in Hong Kong. This Hong Kong joint venture came up with the now famous brand name, Lenovo. In 1993, Hong Kong Lenovo went public on the Hong Kong Stock Exchange, which funded Lenovo's investments in China. Chinese state finance was nowhere to be seen.

This access to growth-enhancing institutions is an unheralded and, most likely, unintended effect of China's open-door policy. Hong Kong, at China's doorstep, and the globalization of the Chinese economy were two consequential scope-widening conditions. China's open-door policy attracted foreign investment, but it has also made possible an exit option for the indigenous Chinese entrepreneurs who performed an arbitrage of the two systems to lessen their dependency on Chinese statism. In the 1990s, the conservative reformers from Shanghai used its left hand to curtail rural entrepreneurship and used its right hand to aggressively globalize the Chinese economy. This is a balanced evaluation of the leaders of the 1990s: they closed one door, but they opened other doors.

The role of Hong Kong is crucial in this interplay of reforms and anti-reforms. In my 2003 book *Selling China*, I showed that in the 1990s Hong Kong provided the equivalent of early rounds of venture capital to Chinese small and medium enterprises, counteracting the rising financing constraints faced by the private sector. Using a large-scale dataset, my coauthors and I show that the more credit-constrained private firms ceded more equity controls to foreign investors, controlling for many conditions.[54] Hong Kong was a lifeline to China's indigenous private sector and without Hong Kong, it is hard to imagine how Lenovo would ever have developed into the global brand it is today.

## *Accessing the Rule of Law*

Among Chinese high-tech firms, how widespread is this practice of registering asset claims outside of mainland China? Very widespread. We can use the registration information of Chinese business units to illustrate this point. The registration record has information about a firm's sources of equity capital, in particular whether the capital comes from three overseas

Chinese territories, Hong Kong, Macao, and Taiwan. I used two Chinese websites specializing in collecting registration information, Qichacha and Qixinbao.[55] Firms have layers of business operations when they establish new subsidiaries. The relevant registration information is a business unit first established in China. In the Chinese registration system, a subsidiary of a foreign-owned unit is usually registered as a domestic firm. To ascertain the nationality of the ultimate ownership requires looking up the first business unit established in China.

Consider BAT, an abbreviation for Baidu, Alibaba, and Tencent, the three internet giants in China. Of these three, only Tencent is domestically registered in China, in Shenzhen. Alibaba Holding is registered in the Cayman Islands, according to one registry. Another registry shows that its Chinese operating unit was established in 1999 as a joint venture between a Hong Kong concern and a Chinese concern. The Cayman unit probably established its Chinese operating unit through a holding company in Hong Kong. Baidu Holding is registered in the Virgin Islands and its Chinese operating unit, established in 2000, is a wholly owned foreign firm, which gives it the same legal status as Lenovo (Beijing) and Lenovo (Shanghai). The biggest facial recognition firm in China, SenseTime, which the United States government has blacklisted, is registered in Hong Kong. China's second largest e-commerce company, JD.com, is registered in the Cayman Islands. Zijietiaodong, the ultimate holding company of TikTok, also known as ByteDance in English, is registered in Hong Kong. *MIT Technology Review*'s special issue on China lists nine Chinese high-tech firms among the world's twenty biggest tech companies. Of these, only three are purely domestically domiciled firms: Tencent, Xiaomi, and Ant Group (whose parent firm is foreign registered). The other six—Alibaba, Bytedance, Baidu, Didi Chuxing, Meituan, and JD.com—all have domicile connections to Hong Kong or other overseas territories.

Chinese high-tech entrepreneurs have benefited from a combination of factors. They ride on the scale advantage of being able to employ millions of well-trained technical personnel and the growth opportunities of a rapidly growing GDP. They also benefit from access to the rule of law and market-based safe harbors offered by places such as Hong Kong. China is unique in that some of its capable entrepreneurs have the option of accessing one of the most efficient financial markets and legal institutions in the world. The beneficial effects of globalization go beyond bringing in foreign capital and technology. An under-appreciated aspect of globalization is that it has widened scope conditions for Chinese entrepreneurs.[56]

## "The New Argonauts"

In her book *The New Argonauts*, AnnaLee Saxenian argues that the future international business landscape is being created and shaped by "new argonauts"—those entrepreneurs who have been trained in the United States and then returned to their homelands to start new companies, all while retaining intimate ties with the venture capital and business communities in the United States.[57] That business landscape has arrived in China, in the life sciences. The new argonauts run China's biotech and pharmaceutical sectors and they have contributed to China's meteoric rise in the life sciences. The life science workforce is far more global in training and orientation than China's IT sector. The founders of Huawei, Alibaba, and Tencent were educated in China, but the best biotech firms in China are all run by the returnees.

My work with Fiona Murray shows that international collaborations in the biological, medical, and agricultural sciences have been the most advanced. Businesses in these sectors are research-intensive and have benefited from the research collaborations I discussed earlier. Patent data from the Patent Cooperation Treaty (PCT) show that as recently as 2010, China produced only about 5.5 percent of the number of U.S. biotech patents and 7.8 percent of the number of U.S. pharmaceutical patents. These two proportions rose to 15 percent and 17 percent in 2015, respectively, and shot up to 42 percent and 39 percent in 2021. China is closing in on the United States.[58]

Academic literature suggests that the status of a region as a technological powerhouse can be tied to a clustering of a critical production input—star professors and entrepreneurs. The rise of Boston, San Francisco, and Seattle as innovation clusters is traced back to the decisions made decades ago of a few star professors and entrepreneurs to settle and move there. It is unlikely that Seattle would be the high-tech hub it is today without Bill Gates's decision to launch Microsoft there.

Knowledge spillovers are often localized.[59] Thus, production of knowledge and commercialization have to be co-located and clustered together. In other words, location matters—an insight that the Chinese government mastered quickly. Kai-fu Lee recalled a conversation he had with an official from Zhongguancun many years before Zhongguancun had become known as the Chinese Silicon Valley. Lee said that the success of Silicon Valley was due to the clustering there of a few innovative high-tech firms that then drew in talent from elsewhere in the United States. Within the blink of an eye, the official decided to offer huge incentive programs to lure a whole group of firms to Zhongguancun.

The Chinese government has systematically targeted academic stars to move to China. One of the most successful programs is in the life sciences. Many Chinese graduates with degrees in the life sciences from American universities have moved back to China, sometimes immediately after graduation, but often after a number of years of working in the United States.

In terms of talent, a higher share of bachelor of science degrees granted in China, 11 percent annually, is in the life sciences compared with 6 percent in the United States. (And many granted in the United States have been earned by Chinese students.) In addition, life science returnees constitute the largest proportion of the pool of Chinese returnees. Between 2011 and 2014, the life science returnees accounted for 18 percent of the total.

A measure of the star power of Chinese life science talent is the shifting composition of the Chinese American BayHelix Group, a group of elite bilingual biotech and pharmaceutical professionals based in San Francisco.[60] In 2001 when the group was founded, 100 percent of BayHelix members resided in the United States. By 2011, this share had declined to 47 percent and the Chinese share was 44 percent. By 2016, the U.S. share had declined further, to 38 percent, while the Chinese share had risen to 57 percent. (The remaining 5 percent were in the rest of the world.) These are "new argonauts" in the life sciences, and China is emerging to be the center of gravity in that area.

These elite argonauts founded China's leading biotech firms.[61] Take, for example, three biotech startups, BeiGene, Wuxi AppTec, and Zai Laboratories. BeiGene was started by serial entrepreneur John Oyler and Professor Wang Xiaodong, and it is the leading oncology company in China. Its collaboration with Celgene, now part of Bristol-Myers Squibb, around its PD-1 inhibitor program is viewed in the medical world as a sign that China-based biotech companies are poised to invent and develop best-in-class cancer therapeutics. Wang was educated in the United States. He is a member of the U.S. National Academy of Sciences and a biochemist and cell biologist from the University of Texas Southwestern Medical Center.

Another returnee and an entrepreneurial star in the biotech space is Li Ge. Born and raised in China, he received his bachelor's degree in chemistry from Peking University and a Ph.D. in organic chemistry from Columbia University. He was a founding scientist at Pharmacopeia in New Jersey before returning to China in 2000, the year he founded WuXi

AppTec.[62] The people listed on WuXi AppTec's management team page are mostly returnees, having received their life science education and professional training in the United States. Wuxi AppTech started as a contract research organization, but now actively pursues its own discovery and development of drugs. The company was profiled in 2006 in the *Harvard Business Review*.[63]

Samantha Du, the founding CEO and chair of Zai Lab, was born and raised in China, received her Ph.D. in biochemistry from the University of Cincinnati, and began her industry career at Pfizer, where she was involved in the development and launch of several drugs. From 2001 to 2011, she was founder and CEO of Hutchison Medi-pharma, one of the first Western-style drug-discovery companies in China. She pioneered China-based global biopharmaceutical innovation by bringing to clinical trials five internally discovered drug candidates, including two global Phase III–ready drug candidates. Prior to founding Zai Lab, she spent two years spearheading healthcare investment at Sequoia Capital China.

═══════

In 2019, as China was cracking down on free speech in Hong Kong, Eswar Prasad of Cornell University wrote that in 1997 Hong Kong's economy was one-fifth the size of China's while in 2018 it was only one-thirtieth. That was the data point behind his argument, "Why China No Longer Needs Hong Kong," published in the *New York Times*.[64] Let me cite a different set of statistics. The three leading biotech firms I profiled—Beigene, Wuxi AppTec, and Zai Lab—are all registered in Hong Kong. So are many of China's most dynamic high-tech firms. It is only a slight exaggeration to say that Hong Kong owns China's high-tech space.

Prasad's article is revealing because it may very well mimic the way that Beijing thinks about Hong Kong. But that mindset is dead wrong. Relegating Hong Kong to the status of just another Chinese city puts an end to the legal arbitrage opportunities and the associated upsides for countless Chinese high-tech entrepreneurs. Under Xi Jinping, it is not just the de facto scope condition of Hong Kong that is damaged; the political and economic recentralization and China's hostile foreign-policy posture have cut deeply into the heterodox model that the pragmatic, reformist CCP devised. The curtailing of the scope conditions from the reformist era has had significant implications for the Chinese economy, its politics, and its relations with the world. So far my discussion of the PRC period has mainly focused on the reformist era, defined in this book as the period leading up to 2018. Next, let me turn to the era of Xi Jinping.

# PART V

# The Future of the EAST Model

# CHAPTER NINE

# The CCP of Xi Jinping

*Village leader:* Good news! The chairman of the party, chairman
of the state, leader of the foreign affairs group, leader of the
agriculture group, leader of the finance group, and leader of the
education group will visit you.

*Villager:* Good! But I don't have so many chairs.

*Village leader:* No worries. You only need one chair.

—Joke on the Chinese internet during Xi Jinping's early days

IN THE 1970s, TIAN Jiyun worked under Zhao Ziyang when Zhao was
party secretary of Sichuan. In 1980, Zhao, as premier, brought Tian to
the State Council, where he served as a vice premier from 1983 to 1993,
first under Zhao and then under the conservative Li Peng. Tian was a
reformer, which meant that his political career was derailed after Tiananmen. In the 1990s, he was largely sidelined.

In 1992, Tian gave a famous speech at the Central Party School in
which he proposed to establish a special economic zone for socialism.
Brimming with sarcasm, Tian envisioned a place where "salaries and the
prices of goods would be low, queuing and rationing would be common-
place, there would be no foreign investment, foreigners would be excluded, and no one would be able to travel abroad."[1]

No Chinese leaders ever took up Tian's proposal—until Xi Jinping. Since Xi came to power in 2012, he has engineered the biggest reform reversals in the history of the PRC. He has reduced credit flows to the private sector, targeted high-profile private firms in the name of regulatory restructuring, and renationalized private firms.[2]

Xi is a shock to the system that the reformist CCP has patched together, in two ways. Recall from Chapter 4 that the post-Tiananmen leaders retrogressed in some areas—rural finance—but reformed in others (privatization and globalization). Xi Jinping has enacted sweeping changes across the board, from foreign policy to domestic politics, social media and economy, all in a consistently hardline direction. The post-Tiananmen leaders eroded the political scope conditions of the country, but they expanded economic and social scope conditions. Under Xi, none of the scope conditions are left. China now is a frictionless autocracy. The other way is the speed of his actions. China is famously known for its incremental and gradualist approach.[3] Not Xi Jinping. His anti-corruption campaign brought down millions of officials and his simultaneous crackdowns on real estate, gaming, private educational services, and fintech wiped out trillions of dollars in wealth and hundreds of thousands of jobs in the real economy.

Many of the shocks unleashed by Xi are still working through the system, and I can only offer a conjecture of their eventual impact. I believe that Xi has weakened the modernized features of the EAST model, such as its systemization, regional autonomy, and the scope conditions for the private sector. Unwittingly, Xi may have loosened the conditions that have helped the CCP endure, for it is hard to see how his approach can stay still. The political system could slip further back to autocracy or it could be forced to move to embrace more openness. The status quo is not in equilibrium.

Economically, China is trending in the direction of a South Korea, but politically it is embracing the North Korean model, minus one advantage that North Korea still has: hereditary rule. Hereditary rule tames succession conflicts just like term limits can. Xi, however, is charging forward without any rule-based succession arrangement. With the surges in COVID-19 cases, the economically and politically damaging lockdowns of Chinese cities, the slowdown in growth, policy mishaps, a sense of anxiety and fear among Chinese elites, crippled incentives of the private sector and local officials, and an adverse global environment, this is as close to a perfect storm as one can get. In an ominous sign of things to come, in

November 2022, protests broke out simultaneously in multiple Chinese cities against the country's zero-COVID policy. Some protestors even called for the ouster of Xi Jinping.

These protests show that COVID-19 is adding an extra layer of uncertainty, on top of the fear and anxiety that have been perpetuated by Xi's policies since 2012. Xi gained confidence from his extreme zero-infection approach in 2020 and 2021, which brought the initial outbreak under control. But he has persisted with it, even after conditions have changed, and despite the exorbitant economic and social toll on the country. Xi, the autocrat, has gained the capacity to make policy and policy changes but, as we have seen in other similar situations, the capacity by an autocrat to make changes is inversely correlated with his willingness to make changes.

Rather than drawing a clinical lesson about China's experience of the pandemic, and being guided by a data-driven approach, Xi Jinping has elevated zero-COVID as the standard-bearing benchmark for himself and for his government. He is exuberantly confident about his decision, claiming that "the East is rising and the West is declining." He has rejected science in favor of administrative compulsion, and he rejected foreign science, in the form of Pfizer and Moderna vaccines, in favor of the weaker domestic science, the Sinovac vaccine, and in favor of pseudo-science in the form of various herbal tonics. His grand vision has spilled over into economics. His one-two punch crackdown on high-profile private firms in the second half of 2021 directly followed his triumphant proclamation about the changing global order.

This is hubris of the highest order. A rational politician will leave some wiggle room for himself and set realistic expectations. By setting the bar so high, he simultaneously raises the expectations of his citizens and lowers the probability of delivering it. Despite the draconian measures and the enormous economic toll of the zero-COVID policy, China has not reduced its COVID numbers to zero, even if we go by the (very suspect) official statistics. Yet the policy has soldiered on possibly because there is not any "team of rivals" and no one dares to tell Xi the truth. Given the complexities of the Chinese economy and society, and of the virus transmission dynamics, it defies common sense that the system defaults to the wisdom of one person and one person alone. Sadly, hubris is often accompanied and compounded by policy missteps and errors.

The next two chapters are admittedly speculative. The topics addressed are fluid and are very close to current events. I humbly accept that the topic is so fluid that the dynamics and developments recorded here may look different by the time this book hits the bookstand. My exposition on the Xi era can be viewed as an out-of-sample application of the scope and scale framework I posited in the introductory chapter. As in many such applications, there will be errors due in part to unforeseen events and to the inability of any framework to capture all the contingencies. As flawed as it can be, the general proposition that Xi has decimated all the residual scope conditions is factually correct. How and in what manner China will get out of this scopeless situation is harder to predict; we can, however, speculate.

## The Xi Jinping Shocks

To its credit, the reformist CCP modernized the EAST model and broke the curse of its forebears by delivering both growth and stability. The model experienced strains and degradations through wear and tear, but most analysts and the CCP insiders expected refinements and course corrections, not a wholesale revamp.

Had I written this book in 2012, I would have ended it there. But this is not what happened. Against all expectations, Xi has thoroughly disrupted the modus operandi of the CCP of the reform era. He has undermined the institutional underpinning of China's peaceful power transition. He has crippled the crown jewel of China's high-tech private sector. He has jeopardized the productive economic and technological collaborations with the West. He has made CCP rule more personalistic and degraded its institutional quality. This is the era of Xi Jinping, defined in this book as commencing in 2018, the year the term limit was abolished. It will be a consequential era, an era of drama, surprises, and convulsions.

### Crossing the Political Rubicon

No matter how powerful they are, autocrats are mortals just like rest of us. Now that Xi has secured his third term, the speculation du jour will be how he will exit from the political scene. The window for a voluntary exit option has become vanishingly small. Xi has made Chinese politics "nasty, short, and brutish" again. Put yourself in his position. You have purged more than four million officials since 2012, jailed many of them, executed a few, destroyed their political careers, taken away their power and privileges, subjected them to the same inquisitions usually reserved for political dissidents, and confiscated their assets. Some of these people were once powerful figures in the military and security apparatus. Would you voluntarily step down without fearing retributions and reprisals?

Term limits lower exit costs by curbing the excesses of power struggles. Jiang and Hu performed surgical operations on corruption because of the certainty of exit after two terms. It would have been foolish for them to burn all the bridges. "Corrupt and let corrupt" is an act of self-preservation. Term limits have another embedded guarantee: they ensure the safety of the predecessors. Who wants to be a predecessor if his post-politics safety is not assured? The difference in the "retirement package" explains why the CCP achieved peaceful power transitions whereas the former Soviet Union struggled.[4] Xi has derailed this "socialist contract" and inadvertently increased future risks for himself.

As noted earlier, the strongest constraint on incumbent leaders in the Chinese system is their predecessors. Early on, Xi's anti-corruption campaign aimed to undercut his predecessors. The first victim to fall was Ling Jihua, a Politburo member and an ally of Hu Jintao.[5] Because Hu did not have many allies, losing Ling deprived him of any residual power he might have wielded after leaving office. Taking on Jiang Zemin was more challenging. By one account, in 2012 five of the nine PBSC members belonged to the Jiang faction, and of the twenty-five Politburo members, fifteen or sixteen could be classified as Jiang loyalists. Xi began by targeting three Jiang loyalists who were former or sitting members of the Politburo—Zhou Yongkang, Xu Caihou, and Guo Boxiong—all on charges of corruption. These moves sent an unmistakable message to Jiang that he had exposure. Already waning because of his advanced age, the influence of Jiang declined.

Zhou Yongkang had already retired from the PBSC, but his background in China's security apparatus afforded him extra muscle. Going after Zhou killed two birds with one stone. Xi cut off Zhou's security connections and he served notice to the other predecessors that their retirement status enjoyed no immunity. By going after his predecessors and their proxies, then abolishing the term limit, Xi has completely destroyed the safety net granted to the predecessors. Is it any wonder that he does not want to become a predecessor?

No doubt Xi's anti-corruption campaign has rooted out truly corrupt officials. The scale, some four million officials at the time of this writing, seems too large for simple political cleansing, but clearly there was a political agenda. During his first term, Xi purged and jailed six powerful CCP leaders. During his second term, the purges continued unabated. There is an endogenous quality to his anti-corruption campaign. Even if the original agenda was all about corruption, given the severe losses caused to those caught in the dragnet, the campaign itself has seeded enmity and opposition, which then further intensifies the campaign. There is a feedback loop dynamic, and disentangling the anti-corruption agenda from a political agenda becomes difficult. The two are closely bundled.

Xi's anti-corruption campaign has become a search for greater political and personal security. Susan Shirk remarks, "Xi Jinping is preoccupied with shoring up loyalty to the party and himself. Despite his apparent grip on power, his insecurity is glaring."[6] The aggravating effect of the weaponized anti-corruption campaign and the decimation of residual norms and scruples are painting Xi into a corner. He has crossed the Rubicon.

## *The Great Purge*

Insecurity begets insecurity. In some ways, whether the insecurity is psychological or material does not matter. Both lead to purges, and more purges sow the seeds of further antagonism and dissent, in a vicious cycle. The anti-corruption campaign is now in its tenth year. It is no longer a "campaign"; instead it would be better to describe it as one of those many oxymoronic concepts the CCP has invented, such as "permanent revolution."

Corruption is pervasive in the Chinese system, and it is corrosive, but it is also a necessary evil. It ameliorates the rigidities of central planning and enables the growth that has helped the CCP stay in power. Xi, however, sees corruption as an unblemished threat. Corruption has "weakened the Party's creativity, cohesiveness, and ability, and posed a serious test to its exercise of national governance" according to the "Resolution on Major Achievements and Historical Experience of the Communist Party of China over the Past Century" adopted by the CCP in November 2021 (the "Resolution"), a document that serves as the manifesto for Xi's third term. Xi insists that statism is the solution to corruption. He has sought to reverse the "lax and weak governance" of the CCP and stamp out the evil nature of capitalism.

Scholars have long suspected that Xi's anti-corruption campaign is political, targeting his rivals who are incidentally corrupt.[7] We no longer need a regression analysis to make this inference. The CCP openly acknowledges it. The resolution states: "The Party has focused on dealing with cases involving both political and economic corruption, prevented interest groups from arising within the Party, and investigated and punished corrupt officials such as Zhou Yongkang, Bo Xilai, Sun Zhengcai, and Ling Jihua for their serious violations of Party discipline and the law." The officials named in this paragraph were all contenders for power with Xi Jinping.

Xi's anti-corruption campaign is popular among the masses and has antagonized the elites. The masses in an autocracy lack agency, and from the point of view of regime survival, antagonizing elites is not a rational move. Is the elites' resentment dangerous for Xi? In the past the CCP was able to survive the Lin Biao affair, which occurred during the traumatic Cultural Revolution when there was pent-up angst among the Chinese political elites. Keep in mind that back then it was Mao Zedong who kept things under control; a lesser leader may be unable to repeat the feat. Also, the Chinese political elites experienced a psychological closure when Lin fell. Lin had mercilessly tormented and persecuted them, and now Mao was getting rid of him. A comparable situation today would have Xi Jinping dismantle a succession arrangement on the ground that the chosen one is not corrupt enough!

Xi's anti-corruption campaign is truly massive. According to one tally, between 2012 and 2017, Xi Jinping purged the same number of full and alternate members of the Central Committee on corruption charges as the CCP did during the previous sixty-three years of the PRC. Between 2012 and 2021, some four million officials were investigated and punished on corruption charges, and 392 officials at or above ministerial and provincial levels were investigated.[8] The discipline procedures have even been invoked against those local officials who failed to implement central policies on the economy and environment.

There is no sign that things are letting up. A genuine anti-corruption campaign responds to actual levels of corruption, while a politically motivated campaign is not bound by anything. As long as there is politics, there is going to be political rivalry, and insecurity is contagious. When you see a rival in one place, you see rivals everywhere. Finance is usually viewed as a technocratic and politically distant arena of the Chinese state. Still, in October 2021, the CCP launched a high-level inspection into top state-owned Chinese financial institutions. The mandate was explicitly political rather than financial. We do not know why but one clue is that Wang Qishan, the vice president, has built an extensive network of ties and controls in finance. In 2021, a longtime aide to Wang, Dong Hong, was given a commuted death sentence, with his crimes enumerated so that their timing aligns closely with when he worked with Wang. In 2022, another of Wang's former aides, Fan Yifei, was placed under investigation.

The political instrumentalization of corruption creates a self-perpetuating dynamic. Targeting political rivals itself sparks political rivalries, and so can have a rebound effect. Since corruption is so pervasive, Xi's future rivals can accuse his own allies of corruption to gain an advantage. This is why Xi's predecessors were careful and surgical in their own anti-corruption drives. The politically motivated anti-corruption drive lays down a trap of a perpetual cycle of purges and counter-purges, with each round of purge planting the seeds for another round. In such an unappetizing environment, standing still invites challenges, while not standing still creates challenges.

## Sliding into Personalistic Rule

A political system can be run in one of three ways. One is to delegate some decision rights—critically, the rights to choose personnel—to the citizens. This is democracy. Or you can delegate decision rights to functionaries of the state. This has been the approach of the reformist CCP for the better part of the reform era. The third option is to keep all the power in the hands of the autocrat himself, an option that Xi has chosen. If you do not democratize or trust the state's functionaries, then the only option is personalistic rule.

China is rapidly sliding into personalistic rule, an outcome predicted by Shirk.[9] Shirk cited several developments, including the revival of the Mao-era practice of requiring major officials to pledge personal loyalty and the abandonment of straw polls by the Central Committee, which had been used as a guide for nominating leaders. The nullification of the two-term rule sets China back to the era of Mao, when successions were arbitrary and chaotic. This descent to personalistic rule has occurred without the personal charisma of Mao and Deng, who could limit factional strife. As Hua Guofeng quickly learned, under a personalistic rule leadership traits such as legitimacy and credibility are often not transferable.

Xi Jinping has openly embraced personalistic rule. Consider the following paragraph from the 2021 "Resolution" about criteria for the selection of officials:

> In appointing officials, the Party has adopted a rational approach
> with a greater emphasis on political integrity. It has adhered to the

principle of selecting officials on the basis of both integrity and ability, with greater weight given to the former, and on the basis of merit regardless of background, and it is intent on appointing those who are dedicated, impartial, and upright. *The Party has opposed the selection of officials solely on the basis of votes, assessment scores, GDP growth rates, or age, or through open popularity contests.*[10]

Notice the criteria that Xi has sought to marginalize and compare them with the ones he has endorsed. Votes, assessment scores, GDP, age, and peer opinions have a grounding in facts and objective conditions. Except for age, these criteria depend on tacit coordination and a convergence of views among the CCP peers. This is what I call horizontal power.

Xi's CCP is curtailing horizontal power to advance its vertical power. Consider those norms that Xi champions—"political integrity" and "dedicated, impartial, and upright" qualities. But what is "political integrity?" Whose definitions of "dedicated, impartial, and upright" should prevail? The following two statements, "Party, government, military, civilian, and academic; east, west, south, north, and center, the Party leads everything" and "The court should lock power in a cage," are both from Xi Jinping. Which one do you follow? A hallmark of an unaccountable leader is his ability to be wildly inconsistent. When the values are subjective, amorphous, and contradictory, we need a final arbiter to settle any resultant disputes. In a centralized autocracy, that arbiter is the autocrat himself. The delay in the initial reporting on COVID-19 within the Chinese bureaucracy is a sign of an autocrat's isolation bubble. No one has an incentive to deliver bad news to the person who holds all the vertical power. Compounding the problem is that Xi, unlike Mao, is a micro-manager and insists on making all the decisions himself. This is a prescription for policy mishaps and paralysis.

A tool of intra-party democracy, straw polls, was abolished. In its place, Shirk wrote, the CCP nominates candidates based on interviews and chosen "elite opinions." The pre-*Keju* imperial bureaucracy ran on personal recommendations, but it was a much smaller operation and more minimalist in its objectives than the CCP. The CCP of Xi Jinping runs a massive bureaucracy but increasingly with an instrument better suited for a boutique operation. A likely scenario is that the system will produce results that are inconsistent over time and will make many mistakes in policy and personnel. The iron law of personalistic rule is that it cannot be scaled without inconsistencies and randomness. Perverse incentives abound in such a system, with subordinates highly motivated to create opacity, with citizens but also with their superiors, creating what James Scott describes as a "legibility problem."[11] The system will favor sycophants and license doublespeak, strategic gaming, and calculated signaling. The noise to information ratio will rise. There will be more Lin Biaos who despise their leader (in Lin's case, Mao Zedong) in private diary entries but effusively praise him in public. There will be fewer Hu Yaobangs who speak their minds with forthrightness and candor. The institutional quality will deteriorate.

## From Targeting GDP to Targeting Conduct

At an economic forum in 2021, Ma Jun, a policy adviser to China's central bank, called on the government to permanently drop GDP as its target.[12] Throughout the era of Xi Jinping, GDP targeting has slipped in importance, a shift in priorities that is evident not only in the CCP's pronouncement on merit evaluation of officials but also in policy actions. An unfortunate aspect of statism is that growth is corruption-dependent, so targeting corruption is anti-growth. Project approvals have slowed down, and officials have become wary in their dealings with private entrepreneurs. Xi's other actions, such as crackdowns on the private sector and economically ruinous lockdowns, also signal the end of GDP targeting.

GDP targeting has produced many well-known pathologies, such as statistical falsifications, corruption, pollution, and excessive debt. In my writing, I too have criticized GDP targeting when that targeting leads to a divergence between GDP growth and those performance dimensions that are closer proxies of welfare, such as household income.[13] But before we dismiss GDP targeting altogether, we need to ask, "What will be the replacement targeting scheme if the CCP drops GDP?"

A top-down political system needs to target something. The more top-down an organization is, the more necessary it is to specify a clear, objective function. For all its woes, GDP targeting is partially based on the objective conditions on the ground, such as labor supply, productivity, and conditions of the global economy. As powerful as the Chinese leaders are, not everything is under their control. By default, GDP targeting anchors the government's actions to the exogenously given conditions, and government decision making is more grounded. There have been more pushbacks against Xi on the economy than on any other issue. Li Keqiang, reduced in stature to the point of invisibility but probably emboldened by his impending departure, sometimes speaks in tunes different from Xi on economic matters. An optimistic—but slim—scenario in the future is ascension of a strong premier who is willing and able to check and balance Xi Jinping on economic policy. It would still be Xi's autocracy but one that would navigate with some frictions. An economic anchor would inject a modicum of objectivity, a valuable attribute in a political system that sorely lacks any.

GDP is a composite metric, the sum of investment, consumption, and net exports. Targeting GDP is targeting multiple metrics. An alternative is to use a single metric. The *Wall Street Journal* reported that local officials whitewashed peasant homes to fulfill Xi Jinping's call to eradicate extreme poverty.[14] The irony is rich that whitewashing was used to prove the existence of Goodhart's Law. (Goodhart's Law states that a measure stops being a good measure once it becomes a target.) During the Deng era, local officials in Guangdong, propelled by the GDP imperative, pushed the economy to open further to foreign investments and trade, often resorting to methods frowned upon by the central government.[15] That era is long gone.

Or the conduct of officials can be targeted. In 2019, the CCP unveiled an app called "Study the Great Nation." Chinese officials are required to download the app and to keep themselves abreast of the latest activities and instructions of Xi Jinping. Watching a video about his visit to France will get you one point, and acing a quiz on Xi's economic policies will get you 10 points. As of 2019, the app had more than 100 million registered users. This shift from outcome to conduct targeting is designed to homogenize the Chinese officialdom. GDP targeting is permissive of diverse approaches (up to a point); it is problematic on many levels, but alternative targeting schemes are even more distortionary. To paraphrase Dani Rodrik, GDP targeting is second best, at best.[16]

Creating GDP reflects an aggregation of decisions, conduct, and preferences on the part of millions of individuals working interactively and iteratively with factors of production such as capital and labor. Targeting GDP rewards an official's ability to coordinate activities as well as people, including with private and foreign businesses. It is a scope-opening move that rewards a broad set of capabilities and skills. Even statistical falsification requires a degree of coordination. One way to falsify statistics involves altering the time stamp of tax receipts, a collaborative act between tax collectors and business owners.

By contrast, conduct targeting scrutinizes the singular actions of an official rather than the broad effects of his or her actions. An official busily watching Xi Jinping's visit to France on the "Study the Great Nation" app coordinates only with himself. Conduct targeting can also make the Chinese system more repressive. Unlike GDP, opportunities to showcase one's allegiance are limited, and one way to generate new opportunities is to deliberately create tensions between the state and the society and then take actions to have the state prevail over the society. During the lockdown of Shanghai, newborn babies who tested positive for COVID-19 were snatched away from their parents and forcibly quarantined. The action had no public health benefit other than exhibiting the fealty of Shanghai to the lockdown mandate of the central government. In the future, as the Chinese economy slows down, local governments may escalate predatory actions against the private property rights of households and entrepreneurs both to clamor for their shrinking portion of the economic pie as well as to act out their allegiance to the CCP.

The pre-Xi, reformist CCP did give regional officials a considerable amount of autonomy, but it made sure that whatever leeway it offered was consistent with its desired outcomes. GDP targeting imposes boundary conditions and discipline on that scope. It reminds me of a famous quotation attributed to Henry Ford: "Any customer can have a car painted any color that he wants, so long as it is black." By targeting GDP, the reformist CCP could extricate itself from micro-management of everyday affairs as long as the aggregate outcome was satisfactory. This is Management 101. Selecting the right metrics empowers agency; picking the wrong metrics decimates agency.

GDP targeting has another upside. It orients the CCP away from its well-worn path of endless class struggles, destructive power rivalries, ideological brainwashing, aggressive foreign policies, and red terror. For this reason, we often consider the economic technocrats such as Liu Shaoqi, Zhou Enlai, and Chen Yun as "moderates" even though they were ardent supporters of one-party rule. For the same reason, I suspect, economic reformers like Hu Yaobang and Zhao Ziyang were inept at power struggles. In a hyper-political system, anything that nudges government priorities away from politics produces a net benefit. It lowers the ideological temperature and makes Chinese society more normal.

Conduct targeting chips away at the operational autonomy of Chinese officials and the pragmatism of the Chinese system. It runs counter to Deng's famous aphorism, "It does not matter whether the cat is black or white as long it catches mice." The color of the cat matters now, and it matters more than the outcome of catching a mouse. Conduct targeting also undermines the state's performance incentives. Even Xi himself has lamented this problem. In several speeches, he harshly criticized the "lazy government" (懒政), that is, its failure to promote economic growth, without a hint of irony that his policies are its root cause. For all its woes, GDP is based on a degree of standardization in a way that political behavior is not. Setting aside GDP as a metric means that the CCP will lose its anchoring to a precious few moorings outside of its supervision and the rudimentary organizational coherence that the reformist CCP has stitched together.

## Further Thinning the Political System

Soon after he came to power in 2012, Xi Jinping offered this diagnosis about the fall of the Soviet Union: "Why did the Soviet Union disintegrate? Why did the Soviet Communist Party collapse? An important reason is that their ideals and convictions wavered. Finally, all it took was one quiet word from Gorbachev to declare the dissolution of the Soviet Communist Party, and a great party was gone." He insinuates that the CCP is stronger because of its ideological coherence.

That is just not true. In 1989, the reformist CCP survived Tiananmen when the Communist ideology was at its lowest ebb. Its strength was its flexibility and pragmatism. The reformist CCP permitted as much scope as was needed to enable growth—regional autonomy and private sector development—but not enough to endanger the political status quo. A great innovation of the CCP, the M-form economy, encouraged policy innovations and experimentation, but the M-form autonomy was nestled in a centralized architecture of personnel management, monitoring, and evaluations. There was an added benefit. The distributed nature of the Chinese economy dissipated risks emanating from Beijing. The 1989 Tiananmen turmoil paralyzed decision making in the central government, but the Chinese economy survived largely intact. A similar shock today would be far more debilitating.

The former Soviet Union got the combination wrong. Its rigid U-form economy failed to produce growth, and the Soviet central state was cavalier about "regional factionalism." The regional officials of the former Soviet Union served in their posts twice as long as the Chinese regional officials. The elaborate organizational devices that I modeled as overcoming agency problems in Chapter 2 did not have their Soviet counterparts.[17]

The reformist CCP survived its own near-death experience of Tiananmen because of reforms. On this matter, Deng was far more perceptive than Xi. During his famous 1992 Southern Tour, in his characteristically blunt fashion, Deng stated, "Had it not been for the achievements of the reform and the open policy, we could not have weathered June 4th. And if we had failed that test, there would have been chaos and civil war."[18] In many ways, Xi's diagnosis that the Soviet Union collapsed due to its ideological wavering vastly understates his own system's strengths and sophistications.

Since 2012, Xi has steadfastly implemented his diagnosis of the Soviet collapse. Hong Kong's autonomy—a crucial source of outsourced property rights security—has been dismantled. Social media has been curbed. Teachings of Communist ideology, heavily dosed with the ideas of Xi, are now a core curriculum on Chinese campuses. Instead of wracking their brains to grow GDP, local officials are engaged in a fierce tournament with each other to showcase their nauseating loyalty to Xi Jinping. Unlike GDP, which subjects state actions to a degree of objective constraints on the ground, personal allegiance to the leader can be generated ad infinitum—subject only to a person's capacity to stomach it.

Earlier I described the Tudor system of Henry VIII as "thick politics," that is, politics that has multiple layers and dimensions. The politics that Xi inherited from Hu Jintao, by contrast, were thin—hierarchical, straightforward, enumerated, and ossified—and Xi has thinned them further. He has scaled the power of the CCP. In the 1980s, the CCP began to withdraw its branches from select government departments and state-operated enterprises, in keeping with the core idea of Zhao Ziyang's reform program at the Thirteenth Party Congress in 1987. And although under Jiang Zemin and Hu Jintao, the CCP reinstated the CCP branches in the administrative units of the state, it still delegated responsibility for the day-to-day functions to these administrative units. The CCP was content with an arm's-length relationship with the private sector.

Xi has rigorously enforced a previously ignored provision in the CCP Constitution that mandates the establishment of a CCP branch when the number of CCP members in an organization exceeds three. By the end of 2020, 92 percent of the top five hundred private companies had a CCP branch, putting them under the direct tentacles of CCP control. This "influence without ownership" has decimated the remnants of civil society lingering from the reform era.[19] In 2014, 1.58 million of the 2.97 million registered non-state-sector firms established CCP branches.[20] Xi has also nationalized private enterprises, through outright nationalization but also through an indirect mechanism known as "pressured liquidations." Between 2014 and 2019, thirty listed companies were nationalized through such pressured liquidations.[21]

Xi has sharply diminished the authority and autonomy of the state's administrative apparatus. He has centralized decision making in the hands of the CCP apparatus at the expense of the State Council. Economic decision making, traditionally a prerogative of the State Council, is now in the hands of the Central Financial and Economic Group, which Xi chairs. He abolished the State Administration of Civil Service and placed its functions under the central Department of Organization. He reassigned cybersecurity from the Ministry of Industry and Information Technology to a CCP organ, the Central Cyberspace Affairs Commission. He transferred the oversight responsibilities over media from the State Administration of Press, Publication, Radio, Film, and Television to the Central Publicity Department of the CCP.

Those who ran these agencies of the State Council were not rebels or renegades. All of them were card-carrying loyal CCP members who had been carefully vetted and regularly evaluated by the Department of Organization. The party secretary always outranked the minister; or in some cases, a CCP secretary served concurrently as the minister. Yet Xi did not trust even this level of delegation. The fusion of the CCP and the state has reverted to a level that prevailed during the Cultural Revolution, at the expense of professionalism and expertise.

## Rising Discretionary Power

The very definition of an autocracy is that it places a great deal of discretion in the hands of the autocrat. Such discretion sometimes acts as a source of power, but sometimes it can be a source of instabilities—instabilities associated with open-ended successions and policy mishaps.

The post–Cultural Revolution leaders created a more defused power structure. They rescinded the title "chairman of the CCP," and adopted "general secretary of the CCP" to deliberately circumscribe the power of the person in that position. Term limits were introduced for the same purpose. But in the early 1990s, power was recentralized in the hands of the CCP general secretary, and in 2018, Xi Jinping removed the last vestige of the reforms that dated back to the 1980s—the two-term limit on the presidency. In other words, discretionary power has been fully restored to the general secretary, betraying the original design principle to have the position perform coordinating rather than commanding functions.

A spokesperson for the National People's Congress, Zhang Yesui, justified the abolition of the term limit on the grounds that it was important to make the president's position consistent with the offices of the general secretary and the chairman of the MAC, which did not have term limits.[22] This is manifestly disingenuous. The same consistency could have been achieved by adding a term limit to the other two positions. Zhang also neglected to mention that the term limit on the premier was not removed; it was removed only for a position held by Xi Jinping.

The amassing of power by Xi is unprecedented since the days of Mao Zedong. Xi also has a level of operational control and micro-management that Mao never exercised. Mao is famous for his hands-off approach to daily affairs. He often spent time reading and writing classical poems in his residence and routinely skipped Politburo meetings. Xi is much more hands-on. As of 2021, he headed no fewer than nine leadership groups. The "chairman of everything" has solved the villager's conundrum about chairs.

A wise dictator, Tullock writes, does not choose a successor; but not choosing a successor does not solve the crown-prince problem.[23] It merely postpones it. No obvious successor has emerged from the Twentieth Party Congress in late 2022, based on information available publicly. Under Jiang Zemin and Hu Jintao, it was implicit that the vice president would be the chosen successor, but the current vice president, Wang Qishan, is older than Xi Jinping and is not a member of the Politburo. He thus is not in a position to succeed Xi.

Postponing a succession decision empowers everyone to think that he has a shot. (And it is always a he.) The playing field is leveled, intensifying illicit political competition. Deng's term limits did not eliminate power struggles, but at least they shortened their duration. Both Jiang and Hu had settled the issue of their respective successions by the beginning of their second terms. Infinite time horizons fan and incubate speculations, misperceptions, suspicions, and ambitions. They seldom end well.

There are already signs of succession conflicts to come. In July 2017, Sun Zhengcai, a Politburo member and CCP party chief in Chongqing, was dismissed and placed under investigation. In May 2018, he was sentenced to life in prison.[24] One charge leveled against Sun stands out in particularly jarring terms: he "conducted a wanton discourse on the affairs of the CCP Center" (妄议中央). Keep in mind that Sun was a Politburo member, and in that capacity he was a constituent and core member of that CCP ruling group. For his "offense," Sun will spend the rest of his life in prison.

## What Lies Ahead?

In the late 1990s, I was in Shanghai doing field research for my book *Selling China*. The basic theme of the book is that China was unusually dependent on foreign capital because its own financial system constrained the ability of China's indigenous private sector to raise capital. In places like Shanghai, the private sector had turned instead to foreign capital.

In an interview, I asked a Shanghai official to introduce me to some private entrepreneurs. He looked at me in shock as if I had asked an inappropriate question about his private life. He frowned and then asked, "Aren't you a Harvard professor? As a Harvard professor, why are you interested in talking to people who sell hot tea and watermelons on the street?" (At that time, I was at Harvard Business School.) One of the unpleasantries for Chinese officials talking to foreign scholars is that some of us push back. And I did. I said, "With due respect, there is no reason why private firms cannot also do technology. Microsoft and GE are all private companies." I further ventured, "Could it be that private entrepreneurs in Shanghai sell hot tea and watermelons on the street because these are the only things you allow them to do?" To accentuate my point, I added that Harvard is a private university.

I will always remember that exchange. I do not think my answer changed his view; nor do I think forty years of Chinese growth has influenced the official perspective on the private sector. Even after all the economic growth powered by the private sector, the CCP has never explicitly acknowledged it as the true engine of Chinese economic growth. The Chinese state recognizes the employment contributions of the private sector, but one is hard-pressed to find a straightforward affirmative statement by the CCP on the private sector as the source of productivity, technology, and innovations.[25] Rarer still are formal declarations of the sanctity of private property rights.

Foreign observers are puzzled that Xi Jinping would purposely damage private companies and entrepreneurs such as Alibaba and Jack Ma, long considered China's crown jewels. There must be a compelling technocratic rationale, they reason—for example, to curb monopoly. Leaving aside the fact that Xi has left intact the biggest monopolies in the country, its SOEs, we are projecting our own views onto Chinese leaders. Chinese leaders may not view the private sector as a crown jewel. Just like that Shanghai official I interviewed, they have an entirely different take on how and why China has grown over the past forty years. They genuinely believe that China has grown because of their own design wisdom rather than because China has given space and freedom to entrepreneurs and the private sector. Some observers argue that by taking down the private sector, Xi is willing to incur a large economic cost in order to achieve a political end. We are again projecting. He may not believe that there is any economic cost to his actions.

One of CCP's costliest cognitive errors is its failure to appreciate the value of the private sector *to itself.* The crackdown on the private sector in 2021 and the previous underreported large-scale curtailment of the private sector since 2013 are detrimental to growth but also to the CCP's ability to rule. Tian Jiyun's proposal to establish a socialist special economic zone was an economic experiment; it is also a political experiment. Xi started his tenure with a dire warning about the fate of the Soviet Union, but his policies amount to preempting a Soviet-style collapse with a Brezhnev solution. If the CCP were to fumble, it would have only itself to blame.

## Biting the Helping Hand of Capitalism

In a famous paper, Timothy Frye and Andrei Shleifer made a distinction between a government with "helping hands," which helps businesses grow, and one with "grabbing hands," which extracts rent from businesses.[26] Let me turn this idea around and distinguish between the helping-hand capitalists and the grabbing-hand capitalists. Capitalists help a government make up for the inefficiencies of the state sector in multiple ways. They soak up the excess labor not absorbed by the state sector. Their tax contributions make up for the revenue shortfalls in the state sector. Their development projects elevate the value of land transactions, which enriches the state as the ultimate owner of the land assets as well as funds the ambitious industrial policy programs. And of course, on the side and under the table, they help the bottom line of individual officials by returning to them a portion of the rent allocation, the supply side of the corruption.

There is another kind of capitalist, though. These capitalists grab from the government. They want power-sharing, a seat at the table where policies are decided, a voice to compete with and contradict the official positions, and protection from an independent judiciary. In other words, they want to grab a piece of the political system from the state.

Overwhelmingly the Chinese capitalists are of a helping-hand variety rather than a grabbing-hand variety. Take Jack Ma, the founder of Alibaba and China's most visible entrepreneur. The fintech arm that he ran, Ant

Group, was a savior to the CCP. It supported economic growth, alleviating the mammoth drag of the state-owned banking system through its efficient matching of the demand and supply of credits and by funding the neglected small and medium enterprises, the backbone of the Chinese economy. And Jack Ma was no political rebel. The media reveal that he has been a member of the CCP since the 1980s.[27] The foreign press often singled out his criticism of the Chinese financial system, but far more interesting is how frequently Jack Ma has defended the CCP. In 2017, he mused that artificial intelligence and the big data revolution could make central planning more feasible, a surprising—and wrong—view for someone who had thrived because of the loosening of central planning.[28]

Academic research has not uncovered any evidence that the Chinese private sector is demanding political openness, or even wants it. Jiang Zemin's co-optation strategy was successful. Bruce Dickson writes that the CCP co-opted "entrepreneurs into the Party and encourag[ed] current Party members to go into business."[29] Private entrepreneurs achieved success by embedding themselves in the CCP network.[30] Crony capitalism delivered both economic and political dividends to the CCP. The Soviet Union collapsed because it did not have a GDP-growing and revenue-contributing private sector that was also politically compliant. The Chinese reformers embraced what Fyre and Shleifer prescribed—they offered a helping hand to the Chinese private sector (and a grabbing hand on the side) in exchange for taxation from a private sector that did not demand representation.

Some observers bought into the narrative that a strong private sector poses a threat to the CCP. But keep in mind that crony capitalism is a powerful mechanism for aligning the incentives of the private sector with the stability objective of the CCP. Chinese political stability is growth-intensive. The CCP's spending on domestic stability outstrips its spending on defense, and it pours a massive amount of financial resources and manpower into influencing, policing, and censoring social media.[31] The costs of zero-COVID measures—both actual and opportunity costs—are astronomical. China also spends liberally abroad in developing countries, using its hard power to make up for its deficits in soft power. "Republic of Government" industrial policy programs and technological ambitions are extraordinarily expensive, both because of the high costs of these undertakings and because of their exorbitant transaction costs in the form of corruption. (China's forays into the advanced semiconductor industry have been plagued by corruption.) China's dynamic private sector is the ultimate underwriter of all this largess of the Chinese state. In the final analysis, "It's the economy, stupid."

We need to distinguish between the CCP as a legal person and the CCP as a natural person. The upside of the private sector has accrued to the CCP as a legal person—tax revenue, job creation, and GDP growth that advances the careers of the members of the CCP. But it is a threat to the CCP as a natural person—the person at the top of the political hierarchy. The crony capitalists' cultivations of political ties, and their pre-IPO sweetheart deals with venture capital funds run by the powerful political families (one run by a son of Jiang Zemin), are viewed as an alarming threat to the power base of Xi Jinping.

By biting the hand that has done so much to shore up CCP rule, Xi may have undermined the institutional interests of the CCP. In a series of shocking moves in 2020 and 2021, he canceled the initial public offering of Ant Group just a few days before its scheduled debut, and the usually visible Jack Ma subsequently disappeared for months without a trace. Xi then cracked down on real estate, private educational services, the sharing economy, and gaming businesses.

But Xi's assault on the private sector has gone far beyond these high-profile moves. Nicholas Lardy at the Peterson Institute of International Economics, for example, points to a switch in the patterns of credit allocation immediately following the ascension of Xi Jinping.[32] In 2013, about 35 percent of bank credit destined for nonfinancial enterprises went to state companies and 57 percent to private companies. But in 2014, this was reversed: 60 percent went to the state sector and only 34 percent to the private sector. (Enterprises with foreign or mixed ownership accounted for the rest.) By 2016 the imbalance had become even more lopsided: 83 percent of credit was going to state-owned or state-controlled companies and just 11 percent to private firms. Many private firms have been nationalized or surrendered into the receivership of the state. China's private sector has been dealt a terrible blow.

## Technology and the Private Sector

Recall in Chapter 8 that Tencent and Alibaba rolled out China's health codes in the early days of the COVID-19 pandemic. They were not alone. Other private-sector companies deployed their "black technologies" in the pandemic response. Cambricon, one of China's most famous startups in microchips, used deep-learning techniques to aid medical diagnostics.

SenseTime and Megvii, known for their facial recognition technology, developed and deployed AI-based contactless temperature detection software. SenseTime's "Smart AI Epidemic Prevention Solution" integrated AI algorithms with infrared thermal technology. It detects a fever within 0.3-degree accuracy and identifies individuals with COVID-19 more than 99 percent of the time. In the health-codes rollout, private high-tech firms controlled the data and the capabilities used for cross-referencing and verification.

We may celebrate the Alipay Health Code as a public-private partnership for the greater good, but to Xi Jinping, the degree of private sovereignty of so much data and the analytical capabilities exhibited in the rapid rollout of the health code were alarming. It could be a notional threat—a threat to the psychology rather than the physicality of state control, but to someone who wants to control everything, threats can emanate from many quarters.

After Donald Trump was elected U.S. president, Jack Ma flew to meet with him to defuse tensions with the United States. He valiantly promised to create one million jobs in the United States if Trump would let go of his trade war against China. Desmund Shum, another businessman, describes his efforts to bring former European officials to China to improve their understanding of "a real China," the one that is prosperous and open, rather than the one portrayed in the Western media.[33] These private initiatives to help the CCP not only fell on unappreciative ears; they were reportedly interpreted as a sign that the CCP was losing control over its messaging. Rather than being grateful, the CCP became alarmed instead.

The CCP wants to seize controls over technology, but if what happened during the 2022 lockdown of Xian is any indication of how a technological project by the government will perform in the next pandemic, there are plenty of reasons to worry. In December 2021 and January 2022, Xian implemented a lockdown when cases of COVID-19 emerged in the city. PCR testing was mandatory, but the government's QR code crashed, multiple times, hampering the PCR tests from being administered. The IT products developed by the Chinese government are notoriously unreliable.

The history of China's industrial policy is littered with failures of technologies developed by state-owned enterprises. With fanfare, in 2014 the government unveiled Chinaso.com, the search engine it had developed at a tremendous cost.[34] If you have not heard of Chinaso.com, you are not alone. In 2021, the top six search engines in China accounted for 99.69 percent of the market share. Baidu by itself was 70.3 percent.[35] Chinaso.com is not one of those six search engines, and it is vying for a portion of the remaining 0.31 percent. To add insult to injury, Google, which is banned in China, commanded a market share of 2.57 percent.

China's technological success stories are overwhelmingly ones of the private sector. One of the undisputed success stories of China's high tech is Huawei, a Chinese telecommunication equipment company and a leading Chinese firm in 5G. A prevailing view is that Huawei was propped up by the Chinese government. This is true, but it is not the whole story. In the early 1990s, there were four major telecom equipment makers in China: Julong, Datang, ZTE, and Huawei. The two state-owned enterprises, Julong and Datang, were favored by the government and so were showered with subsidies and given privileged access to China's lucrative market. Huawei and ZTE, which was privatized from a state-owned enterprise, operated in the more free-market environment of Shenzhen. Huawei focused on the rural markets neglected by the state-owned enterprises and in foreign markets out of their reach. Today Huawei is a giant in the industry, followed by ZTE. Julong went bankrupt a long time ago and Datang is a miniscule player in the market.

First through IP piracy and then through its own innovations, Huawei has become a private-sector success story. Before Trump's trade war, in 2018, Huawei ranked fifth in the world on R&D spending, ahead of Intel and Apple. Yes, it has a tainted history, and the firm has itself admitted as much, but Huawei in recent years has evolved from an imitator to an innovator.[36] Government support is a part of the story, but it does not explain why it was Huawei, and to a lesser extent ZTE, that eventually claimed the mantle of technological leadership in 5G. Even with more support from the government, the SOEs failed. A tolerant business environment that nurtures private-sector startups has been a crucial factor in China's technological development.

## Unraveling Collaborations

Even the reformist Chinese leaders viewed the United States with suspicion, but they were more circumspect and conflicted. Not Xi. Xi has defined the threat from the United States in existential terms and has mobilized the entire Chinese society in an almost warlike movement against his perceived threats from the West. To tighten security, he has enacted policies and laws that completely eradicate any space between the state and the society and between the government and the private sector. His anti-private-sector policy will prevent future Huaweis from emerging and his escalation of tensions with the United States will damage a pillar of China's technological development—international collaborations.

Soon after he came into office, Xi enacted a raft of legislation aimed at tightening security. These laws blurred any distinction between a private and a public entity in terms of the rights of government and the obligations of citizens and organizations. They include the laws on Counterespionage (2014), National Security (2015), Counterterrorism (2015), Cybersecurity (2016), and Foreign NGO Management (2016), as well as the National Intelligence Law (2017). The language and the coverage of the National Intelligence Law, in particular, are sweeping, broad, and open-ended. According to a detailed analysis, the intelligence law "obliges individuals, organizations, and institutions to assist Public Security and State Security officials in carrying out a wide array of 'intelligence' work." It stipulates that "any organization or citizen shall support, assist, and cooperate with state intelligence work according to law." The intelligence agencies "may demand that concerned organs, organizations, or citizens provide needed support, assistance, and cooperation." They have "the right to enter otherwise restricted facilities, examine private records, investigate and question personnel, and access or even requisition communications or transport equipment owned by companies or individuals."[37]

This is the broader context in which Huawei now operates. Huawei is on the front line of the tensions in U.S.-China relations. Huawei claims that it could resist the entreaties from the Chinese state on the ground that it is privately owned, but this is no longer credible. The debate on the nature of Huawei's ownership is mostly academic, in the sense that policy practitioners use that word.[38] Huawei is private, but the ownership status of Huawei is only meaningful if the revenue rights of the firm overlap with its control rights to a substantial degree. Under Xi Jinping, however, that overlap has evaporated and Huawei's protestations that it is an employee-owned firm are technically correct but substantively immaterial.[39] There are no longer any boundaries between private revenue rights and the state's controlling rights.

Xi Jinping has helped to settle many long-standing academic debates about the boundary between the state and society—for the Chinese laws have legislated that boundary out of existence. Xi has resolved the uncertainty decisively in favor of those foreign-policy hawks in the United

States who portray the threat from China as "whole-of-society." All the nuances and ambiguities are gone, clarifying the following to the United States: "Feel free to do business with us but please know we have the right to your data," furnishing a justification to the rest of the world why they should decouple from China.

U.S. policymakers acted on cue and are determined to decouple from China-based technologies. In May 2019, the U.S. Department of Commerce put Huawei on its entity list, meaning that the only way U.S. firms can supply to Huawei is with a waiver. The entity list also prohibits firms in a third-party country from supplying to Huawei if they have commercial relationships with U.S. firms. In 2020, the United Kingdom decided to bar Huawei equipment from its wireless networks. So did countries like Australia, Sweden, Norway, Denmark, Belgium, France, and Estonia.[40] In 2021, India did not select Huawei in its 5G trials, clouding Huawei's future in that country. Such sanctions have severely damaged the company. Huawei's overseas shipments of handsets dropped by 42 percent in 2020 and in China it is also losing market share to its domestic rivals.

These effects are entirely foreseeable. Huawei has succeeded in the same manner as many entrepreneurial high-tech companies elsewhere— by forging close collaborations with the most advanced companies in the world. Huawei had over 130 suppliers from the United States and its highly rated triple-lens camera was developed in collaboration with the German company Leica.[41] It sourced two-thirds of its software and vital chips for its smartphones and 5G from the United States and United Kingdom, and it relied on Google's operating system and the microprocessors supplied by ARM, a UK firm. One effect of the U.S. moves against Huawei is that the company has been pushed to rely increasingly on China's domestic market. In 2016, domestic sales were about 45 percent of Huawei's sales; by 2020, that figure rose to 65 percent. Huawei now operates in a homogenous domestic environment, forsaking a key factor for its success— diversity of global competition and synergistic collaborations.

China's hostile foreign-policy postures toward its own closest economic and technological partners have inflicted irreparable damage on the complex web of networks that Chinese high-tech firms and research institutions took decades to build and cultivate. The Chinese scientists generated high-impact research through international collaborations. According to the National Science Foundation, in 1995, coauthored papers between Chinese and American scientists accounted for 38.1 percent of the China-world coauthored papers; by 2010 this proportion rose to 45 percent. For the American scientists, the share of their Chinese coauthored papers rose from 3 percent to 13 percent of U.S.-world co-authored papers.[42]

In AI, a field in which Eric Schmidt describes China as "a full-spectrum competitor," the Chinese advances are built on international collaborations. According to Tsinghua University, 60 percent of the papers on AI were coauthored with American scientists, easily eclipsing coauthorship with scholars from Singapore (7.8 percent), Australia (7.3 percent), England (5.8 percent), and Canada (5.8 percent).[43] One might try to use this data to argue that the U.S. researchers in AI depend on collaborations with Chinese researchers, not the other way around. According to a report by Tsinghua. the United States has six times the number of top scholars in AI as China does. The research capabilities are lopsided in favor of the United States.

There are many collaborative and complementary dimensions that are less obvious but are equally and mutually beneficial to China and the United States. For example, the R&D expenditures of the United States are more heavily weighted toward basic research than Chinese R&D expenditures, which are oriented toward applications and experimentation. Furthermore, the U.S. R&D expenditures are more concentrated in a few disciplines; the Chinese R&D expenditures are more distributed. (U.S. R&D expenditures are overweighted toward the life sciences, whereas the Chinese spend more on hard technologies.) These structural differences have created opportunities for fruitful collaborations. On economic grounds, the argument for synergy and complementarity is impeccable.

The decoupling is a lose-lose proposition, and it damages the United States as well as China. Before Trump's trade war, according to a 2018 report by the Jefferies Investment Bank, China generated between US$100 billion and US$150 billion in revenue to the U.S. technology companies.[44] The decoupling reduced these revenue flows.

Which side will lose more in the long run from a high-tech decoupling between China and the United States? There are two ways to approach this question. One is to distinguish between a financial hit and a technological hit. In industries such as semiconductors, the damage to the U.S. companies is mainly financial, whereas that to China is technological. There are more suppliers of finance than suppliers of critical and leading-edge technology and a more active stance of the U.S. government in technology may spawn more resources and make up for some of the revenue losses from China. Technological risks are less diversifiable. In semiconductors, for example, one or two firms control the entire supply chain of critical components. ASML, a Dutch firm, is the only firm in the world capable of making the most advanced lithography equipment. NVIDIA of the United States dominates the market for graphics cards, and all specialty chemicals used in semiconductor manufacture are made by Japanese firms.

Second, how one predicts China's future technological trajectory depends on how one explains the rise of China as a technological power. The research reports by the China Strategy Group and by Harvard's Kennedy School of Government, cited earlier, lean heavily toward scale as an explanation.[45] International collaborations are not viewed as a primary factor in these reports; instead they make linear projections based on the willingness of the Chinese to outspend the United States, and on the Chinese organizational and integration capacities.

In this regard, it is worth noting how Chinese researchers—none cited by the aforementioned reports produced by American researchers—present a very different perspective. The report by Tsinghua University on AI lists 185 top AI scholars at Google, 91 at Microsoft, and 59 at Facebook. Despite the vaulted valuation of SenseTime and the fintech of AliPay, not a single Chinese firm is listed as having any top AI scholar. The lone Chinese institution listed is Tsinghua University, with 27 top AI scientists. A report by a group at Peking University is more pointed on the implications of a technological decoupling for China: "in both technological and industrial development, both China and the United States face damages from 'decoupling,' but based on current information the damages to China are probably greater."[46]

## *The Rising East?*

In 2021, Xi Jinping proclaimed his assessment of the post-pandemic global order: "the East is rising and the West is declining." That was the year in which Xi's CCP celebrated the centennial of the CCP's founding and concluded that it had successfully brought COVID-19 under control. The political tumult in the United States after the 2020 presidential election and its high death toll from COVID-19 had emboldened the Chinese leader to proclaim and project his exuberant triumphalism.

He acted accordingly. In the second half of 2021, Xi launched a series of high-profile crackdowns on private companies. The economy responded swiftly and slowed down in the second half of 2021.[47] In 2022, further dragged down by the zero-COVID policy, the Chinese economy slowed down to its lowest level since the early 1990s.

Bill Emmott, a former editor-in-chief of the *Economist*, once observed that Japan began to commit more policy mistakes when it became arrogant about its economic success.[48] One wonders if the "rising East" narrative may turn out to be that hubris moment for China. The ability to bring COVID-19 under control in 2020 owed a lot to an ancient source of Chinese strength—the regime's ability to control population movements. Fundamentally, this state capacity is rooted in the backwardness and marginalization of civil society. During antiquity, states excelled at it in ways that are difficult for modern states to replicate. In "To Take on the Coronavirus, Go Medieval on It," Donald G. McNeil Jr. wrote that the United States successfully enforced a national quarantine in 1892 to keep a raging cholera outbreak from Hamburg off its shores.[49] Communist Cuba forcibly quarantined HIV patients in the 1980s and incurred a lower AIDS mortality rate than New York as a result. And during the Spanish flu of 1918–1919, the Chinese mortality rate was 1.3 per thousand compared with 2.5 percent or more in other areas of the world.[50]

Cuba in the 1980s was not an example of advanced institutions, science, or technology; nor was China at the time of the Spanish flu. China then was so weak that at the Versailles Peace Conference, Shandong, a Chinese province formerly held by Germany, was transferred to Japan rather than back to China. The relevant state capacity here is controlling the movement of a population, a capability that China's first dynasty, the Qin, already possessed in abundance. The first emperor relocated 120,000 families close to the capital and put them under surveillance. China's population control is a showcase of China's early evolution out of a tribal society.[51] Yes, the CCP could draw legitimate pride from its initial pandemic controls, especially its ability to use its administrative capacity to scale the health code, but resting a triumphant assertion of a rising East on a primitive method of population control is factually tenuous and conceptually problematic. Maybe an adage from Zhou Enlai on the French Revolution is apropos here: "It is too early to tell." Or to act on.

## Political and Economic Risks

China appears poised to enter into its most uncertain and complex period since 1978 and possibly since 1949. Uncertainties abound on the economic front—bad debt, unfavorable demographics, low productivity growth, an economic slowdown, and a middle-income trap. In the opinion of George Magnus, "Xi's China is in jeopardy."[52] Magnus's risk factors are relatively long-term, and Chinese leaders and the population have time to adjust their expectations. More worrisome is a prospect of economic and political risks converging with each other.

As Xi intensifies his lock on his third term with all the attendant political complications, the Chinese economy has been rocked by economic turbulence. In August 2021, half a trillion dollars of value was wiped out from Chinese and Hong Kong stock markets in one week, with a steep fall in the value of Chinese real estate likely to happen next.[53] These events will hit the net worth of the urban middle class hard, and so too the revenue flows to local governments. Many of the mega projects, including CCP's ambitious industrial policy initiatives, are funded by the proceeds from land sales. The CCP, then, may find itself in an unenviable position of budgetary retrenchment. Several local governments have already experienced steep revenue falls and announced pay cuts to their civil servants.

An autocracy struggles with two kinds of instabilities. One is an intra-elite instability—where elites fight with each other for power, resources, and graft. The other is inter-elite instability, which arises from popular rebellions against elites. In the past, a prosperous economy enabled the CCP to grow itself out of these two types of instabilities. A bigger economic pie palliates labor, capital, and the state and alleviates distributional conflicts. China's distributional tensions have been manageable, even with the country's extraordinarily high score on the Gini index, a measure of income inequality.

A few years ago, Martin Whyte debunked the notion that China was on the cusp of a social volcano of unrests and instabilities because of the widening income gap between the rich and the poor.[54] His survey data show that Chinese respondents have a higher tolerance for income inequality than many scholars assumed. But it is important to note the larger context of his findings. His book was published in 2010 and based on data from an earlier time, when economic growth was still robust. The social volcano did not erupt because the effect of the absolute income gains bested the effect of the relative income losses.

Absolute income gains are critical to political stability. A smaller economic pie, resulting from an economic downturn, increases distributional conflicts both among elites and between elites and non-elites. These conflicts are difficult to manage in any circumstance, but are even more fraught when politics is less rule-based, power struggles are more intense, information to decision makers is more distorted, and an unbridled autocrat is overly confident. The single biggest threat to Xi's stewardship of his third term is a mishandling of the economy and the associated political ramifications of an economic slowdown.

An economic downturn can also make the Chinese state more predatory, which creates social antagonism. The political dynamics among three actors of the economy—the state, the capitalists, and the household—are very different under an expanding economy as opposed to under a shrinking economy. The primary claimant to income is the household sector. During the reform era, the labor share of income declined, but that decline was politically and psychologically palatable since there were still absolute income gains. The secondary claimants to income are the state, through taxation, and capitalists, through retention of profit. Historically, both have reaped an outsized benefit through rapid income gains and through shifting income distribution in their favor.

Now imagine a shrinking economy. In that scenario, the only way to appease the household sector—so that it remains politically pliable—is to engineer an income shift in its favor. The option of an absolute income gain is no longer available. The state can reduce taxes, but the Chinese state is astonishingly unwilling to give up its income claims. Capitalists become vulnerable in this scenario. Xi Jinping's method of assuring a common prosperity through shaming Chinese capitalists, and through a tertiary income redistribution funded by massive charity donations, is exactly this predatory tactic. According to press reports, Tencent, a high-tech firm, agreed to donate US$15 billion to social aid when the Chinese government stepped up its scrutiny of the company.[55] Other high-tech firms, like Alibaba, Pinduoduo, JD, and Meituan, have made similar pledges.

As sizable as these donations are, they are more optics than substance. In a country of 1.4 billion people, they do not come close to offsetting the lost income gains from economic slowdowns. Unless there was a coincidental rise of conscience among Chinese high-tech billionaires, the simultaneity of their charity pledges indicates coercion in the background. A coerced redistribution undermines private incentives and wealth accumulation not only by the ultra-rich, but also by China's middle-class shareholders. The large donation pledges made by Alibaba, Tencent, and other high-tech firms drew from company funds, that is, investors' money, not from the wealth of individual entrepreneurs. Not surprisingly, the announcements of these donations were followed by declines of stock prices, which in turn led to layoffs in the high-tech sector, undermining the income positions of the Chinese professional labor force.

## The Return of Tullock's Curse

The ultimate badge of honor for a Communist autocrat is a natural death on the job. Joseph Stalin, Mao Zedong, Leonid Brezhnev, the two Kims of North Korea, and Fidel Castro of Cuba are the fortunate ones, even as their citizens bore a heavy price in the form of repressions and poverty. The alternatives are all unpleasant: execution in the case of Nicolae Ceaușescu, being deposed in the cases of Nikita Khrushchev and Hua Guofeng, and unceremonious dismissals of Hu Yaobang and Zhao Ziyang.

In 2002 and 2012, China accomplished a remarkable and rare feat for a Communist country: two peaceful transitions of power in a row. Today, however, there is no framework in place to guide the transfer of power in the future and there is no successor in sight. The CCP has now entered unchartered territory without a succession plan or the legitimating power of a charismatic leader. Will Tullock's curse raise its ugly head once again? We cannot rule it out. In Chapter 6, I explained that the proscriptive features of term limits worked in conjunction with "gentle politics" to contain the risks of the succession failures and to reduce their incidence. By eliminating term limits and escalating power struggles, Xi has unleashed the genie that Deng Xiaoping had put in the bottle—Tullock's curse.

The case of Sun Zhengcai may be a preview of succession storms to come. In 2018, Sun received a life prison sentence for the ostensible crime of taking US$26 million in bribes. Maybe corruption was involved, but the official pronouncement on his case put politics front and center: he was singled out for being ineffective in rooting out the residual influences of Bo Xilai, a rival to Xi in the run-up to the power transition in 2012. Sun, however, is one successor removed from Bo. Linking the two tenuously together is either a sign of a "deep state" or reflects the extent of paranoia about succession dynamics.

The timing of the Sun affair is closely tied to succession. He was taken down in 2017, one year prior to Xi's removal of the term limits. This sequence suggests a coordinated and calculated move to first eliminate a potential successor and then remove the constitutional constraint on a third term. Sun was singled out because of his heir natural status. At the age of fifty-four, he was "one of only two next-generation leaders on the party's Politburo" and "was at least tentatively earmarked to succeed President Xi Jinping or Premier Li Keqiang at the 20th National Congress in 2022." Sun's youth rendered him a potential threat.[56] A statement by the Central Commission for Discipline Inspection (CCDI) in September 2018 cites Sun's calling himself "China's youngest political figure" as evidence that he attempted to undermine the unity of CCP leadership.[57] Tullock's curse has just announced its arrival.

Another stabilizing factor is absent in China today—the charisma of leaders. The ability of the CCP to contain the spillover effects of past succession failures owed much to the sheer force of personality that Mao and Deng symbolized. Has Xi Jinping attained the prestige of a Deng or a Mao? Unlikely. One clue is the moniker he has acquired: chairman of everything. His authority exclusively rests on "legal authority," one of the three sources of power in the conception of Max Weber. The other two are charisma and tradition.[58] In the CCP-type of system, charisma and legal authority are partial substitutes for each other. Mao easily removed two consecutive defense ministers not because he ran the Chinese military on a daily basis (as Xi does today), but because of his prestige. In 1992, Deng renewed economic reforms from his perch as the honorary chairman of the China Bridge Association. All he had was charisma.

By the ubiquity of Xi's portraits in public places, we can say that Xi has succeeded in establishing a form of a personality cult, but Hua Guofeng had that too (and his calligraphy). The question is whether Xi's personality cult denotes real legitimacy and power. That is harder to know. On any objective grounds, the achievements of Mao and Deng—defeating the Nationalists, establishing the PRC, and putting China on track to be the second largest GDP in the world—are a high bar. Even Mao's prestige did not give him unlimited power. It ensured the ascension of Hua Guofeng, but not Hua's political viability. The very fact that Xi has been so eager to accumulate titles is proof that he does not perceive himself as a charismatic leader. Charisma is intangible, fungible, and axiomatically legitimate—in other words, something that formal titles could never confer on their own.

Historically, the CCP's succession conflicts have not escalated to a systemic crisis. The question is whether China will be lucky again next time. Will a future succession conflict spill over into the broader political arena?

Two factors are crucial. One is whether China's military and security apparatus will intervene in a future succession conflict. This is the darkest corner of the black box of Chinese politics, and it is hardest to predict. The CCP has been mercifully spared unconstitutional seizures of power and military coups due to a combination of factors, including the prestige of individual leaders, the institutional norm of civilian primacy, and the largesse conferred on the military.

Xi, however, does not take the "coup-proofing" feature of the Chinese military system for granted. During his first term, he purged six high-level officials for political reasons, according to Susan Shirk.[59] Shirk, quoting a specialist on the Chinese military, states, "No other Chinese Communist Party Leader, not even Mao Zedong, has controlled the military to the same extent as Xi does today." He, not the generals, runs the PLA on a day-to-day basis, and he has taken over control of the Chinese paramilitary police.

Xi has also targeted China's security apparatus. He opened his anti-corruption campaign by bringing down Zhou Yongkang, then followed up with serial purges of four vice ministers of public security between 2013 and 2021. One of these vice ministers, Fu Zhenghua, was expelled from the CCP for his "inflated political ambitions" and for "carrying firearms," an ominous combination of charges.[60] Fu had been promoted under Xi's own watch, and had gone to extraordinary lengths to demonstrate his allegiance to Xi. On July 9, 2015, Fu supervised mass arrests of hundreds of rights lawyers and civil society activists, an early sign of Xi's hardline stance. Even so, Xi targeted him. In November 2021, Xi suddenly elevated Wang Xiaohong to party secretary of the Ministry of Public Security, sidelining the much more senior Zhao Kezhi, the minister. Wang worked under Xi in the 1980s when Xi was a local official in Fujian. It seems that Xi's circle of trust is getting tighter and cliquish, a sign of distrust and insecurity. This is not a comforting thought.

The other factor involves a combination of contextual factors and succession conflicts. The most salient factor here is a slowdown in economic growth, whether induced by bad policies or by mismanagement of COVID-19. The economic context sets the Xi Jinping era sharply apart from the previous ones. Deng Xiaoping unwound the succession arrangements for Hu Yaobang and Zhao Ziyang at a time when the growth potentials of the Chinese economy were substantial and China was continuing with aggressive economic reforms. Today, the economic landscape is far less benign.

A secular slowdown of the Chinese economy, compounded by the self-inflicted wounds to Chinese economic productivity, will increase distributional conflicts. A sudden stop of Chinese growth is more politically damaging and psychologically unnerving. In the near term, the biggest economic risk factor is the zero-COVID strategy of the CCP. The conservative estimate by Professor Michael Song of Chinese University of Hong Kong puts the complete lockdown of Shanghai alone as costing China 4 percent in lost GDP. The worst-case scenario would be a lockdown of all cities for one month, which would lead to an estimated 53 percent loss in GDP.[61]

One of the CCP's biggest mistakes was wasting the two-year window of opportunity in 2020 and 2021 to beef up its hospital capacity and general healthcare, and to vaccinate its population with the effective Pfizer and Moderna vaccines after the vaccines became available. At some point, the CCP has to decide whether to persist in its economically damaging and socially antagonistic lockdown strategy or to accept a high death toll that is likely to occur once the transmission of the Omicron variant is not contained by the lockdown. Contingencies such as this could spill over into the inner politics as the CCP wrestles with economic slowdowns, global tensions, and succession issues while Xi navigates his third term.

While worries about unrest and words like "social volcano" pepper the discourse on China, we should bear in mind that barring extraordinary events and developments, the Chinese system gravitates toward stability rather than to sudden convulsions, ceteris paribus. Axiomatic legitimacy and psychological compliance help the CCP steady itself.

Have the reign of Xi and his policy hubris upended that ceteris paribus condition? The privations of the Great Leap Forward victimized China's rural masses, who were kept isolated from each other and who did not have real-time knowledge of the toll of the unfolding disaster. In this regard, the zero-COVID policy is a game changer. The extreme lockdown of Shanghai was inflicted on a vibrant, educated, well-connected urban population, and the collateral damage to the economy is being felt in real time. The ghastly fire in a high-rise in Ürümqi of Xinjiang galvanized the protests in November 2022 by triggering a sense of empathy and resonance across the nation. The affluent Shanghainese, who normally have very little in common with those in Ürümqi, live in similar high-rises themselves. Their fire exits, just as in Ürümqi, were padlocked per the lockdown order. Chinese society lacks a tradition of collective action, but Xi just provided it. The two types of instabilities, intra- and inter-elite, may intersect with each other more frequently than before.

Ignore heterogeneity at your own peril. This is a critical lesson from the Dazexiang Uprising and a lesson that Xi has ignored. He is imposing homogeneity on a Chinese society and economy that are far more complex and diverse than they were during the Mao and Deng eras. Contradictions and dissensions are rising. Term limits, a mechanism on which Xi relied in 2012, no longer exist. Under Xi Jinping, political rivalries have again become "nasty, brutish, and short." These developments do not bode well for the ability of the CCP to deal with contingencies and crises in the future.

A big test is whether the institutional and civilian controls over the Chinese military and security apparatus will remain as strong as they have been. We have very few reliable insights on this issue. The stability of the CCP thus far has depended on multiple conditions reinforcing one another in ways that we cannot fully isolate or disentangle to pinpoint one single determinant. History is conjunctional and is seldom made by one isolated development. While the risks of Tullock's curse have become more pronounced, whether these succession risks will translate into wider systemic risks is difficult to say, and we may never find out until the moment that they materialize.

Barry Naughton's *Growing Out of the Plan* is perceptive.[62] Growth has enabled the CCP to solve so many seemingly intractable problems, including political stability, distributional conflicts, and the simultaneous appeasement of the masses, civil servants, and capitalists. After forty years of robust growth, a moderation of the growth rate is neither surprising nor alarming on its own, but it does raise the question of whether the existing political arrangements can withstand this change. Political complexities may have to be resolved directly and on their own accord, by political institutions and policies, rather than intermediated through economic growth. Change—of whatever stripe or direction—may emerge as a gathering theme in the next stage of Chinese politics. My EAST framework has emphasized persistence as the defining feature of China; now let's ask, "Can China break out of its EAST model?"

# CHAPTER TEN

# Breaking Out of the EAST Model?

*Official:* Why do you want to immigrate to the United States? Doesn't our government pay you a high salary?

*Citizen:* Yes.

*Official:* Doesn't our government protect your safety?

*Citizen:* Yes.

*Official:* Doesn't our GDP grow very fast?

*Citizen:* Yes.

*Official (exasperated):* Then why do you want to immigrate to the United States?

*Citizen:* I want to go somewhere I can say "No" sometimes.

—CHINESE JOKE

JUST BEFORE THE LUNAR New Year, traditionally the busiest travel time for Chinese families, the authorities issued a lockdown order and shut down many crucial transportation routes. The fear was that a deadly pneumonic disease was lurking silently among the Chinese population. School buildings were converted into hospitals, and in a stark contravention of Chinese tradition, the government took over the burial of those who had died from the disease. Troops were dispatched to enforce the lockdown order, and new government apparatuses were created to coordinate various measures.

Is this a description of the famous lockdown of Wuhan, a city of 11 million people, to contain the outbreak of COVID-19 on January 23, 2020? (And a few days later, of Hubei province, with a population of 59 million?) Actually, this is a description of January 1911, when the Qing dynasty government mounted a ferocious battle against the "great plague of northeastern China." Like COVID-19, this pneumonic plague was a zoonotic disease and it had a high transmissibility rate, spreading rapidly throughout much of China's northeastern corner.[1]

The Qing court soon brought the contagion under control. The quarantine worked. It also worked in China in 2020. The COVID infection curve began to flatten three weeks after the Wuhan lockdown. On February 13, 2020, daily infections peaked at 15,141 new cases, then dropped precipitously, to 2,538 on February 15 and below a thousand after February 19.[2] Until the arrival of the Omicron variant in March 2022, the low infection rates in China stood in sharp contrast with the policy disarray and high death tolls in the United States.

Let's give credit where credit is due. In 2020, the Chinese Communist Party performed well in terms of lives saved and an economic downturn averted. The CCP, however, elevates this performance to a meta point about the overall superiority of its system. In a 2021 white paper portraying itself as an effective and responsive government, the CCP claims that its record on controlling COVID-19 is evidence of the superiority of the CCP system.[3] That, as Monty Python would put it, is something completely different.

To make the claim of CCP's superiority requires answering a counterfactual question: "What would have happened if China had a more open political system that protected free flows of information and speech?" A rejoinder to the CCP's claim is that its mitigation was achieved at the expense of an early detection of the virus outbreak. Early detection requires free information flows and professional and non-political surveillance of virus outbreaks. The CCP fumbled badly in this task, and its failure in early detection permitted the virus to reach an exponential phase of transmission—which only then activated the strong suit of the CCP's mitigation measures. In declaring triumph, the CCP conveniently skipped this important part of the story.

We need to tell this broader truth: the CCP excels at solving problems, but these problems are often created by itself. A good system solves problems; an even better system excels at not creating problems, and at preventing problems from spiraling in the first place. In terms of the first criterion, the Chinese system has excelled; in terms of the second criterion, the Chinese system has failed, and it has failed repeatedly. In this chapter, I will take stock of the strengths and weaknesses of the CCP system. This accounting exercise does not support the simplistic claim of the CCP. The best it can claim is a draw in the grand scheme of things: its accomplishments are either wholly or partially offset by its failures. This verdict does not amount to a condemnation of its system, but it is hardly a validation of its superiority. There is, to put it mildly, much room for improvement.

The question is how. Let me propose the following way to think about this issue: any flexibilities in that system are a welcome development. Left to its own devices, ever since the Sui dynasty, the Chinese system instinctually inclines toward political singularity and a monopoly of power and ideas. Any policy moves that can make Chinese autocracy a bit more frictional constitute progress. Polarizations of any stripes, whether conservative or reformist, help nudge China toward more space and more, in the language of this book, autocratic scope.

The United States has not been a bystander when it comes to Chinese politics. Until the Trump administration, the United States pursued an engagement policy toward China. By the criterion of seeding incremental changes in China, the engagement policy failed. Let me begin with an assessment there.

## U.S. Engagement Meets Autocratic Persistence

China has a powerful autocratic lineage. After more than a millennium of imprinting and entrenchment of the cognitive methodology and values based on *Keju*, a path dependency rooted in the autocracy way of government is neither unusual nor unnatural. As a factual statement, Chinese history is stacked against democracy. Survey research shows that nearly half of those who oppose China's current system also reject multi-party democracy.[4] Many of the self-avowed Chinese liberals fit into this category. Maybe the anchoring effect of history is too overwhelming.

A realistic vision for a future China is not likely to be a liberal democracy crafted in the Western image, at least not within a reasonable time frame. China has defied the democratic pulls of economic development and geography. The East Asian region is vibrantly democratic, and South Korea and Taiwan began their regime transitions at an income level not much higher than that of China today. China and North Korea are striking exceptions to this East Asian pattern. The "third wave" of democratization did not reach Chinese shores.

North Korea is easy to explain. Its economy and politics are stuck in a backward equilibrium of the medieval age, a situation in which there is no identifiable first mover of change. China is a different story altogether. It has all the cognitive capabilities due to its high literacy rates; it has registered rapid growth; it has created a massive middle class; and it has globalized its economy. Yet China has stubbornly refused to join the global trend toward democracy. The sobering reality is that as its per capita GDP trends toward that of South Korea, its political system is inching closer to that of North Korea.

Since the sixth century, deviations from China's authoritarian path have been few and far between. During the PRC period, China experienced a brief liberal interlude in the 1980s but under Xi Jinping, the country has retrogressed beyond recognition. The working relationship that reformist leaders carefully crafted with the West has all but collapsed. The Taiwan issue, which Deng Xiaoping set aside wisely in deference to economic priorities, is now threatening to unravel the peace and stability of East Asia. For all practical purposes, Hong Kong is just another Chinese city now. Within China, the CCP has reasserted its power and has eradicated the autonomous residues of NGOs, lawyers, social media, universities, and the private sector. To say that China has returned to the Maoist era is an understatement. Mao never had to rein in as many heterogenous forces as Xi has done.

The United States, and the West in general, has invested heavily in a democratic scenario for China through a policy of "engagement." This policy is based on a variant of what is known as modernization theory. The idea dates back to Martin Lipset, a Stanford sociologist, and can be summed up as "the level of economic development drives the creation and consolidation of democracy."[5] Partially based on this theory and partially based on the experience of the rest of East Asia, many in the West believed that economic development, marketization, a rising middle class, and globalization would eventually bring democracy to China. It has not worked out that way.

What went wrong? One reason is that the marketization of China was exaggerated. It is not uncommon to find in economics papers and the business press the claim that the Chinese economy was fully market driven, even more so than the U.S. economy. A 2004 article in the *Wall Street Journal* reported the views of a number of Nobel laureates in economics on the quality of the Chinese economy.[6] The views ranged from "a tie between Norway and the United States—with China the runner-up" to "grudging respect." As I noted earlier, China reversed rural reforms in the 1990s and has substituted—rather than augmented—its domestic reforms with external reforms. I myself have never believed in these exuberant claims about Chinese reforms and have used data and detailed archival research to show that these claims are false.[7]

A bigger problem is that our understanding of modernization, at least in the foreign policy context, is too simplistic. A crude version of the modernization theory centers on one variable—per capita GDP—while more sophisticated versions stress other related or derived variables such as technology, marketization, the middle class, and the private economy. Their common failing is treating politics as purely endogenous of economic and technological forces. Recall the claim that literacy, printing, and gunpowder unleashed political changes in Europe. I call claims such as these the "political endogeneity" school.

The evidence marshaled in this book suggests an opposite causal order. Instead of political change flowing causally from the mechanics of economics and technology, the reverse is true. The political and ideological homogeneity after the sixth century altered China's technological trajectory, and under the CCP, strong political commitments along with an expansion of scope conditions advanced technology and economic growth. Technology itself does not produce a liberalizing effect. The peak of the Chinese inventiveness of the Han-Sui Interregnum was followed by more than a millennium of autocracy. China today, a technological and economic power in its own right, is hardly trending democratic.

The experience of the East Asian Tigers has often been cited as evidence of political endogeneity.[8] A deeper immersion into their history, I believe, would have uncovered the fallacy of this supposition. South Korea and Taiwan transitioned to democracy with a crucial preexisting condition that is missing in China today: political, institutional, and societal flexibilities that enabled a degree of individual agency and autonomy. Human agency, with all of its foibles and uncertainties, was a vital attending factor in the political transitions of East Asia. Another difference is that the United States bundled commercial and political engagements together in its policy approach toward South Korea and Taiwan, in contrast to the aloofly economic nature of U.S.-China relations.

Another way to illustrate that economics alone did not make East Asia democratic is to draw a distinction between the demand side of democracy and the supply side of democracy. The rising middle class, an expanding private sector, and globalization work on the demand side. They bring about awareness of rights, raise expectations for the future, and cultivate individual values. But to translate these into political changes requires a mechanism to voice and activate these demands. In the 1980s South Korea and Taiwan had such a mechanism—though it was restricted to be sure—whereas China today does not. The supply-side condition is missing in China.

A fundamental error of the U.S. approach is a failure to recognize this distinction between these demand-side and supply-side conditions for democracy. U.S. administrations have assumed that demand-side conditions would, on their own, translate into democracy. A 2000 speech by President Clinton illustrates this thinking. He gave an example of a local election in China and portrayed that local election as a response to the increasing employment freedom of the Chinese people in the age of globalization.[9]

Little did he know that rural elections were held in China in the 1980s long before Chinese economy was opened to trade and foreign investments. Clinton appeared unaware that by 2000 these local elections were more restricted than the ones held in the 1980s, in a broader trend of autocratic reversion after Tiananmen. Yes, the village heads were elected, but the real village leaders were the party secretaries appointed from the top. (This brings up another topic. Despite legions of China scholars in U.S. academia who know the country really well, very few of them are ever consulted by U.S. policymakers. It takes some effort to maintain this level of ignorance about China.) Operating on wrong facts and an erroneous premise, the U.S. policy toward China never even attempted to incorporate the supply-side dynamics into policy deliberations.

The U.S. engagement policy was overly grandiose in its goals. The goals should have been bite-size changes and incremental flexibilities in the Chinese system, nudging China not to become the South Korea of today but rather the South Korea of the 1980s. These nudges are not overly political and are well within the reciprocal gives and takes in bilateral negotiations, amenable to interventions through the normal tools of economic engagements. The United States did exactly the opposite. It talked up the grandiose goals of democracy and human rights while failing to press for tangible, incremental milestones of progress.

## Political Endogeneity

Market economics is often touted as an agent of political change. So is technology. On June 20, 1989, the *New York Times* reported, in a piece titled "China's Fax Invasion," that Chinese students outside of China faxed into the country "a steady flow of uncensored news about the tumult in Tiananmen Square and world reactions to it."[10] A year later, the newspaper recounted this episode of fax invasion, this time with the title, "Faxing Democracy."[11] Yet not only did fax machines fail to fax democracy into China, they did not even fax Tiananmen into China. Today, many young Chinese have no memory of the Tiananmen demonstrations.

In 1989, the technology du jour was the fax machine; in the twenty-first century, it was the internet that would supposedly set Chinese minds free. In his 2000 speech, Bill Clinton chuckled at the notion that China could control the internet. He compared internet controls to "nailing Jell-O to the wall" and wished "good luck" to the Chinese leaders, a comment that elicited knowing laughter from his audience at the School of Advanced International Studies of Johns Hopkins University. Well, the Chinese did nail Jell-O to the wall, via the "Great Firewall." The Chinese regime has used advanced tools and deployed manpower to censor and scrub critical posts, and to propagate social media with official lines.[12]

Forget about weakening the CCP system. When given the opportunity to search for political information through VPN, young Chinese choose not to do it.[13] Worldwide, authoritarian regimes are eager to embrace technology, and are apparently unfazed by its alleged innate liberal bias. They instead tailor surveillance technologies in order to better execute their Orwellian agenda. Digital autocracy puts the KGB and Stasi to shame. Technology may not have flattened the world for everyone, but it has flattened the world for the autocrats.[14]

The *New York Times* piece on the so-called fax invasion hints at what truly drives political change. According to the article, "from Hong Kong comes word that in China, police and security officers have been posted at all fax machines." This is a crucial—if incidental—insight from that article. The political effects of technology are mediated by human beings, who can move society in a liberal or in an illiberal direction. In 1989, the central government issued instructions via the same fax technology to local governments, ordering them to put down protests in their regions.

Karl Marx opined that "gunpowder, the compass, and the printing press were the three great inventions which ushered in bourgeois society. Gunpowder blew up the knightly class, the compass discovered the world market and founded the colonies, and the printing press was the instrument of Protestantism and the regeneration of science in general; the most powerful lever for creating the intellectual prerequisites."[15] Marx may very well be right about this in the European context, but not as a general proposition. The error is especially pronounced in this case, since Marx was aware that the Chinese invented these three technologies and he knew that the bourgeoisie was conspicuously absent in imperial China. He coined the concept of "the Asiatic mode of production" to mean the absence of private ownership and a primitive agrarian economy. (By contrast, Francis Bacon made a similar claim about the magical power of these three inventions, but he was referring only to their technical prowess, and he was unaware of their Chinese provenance.) Ancient China led the rest of the world in inventions, but it was Europe during the post-Roman era that pioneered economic growth and democracy. Today's China, the land of quantum communications, hypersonic missiles, a moon landing, and WeChat, directly contradicts the idea of political endogeneity.

That technology instigates profound social and political changes is a fallacy, "a technological fallacy," in the words of Mark Kurlansky.[16] By itself, technology does not change society or politics. Technology may change the method of politics, and it may be used to reinforce the political status quo rather than disrupt it. Literacy and the inventions of paper, printing, gunpowder, and the compass induced transformational changes in Europe, but only because with its fragmentations and fierce competitions, Europe was already primed for such transformations. On the other side of the globe, the thin politics of imperial China thwarted these conjunctural dynamics, in the end stalling technological advances and sending the country into a long period of stasis. The CCP autocracy today takes great pains to inoculate its politics against economic and technological forces and has largely succeeded in heading off political change.

### Incipient Flexibilities

Japan, Taiwan, and South Korea are not only educated, industrialized, and rich; they are also vibrantly democratic, completing the WEIRD checklist—minus the W—drawn up by Joseph Henrich.[17] Singapore, too, is gradually trending democratic. (And Hong Kong no doubt would be a democracy without Chinese intervention.)

All of these societies had the demand-side conditions for democracy in great abundance. Since the early 1960s, South Korea and Taiwan had fast growth, a rising middle class, and then, in the 1980s, they democratized. The sequence fits with our modernization priors. By coincidence, the East Asian Tigers democratized just as the United States was debating what to do with China after Tiananmen. The democratization experience of East Asia heavily influenced policy discussions on China. On June 5, 1989, President George H. W. Bush had both China and the East Asian Tigers in mind when he remarked, "I think as people have commercial incentive, whether it's in China or in other totalitarian systems, the move to democracy becomes more inexorable."[18]

But the East Asian tiger story is not that simple. Yes, economics played a role, but it did so in the presence of favorable supply-side conditions. South Korea and Taiwan were authoritarian, but they were frictional autocracies, not nearly as watertight as the CCP. As I showed in Chapter 4, the CCP tightened political controls and centralized power in the position of the general secretary. The supply-side conditions evaporated. The U.S. engagement policy toward China was based on projecting a flawed conception of East Asia to China. Market economics had nudged South Korea and Taiwan to democracy, but it was the human mediation and existing social and political conditions that fermented the actual change. In the 1990s, when the United States was debating about granting China most-favored-nation trading status and membership in the World Trade Organization, few bothered to check these details.

After his 1961 coup, South Korean general Park Chung-hee restored civilian rule and the formalities of presidential elections under pressure from the Kennedy administration.[19] Rupert Emerson, a Harvard academic, was recruited to draft Korea's constitution. Korea held regular elections under Park, and in 1971 Park came close to losing the presidential election to an opposition candidate, Kim Dae-jung. Park then launched a wave of repressive policies by suspending the constitution, dissolving the legislature, closing the universities, and banning all political parties. He arrested and sentenced to death Kim Dae-jung, only staying the sentence at the last moment when President Jimmy Carter personally intervened.[20]

Before 1987, Taiwan held regular local elections. The Nationalist state maintained the fiction that it ruled all of China by maintaining two positions in the government, one in the central government and the other in the local government system. The opposition was banned, but some opposition candidates competed within the Nationalist party and periodically they won some of these elections. Authoritarian elections are more show than substance, but formalities matter because they provide a platform from which to coordinate and make demands. Taiwan in the 1970s was rated in civil and political rights about the same level as Spain and Portugal, well ahead of China at that time and China today in comparable terms.[21]

After Park was assassinated in 1979, three opposition leaders—Kim Jong-pil, Kim Dae-jung, and Kim Young-sam—vowed to run in the forthcoming election, only to be met by repression at the hand of another military strongman, Chun Doo-hwan. Civil society was weak but it existed. Student protests and labor strikes occurred with some frequency. A sizable portion of the South Korean population was Christian, including many political elites. In Taiwan, too, there was a de facto political heterogeneity created by the divisions and schisms between the native Taiwanese and the mainlanders.

Imagine Zhao Ziyang contending with Hu Jintao in 2002 for the office of the presidency. Imagine the National People's Congress including many non-CCP legislators on behalf of their constituents. These would have been the analogs to what was happening in South Korea during the 1970s and the 1980s. China is missing that crucial mediation mechanism, which is why the CCP has been insulated from the effects of a middle class, globalization, and technology.

Yet another illustration: the divergent responses of Meiji Japan and Qing China to Westernization pressures during the nineteenth century. Meiji Japan adroitly modernized its economy and society while being able to preserve the basic fabric of its politics and culture. By contrast, the Qing dynasty crumbled under the forces of globalization and gunboat diplomacy. What explains this difference? Japan learned about politics and culture from Tang's China, a period in Chinese history that was ideologically diverse and flexible. It implemented *Keju* but only briefly. Meiji Japan reformed on that baseline, rather than looking to the sclerotic autocratic systems of the Song, Yuan, Ming, and Qing.[22] Meiji Japan had the good fortune to confront and embrace Westernization with an agile version of the Chinese system in place. The Qing, by contrast, was beset with all the rigidities of Tang's autocratic progenies—the marginalization of society, ideological homogeneity, and the stifling of intellectuals by the state. There were no incipient flexibilities by the time the Qing responded to the Westernization shocks and thus it responded in the only way it could—by collapsing.

## A Lopsided Engagement

U.S. engagement with China succeeded on the economic side. Never in history have two economies so diametrically opposed politically and ideologically been entangled to this degree. Economics textbooks frame trade and foreign investments in terms of comparative advantage, the asset-specificity of foreign firms, and profit maximization of multinational corporations, but politicians need extra ammunition to justify doing business with a foreign country. Since Tiananmen, consecutive U.S. administrations have defended commercial engagements with China on the grounds that economics could change Chinese politics. Given the political origin of economic engagements with China, it is all the more remarkable that the purported goal and the deployed method were so disconnected. There were very few occasions that economics was adjusted according to the political developments on the ground.

President Bill Clinton offered the most cogent articulation of the engagement policy in a 2000 speech at Johns Hopkins University, where he argued forcefully for Chinese membership in the World Trade Organization. He laid out an economic argument, but he articulated a political rationale as well.

> By joining the W.T.O., China is not simply agreeing to import more of our products; it is agreeing to import one of democracy's most cherished values: economic freedom. The more China liberalizes its economy, the more fully it will liberate the potential of its people—their initiative, their imagination, their remarkable spirit of enterprise. And when individuals have the power, not just to dream but to realize their dreams, they will demand a greater say.[23]

President Clinton presented a binary choice—accepting China into the global economic order or denying that membership to China. There was no layout of how the economic engagement might be calibrated to meet or advance political goals. There was no road map of the intermediate milestones of progress, and there was no framework to link these milestones incrementally in order to achieve the eventual objective. Instead, the United States has operated on an eerily Marxian faith that politics is automatically endogenous of economics. The Chinese citizens "will demand a greater say," as President Clinton put it, but how that demand could translate into an actual greater say in a tight one-party system remains undefined and unspecified.

Imagine hearing a pitch from an entrepreneur promising US$100 billion in sales but never telling you how he will acquire the customer base, build a management team, or set up and meet performance metrics. If you invest in this business, you have committed the same mistake that the U.S. policymakers have made when engaging with China.

The definitive post mortem on engagement policy is a 2018 *Foreign Affairs* article by Kurt Campbell and Ely Ratner, both now in the Biden administration with policy responsibilities related to China.[24] In the article, they provide a long list of visions and hoped-for scenarios proclaimed by the various American administrations, but few details on how commercial ties were actually used to advance Chinese political developments on the ground. The United States has pursued engagement; it has not pursued an engagement strategy.

Counterintuitively, a hallmark of an engagement strategy is a readiness to disengage. Chinese have pursued an engagement strategy with intentionality and relentlessness. The Chinese government punished Norway for awarding Liu Xiaobo a Nobel prize, Australia for calling for an independent investigation into the origins of COVID-19, Japan for its territorial claims, South Korea for its installation of the THAAD missile defense system, and the National Basketball Association for the exercise of free speech by one of its members. The Chinese have never assumed that closer commercial ties would, on their own, elicit favorable diplomacy. They apply a strategy that switches between engagement and disengagement, sometimes successfully.

By contrast, the United States wavers between issuing largely empty threats—"Improve human rights and respect IP or no further investments"—and justifying deeper ties on the basis of political-endogeneity thinking. One exception was when President Donald Trump accidentally applied an intentional engagement strategy. Although the pros and cons of his approach can be debated, his tariffs on China were tied to concrete milestones—tariff treatments of U.S. products, intellectual property rights, subsidies, and so on. The trade war had some teeth and credibly signaled a willingness to disengage.

U.S. policymakers have often affirmed democracy, human rights, and the rule of law while setting aside small-bore, concrete, incremental milestones that could lead to some meaningful openness. Take the example of the Public Company Accounting Oversight Board, created by Congress through the passage of the Sarbanes-Oxley Act of 2002. After its launch in 2003, the board was supposed to inspect information and documents used to audit companies issuing shares in the United States, regardless of their national origins. China refused to comply, and for twenty years, inexplicably, the U.S. government simply looked away and permitted Chinese firms unimpeded access to the American capital market. The Chinese argument against the rule—that the inspection might lead to exposure of national security information—is self-defeating. If the firm in question is involved in national security, why should the United States permit access to its capital market by such a firm? The Biden administration's decision to enforce this rule on China is a step in the right direction.[25]

## Nudging China to Change

The history of the U.S. engagement policy with China is long on goals and short on tactics. Given the massive stakes, it is extraordinary that there has never been a serious effort to gather the best minds in government, industry, and academia to collectively ponder the question, "How will sourcing widgets from Guangdong and building a car factory in Shanghai miraculously bring a constitutional form of government to China?" For decades, U.S. foreign policy operated on faith and on an unstated axiom rather than on an articulated and intentional rationale.

There is a saying in business, "Do not tell me that you have a million customers. Tell me about your first customer." In the follow pages, I will lay out a case for a grounded and contingent strategy that aims at nudging rather than transforming China, a strategy that engages China in economics on a conditional basis and in a realm of ideas through exchanges rather than exhortations. Think small and think concrete. That should be the mantra of our engagement with China.

### Reciprocity

Nudging can only succeed if the goal is modest and the tactic is calibrated. So here is a straightforward goal for economic interactions between China and the United States: reciprocity. Reciprocity, which happens to be the most effective way to achieve cooperation, has been largely missing from U.S.-China relations.[26] Google's search engine is blocked in China, whereas Baidu operates freely in the United States. The *New York Times* has been banned from China since 2012, whereas one can pick up a copy of *China Daily* and *People's Daily* in the United States with ease (and often free of charge). Chinese companies such as Alibaba operate cloud-computing services in the United States without restrictions, whereas Amazon and Apple face many regulatory hurdles in China. There are legions of similar asymmetries.

The various U.S. administrations did apply pressure to the Chinese, but only in order to open markets to American businesses rather than to correct these blatant imbalances. The United States clamored on behalf of Wall Street to get into China's lucrative investment markets, but not on behalf of Google and the *New York Times*, who could open up China's information space. From the perspective of nudging Chinese politics, this was one of the worst mistakes the United States has made—actively helping Chinese elites to raise capital while failing to help those in the information business and those who could plant some political externalities down the road.

The Biden administration has compounded these historical mistakes by going to the other extreme. Rather than demanding that China open itself to American institutions, the U.S. government has pressured American universities to close Confucius Institutes on their campuses. (Confucius Institutes are funded by the Chinese government to propagate Chinese culture and values.) And the Trump administration canceled the Fulbright program that sent American scholars to China. Are we so insecure that we are afraid of engaging with values different from ours? A superior approach is to require, on a case-by-case basis, the opening of U.S. NGOs in China in exchange for the continued operations of the Confucius Institutes here. A similar approach can be adopted by the Committee of Foreign Investment in the United States (CFIUS)—evaluate investment from a country by considering how that country treats investment from the United States.

The United States is now trying to unwind the extensive scientific collaborations with China, even going as far as fabricating charges of economic espionage against Chinese American scientists under the "China Initiative." These scientific collaborations with China are not the mistake. They benefited the United States and science in general. The mistake was undertaking these collaborations without symmetry. During his visit to China in 1978, Frank Press, science adviser to President Jimmy Carter, relayed a request by Deng Xiaoping to send seven hundred Chinese students to the United States to study science and technology. Carter agreed, but he did not lay down any reciprocal conditions from China.[27]

Acquiring foreign science and technology was of the highest priority to Deng Xiaoping, as we can see by the unusually extensive coverage that *People's Daily* gave to Press's visit. The United States should have used this leverage to demand that American academics have the freedom to give lectures and organize conferences in China, not just on scientific subjects but on a range of topics, without restrictions. The United States could also agree to open its labs and research institutions to Chinese researchers on the condition that China allow American scholars to access its own data and research. MIT, for example, runs collaborative research projects in Saudi Arabia on the well-defined condition that female Saudi researchers have complete freedom to participate.

In the 1980s, Chinese academia was more open and was moving, on its own, toward a Republic of Science model. But after 1989, when the Chinese tightened controls over education and the collapse of the Soviet Union diminished China's strategic balancing value for the United States, the United States should have used its tremendous leverage more wisely. China was isolated and eager to reengage with the international community, a welcome development but the United States should have demanded more reciprocity. An opportunity was lost.

## *Human Rights*

There is one issue on which the United States has sought to engage with China outside of economics—human rights. But the U.S. engagement is often formulaic, defaulting to the familiar and sacrosanct language of universal values and individual autonomy. The rationale the United States offers to defend its human-rights policy comes off as defensive, arrogant, and self-serving. President Biden, when explaining why he raised human rights with President Xi Jinping, put it this way, "I point out to him no American President can be sustained as a President if he doesn't reflect the values of the United States." In 1989, President George H. W. Bush used the same language in a private letter to Deng Xiaoping.[28] Would the United States accept Chinese criticism of U.S. democracy if the Chinese leader insisted that he had to do so because of his country's autocratic values?

The United States should rethink its discourse on human rights and capitalize on those moments when engagement presents itself as a reciprocal exchange. In March 2021, at the first high-level meeting between the new Biden administration and the Chinese leaders, the head of the Chinese delegation, Yang Jiechi, launched a scathing critique of the U.S. record on human rights. Whether his critique is correct or not is of secondary importance. What escaped notice by both Yang and Secretary Antony Blinken is that by offering this critique, Yang made a considerable concession to the United States—that human rights are a legitimate topic for discussion between the two countries. Blinken failed to recognize that concession and missed an opportunity to put Chinese officials on record to embrace this stance or walk away from it.

The United States should engage with the Chinese on human rights with humility and openness about its own failings. To his credit, Secretary Blinken acknowledged that the United States is not "a perfect union," but he could have been more detailed and candid in his assessment. He could have turned the Chinese criticism on its head and argued that America fell short in precisely those areas where it has not been fully democratic. The Electoral College, the filibuster, and gerrymandering, for example, are anti-democratic features that have contributed to dysfunction and poor accountability in the American political system. Democracy is not the disease; the problem is that America is not democratic enough.

U.S. policymakers should also appeal to the enlightened self-interests of the Chinese. After listing Chinese actions in Xinjiang, Hong Kong, South China Seas, and cyberattacks at the Anchorage meeting, Blinken said, "Each of these actions threatens the rules-based order that maintains global stability." To the uninitiated, Blinken is defending a global order created by and for the United States and its allies. An ordinary Chinese may legitimately react in the following way, "You have your order, and we have our order. You challenge mine, and I challenge yours."

In fact, this global order has delivered immense benefits to China and it is against China's self-interest to undermine it. Blinken could have quoted Deng Xiaoping, who famously remarked, "Look back at the last several decades. All the countries that foster good relations with the US become rich."[29] Or he could have mentioned that historically Russia has been China's biggest bully, forcing China to cede territories equivalent to 10 percent of China today through the Russo-Chinese Convention of Peking (1860) and the Treaty of Tientsin (1858). None of this rhetoric will alter Xi's foreign policy, but it may win over Chinese intellectuals, reformist establishmentarians, technologists, and other segments of the Chinese society.

The United States has alienated mainstream segments of the Chinese population by lending moral support to a tiny number of dissidents—the anti-establishment individuals and those operating on the fringe of Chinese society. (One research paper shows "that discontented citizens in contemporary China are more fearful, disagreeable, and introverted, lacking close emotional attachments to others").[30] Western leaders showcase their support for human rights in China by orchestrating choreographed and substance-free photo meetings with the Dalai Lama—an individual demonized in China as a separatist and one about whom the vast majority of the Chinese have a neutral or a negative opinion. Whether the Dalai Lama is a separatist is beside the point; the reality is that this is the Chinese perception and the purely symbolic gestures showered on the Dalai Lama reinforce that idea without doing anything for human rights in China.

Some of the dissident protest movements have been detrimental to nudging China in a liberal direction. They have often ended up punishing the establishment reformers and rewarding the most entrenched forces of the Chinese political system. The history of the "democracy movement" in China, sadly, is one of provoking counterreactions that have moved China uniformly toward a more repressive society. It is not the fault of individuals in these mass movements that this happened, but the fault of the nature of the autocracy. In a dictatorship, individuals lack agency, but a mass movement confers a sudden windfall of individual agency power without a norm for how to apply that agency power purposely and responsibly. This overnight transition from minimum to maximum agency power presents perilous risks. Admittedly, the United States has very little leverage affecting the dynamics on the ground, but it should refrain from inadvertently lending moral support to an unthinking and reckless application of that agency power.

Compromise is a virtue of democracy and a necessity for a functional democracy. When extremist Republicans were calling for stripping the committee memberships of their colleagues who voted for Biden's infrastructure bill, their uncompromising extremism was widely criticized in the media. But some of the Chinese "freedom fighters" behave as these uncompromising Republicans do. In 1989, the student demonstrators were able to secure unprecedented face-to-face dialogues with CCP leaders, but instead of settling for more dialogues and capitalizing on the legitimacy these dialogues conferred, they demanded concessions that the government could not possibly meet.[31] Their radicalism directly caused the downfall of Zhao Ziyang, burying China's best hope for a gradual and incremental reform path. A similar situation unfolded in Hong Kong thirty years later. In 2019, the Hong Kong demonstrators refused to accept the Hong Kong government's concessions to their demands. The radical protestors set fire to public buildings and ransacked university campuses. They blocked streets and mass transit for days on end, disrupting the daily lives of Hong Kong residents.

One sign of undisciplined agency power is a refusal to build alliances across the aisle. The Hong Kong protestors violently attacked innocent mainland-Chinese bystanders, falsely equating ordinary Chinese with the Chinese political regime. They were their own worst enemies and turned Chinese public opinion, which was initially sympathetic and supportive, against them. Meanwhile the Western governments and human rights organizations remained largely silent about the protestors' violent tactics, a silence that was interpreted by the Chinese as tacit approval.

The CCP excels at capitalizing on wedge issues. The actions of the Hong Kong protestors furnished the proof of an idea the CCP has perpetuated—that democracy breeds chaos. The authoritarian regime seized on the upheavals as a pretext to quash the precious freedoms remaining in a Chinese territory. No one can argue with a straight face that Hong Kong today, from the vantage point of freedom and democracy, is a better place than Hong Kong before 2019.

## *A Performance-Based Argument for Democracy*

One lesson from Tiananmen and Hong Kong is that we need a situationally specific approach on human rights and free speech. It should appeal to a "median" Chinese—an individual who is not dedicated to the destruction of the current system nor to a staunch defense of the status quo. The narrative should showcase the tangible benefits of human rights, the rule of law, and democracy for most Chinese citizens and even for some of the CCP elites.

The argument for democracy is typically delivered with a sweeping moral tone, that is, touting the universality of human rights and human beings' innate aspirations for freedom and autonomy. This argument has always run hollow, but it sounds vacuous today. More than 74 million Americans voted for a manifest authoritarian in the 2020 presidential election, and 26 percent of Americans score high on a measure known as right-wing authoritarianism.[32] Democratic values are not even universal within the United States, let alone across cultures and nations.

There is a deep gulf of values between China and the West. The Chinese have a utilitarian concept of "rights"—rights that advance the greatest good for the greatest number. The West views rights as protections against encroachments on the disenfranchised few, such as political dissidents. This notion of rights does not resonate broadly with the Chinese population. In an ethnically homogenous society and in a political culture that celebrates convergence, the thinking that a subgroup of the population has immutable, distinctive characteristics is not easily accepted.

One way to engage with the Chinese is to appeal to a performance-based reasoning about democracy. We know this will engage the Chinese because this is the logic the CCP invokes. The CCP denies that it is an autocracy and claims that it is more democratic than the West because it has delivered a superior performance. On the eve of a 2021 "Summit of Democracy" convened by the United States, the State Council issued a white paper, "China: Democracy That Works," a full-throttled defense of the CCP system that takes Western democracy to task for its multiple failures, such as COVID-19 infections and death tolls.

It is critical that the West takes this narrative seriously and confronts it directly. It is not that hard. The CCP's argument is based on cherry-picking performance metrics, slicing and dicing the cited evidence, and conflating a general proposition with one that is specific to a country and to a time period. The CCP wants you to believe that during the reform era it developed a superior system to deliver growth, but it fails to account for its dismal failures before the reform era began. The CCP touts the lives saved under its draconian COVID-19 mitigation measures, omitting that stifling the free flow of information possibly caused a delay in the government's response during the initial phase of the outbreak. It extolls its impressive performance on alleviating poverty since 1979, while failing to mention that it was the policies of the CCP before 1978 that mired the Chinese peasants in poverty and privations in the first place.

Economy is the favorite performance metric of the CCP, but presentations of China's economic data are often based on crude cross-country comparisons—usually just China benchmarked against some unnamed democracies—and are plagued with selection biases and causal misattributions. A researcher armed with this kind of logic and social science skills is unlikely to survive for five minutes at an MIT seminar.

A discourse on democracy on our side should be factual and evidence-based. There is an emerging body of evidence showing that more open systems outperform closed polities across various performance dimensions.[33] In the East Asian context, autocracies with more scope conditions—such as South Korea of the 1970s and the 1980s, imperial China during the

Han-Sui Interregnum, and China in the 1980s—outperformed their scope-restrictive counterparts. Democracies may not command a decisive edge over autocracies when it comes to economic growth, but there is no compelling evidence that autocracies command a compelling edge over democracies.

Perhaps the strongest evidence in favor of liberal democracies is protection of personal security. Steven Pinker cited a study showing that during the twentieth century the number of unnatural civilian deaths in totalitarian countries was 120 million; for democracies, that number is two million.[34] Two million is still a gigantic number, but one cannot possibly make a good-faith argument that democracies and autocracies are equivalent on that score. No, the CCP is not a democracy. It walks like an autocracy, it quacks like an autocracy, and it performs like an autocracy.

When discussing personal security, U.S. diplomats should stress that a system with rights confers protection on everyone, including CCP elites. Chinese elites intuitively grasp this point. The police chief of Chongqing, Wang Lijun, did not flee to the Russian or Iranian embassies; he sought refuge in a U.S. consulate. Many Chinese officials have sent their family members to the United States, placing implicit trust in the security of persons and property offered by a democracy. I am puzzled why American leaders do not use this line of argument more often with their Chinese interlocutors. Wouldn't the Chinese elites like a little more of that security closer to home? Instead of framing the Uyghur situation as an ethnic genocide, wouldn't it be wiser to link Xinjiang to the reeducation camps of the Cultural Revolution and so rekindle memories of the suffering of so many Chinese who lived through that traumatic era?

## A Case for Political Openness

Chinese economic growth is slowing down and, more importantly, its engines of growth—the private sector, globalization, incentives, and decision-making autonomy—are damaged. The stability component of the EAST model has become compromised as the CCP reverts to the discretionary succession method of the Mao era. There may come a time when China can use introspection, soul-searching, and self-reflection when discussing its politics, its economic system, and its foreign policy, rather than defaulting to platitudes and wolf-warrior polemics. I am agnostic about when or if that moment will arrive, but in case it ever does, let me lay out an argument for why China should embrace more political openness and rebalance its scale and scope portfolio in favor of more scope.

I want to be clear: an argument for political openness is not an argument for any particular form or pace of political openness. A transition to democracy constitutes political openness, but to me, returning China to the China of the 1980s also constitutes political openness. Evolution, not revolution, should be celebrated and encouraged, and any steps to restore decentralization policies and reinvigorate private-sector autonomy would be welcome developments. A pragmatic, problem-solving, and solution-based approach toward the West is a step toward political openness. Many want to see democracy in China, but regime transition entails risks, and I believe that those risks should be explicitly incorporated into deliberations of the larger pros and cons of making that transition. I will leave this topic on regime transition to others and my future writings; for now, I will not impose a rigid definition of political openness, leaving it to mean movements that scale in such a way that they don't cause an undue loss of scope.

Hu Xijin, the ultra-nationalist former editor of the *Global Times* and a combative wolf warrior, once wrote that if China had experienced a similar death toll of COVID-19 as the United States, the Chinese people would have rebelled. Unbeknownst to Hu, his comment was an underhanded compliment to democracy. Democracy is stable even at moments of high stress. Voting and criticisms of government operate as an open valve that periodically vents anger and frustration so the pressures do not build up to a breaking point. The January 6 insurrection is on a more extreme end of democratic instability, but this insurrection, cheered on by a sitting president no less, does not remotely compare to the mayhem of the Cultural Revolution and the enormity of Tiananmen. The shock is that it happened at all in the United States.

I will build on the compliment by Hu Xijin and argue that greater political openness would offer enormous benefits to China. But to make that case requires us to assess those arguments the CCP has invoked to defend its power and the political status quo.

## Efficiencies

Is the one-party Chinese system more efficient and effective in tackling the economy, society, and future challenges facing humanity (such as disease and climate change)? Thomas Friedman once wished that the United

States could be China for a day. He wanted the United States to emulate China's efficiency in rolling out infrastructure improvements and sustainable energy solutions.[35] Friedman's musings about China evoke "authoritarian envy," an affliction particularly prevalent among Western liberal intellectuals. One reason, I suspect, is that liberal intellectuals are critical of their own system and are always on the lookout for an alternative.

But which Chinese day would Friedman fancy? Is it a day in 1958 when Mao launched the Great Leap Forward? Or May 16, 1966, the day he unleashed the violence of the Red Guards? Or maybe June 4, 1989, when tanks rolled into Tiananmen Square? Or January 3, 2020, when the Wuhan Public Security Bureau interrogated Dr. Li Wenliang, an ophthalmologist who had just sounded the alarm about a SARS-like pneumonia spreading through the population?

The point is not that Friedman is completely wrong—the Chinese system has its efficient aspects—but we need to consider the CCP system as a package. Friedman celebrates China's alternative energy investments, but he does not know that in the 1990s, without any thoughtful discussions and public debates, the Chinese government designated the automobile as its pillar industry, setting the stage for a car culture, with its higher carbon emissions, the air apocalypse, exurban commuting, and energy-intensive GDP. To add an exclamation mark to that heavy-industrial drive, the Chinese government imported turnkey production of one of the world's top gasoline guzzlers, GM's Buick.

The CCP system is efficient in rolling out high-speed rail systems, but it is also efficient at exiling intellectuals as part of its anti-rightist campaign. These two types of efficiencies cancel out each other, and in the long run, at best they produce a draw in economic development. The fast growth that China has achieved since 1978 has not been enough to tip the balance and make up for the tremendous losses suffered during the Great Leap Forward and the Cultural Revolution. In 2020, China's per capita GDP was US$10,500 (based on exchange-rate conversions), roughly a third that of Taiwan (US$28,894) and South Korea (US$31,346), and about a fourth that of Japan (US$39,484).[36] A bigger question is not why China has grown fast in recent decades, but why it is not as rich as the rest of East Asia.

One may dispute this comparison. There are many differences between China and the rest of East Asia, and their differences in economics and politics are only a part of the picture. Also isn't the so-called East Asian miracle proof positive of authoritarian superiority in economic development? All fair points. Let's make a head-to-head comparison between the two halves of a peninsula, North Korea and South Korea, which are identical in every economically relevant dimension we can think of—culture, tradition, literacy, and genetic makeup of the population. But they differ, crucially, in their economic systems and partially in their political systems.

Today North Korea's GDP per capita is a dismal US$1,700, 5 percent of its southern counterpart. Its men are three inches shorter than their brethren in the south.[37] A satellite photo of Asia reveals a dark patch of land in a sea of brightly lit regions. That dark patch of land epitomizes both the power of the system as well as history's cruel randomization of the fates and fortunes of people caught in it. In 1945, as the Soviet army was advancing, the task to partition Korea fell on two lieutenant colonels of the U.S. army, Dean Rusk and Charles Bonesteel.[38] Without consulting a single Korean, the duo initially drew the partition line at the 39th parallel, then changed it to the 38th parallel. The basis for their decision: a 1942 *National Geographic* map that did not even show the provincial boundaries. The partitioning of Korea took a total of thirty minutes and it sealed the fates of tens of millions of people. Years later, Dean Rusk, who became U.S. secretary of state, acknowledged it as a "fateful" decision.

Some hold the success of East Asia as evidence of an autocratic edge, connecting the region's GDP growth to the authoritarian nature of the regimes in South Korea, Taiwan, and Singapore. This conclusion suffers from a classic selection bias. It ignores the other East Asia, the one that is more authoritarian, minus the economic success of the tigers. For each East Asian authoritarian success story, there is an East Asian authoritarian failure. Taiwan grew rich, but authoritarian Mao's China did not. South Korea developed rapidly, but North Korea floundered. A strong one-man rule in Singapore succeeded, but so did laissez-faire Hong Kong. Yes, the neo-authoritarian China since 1989 has performed well, but its more liberal counterpart of the 1980s performed even more impressively. In its totality, the East Asian experience does not offer supporting evidence of an autocratic edge. In fact, to the extent that there is a difference, the less autocratic regimes, such as South Korea, outperformed the extreme autocracies such as North Korea.

The CCP put out a North Korean performance between 1949 and 1978 and a South Korean performance since 1978, scoring a draw in the grand scheme of things. It is capable of delivering rapid growth, but also of causing famine (the Great Leap Forward) and bringing about destruction (the Cultural Revolution). Yes, China has lifted more than half a billion of people above abject poverty during the reform era, a much heralded and well-deserved accomplishment, but who was responsible for the commune system and for the forced industrialization that mired the Chinese peasantry in poverty in the first place? The stern mitigation measure to contain COVID-19 garners kudos from some Western observers, but the same CCP was in the thrall of a zero-COVID policy regime that was destroying the economy and ruining the livelihood of ordinary Chinese.

One can go further and ask whether the achievements of the CCP should be evaluated in a framework that clinically compares costs and benefits. The catastrophic Great Leap Forward and the Cultural Revolution were acts of deliberate decisions and actions of the Chinese state. By contrast, its enviable record of economic success is due to its willingness to step out of the way. The virtues of an omission cannot fully make up for the errors of a commission. When evaluating the claim of the CCP's superiority, the burden of proof should fall more heavily on those actions a system is designed to execute rather than those that a system refrains from undertaking. In that sense, there is no symmetry between the pros and cons of the CCP system.

Is this type of dual assessment unfair? One can argue that since 1978, the CCP has transformed and modernized itself and has moved away from its former identity. As an analogy, it would be absurd to lump the Democratic Party today in the same category as its former self that supported slavery and segregation. The problem is that the CCP itself does not acknowledge that binary discontinuity in its history. Deng's CCP was more forthcoming about its failings and drew a line at 1978. Not Xi Jinping. The "Resolution" adopted by the CCP in 2021 portrays the CCP as a glorious uninterrupted whole, going as far as to suggest that the CCP before 1978 laid the foundation for the CCP after 1978. It blames the Great Leap Forward and the Cultural Revolution not on the CCP, but on its inability to rectify the mistakes of Mao Zedong. This is surreal. It is as if an abstract entity, a legal person known as the CCP, possessed a will and agency of its own separate from its almighty chairman. The insinuation is that the CCP is perennially immaculate even during its darkest days. (This grand claim is simply false. The Great Leap Forward and the Cultural Revolution were launched in the name of the Central Committee of the CCP, not in Mao's personal capacity.) If the CCP views its history as a smooth curve on a continuous scale, then it should be judged accordingly.

## Balancing Scale and Scope

According to Statista.com, as of November 2022 more than one million Americans have died of COVID-19 compared with China's 5,229.[39] Even if the Chinese number is seriously underreported, the error is unlikely to be big enough to explain all the difference between China and the United States. Before the vaccine became available, there is no question that the Chinese ability to control its population worked. The West has limited ability to quarantine its population and could only rely on science as the solution, but science took time, and during the waiting period, the West paid a price.

This is a calibrated, and, I would argue, factually defensible view. China's approach, however, was greeted with bountiful accolades in the West. One observer went so far as to pronounce that China's pandemic controls show that China is more modern on many dimensions than the West.[40] Another unabashed admirer of the Chinese system, Martin Jacques, echoes this sentiment.[41] Eric Li was invited by the *Economist* to tell us how advanced the Chinese COVID management is.[42]

This is a surreal claim. China's weapon is its administrative ability to restrict population mobility. It is modern only insofar as it is a hallmark of a successful transition out of a tribal society in ancient times. There are genuinely modern aspects to China's mitigation measures, such as its health code, but the strict lockdowns of Chinese cities have been enforced by the sheer mobilization of a massive labor force—to barricade residential buildings, erect physical barriers, conduct PCR tests, and, when necessary, use force to haul infected people into field hospitals. Ultimately, the power of the CCP rests on psychological compliance, on the one hand, and a primordial strength to mobilize people, on the other. It served a useful function before the vaccine became available, but there is nothing modern about a contemporary equivalent of building the Grand Canal of the Sui dynasty. Modern for the seventh century maybe, but not for the twenty-first century.

As I am writing this paragraph, China is experiencing a surge in COVID-19 infections, warranting extreme or targeted lockdowns in a number of cities, including Beijing, Guangzhou, and Chongqing. Yes, the CCP has an impressive capacity to mobilize, but there is a difference between enforcing zero-COVID in one or two locations, such as Wuhan and Shanghai, and doing the same in multiple locations simultaneously. The three years of extreme lockdowns are straining government finances as well as public health resources and capacity, suppressing the economy, destabilizing an unhealthy real estate sector, and producing collateral damages that are arguably worse than COVID-19 itself. The high psychological toll of what amounted to an incarceration of hundreds of millions of people in their homes and field hospitals has probably permanently damaged whatever support Xi's CCP enjoys from the public.

Also, the initial Chinese success in pandemic controls is not unique. South Korea, Israel, and Taiwan, all with high population densities susceptible to virus transmissions, were able to bring COVID-19 under control without resorting to inhumane lockdowns. They used their administrative capacity and high trust from the public to minimize the death toll before the science came to the rescue. An even bigger contrast is in learning curves and capacity for self-correction. South Korea learned from its mishandling of the 2015 MERS in a way that China never did from its response to the SARS of 2003.[43] Both SARS and COVID-19 are believed to have originated from live animal markets, but the Chinese government only temporarily suspended these markets in response to the outbreaks.[44] Today, many wet animal markets still operate in China, setting the stage for another potential zoonotic disease outbreak in the future.

China's disease surveillance strategy, which the government rolled out after SARS, completely failed. The director of the Chinese Center for Disease Control and Prevention, Gao Fu, first learned about the virus outbreak "rumor" on social media rather than from the official reporting system. A Chinese economist who made this revelation, Hua Sheng, commented, "Within seventeen years of SARS, we have fallen into the same river of virus twice."[45] He did not give a reason, but in 2020 the Chinese system was so centralized that nobody wanted to be the messenger bearing the bad news.

Once an epidemic was under way, China's autocracy mobilized resources quickly to cut off the virus transmission, after having failed at detecting an incipient outbreak. An analogy is fighting a fire. The Chinese autocracy excels at putting out a fire once it breaks out, but it is terrible at sounding the alarm about one. This is all the more remarkable because China experienced an identical situation in 2003 when the government suppressed information that would have aided early detection. From a design perspective, a system that prevents a crisis from breaking out is superior to one that mitigates and controls a crisis.

Censorship impedes the timely surfacing of information. We cannot be definitive here, and counterfactual analytics never is. Still, it is legitimate to ponder whether the COVID-19 pandemic may go down in history as one of the costliest mistakes of censorship. On December 30, 2019, a Wuhan doctor, Li Wenliang, posted to his WeChat group about a "SARS-like pneumonia." Instead of following up on his lead, the police forced Dr. Li to recant his message. (Dr. Li himself later died from COVID-19.) China had experienced an uncomfortably similar situation during the SARS episode of 2002–2003.[46] Local officials hid the information and punished those who sounded the alarm. According to Dr. Jiang Yanyong, a doctor at a military hospital in Beijing who took the information public, his hospital was informed about SARS in Beijing but was instructed not to disclose the information for fear of disrupting the annual gathering of the National People's Congress. Unlike the Western governments, which are much less experienced in zoonotic diseases, the Chinese government should have possessed situational awareness, historical recall, policy know-how, and ample knowledge of the harm caused by impeding free flows of information about public health. Yet it repeated the same mistake in 2020.

One can argue that the situation was objectively difficult and fluid during the initial outbreak of the virus. The authorities lacked complete and accurate information about the virus's transmissibility and lethality. SARS-CoV-2 was a novel disease, and uncertainty abounded. But there is a fundamental difference between a delay caused by technical uncertainty and a delay caused by systemic opacity. It is illogical to excuse the initial delays on the grounds of a shortage of data and information and then turn around to praise a system that exacerbates that shortage. An explanation attributing the initial delay solely to an information shortage would be far more convincing if Dr. Li and other doctors had not been silenced and if authorities had actively investigated and solicited information during those crucial early days of the outbreak.

We ought to adopt a balance-sheet perspective, acknowledging the advantage of scale while giving due deference to the utility of scope. As I showed in Chapters 7 and 8, scope conditions contributed to China's technological development, but this is not the official line of the CCP. The CCP actively curtails scope and extolls the ability to do so as its strength. Apart from COVID-19 controls, another example the CCP likes to cite is its ability to build infrastructure. Yes, the CCP did build out an impressive network of infrastructure, but let's be clear: its infrastructural power is based in part on forcibly taking land from Chinese peasants. Its control of people comes into play again.

Would the Chinese economy have failed to take off if China had private land ownership and stronger contract rights? Not necessarily. China would have grown with a counterfactually different economic model. The construction costs of China's infrastructure would have been more elevated, but the flows of income to Chinese households, especially rural households, would have been larger. Forcible taking of land is not the only solution to the stickiness of private ownership. The state could have assigned a portion of equity shares of the infrastructure projects to the original rural landowners, aligning their incentives with the future growth enabled by that infrastructure. With private ownership, China would have a more balanced and sustainable growth model driven by consumption rather than by debt-laden investment. Let's recall from Econ 101 a circular flow of money: a cost to one agent in the economy is an income to another agent. In the 1980s, the Chinese economy thrived without the infrastructure that the country later became known for. Household consumption was growing, fueled by rapid gains in income.

Making a normative statement requires taking into account the history that has happened as well as the history that could have happened. The CCP and its advocates in the West fail to meet this basic counterfactual threshold. We should greet their claims with a healthy dose of skepticism.

## Compatibilities

In the 1990s, a school of thought known as "Asian values" emerged as a counternarrative to Western values. Its core claim is that the Western system—with its rule of law, democracy, and free speech—is fundamentally incompatible with and unsuited for countries rooted in Confucianist ideology.

The argument is flawed. There is nothing "genetic" about Western values. Freedom of expression and individual rights came to the West first, but their origins and arrival are sometimes debated. David Graeber and David Wengrow believe that some of the canonically "Western" ideas came from exchanges with indigenous populations.[47] Isaiah Berlin, when answering a question about when the notion of individual liberty emerged in the West, was overheard saying: "I have found no convincing evidence of any clear formulation of it in the ancient world."[48]

We use ideas invented by others all the time in part because some of the values created by our own ancestors are horrible. Nobody would defend the foot-binding of women in China today. The nationality of an idea is irrelevant. What matters is whether an idea is right or wrong and whether it produces benefits. Then we engage in a debate on utility and on what makes sense and what does not. An outcome of this debate may very well be a rejection of some Western values and practices, but here is a catch: in order to reach that conclusion, we need a modicum of freedom— freedom to state a point of view, freedom to criticize and to be criticized, and freedom to debate, that is, maybe "discussion democracy," if not full- fledged democracy.[49] In other words, we need to affirm some Western val- ues—free speech and debate—in order to affirm Asian values and in order to reject those Western values we deem to have low utility.

Should the Chinese reject democracy on the ground of its incompat- ibility with Confucianism? The proponents of this view seem to define Japan, South Korea, and Taiwan out of their Asian existence, and then conflate two entirely different concepts. One is inventing something; the other is applying and utilizing an existing invention. The *Keju* system pre- empted the idea of market economics and democracy, but today Japan, South Korea, and Taiwan are living proof that Confucianism is perfectly compatible with market economics and democracy. True, the Chinese did not invent individual rights and freedom, but I did not invent the com- puter either and I still use it every day. We do not only use things we invented; in fact, there are advantages to adoptions as opposed to inven- tions. Adopters have an "advantage of backwardness" in the sense meant by Alexander Gerschenkron.[50] By being adopters rather than inventors, we learn from the pioneers' mistakes and avoid startup costs. Surely, we should be methodical and thoughtful in our selections, but "not invented by us" is an incorrect basis for making such a judgment.

Another argument against Western values is that the history of the West is tainted. How can we accept values from those who have done many terrible things, such as mass killings of indigenous populations in America and Australia, slavery, racism, and the late arrival of universal suf- frage? This criticism of the West is entirely fair and factually accurate, but there is a difference between making this criticism to learn from history and making this criticism to justify similar deeds being perpetuated by autocracies today. Cui Zhiyuan, a Tsinghua professor, at one point a policy adviser to Bo Xilai, drew a parallel between Tiananmen and the Hoover administration's 1932 crackdown on protesting U.S. veterans.[51] Leaving aside the vast factual differences between these two episodes, this is a strange defense of the Tiananmen crackdown. Imagine an argument that every astronomy student today should still repeat the Ptolemian error. It is a nonsensical argument. We should instead turn this argument around and say that precisely because the West has made those horrible mistakes, we should learn not to make them again. Should we also add that when the West committed those dreadful deeds, its less democratic political system was more similar to the Chinese autocracy today? The same goes for the argument that the West has polluted and has pirated intellectual property rights in the past and therefore we should do it too. This argument ignores the fact that countries today can learn from the mistakes of the past and can design a developmental path that takes advantage of technologies and options that were previously not available.

## *Self-Preservation by the Elites*

An autocracy showers elites with privilege and power. Ultimately, it is also the elites who decide the future of their country. Is there a self-interested argument in support of democracy that might appeal to the Chinese elites? To develop this argument, we can invoke a famous thought experiment known as a "veil of ignorance" proposed by John Rawls in his influential book, *The Theory of Justice*.[52] In this thought experiment, an individual is assumed to be rational, self-interested, and unconcerned about the welfare of others. Under what circumstances, Rawls asks, can this individual choose a set of organizing principles for a society that can be considered "just?" The answer: when the individual in question is denied the knowledge of his/her particular situation and conditions, such as gender, race, talents, and social status. Under a veil of ignorance, it is in the self-interest of this individual to choose to organize the society without prejudice, discrimination, and oppression. A vision of this society is one that benefits a universal person rather than a particular person. The society that thus emerges is "fair," and it is axiomatically just.

The Rawlsian principle offers a way to appeal to the self-interest of the Chinese elites. One helpful fact is that the Chinese system has been cruel to some of its own elite members, for example during the Anti-Rightist Campaign and the Cultural Revolution. Since 1989, Chinese politics has become more precarious after a brief interlude of gentle politics. One day you may have power and privilege at your fingertips, then suddenly you can vanish without a trace.

Liu Shaoqi, the aborted heir apparent to Mao, died alone, buried under a fake name and wrapped in a rag. The two military giants who clashed at the 1959 Lushan conference, Marshalls Lin Biao and Peng Dehuai, died horrible and agonizing deaths—Lin in a fiery plane crash fleeing from China, and Peng from an untreated cancer in jail. Chinese politics today is less lethal, but it can still be a life-or-death affair. In 2007, a vice chairman of the National People's Congress and a director of China's Food and Drug Administration were executed. So was Wen Qiang, the deputy police chief of Chongqing, in 2010. Lai Xiaomin, a finance executive, was executed in 2021. More commonly, the high-pressure technique is used to extract confessions. The *New York Times* reported on Wang Guanglong, a fallen official in Fujian province. He was "starved, pummeled, and interrogated for days on end in an ice-cold room where sleeping, sitting, or even leaning against a wall were forbidden."[53] Bo Xilai hinted that he had confessed under "psychological pressures."[54]

An astonishing number of Chinese political elites have been falling from power. Over the past two decades, the party secretaries in three of the four most important municipalities, Beijing, Shanghai, and Chongqing, went straight to jail from their top posts. Xi's anti-corruption campaign has intensified pressures, psychological or otherwise, on the Chinese officialdom. Between 2012 and 2016, some 120 officials committed suicide, a sharp increase from the already high figure of sixty-eight between 2003 and 2012.[55] In "Why China's Elite Tread a Perilous Path," *Financial Times* columnist Gideon Rachman wrote about Rui Chenggang, a TV personality in China and a man once brimming with self-confidence (for no apparent reason, in my opinion).[56] One year, he was hobnobbing with the rich and famous at Davos; the following year, he landed in jail. Quoting from Chinese media, Rachman reported that as of 2011, of seventy-two Chinese billionaires, fourteen had been executed, fifteen had been murdered, seventeen had committed suicide, seven had died from accidents, and nineteen had died from diseases.

Overnight, a tormentor can turn into one who is tormented, as a famous Chinese legend illustrates. According to this legend, Empress Wu Zetian dispatched an official of hers, Lai Junchen, to investigate Zhou Xin, another official. Lai asked Zhou for advice on how to get a criminal to confess. "Easy," Zhou said, "you take a jar and set fire to it, and you invite the criminal to step into it." Lai then had a jar brought in, lit a fire, and invited Zhou to step in. Ever since, "Please kindly step into the jar" illustrates the boomerang character of Chinese justice. (Lai did not escape the curse of the legend he created. He was executed by Wu Zetian.)

In 2016, Interpol chose a vice minister of public security, Meng Hongwei, as its new president. The appointment raised widespread concerns that China might use Interpol to track down political dissidents. While on a business trip to China in 2018, Meng texted his wife two messages, the first, "wait for my call"; the second, an emoji of a kitchen knife. Meng's wife interpreted the emoji as a signal of danger, which it was. Meng was arrested, but the emoji was more than a danger signal. The Chinese word for knife handle (刀把子) refers to the law enforcement apparatus. Meng was telegraphing that he had stepped into the same jar that he had prepared for Chinese dissidents. Of the nine vice-ministers of public security since 2018, three have gone to jail: Meng in 2018, Sun Lijun in 2020, and Fu Zhenghua in 2021. Another vice minister, Li Dongsheng, was arrested in 2013.

The knife holders often find themselves at the edge of that knife. The chief of police under Stalin, Lavrenti Beria, once said: "Show me the man, and I will find the crime." He died proving the wisdom of his own words, executed by the successors of Stalin and so meeting the same fate as his two predecessors. The man who once ran the entire security apparatus of China, Zhou Yongkang, is now languishing in a Chinese jail. Wen Qiang, the executed Chongqing police chief, carried out multiple executions in his career. Wang Lijun, who oversaw Wen's execution, was himself arrested and sentenced to jail. So many administrators of the state's monopoly of violence have ended up having that same violence administered to them. In the wise words of a Chinese proverb, "Accompanying the king is like accompanying a tiger."

When you hear Chinese officials criticizing the individual rights of the West, you can safely bet that they are enjoying plenty of individual rights at the moment they issue these diatribes. Chinese wolf-warrior diplomats often condemn the hypocrisy of the West, on Twitter, a communication medium denied to their fellow citizens. The irony is for all to see, except the wolf warriors themselves. In a 1998 book, Gu Kailai, the wife of a CCP rising star, Bo Xilai, mocked the American judiciary's obsession with individual rights and praised the swift justice of the Chinese system. In 2012, after her patron husband fell from power, Gu was given a commuted death sentence for the murder of a British businessman in a one-day show trial. It's safe to assume that she came to a different view on judicial swiftness now, with her own neck on the line.

The Chinese system does confer rights in great abundance, but one must have power to access those rights. A motivation to reform the system is to recognize the precariousness of that arrangement. Suppose you cannot know the probability distribution of being on the Politburo or landing in jail, which system would you favor? A rational and self-interested person would choose a system of universal rights—rights that are conferred on all persons, whether a sitting Politburo member or a former one. Democracy is like an insurance policy. When you do not know whether you will have an accident, a smart thing to do is to take out insurance.

The trap of the Chinese system is that by the time the merit of the Rawlsian principle is recognized, it is too late. As Red Guards dragged him out for a struggle session, Liu Shaoqi waved a copy of the constitution and feebly protested that he had rights. Zhao Ziyang, the premier and the general secretary of the CCP in the 1980s, became a convert to democracy, but only under house arrest. His confession was published in his book *The Prisoner of the State*. In 2021, Wen Jiabao, China's premier between 1998 and 2002, published a memorial honoring his mother in an obscure paper in Macao. The article was censored and scrubbed from the Chinese internet because it expressed mild yearnings for freedom and democracy. Did he foresee this scenario when he could have done something about press freedom as China's premier? It never occurred to Hu Jintao that one day he could be ejected from the stage of a CCP conference by a strongman whose power he, as CCP's general secretary from 2002 to 2012, had steadfastly refused to dilute through political reforms and rule of law.

Would the Rawlsian reasoning resonate in China? It will critically depend on how unpredictable and erratic Chinese politics becomes. The person who keenly recognized this point is the mercurial Lin Biao. Sensing danger after the state chairmanship fiasco, he drafted a letter to Mao. In it, Lin proposed a "four no" policy. No arrest, no detention, no execution, and no firing of the current and alternate Politburo members and the top regional military commanders.[57] Lin qualified for one or more of those categories he listed, but he was surely speaking to the anxiety of a large number of the Chinese political elites at the time.

China missed a window of opportunity to permanently move away from "a world of living dangerously" immediately after the Cultural Revolution, which had targeted elites and destroyed many lives and livelihoods. Back then, the fall from victorious to vanquished was so abrupt that it blurred the line between power and powerlessness, providing an approximation of a "veil of ignorance" situation. The CCP of the 1980s enacted genuine political reforms, designed to prevent another internecine fratricide. The Cultural Revolution had taught these leaders empathy—the ability to see politics from the perspectives of both the victorious and the vanquished. The gentle politics of the 1980s ensured a degree of "live and let live."

One can hope that the wholesale assault on the Chinese elites under Xi may create a similar moment as the one after the Cultural Revolution. In this scenario, more people, including those currently in positions of power, would hopefully come around to the view that placing limitations on power is an act of self-preservation and that granting all the power to a single ruler, or to one part of the state, is inherently dangerous.

———

I opened this book with the Dazexiang Uprising, which is often used to describe the cruelty of the Qin dynasty. The real moral is more profound: it is about ignoring heterogeneity at your own risk. The *Keju* system took care of the heterogeneity problem for the Chinese emperors by restricting opportunities for new ideas to emerge. Imperial China gained in political stability from this approach, but it also paid a steep price. It lost its technological lead.

History may not repeat itself, but it rhymes. Xi Jinping is now re-imposing ideological homogeneity and everyday autocracy—now powered by the health code on everybody's phone—on a nation that is no longer in the "high-level equilibrium trap" of the imperial era. Will there be backlashes against his actions when the long-term consequences of his policy course become truly dire and unbearable? Could the zero-COVID policy, born out of CCP's supreme confidence about itself, become its undoing and its effects so extreme that it breaks the habitual psychological compliance of the Chinese society? Could Chinese elites pivot away from a ruler-centric worldview to one that is more systemic? Could another Tocquevillian moment occur?

We do not know the answers to these questions. China has surprised us before and it will surely do so again. What we do know is that the era of Xi Jinping puts back on the table many of these questions that we thought were already resolved. Under normal circumstances, China gravitates toward stability rather than convulsions, but the era of Xi is not normal and his forceful disruptions to the innovative components of the EAST model created by the reformist leaders are turning into a source of convulsions, as manifested by the nationwide protests in 2022 against his zero-COVID policy. Tumult, or small everyday acts of defiance, may be a signature of his coming era. While it is difficult to predict the lifespan of the CCP, it is not that difficult to prove that its health span has deteriorated.

Change will come when unanticipated contingencies, such as a financial crisis, a meltdown in the social order, or an abrupt and disorderly change in politics, occur. The extremity of Xi's policies, such as COVID lockdowns, may inadvertently awaken the Chinese elites to the Rawlsian proposition. China's vibrantly self-centered middle class may finally come to empathize with the small peddlers and shantytown dwellers who have been abused for years right in front of their eyes—through asset seizures, detentions, and evictions. Maybe Shanghai's white-collar professionals will come to appreciate why their Hong Kong counterparts clamored for democracy.

China may retrench further back into its autocratic past—in keeping with the persistence so characteristic of Chinese history. Or it may break out of its EAST equilibrium. Let's hope that whatever the direction and the manner of future political change in China, the long-suffering Chinese people, blessed with a semblance of normalcy between 1978 and 2018, can still reside in peace and with their livelihoods intact. Politics is statecraft for some, a passion for others, and a profession for the rest, but the Chinese people deserve better, and they deserve to be left alone.

# Chronology

## Imperial China

Spring and Autumn: 770–476 BCE
Warring-States period: 475–221 BCE
Qin dynasty: 221–207 BCE
Han dynasty: 202 BCE–220 CE
Han-Sui Interregnum (or Wei, Jin, Southern and Northern Dynasties): 220–581 (589)
Sui dynasty: 581–618
Tang dynasty: 618–907
Fives Dynasties and Ten Kingdoms period: 907–979
Song dynasty: 960–1279
Yuan dynasty: 1271–1368
Ming dynasty: 1368–1644
Qing dynasty: 1644–1911

## Contemporary China

Republic of China: 1912–1949
People's Republic of China: 1949–
—Mao Zedong: 1949–1976
—Hua Guofeng: 1976–1981
—Deng Xiaoping, Chen Yun, Hu Yaobang, and Zhao Ziyang: 1978–1989
—Jiang Zemin: 1989–2002
—Hu Jintao: 2002–2012
—Xi Jinping: 2012–

# Notes

## Introduction

*Epigraph:* Quoted in U.S. Department of State, "Foreign Relations of the United States, 1969–1976," 240.

1. Unless otherwise noted, I use the chronological dates published on the website of the Chinese government, http://www.gov.cn/guoqing/2005–09/13/content_2582651.htm, accessed March 20, 2020.

2. The figures cited here are from the website Heyzhen.com, https://www.heyzhen.com/%E4%B8%AD%E5%9B%BD%E5%8E%86%E4%BB%A3%E7%9A%84%E7%96%86%E5%9F%9F%E9%9D%A2%E7%A7%AF/#%E5%85%83%E6%9C%9D1400%E4%B8%87%E5%B9%B3%E6%96%B9%E5%85%AC%E9%87%8C.

3. Historical estimates of these geographic areas are not precise or uniform. I have consulted four sources for the estimates that have the longest time-series observations. Using all available estimates and averaging them provides the same conclusions.

4. Guowuyuan, *Zhongguo Disanci Renkou Pucha Ziliao Fenxi.*

5. Between the two Hans, Wang Mang (45 BCE–23 CE) usurped power and created the Xin dynasty (9 BCE–24 CE).

6. Spence, *Search for Modern China*, 194.

7. Nathan, "China's Changing of the Guard."

8. Huang, "Why China Will Not Collapse."

9. Sng, "Size and Dynastic Decline."

10. Alesina and Spolaore, *Size of Nations.*

11. Scheidel, *Escape from Rome.*

12. Ibid.

13. Grandin, *End of the Myth*, 27.

14. The discussion in this section is based on Grandin, *End of the Myth.*

15. Stasavage, *Decline and Rise of Democracy.*

16. Langworth, *Churchill by Himself.*

17. Quoted in Sen, "Contrary India."
18. Fearon, "Ethnic and Cultural Diversity by Country."
19. Hasan and Jandoc, "Distribution of Firm Size in India."
20. Subramanian, *Of Counsel*.
21. Science is advanced through forming consensuses among scientists. See Oreskes, *Why Trust Science?* for this view.
22. Hale et al., "Russia May Be about to Invade Ukraine."
23. This entry was deleted. See forty-two "notable" names on Wikipedia's "List of Chinese Dissidents": https://en.wikipedia.org/wiki/List_of_Chinese_dissidents, accessed July 12, 2020. Keep in mind that most of the forty-two individuals have been dissidents during the reform era, a far more open period than the Soviet era.
24. Strittmatter, *We Have Been Harmonized*.
25. Wang, *The China Order*.
26. I heard this from the late Professor Roderick MacFarquhar.
27. Fu, *Autocratic Tradition and Chinese Politics*.
28. Scheidel, *Escape from Rome*.
29. Bell, *China Model*.
30. This is my own coinage. In the official historiography, this period is known as "Wei, Jin, and Southern and Northern dynasties."
31. Acemoglu and Robinson, *Narrow Corridor*.
32. Lee, *AI Superpowers*.
33. See China Biographical Database Project at Harvard University, https://projects.iq.harvard.edu/cbdb/home, accessed July 8, 2014.
34. Needham, *Grand Titration*.

## Chapter One. *Keju* as a Scaling Instrument

*Epigraph:* Quoted in Chen, "Civil Service Examination and Culture of Two Song Dynasties."

1. For a detailed review of *Keju*'s influence in Asia, see Liu, "Influence of China's Imperial Examinations on Japan, Korea and Vietnam." For an interesting look at how anonymized auditions led to more female musicians being hired in orchestras, and benefited women and minority candidates in the Swedish labor market, see Goldin and Rouse, "Orchestrating Impartiality," and Åslund and Skans, "Do Anonymous Job Application Procedures Level the Playing Field?"
2. Têng, "Chinese Influence on the Western Examination System."
3. The literature on *Keju* is substantial in both Chinese and English. My sources include Bai and Jia, "Elite Recruitment and Political Stability"; Chen, *Tang Song Keju Zhidu Yanjiu*; Chen, Kung, and Ma, "Long Live *Keju!*"; Ch'ien, *Merits and Demerits of Political Systems in Dynastic China*; Guo, "Size and Admission Rate of Keju in the Ming Dynasty"; Guo, *Mingdai Xuexiao Keju Yu Renguan Zhidu Yanjiu*; Huang, "Study of the Chinese Civil Service Examination System in Ming Times"; Hucker, "Governmental Organization of the

Ming Dynasty"; Jiang and Kung, "Social Mobility in Pre-Industrial China"; Liu, *Zhongguo keju wenhua*; and Miyazaki, *China's Examination Hell*.

4. Fu, *Autocratic Tradition and Chinese Politics*.
5. Huang Liuzhu, *Qinhan Shijin Zhidu*.
6. Ibid.
7. Chi'en, *Traditional Government in Imperial China*.
8. Chen, "An Explanation on 'Han Official Needs to Be Able to Recite 9000 Words.'"
9. Chinese Government, "Sao Chu Wen Mang Gong Zuo Tiao Li."
10. Yuan, *Sinitic Civilization*, vol. 2, 389.
11. Zhang Chuangxin, *Zhongguo zhengzhi zhidushi*; Ho, *Ladder of Success*.
12. Fu, *Autocratic Tradition and Chinese Politics*, 97.
13. Sun, *Collection on Tang and Song History*.
14. This section is based on Brook, *Troubled Empire*, 2013.
15. Bol, *Neo-Confucianism in History*, 118.
16. Fu, *Autocratic Tradition and Chinese Politics*, 97.
17. Spence, *Search for Modern China*.
18. Zhang Chuangxin, *Zhongguo zhengzhi zhidushi*; Guo, *Mingdai Xuexiao Keju Yu Renguan Zhidu Yanjiu*.
19. Elman, *Civil Examinations and Meritocracy*, 227.
20. South refers to Zhejiang, Jiangxi, Fujian, Yingtian, Guangdong, and Huguang; north refers to Shuntian, Shandong, Shanxi, Henan, and Shaanxi; and central China is comprised of Guangxi, Sichuan, and Yungui.
21. An independent website by Erik Jacobsen provides a brief discussion on the history of standardized tests in the United States. See http://www.erikthered.com/tutor/sat-act-history.html, accessed July 3, 2021.
22. Fukuyama discusses the "precociously modern" features of the Chinese imperial system. See Fukuyama, *Origins of Political Order*.
23. Elman, *Civil Examinations and Meritocracy*, 56.
24. History has a way of exacting revenge. Wang Ao cast a far larger influence than Shang's "three firsts." His essay set the standard for the *Keju* essays for the next five hundred years. Wang is credited with creating the essay style known as the "eight-legged essay" that was emulated by future generations of *Keju* candidates.
25. See a review in Björklund and Salvanes, "Education and Family Background."
26. The primary source of the data is the China Biographical Database (CBDB) created and maintained at Harvard University. We used the Ming Jingshi-lu_52y_release.xlsx dataset of the CBDB in our analysis.
27. Fairbank, *China*.
28. Ch'ien, *Traditional Government in Imperial China*.
29. Hart, *The 100*. In addition to his insights on Sui Wendi and other historical figures, the quixotic Hart is also known for his advocacy of white separatism.
30. Central Committee Document Office, *Mao Zedong Duwenguji Piyuji*. Notably, other than Sui Wendi's lack of interest in books, the two men were not that dissimilar from each other.

31. See Fu, *Autocratic Tradition and Chinese Politics*.
32. Sutton and Rao, *Scaling Up Excellence*.
33. Fu, *Autocratic Tradition and Chinese Politics*, 56.
34. Fukuyama, *Origins of Political Order*.
35. Fu, *Autocratic Tradition and Chinese Politics*, 193.
36. Kristof, "Suicide of Jiang Qing."
37. This description of Wu Zetian draws from Paludan, *Chronicle of the Chinese Emperors*.
38. See Wilkinson, *Chinese History*, 898.
39. Paludan, *Chronicle of the Chinese Emperors*, 101.
40. Han, "Political Incentives for Wu Zetian's Keju Reform."
41. Elman, "Political, Social, and Cultural Reproduction."
42. Liu Haifeng, *Zhongguo keju wenhua*.
43. Chen, *Tang Song Keju Zhidu Yanjiu*.
44. Liu Haifeng, *Zhongguo keju wenhua*.
45. Blank, "Effects of Double-Blind versus Single-Blind Reviewing."
46. Ho, *Ladder of Success*, 216.
47. Yang, Wang, and Yang provide details about his anti-corruption campaign in their article, "Probe into the Anti-Corruption Mechanism."
48. Wu, *Zhu Yuanzhang Zhuan*.
49. This discussion on Zhu Yuanzhang is based on Fu, *Autocratic Tradition and Chinese Politics*.
50. In 2018, while the average admission rate for China's top four hundred universities was 12.4 percent, it was 30 percent for Beijing and only 10 percent for Guangxi, Henan, and Shanxi. See Tencent, "Big Data on Gaokao."
51. Ma Mingdao, *Mingchao Huangjia Xinyangkao Chugao*.
52. Fu, *Autocratic Tradition and Chinese Politics*.
53. Elman, *Cultural History of Civil Examinations*.
54. Harvard Yenching Library is one of the creators of the Chinese Text Project; see the website https://ctext.org/, accessed on March 20, 2022.
55. Ho, *Ladder of Success*, 11.
56. This account is based on Deresiewicz, *Excellent Sheep*.
57. Fu, *Autocratic Tradition and Chinese Politics*, 70.

## Chapter Two. Organizing China—and the CCP

1. Micklethwait and Wooldridge, *Fourth Revolution*.
2. Fukuyama, *Political Order and Political Decay*, 3.
3. Young, *Rise of the Meritocracy*.
4. Kung and Chen, "Tragedy of the *Nomenklatura*."
5. Harding, *Organizing China*.
6. Qian and Xu, "M-Form Hierarchy and China's Economic Reform."
7. Williamson, *Markets and Hierarchies*.
8. Chandler, *Strategy and Structure*; ibid.

9. In 1992, the average domestic trade/GDP ratio for the twenty-six provinces for which data are available was 14.7 percent compared with their average foreign trade/GDP ratio, which was 17.5 percent. Trade among the European Community countries was 28.3 percent. Figures from World Bank, *China*, 37–43.

10. See Vogel, *One Step Ahead in China*.

11. Hayek, "Use of Knowledge in Society."

12. Huang, "Information, Bureaucracy, and Economic Reforms."

13. Susan Shirk offers a good critique of this simplistic economistic rendition of the reforms in her book *Political Logic*.

14. Harding, *China's Second Revolution* presents an account of this episode.

15. Bo is the son of Bo Yibo, one of the revolutionary founders of the PRC. See YouTube, https://www.youtube.com/watch?v=MVPvJRB74NM, accessed June 8, 2018.

16. Lawrence and Martin, "Understanding China's Political System."

17. This is a well-established finding by many researchers. In addition, over time, outsiders made up a greater share of governors, party secretaries, and members of the provincial standing committees of the CCP. See Li, "Analysis of Current Provincial Leaders"; Zeng "Control, Discretion and Bargaining"; and Bo, *Chinese Provincial Leaders*.

18. Zeng, "Control, Discretion and Bargaining."

19. Ministerial officials live and work where the top leaders are, giving them access to and ties with the selectorate. The political science literature portrays Chinese politics as riven by informal and factional ties. (See, for example, Shih, Adolph, and Liu, "Getting Ahead in the Communist Party.") This reasoning privileges ministerial officials above provincial officials, but the ministers in Beijing typically do not go very far in national politics. Nor does a particular group of regional officials with ties to the central government, that is, those who rule Beijing. There is something about their geographic proximity to the central government that works against their political proximity to it.

20. On Soviet politics, see Hough and Fainsod, *How the Soviet Union Is Governed*. On the Soviet economy, see Hewett, *Reforming the Soviet Economy*. On the Gorbachev era, see Zubok, *Collapse*.

21. This list does not include Georgy Malenkov, who ruled as a top leader for only several weeks before being replaced by Khrushchev.

22. Landry, *Decentralized Authoritarianism in China*.

23. This view was expressed in the books by Huang and Landry. See Huang, *Inflation and Investment Controls*; Landry, *Decentralized Authoritarianism in China*.

24. Williamson, *Markets and Hierarchies*.

25. Landry, *Decentralized Authoritarianism in China*.

26. Li and Zhou, "Political Turnover and Economic Performance"; Shih, Adolph, and Liu, "Getting Ahead in the Communist Party."

27. Yin et al., "Effect of Air Pollution."

28. For more details on this incident, see Lieberthal and Oksenberg, *Policy Making in China*, 253.
29. A textbook treatment is Milgrom and Roberts, *Economics, Organization, and Management*.
30. Jensen and Meckling, "Theory of the Firm," 308.
31. Nove, *Soviet Economic System*, 93–94.
32. Holmström, "Managerial Incentive Problems."
33. There is firm-level support for this proposition. SOE managers being considered for a political promotion are found to receive fewer explicit incentives (that is, lower pay) compared with those who are not being considered. This is consistent with the theory that implicit incentives related to career concerns can substitute for explicit incentives related to wage and salary. See Cao et al., "Political Promotion."
34. Lieberthal and Oksenberg, *Policy Making in China*.
35. Huang, *Inflation and Investment Controls*; Huang and Sheng, "Political Decentralization and Inflation."
36. Xie, *Brief History*, 171.
37. Fu, *Autocratic Tradition and Chinese Politics*, 83–84.
38. Huang, "Managing Chinese Bureaucrats."
39. These periods are the Cultural Revolution (1966–1976) and the period between 1977 and 1982 when the post–Cultural Revolution leadership mounted a wholesale purge of officials who had been promoted during the Cultural Revolution.
40. Landry, *Decentralized Authoritarianism in China*.
41. Manion, *Corruption by Design*.
42. For the original citation, see Huang, "Managing Chinese Bureaucrats."
43. A counterargument is expertise. Managing the various provinces requires similar skills, whereas managing the various ministries requires different skills. This argument discounts regional knowledge and expertise. In any case, evidence does not support it. In my 2002 paper "Managing Chinese Bureaucrats," I investigated the ministerial promotions and found that cross-ministerial promotions—moving from a junior to a senior position—are not infrequent. Expertise considerations do not drive promotional patterns.

## Chapter Three. A State without a Society

*Epigraph: New York Times*, "Singapore's Lee Kuan Yew."
1. Ray Huang told the famous tale of Wanli in his book *1587*. Unless otherwise noted, my writing is based on this book.
2. Henrich, *WEIRDest People*.
3. Ray Huang states, "From their classical education, including historical lessons, the entire population had learned that fathers must be impartial to their sons, that elder brothers were supposed to command and lead their younger brothers, and that men of rectitude should never be swayed by the

influence of women to modify their public obligations because of private sentiments. These tenets had been repeatedly cited in every school in every village and even passed on to the illiterate to keep the empire in order." Huang, *1587*, 64.

4.  Migdal, *Strong Societies and Weak States*.
5.  Acemoglu and Robinson, *Narrow Corridor*.
6.  Stasavage, *Decline and Rise of Democracy*.
7.  Shue, *Reach of the State*; Szonyi, *Art of Being Governed*.
8.  Khilnani, *Idea of India*, 9.
9.  Anderson, *Private Government*, 37.
10. Fukuyama, *Origins of Political Order*, 273.
11. This section is based on Dincecco and Wang, *Violent Conflict*, and Wang, "Sons and Lovers."
12. This section draws from Zhang, "When Were Marriages between Cousins Banned?"
13. Ebrey, "Concubines in Sung China."
14. Wang, "Sons and Lovers."
15. Scarisbrick, *Henry VIII*, 498.
16. This discussion is based on Zhang Jian, "Zhongguo gudai guojia zongjiao lishitedian yanjiu."
17. Xiong, Bin Ye, and Bihan Cai, "Needham Puzzle."
18. The term applies to those who passed *Keju* and who acquired official positions. See Tackett, *Destruction of the Medieval Chinese Aristocracy*.
19. For excellent treatment of the market economy during the Song dynasty, see Liu, *Chinese Market Economy*.
20. Wakeman, *Fall of Imperial China*.
21. Rajan and Zingales, *Saving Capitalism*.
22. Wu Xiaobo, *Lidai Jingji Biange Deshi*, 100.
23. Mungello, *Great Encounter*.
24. Fukuyama, *Political Order and Political Decay*, 68.
25. This discussion is based on Creel, *Origins of Statecraft in China*.
26. Ibid., 25.
27. Ibid.
28. Fukuyama, *Political Order and Political Decay*.
29. Ibid., 196. Stasavage traced this sequencing development to an earlier era, at the dawn of human civilization; see Stasavage, *Decline and Rise of Democracy*.
30. Acemoglu and Robinson, *Narrow Corridor*.
31. Ho, *Ladder of Success*.
32. Bai and Jia, "Elite Recruitment and Political Stability."
33. Guo, *Mingdai Xuexiao Keju Yu Renguan Zhidu Yanjiu*.
34. Huang and Yang, "Longevity Mechanism."
35. Rawski, *Education and Popular Literacy*, 23.
36. See Liu Yonghua, "Qingdai Minzhong Shizi Wentide Zairenshi."

37. Xu Yi and Leeuwen, "Shijiushiji Zhongguo Dazhong Shizillvde Zaigusuan 19."
38. Rawski, *Education and Popular Literacy*, 11.
39. Brook, *Troubled Empire*, 200.
40. Ibid.
41. Naquin and Rawski, *Chinese Society in the Eighteenth Century*.
42. Rawski, *Education and Popular Literacy*, 11.
43. Zhao Gang, *Zhongguo Chengshi Fazhanshilunji*.
44. Elman, *Civil Examinations and Meritocracy*, 19.
45. The odds vary by race. African Americans in the United States face the lowest odds, at 0.064, according to researchers at the Federal Reserve and reported by Stilwell, "What Are Your Odds?"
46. Guo, "Size and Admission Rate of Keju in the Ming Dynasty."
47. Henrich, *WEIRDest People*.
48. Table 4 in Xu Yi and Leeuwen, "Shijiushiji Zhongguo Dazhong Shizillvde Zaigusuan 19."
49. Henrich, *WEIRDest People*, 7.
50. Buringh and Zanden, "Charting the 'Rise of the West,'" table 4.
51. Ibid., cited by Henrich in *WEIRDest People*, used demand for books to estimate literacy, whereas Rawski used school records. Rawski's figure refers to male literacy, but the methodology used by Buringh and Zanden cannot distinguish between male and female literacy.
52. Oxford University, Our World in Data, https://ourworldindata.org/literacy, accessed February 2, 2020.
53. These figures are from Bao Weimin, "Zhongguo Jiudaoshisanshiji Shehuishizilv Digaodejige Wenti."
54. Ho, *Ladder of Success*, 14.
55. Miyazaki, *China's Examination Hell*.
56. Elizabeth Perry writes that "the meritocratic and impartial reputation of the Confucian examination system made it a mainstay in upholding the legitimacy of the imperial Chinese state."
57. Perry, "Higher Education and Authoritarian Resilience"; Henrich, *WEIRDest People*.
58. Yong Zhao of University of Kansas offers a sweeping critique of standardized tests based on the Chinese model; see Zhao, *Who's Afraid of the Big Bad Dragon?* For a good discussion on liberal arts vis-à-vis standardized tests in an Asian context, see Nussbaum, "Democracy, Education, and the Liberal Arts."
59. Here, I use Chinese and East Asians or Easterners interchangeably.
60. Epicurus argued that "happiness . . . [is] a matter of individual definition, and any a priori commitment of a civic or political kind carried the initial suspicion of being a snare designed to trap the individual and to make him conform to a public definition of happiness." See Wolin, *Politics and Vision*, 72.
61. Sen, *Argumentative Indian*.

62. Weber, *The Religion of China*.
63. Scheidel, *Escape from Rome*.
64. Putnam, *Bowling Alone*.

## Chapter Four. Reversion to the Autocratic Mean

*Epigraph:* Zubok, *Collapse*.

1. This is described in Saich, *From Rebel to Ruler*, 291. The play *What if I Were Real* is a satire of official power and privilege.
2. See "Ranlingdao Xianfei Guiding Zainali?"
3. Li, "In Chinese Corruption Cases, Who's Taking What?"
4. Goldman, *Sowing the Seeds of Democracy*.
5. Saich, *From Rebel to Ruler*, 297.
6. Ibid., 302.
7. Vogel, *Deng Xiaoping*.
8. Zhao, *Prisoner of the State*, 123.
9. Saich, *From Rebel to Ruler*, 291–293.
10. Zhao, *Prisoner of the State*, and Vogel, *Deng Xiaoping*, both have a detailed account of this episode.
11. Deng, *Shierge Chunqiu, 1975–1987*.
12. The literature on TVEs is large. I provided a review of this literature in my 2008 book Huang, *Capitalism with Chinese Characteristics*.
13. This quotation is from the fascinating book by Wu Xiaobo called *Jidang Sanshi Nian 1978–2008*, vol. 1, 3.
14. Vogel, *Deng Xiaoping*.
15. This section draws from my 2008 book Huang, *Capitalism with Chinese Characteristics*. The research for that book was based on detailed archival evidence and numerous records of Chinese banks.
16. Allen, Qian, and Qian, "Law, Finance, and Economic Growth in China"; Tsai, *Back-Alley Banking*.
17. Wu, *Jidang Sanshi Nian, 1978–2008*, vol. 1.
18. Ibid., vol. 1, 55.
19. The following two episodes are from ibid., vol. 1, 85–86.
20. Media coverage attracted the attention of a central leader, who then inquired about the matter. See ibid.
21. Tocqueville, *Ancien Régime and the Revolution*.
22. Fewsmith, *Rethinking Chinese Politics*, 101–108.
23. I discuss this issue in detail in my forthcoming book Huang, *Statism with Chinese Characteristics*.
24. Wu, *Jidang Sanshi Nian, 1978–2008*, vol. 1, 175.
25. Qian and Huang, "Political Institutions, Entrenchments, and the Sustainability of Economic Development."
26. If we use the original data published by the Chinese government, rural household income grew at 12 percent a year in the 1980s, but the deflators

used in the calculation might be too low. So here I am using the growth rate between 1984 and 1988 and projecting it onto the entire decade of the 1980s.

27. Huang and Qian, "How Gradualist Are Chinese Reforms?"

28. Zhang, *Tiananmen Papers*, 151.

29. Naughton, *Chinese Economy*, 322.

30. China.org.cn, "Corruption Is Crucial Threat, Wen Says."

31. Sun, *Corruption and Market*, 48.

32. Another excellent study is Minxin Pei's *China's Crony Capitalism*. The limitation of Pei's book is that most of his data are from 1990 onward, limiting our ability to assess changes over time.

33. Alternative interpretations, such as changes in the anti-corruption targets and in the nature of press reporting, do not hold. In the 1980s, the CCP did target politically important figures, such as those connected with Kanghua Corporation, and the press freedom in the 1980s was substantial.

34. Fewsmith, "Succession That Didn't Happen."

35. Kuhn, *Man Who Changed China*, 164.

36. Ibid., 163.

37. Zhang, *Tiananmen Papers*, 310.

38. Ji, "Jiang Zemin's Command of the Military."

39. Zu and Mukhin argue that this is a key difference between China and the former Soviet Union in how they tackled the exit and the treatment of predecessors. See Zhu and Mukhin, "Modern Regency."

40. Fewsmith, *China Since Tiananmen*, 76.

41. Deng contemplated replacing Jiang in 1993 because he thought Jiang was too conservative. Deng also intervened in the selection of Hu Jintao as Jiang's successor, a decision by Deng that planted some animosity between the two that would plague Hu Jintao's entire tenure from 2002 to 2012.

42. The vote on martial law at the PSC meeting on May 17, 1989, was deadlocked: two for and two against with one abstention. The decision then defaulted to the elders who decided in favor of martial law. There appeared to be a secret resolution by the PSC to refer any stalemate to the elders. See Nathan, "Tiananmen Papers."

43. Kristof, "A Year Later."

44. An institution acquires identity, interests, and new members over time, and it claims resources and allies along the way. Just as the Democrats in the United States have found it extraordinarily difficult to eliminate the Senate filibuster rule, the CCP after Deng and Chen would have encountered many obstacles to terminate an institution comprised of former leaders. Incumbency breeds vested interests in its continuation and builds its own defense mechanisms.

## Chapter Five. What Makes Chinese Autocracy So Stable?

*Epigraph:* Karl Marx, "Revolution in China and in Europe," *New York Daily Tribune,* June 14, 1853, available at https://www.marxists.org/archive/marx/works/1853/06/14.htm.

1. Ray Huang's wonderful book *1575: A Year of Insignificance* gives readers a fly-on-the-wall view of what went on in the inner sanctum of Wanli's court.
2. Preskar, "Roman Emperor."
3. Shiono, *Rome Was Not Built in a Day,* vol. 1.
4. Fu, *Autocratic Tradition and Chinese Politics,* 2.
5. Kuroski, "Lineage."
6. Wang, *China Order,* 48.
7. For a literature survey, see Zhao, *Confucian-Legalist State.*
8. Fu, *Autocratic Tradition and Chinese Politics,* 68.
9. Pines, *Everlasting Empire,* 3.
10. Grieder, *Intellectuals and the State,* 19.
11. Ho, "Presidential Address."
12. Fukuyama, *Origins of Political Order*; Zhao, *Confucian-Legalist State.*
13. Zhao, *Confucian-Legalist State.*
14. Fukuyama, *Origins of Political Order.*
15. Diamond, *Guns, Germs, and Steel*; Morris, *Why the West Rules.*
16. Ho, "Presidential Address," 554.
17. Zhao, *Confucian-Legalist State,* 58–59.
18. This is described in Scheidel, *Escape from Rome.*
19. Gibbon, *History.*
20. Levathes, *When China Ruled the Seas.*
21. Fogel, *Politics and Sinology,* 1980. Unless otherwise noted, this summary of major ideas of the Great Tang-Song Transition is based on the books by Fogel and Miyakawa. See Fogel, *Politics and Sinology,* 1980; Miyakawa, "Outline of the Naito Hypothesis."
22. Pinker, *Better Angels of Our Nature.*
23. Mingxi Lishi, "Economic Analysis."
24. Twitchett, *Cambridge History of China,* vol. 3.
25. Davis and Weinstein, "Bones, Bombs, and Break Points."
26. Tackett, *Destruction.*
27. Hartwell, "Demographic, Political, and Social Transformations."
28. Fu, *Autocratic Tradition and Chinese Politics.*
29. Blaydes and Chaney, "Feudal Revolution"; Kokkonen and Sundell, "Delivering Stability"; Wang, "Sons and Lovers."
30. Svolik, *Politics of Authoritarian Rule.*
31. Hirschman, *Exit, Voice, and Loyalty.*
32. Zhao, *Confucian-Legalist State,* 297.
33. The fit is defined by how close the actual values are to the predicted values of the fitted model. These nine dynasties generate the lowest residuals. The

average of their absolute values is 1.22 compared with 6.84 for the rest of the dynasties.

34. Zhao, *Confucian-Legalist State*.

35. I have also tried two other definitions. One is to include the Sui in the second period, and the other is to define the first period as including the Tang. The results are largely consistent with the results reported in the table. But the statistical significance of the dynasty duration is sensitive to these two alternate definitions.

36. Was the Grand Canal behind an increase in dynastic and emperor durations? That would require a convoluted reasoning, about how, say, lower transportation costs empowered regimes rather than the enemies of the regimes. It is not a parsimonious explanation. I know of no theory, nor do I recognize any reasonable logic, that can connect the Grand Canal with a reduction of premier executions and an increase of their resignations as an exit option. The Grand Canal offers a poor explanation for the emerging symbiotic relationship between emperors and officials after Sui.

37. See Svolik, *Politics of Authoritarian Rule*, 6, for a representation of Machiavelli's view.

38. Bueno de Mesquita et al., *Logic of Political Survival*.

39. Bai and Jia, "Elite Recruitment and Political Stability." In our ongoing research with Clair Yang, we did not find evidence that mass rebellions diminished in the wake of *Keju*, casting doubt on the idea that social mobility was the main reason why political stability prevailed.

40. Björklund and Salvanes, "Education and Family Background."

41. Hucker, "Governmental Organization."

42. Calculated from the imperial court database.

43. Huang, *1587*, 31.

44. Elman, *Civil Examinations and Meritocracy*, 51.

45. This is translated from classical Chinese quoted by Chen, "Civil Service Examination and Culture of Two Song Dynasties," 57. The original Chinese is here: "向者登科名级，多为世家所取，致塞孤寒之路，甚无谓也。今朕躬亲临试，以可否进退，尽革除昔之弊矣。"

46. Elman, *Civil Examinations and Meritocracy*, 101.

47. Please refer to Huang and Yang, "Longevity Mechanism," for details on the database, variables we used and constructed, robustness checks, and the econometrics procedure.

48. After an extensive survey of the literature, Björklund and Salvanes conclude that in all countries for which they have data, more than 50 percent of the variation in years of schooling may be attributed to family background factors, among which family income is among the most important. See Björklund and Salvanes, "Education and Family Background."

49. Eberhard, *Social Mobility*; Miyazaki, *China's Examination Hell*.

50. Elvin, *Pattern of the Chinese Past*.

51. Svolik, "Power Sharing and Leadership Dynamics."

52. Blaydes and Chaney, "Feudal Revolution and Europe's Rise."
53. Fu, *Autocratic Tradition and Chinese Politics*, 122.
54. Hofstede, Hofstede, and Minkov, *Cultures and Organizations*.
55. This is described in Huang, *1587*, 54.
56. This account is based on ibid., 96–101. In his book, Huang spelled Zheng De as Cheng-te.
57. Ho, *Ladder of Success*, 218.
58. Spence, *Emperor of China*, 50.
59. Fukuyama, *Origins of Political Order*; Craig, *Heritage of Chinese Civilization*.
60. Fogel, *Politics and Sinology*, 171.
61. Fu, *Autocratic Tradition and Chinese Politics*, 59.
62. Ibid., 61.
63. Quoted in Spence, *Emperor of China*, 80.
64. Fu, *Autocratic Tradition and Chinese Politics*, 61.
65. Ho, *Ladder of Success*, 189.
66. A vivid account of the Taiping Rebellion is in Platt, *Autumn in the Heavenly Kingdom*.
67. Li and Lin, "A Re-Estimation."
68. Wright, *China in Revolution*, 2.
69. Grieder, *Intellectuals and the State*.

## Chapter Six. Tullock's Curse

*Epigraph:* After Mao died, Hua Guofeng capitalized on Mao's instruction to great effect. Whether Mao also instructed him to seek counsel with Jiang Qing was never confirmed. The rumor in Beijing at the time was that Jiang Qing manufactured the addendum. See an account in "Mao Zedong Yizhuzhimi."
1. In Chinese this is "公道不蠢." See "Ye Jianying Yi Mao Zedong Lingzhong Tuogu."
2. Central Committee Documentation Research Office, *Chen Yun Nianpu*.
3. Tullock, *Autocracy*.
4. Nathan, "China's Changing of the Guard."
5. Chang, *Coming Collapse of China*.
6. Zhu, "Performance Legitimacy." The general theoretical point comes from Huntington, *Political Order in Changing Societies*. Huntington distinguishes between regimes that derive legitimacy from representation and regimes that deliver "benevolent results."
7. For an overview of this perspective, see Girard, "Secret."
8. Dikötter gives the highest estimate, and his book cites other estimates. Even if we accept the lowest estimate, the official 16.5 million, the Great Leap Forward is still among the greatest man-made disasters in modern history. See Dikötter, *Mao's Great Famine*.
9. See MacFarquhar and Schoenhals, *Mao's Last Revolution* for some of the estimates.

10. Naughton, *Chinese Economy*, 214–215.
11. This estimate was given by Cheng Li in a lecture at Harvard's Fairbank Center for Chinese Studies on December 8, 2021. See the video at https://www.youtube.com/watch?v=xn6DxmelkLU, accessed October 15, 2022.
12. Snyder, *On Tyranny*.
13. See *People's Daily Online*, "Xi Jinping Diguode Sange Xuanjin Dinlu Doushisha?"
14. Successful performance on *Keju* in the Ming dynasty was correlated with school enrollments in the twenty-first century. See Chen, Kung, and Ma, "Long Live *Keju!*"
15. Perry, "Higher Education and Authoritarian Resilience."
16. Lim and Blanchard, "Exclusive."
17. Sina News, "Pandian Shaohuai Dianchaoji de Yiwan Tanguan."
18. Cunningham, Saich, and Turiel, "Understanding CCP Resilience."
19. Ibid. Being exposed to a corruption investigation reduces about 0.001 out of a 1 to 10 scale of legitimacy variables, and it is unlikely that the marginal effect of the exposure remains constant.
20. Richard Nisbett states, "What captures one's attention is what one is likely to regard as causally important." See Nisbett, *The Geography of Thought*.
21. Ibid.
22. Cunningham, Saich, and Turiel, "Understanding CCP Resilience."
23. Maybe respondents feared reprisals if they expressed negative opinions about the higher authorities. True, but it is the local officials who are tasked with carrying out reprisals, and citizens freely express their negative opinions about local officials. To make sense of this unusual hierarchical satisfaction requires more than a reprisal calculation.
24. These accounts about aspirational emperors were available at http://mp.weixin.qq.com/s/cpzM_rrN6whlh8NQplvOyQ, accessed January 6, 2018. They have since been deleted.
25. Ongoing research by Yiqing Xu at Stanford University is examining this phenomenon. Personal communication with Yiqing Xu.
26. Pan and Xu, "China's Ideological Spectrum."
27. Tullock, *Autocracy*.
28. See Kurrild-Klitgaard, "Constitutional Economics"; Kokkonen and Sundell "Delivering Stability"; and Wang, "Sons and Lovers."
29. Li, *Private Life of Chairman Mao*, 183.
30. In Chinese: "只有毛主席能当大英雄，别人谁也不要想当英雄，你我离得远的很，不要打这个主意。" This is from Gu and Du, *Mao Zedong He Tade Gao Canmen*.
31. MacFarquhar, *Origins of the Cultural Revolution*, vol. 3, 262.
32. Shirk, "China in Xi's 'New Era,'" 22.
33. Buchanan and Tullock, *Calculus of Consent*.
34. Tullock, *Autocracy*, 151.
35. Herz, "Problem of Successorship," 30.

36. Wertime, "Finally."
37. Osnos, "Born Red."
38. Zhao, *Prisoner of the State*, 169.
39. As early as 1980, in his interview with Italian journalist Oriana Fallaci, Deng made his point clear about the retirement of the entire cohort of elders. See Vogel, *Deng Xiaoping*, 556.
40. Zhao, *Prisoner of the State*, 175.
41. Ibid., 173.
42. Pang and Feng, *Mao Zedong Nianpu, 1949–1976*, 493.
43. Zhou was never formally designated as a crown prince, but he would most likely have succeeded Mao if he had outlived him. For Zhou, the rational strategy was not getting a formal designation, but surviving his purge. Maybe Mao knew this. Zhou's cancer diagnosis was confirmed on May 18, 1972, and his doctors immediately devised a treatment plan. In a bizarre twist, the treatment plan required approval from Mao, but Mao withheld his approval until March 5, 1973, delaying Zhou's treatment during a crucial phase of his illness. The account is based on interviews with people working closely with Zhou Enlai, including his doctor and his official photographer. See Gu, *Zhou Enlai Zuihou 600 Tian*.
44. Dikötter, *How to Be a Dictator*, 109.
45. This section is based on Salisbury, *New Emperors*, 284–285.
46. MacFarquhar, *Origins of the Cultural Revolution*, vol. 3, 258.
47. Quoted in Dikötter, *Mao's Great Famine*, 100.
48. Quoted in MacFarquhar, *Origins of the Cultural Revolution*, vol. 3, 258.
49. Shirk, "China in Xi's 'New Era,'" 23.
50. Jiang, "Nengyuan Fazhan Shishi Ji Zhuyao Jieneng Cuoshi."
51. Lorge, "Entrance and Exit."
52. Huntington, *Political Order in Changing Societies*; Umansky, "Why Is Qaddafi Still a Colonel?"
53. Joffe, *Chinese Army after Mao*.
54. Ji, "Jiang Zemin's Command of the Military."
55. See Worship, "Witness."
56. Saich, *From Rebel to Ruler*, 330.
57. Cheng, "Was the Shanghai Gang Shanghaied?"
58. Gillespie and Okruhlik, "Political Dimensions."
59. Tullock, *Autocracy*, 152.
60. Kuhn, *Man Who Changed China*, 211–218, contains information on this episode. He writes that Deng was considering replacing Jiang with Qiao Shi, a more reformist PBSC member, and that Qiao Shi himself advised some leading comrades who had feigned support for the reforms to step down from power.
61. An early piece on this topic is Cheng, "End of the CCP's Resilient Authoritarianism?"
62. Vogel, *Deng Xiaoping*.

## Chapter Seven. Reframing the Needham Question

*Epigraph:* The English version of this quotation is from septisphere.word
press.com/2014/01/28/four-great-inventions/. Like many Europeans of his
era, Bacon referred to paper as a part of printing.

1. Levathes, *When China Ruled the Seas.*
2. The term is used by Ian Morris in his *Why the West Rules,* 413, to describe
   rulers who made consequential but stupid decisions. He includes Ming emperors in this category.
3. Jones, *European Miracle,* 160.
4. Very few academics have biographies written about them. Needham is one of
   them. See Winchester, *The Man Who Loved China.*
5. Needham, *Grand Titration.*
6. Needham and Harbsmeier, *Science and Civilisation in China,* vol. 7.
7. Rostoker and Dvorak, "Cast-Iron Bells."
8. Ronan and Needham, *Shorter Science and Civilisation in China.*
9. Mokyr, *Lever of Riches.*
10. Temple, *Genius of China,* 9.
11. Landes remarks, "The ingenuity and inventiveness of the Chinese, which
    have given so much to mankind—silk, tea, porcelain, paper, printing, and
    more—would no doubt have enriched China further and probably brought
    it to the threshold of modern industry, had it not been for this stifling state
    control." Landes, *Wealth and Poverty of Nations,* 57.
12. Morris, *Why the West Rules,* 520.
13. North, "Government and the Cost of Exchange," 160.
14. Needham, *Grand Titration,* 27.
15. Ibid.
16. Mao Zhonggeng, "Zhongguo Gudai Kexuejia Zhengti Zhuangkuan Tongji
    Yanjiu."
17. Dai Jianping, "Zhongguo Gudai Kexuejia Lishi Fenbude Tongjifenxi."
18. The compilations are in four volumes. See Ouyang and Hu, *Zhongguo Gudai
    Mingren Fenlei Dacidian.*
19. A potential bias is that since official activities are better documented, those
    with an official status more likely make it into the official record. But even if
    we arbitrarily cut the percentage by half, still 25 to 30 percent of the scien-
    tists and technologists had government backing.
20. Needham, *Grand Titration,* 25.
21. Stasavage, *Decline and Rise of Democracy.*
22. The figures are provided in Dai Jianping, "Zhongguo Gudai Kexuejia Lishi
    Fenbude Tongjifenxi."
23. Wang Qianguozhong and Zhong Shouhua, *Li Yuanse Dadian.*
24. This phrase is most commonly applied to the economic rather than technolog-
    ical divergence between China and Europe. See Pomeranz, *Great Divergence.*
25. The database, the invention measures, and sources are explained in great
    detail in the ongoing book project Huang et al., *Needham Question.*

26. I group the Qin and Han dynasties together in the tabulation of invention counts. Because the Qin is extremely short, only fourteen years, attributing an invention to that dynasty can be inaccurate. The *SCC* and *HCST* are vague about the dating of inventions during that period. Chinese historians often group the Qin and Han together in recognition of the similarities in their political systems. I adopt the same approach here.

27. The patent data are from the World Intellectual Property Organization website, https://www.wipo.int/portal/en/index.html.

28. Mokyr, *Lever of Riches*.

29. In a classic article, Simon Kuznets states, "More population means more creators and producers, both of goods along established production patterns and of new knowledge and invention." Kuznets also notes that the relationship is a loose one. (See his "Population and Economic Growth.") The point here is that the relationship between inventions and populations is not automatically positive nor automatically negative.

30. Glaeser, *Triumph of the City*.

31. Bloom et al., "Are Ideas Getting Harder to Find?"

32. Arthur, *Nature of Technology*.

33. Elvin, *Pattern of the Chinese Past*, 189.

34. I grew up in China reading *The Romance of the Three Kingdoms*. The current generation knows about this period through numerous video games.

35. Dong Jielin, Chen Jun, and Mao Lili, "Congtongji Shijiao Tantao Zhongguo Lishishande Jishufazhan Tedian."

36. Chen, "从李约瑟问题的研究经历看中西科技体制和学风的差距"; Hartwell, "Historical Analogism, Public Policy, and Social Science"; Griliches, "Hybrid Corn."

37. Bray, *Technology and Gender*.

38. Elvin, *Pattern of the Chinese Past*.

39. Needham and Harbsmeier, *Science and Civilisation in China*, vol. 7; Lin, "The Needham Puzzle: Why the Industrial Revolution Did Not Originate in China."

40. This claim is mainly made about the economy. It is known as the "California School." See Pomeranz, *Great Divergence*; Wong, *China Transformed*; Goldstone, *Why Europe?*

41. Mokyr, *Lever of Riches*; Needham and Harbsmeier, *Science and Civilisation in China*, vol. 7.

42. Mokyr, *Lever of Riches*.

43. Cipolla, *Guns, Sails, and Empires*.

44. Headrick, *Tools of Empire*.

45. Davies, "Thousand Years of Science and Scientists."

46. Needham, "Roles of Europe and China."

47. Mokyr remarks on Greek science, "Many classical scholars have noted the abstract and detached nature of Greek science, where experiments were unimportant because of the presumed separation between abstract reality and

its manifestation in the real world. Classical natural philosophy submitted that the natural world could be understood by rational principles, but the insights were their own reward. Science, when it stooped down to the real world, either created toys and gimmicks for the rich and famous, or confined itself to classification and taxonomy. The technological barrenness of classical natural philosophy must be contrasted with the practical and applied bent that slowly surfaced in medieval science." See Mokyr, *Lever of Riches*, 196.

48. This interpretation of Needham is based on Olerich, "Examination."

49. Justin Lin also blames *Keju*, but he dates the decline of Chinese technology to the Ming dynasty, seven hundred years after *Keju* was established. See Lin, "Needham Puzzle: Why the Industrial Revolution Did Not Originate in China"; Lin, "Needham Puzzle, the Weber Question, and China's Miracle."

50. Mokyr, "Market for Ideas."

51. There are other terms in the literature, such as "polycentrism," that are quite similar in concept and meaning.

52. Ouyang and Hu, *Zhongguo Gudai Mingren Fenlei Dacidian*.

53. In addition, the compilation includes information on Islam and Christianity. I exclude these two religions from my calculation because they did not arrive in China until the sixteenth century.

54. In psychological experiments, Chinese subjects, and East Asian subjects in general, are less facilitative in causal thinking and hypothesis development as compared with Western subjects. One experiment identifies whether a subject is surprised when a prior view turns out to be wrong. East Asian subjects are less surprised in such experiments. See Nisbett, *Geography of Thought*.

55. Olerich provides this interpretation by Needham. See Olerich, "Examination."

56. Fraser states that Mohists "were the first in the tradition to engage, like Socrates in ancient Greece, in an explicit, reflective search for objective moral standards and to give step-by-step, tightly reasoned arguments for their views, though their reasoning is sometimes simplistic or rests on doubtful assumptions." See Fraser, "Mohism."

57. Ricard and Singer, *Beyond the Self*.

58. In Frankopan, *Silk Roads*, 181, the Chinese accounts of the outside world contained legions of inaccuracies. In one, melons in Spain grew to six feet in diameter and sheep were the size of a full-grown man. I think these errors occurred for lack of subsequent and repeated contacts with these places, so the initial errors stood uncorrected. These fanciful accounts are meaningful in another sense: they apparently aroused no curiosity from the Chinese to go and witness these extraordinary creatures.

59. Li, "Tang Dynasty."

60. Morris, *Why the West Rules*. Chinese demographers disagree about the estimates for the Song population more than they do for other dynasties. Depending on which population estimates we use, we get a very different CDI index for the Song. One stands at 26.7; the other, at 15.8. A higher CDI

index would put the Song above the Tang, whereas a lower CDI index would suggest that the two dynasties are comparable.

61. This view that Song was "weak and poor" has been popularized by two of China most prominent historians. See Ch'ien, *Traditional Government in Imperial China*; and for a contrary view, Liu, *Chinese Market Economy*.

62. Liu, *Chinese Market Economy*.

63. Mokyr, *Lever of Riches*.

64. Levathes, *When China Ruled the Seas*.

65. Mokyr, *Lever of Riches*.

66. Scheidel, *Escape from Rome*.

67. I blame Confucian historiography for this inverse correlation between knowledge and importance. Confucian historiographers had a penchant to glorify emperors and empires, two standards the Han-Sui Interregnum and the Sui fell well short of. They also glorified longevity and stability, two additional areas in which the Han-Sui Interregnum and the Sui failed spectacularly.

68. Ebrey, *Cambridge Illustrated History of China*.

69. Ouyang and Hu, *Zhongguo Gudai Mingren Fenlei Dacidian*.

70. Morris, *Why the West Rules*.

71. Ebrey, *Cambridge Illustrated History of China*, 210.

72. Sen, *Argumentative Indian*.

73. The anecdote about Ruan Ji is from Ebrey, *Cambridge Illustrated History of China*. The anecdote about Liu Ling is from Craig, *Heritage of Chinese Civilization*.

74. Hui, *War and State Formation*, 171.

## Chapter Eight. A Republic of Government

*Epigraph*: Quoted in R. L. G., "Of Nations, Peoples, Countries and Mínzú."

1. Fisman et al., "Social Ties and Favoritism."

2. Lichfield, "Editor's Letter."

3. Gibney, "Astronomers Closer to Cracking Mystery."

4. Giles, "Man Turning China into a Quantum Superpower."

5. Yin et al., "Entanglement-Based Secure Quantum Cryptography."

6. This term was coined by Eric Schmidt, the former head of Google. He refers to AI, but this term is also applicable to other areas; two reports provide comprehensive coverage of this topic. See China Strategy Group, "Asymmetric Competition." Also see Belfer Center for Science and International Affairs, "Great Rivalry." The more data-driven research is by Acharya and Dunn, "Comparing U.S. and Chinese Contributions."

7. Graham, *Lonely Ideas*.

8. China Strategy Group, "Asymmetric Competition."

9. Demsas, "Voters Already Love Technology."

10. Lee, *AI Superpowers*.

11. Bloom et al., "Are Ideas Getting Harder to Find?"

12. National Bureau of Statistics, *Zhongguo Tongji Nianjian 1981*, 441.
13. Wu Daguang and Fan Wei, *Zhongguo Gaodengxuexiao Benke Jiaoyuzhiliang Baogao*.
14. There is social science literature on the persistence of history and on history as a process to form capabilities and knowhow. Even massive bombings failed to change the long-term economic fundamentals of a country, as a study on Japan shows. See Davis and Weinstein, "Bones, Bombs, and Break Points."
15. For a discussion of this concept, see "Freedom on the Net, 2018."
16. Kostka, "China's Social Credit Systems."
17. China Institute for Science and Technology Policy at Tsinghua University. *China AI Development Report, 2018*, 88.
18. This may change in the future. A team of MIT researchers is working on subnetworks that are a tenth the size of the neural network but are equally capable of learning and training. This new method would reduce substantially the amount of data required for training. See Conner-Simons, "Smarter Training of Neural Networks."
19. Gray and Suri, *Ghost Work*.
20. The statistics cited in this section are from World Bank, "Research and Development Expenditure (% of GDP)." The World Bank classifies China as "an upper middle-income country," which according to the bank's 2021 classification, means that it falls within the range of US$4,096 to US$12,695 per capita GDP.
21. The report can be downloaded at the website of National Security Commission on Artificial Intelligence, https://efaidnbmnnnibpcajpcglclefindmkaj/ https://www.nscai.gov/wp-content/uploads/2021/03/Full-Report-Digital-1 .pdf, accessed December 3, 2021.
22. Moody, "China's Surveillance Plans."
23. This account is based on the case studies on the website of Wisen, https:// www.wisencn.com/cgal_en, accessed April 2, 2020.
24. Iplytics, "Who Is Leading the 5G Patent Race?"
25. Young, "Tale of Two Cities."
26. Reported on Sohu.com, https://www.sohu.com/a/421551077_126758, accessed January 3, 2021.
27. *Economist*, "To Curb Covid-19."
28. Trefis Team, "Is Alibaba Really the Amazon of China?"
29. Polanyi, "Republic of Science."
30. In January 2022, the U.S. government dropped its case against Professor Chen after a review of the evidence showed that it could not satisfy a burden of proof.
31. See the response by Noam Chomsky at https://youtu.be/wqFhyaWQI1Y.
32. Yang, Vidovich, and Currie, "'Dancing in a Cage.'" Studies of Chinese universities are few. A recent one is Kirby, *Empires of Ideas*.
33. The controversial views expressed by Zhu Qingshi have been censored in China. The following account on SUSTech and Zhu Qingshi is based on

the Chinese Wiki at https://zh.wikipedia.org/wiki/%E6%9C%B1%E6%B8
%85%E6%97%B6 and https://baike.baidu.com/item/%E6%9C%B1%E6
%B8%85%E6%97%B6/2733586?fr=aladdin, accessed March 20, 2019.

34. This part of the chapter draws heavily from unpublished research I have
undertaken with my MIT colleague Fiona Murray.

35. Merton, *Sociology of Science.*

36. Shi and Rao, "China's Research Culture."

37. Feng and Huang, "Real Picture of China's Science Enterprise."

38. The analysis is reported in the special 2019 issue of *MIT Technology Review,*
cited in Lichfield, "Editor's Letter."

39. From the *Wall Street Journal* website, https://www.wsj.com/articles/BL
-CJB-27855#:~:text=Tsinghua%2C%20which%20is%20often%20called
,Cambridge%2Dbased%20MIT%20ranking%20second, accessed Septem-
ber 2, 2021.

40. American Association for the Advancement of Science, "Historical Trends in
Federal R&D."

41. This is from the website of Chinese Academy of Science and Technology
for Development, http://2015.casted.org.cn/web/index.php?ChannelID=17
&NewsID=3545, accessed April 3, 2022.

42. See "Introduction on the 'International S&T Cooperation Program of
China,'" 2001, and "The Major Focus on the First Round of 2021 ISTCP,"
2021, ISTCP website, https://www.istcp.org.cn/intro.html; Ministry of
Science and Technology, https://service.most.gov.cn/u/cms/static/202009/
30174925 1itr.pdf, accessed October 8, 2021.

43. See Ministry of Education, People's Republic of China, "Brief Report."

44. National Science Foundation, "Report—S&E Indicators 2018."

45. A better indicator is social science research on China. Social scientists in
China operate in a highly restrictive environment, except for a few highly
technical topics (such as finance). Most likely, social scientists outside of
China have produced far better quality research on China.

46. Graham, *Lonely Ideas.*

47. Baumol, *Free-Market Innovation Machine.*

48. Senor and Singer, *Start-up Nation.*

49. Abrami, Kirby, and McFarlan, "Why China Can't Innovate."

50. The following account on Lenovo is based on my 2008 book. See Huang,
*Capitalism with Chinese Characteristics.*

51. McGregor, "World Should Be Braced."

52. Investments from Hong Kong are classified as foreign investments in China.
This is consistent with the standard country practice and definition. The
definition of "foreign" investment is that the investor resides in a separate
*economic* territory with its own currency and border controls. Before 1997, for
example, all investments from Hong Kong into Great Britain were classified
as foreign investments under British law.

53. See a detailed account in Lu, *China's Leap.*

54. Huang, *Selling China*; Huang et al., "Fire Sale without Fire."
55. Qichacha (https://www.qcc.com) and Qixinbao (https://www.qixin.com) are two websites that collect and publish business registration information with support and recognition from the Chinese government.
56. An alternative hypothesis is that Chinese high-tech entrepreneurs registered their businesses in Hong Kong for tax purposes rather than to access its legal system. To access that tax benefit, the Chinese firms have to book their profits in Hong Kong. There is no evidence that this is done on a large scale.
57. Saxenian, *New Argonauts*.
58. The data were downloaded from World Intellectual Property Organization, https://www.wipo.int/portal/en/ on April 8, 2022.
59. Jaffe, Trajtenberg, and Henderson, "Geographic Localization."
60. This is from the website of BayHelix Group, https://bayhelix.org/, accessed July 8, 2019.
61. In writing this section, I benefited from discussions with Sofie Qiao, a former McKinsey consultant and a founder of a biotech business in China.
62. From the company website at https://www.wuxiapptec.com/, accessed April 8, 2019.
63. Hamermesh and Zhou, "WuXi PharmaTech."
64. Prasad, "Why China No Longer Needs Hong Kong."

## Chapter Nine. The CCP of Xi Jinping

*Epigraph:* This joke is no longer available on the Chinese internet, which has been scrubbed clean by the CCP.

1. Saich, *From Rebel to Ruler*, 322.
2. I will not repeat many of the excellent accounts of his rise and his style of leadership. Interested readers should consult Economy, *Third Revolution*; Shambaugh, *China's Leaders*; and ibid.
3. Naughton, *Growing Out of the Plan*.
4. Zhu and Mukhin, "Modern Regency."
5. Bo, "Downfall of Ling Jihua."
6. Shirk, "China in Xi's 'New Era,'" 25.
7. Lorentzen and Lu, "Personal Ties, Meritocracy, and China's Anti-Corruption Campaign."
8. Department of the United Front, "Zhongbang Fafu Shuju Gongbu."
9. Shirk, "China in Xi's 'New Era.'"
10. Xinhua News, "Full Text: Resolution of the CPC Central Committee." Emphasis added.
11. Scott, *Seeing Like a State*.
12. Yao, "Exclusive."
13. Huang, *Capitalism with Chinese Characteristics*.
14. Wong, "Xi Jinping's Eager-to-Please Bureaucrats Snarl His China Plans."
15. Vogel, *One Step Ahead*.

16. Rodrik, *Globalization Paradox.*

17. I explore in more detail these differences between China and the Soviet Union in Huang, *Statism with Chinese Characteristics.*

18. The translated text is provided by China.org.cn, "Excerpts from Talks."

19. Doyon, "Influence without Ownership."

20. Xinhua News, "Minqi Waiqi Weihe Douyao Jiandangwei?"

21. Tan and Huang, "State Ownership and the Cost of Debt."

22. Gao, "As 'Two Sessions' Open."

23. Tullock, *Autocracy,* 156.

24. Associated Press, "Former Top Chinese Official Gets Life Term."

25. Officials sometimes affirm the private sector in their speeches, usually after the government has taken actions that have damaged the investment confidence of the private sector.

26. Frye and Shleifer, "Invisible Hand and the Grabbing Hand."

27. Kharpal, "Alibaba's Jack Ma."

28. Thornhill, "Big Data Revolution."

29. Dickson, "Integrating Wealth and Power," 852.

30. Dickson, *Wealth into Power.*

31. The 2013 external defense spending was US$117.82 billion compared with US$123.8 billion on internal security. Since 2014, China has stopped releasing these data. See Greitens, "Rethinking China's Coercive Capacity."

32. Lardy, *State Strikes Back.*

33. Shum, *Red Roulette.*

34. Chinese Government, "Guojiaji Sousuo Pindai Zhongguo Sousuo Zhengshi Shanxie Kaitong."

35. "Zhongguo Shida Yinjin Baiming."

36. See Thurm, "Huawei Admits Copying Code."

37. Tanner, "Beijing's New National Intelligence Law."

38. Academics delved into this issue long before Huawei became known to the policymakers. In my 2008 book Huang, *Capitalism with Chinese Characteristics,* I determined that Huawei was an employee-owned company (although it probably issued shares to some state agencies), a status confirmed by the company itself many years later. See Corera, "Huawei's Business Damaged."

39. Corera, "Huawei's Business Damaged."

40. Whalen, "U.S. Campaign against Huawei."

41. Cuthbertson, "Huawei Ban"; Brown, "Huawei P20 Pro."

42. White, "Publications Output."

43. Tsinghua University, "Renkong Zhineng Fazhan Baogao." The Tsinghua report draws from the data originally presented by "The Global AI Talent Tracker" released on the website of MacroPolo of the Paulsen Institute. Their data are a sample of authors of papers accepted at NeurIPS 2019. See Paulsen Institute, "The Global AI Talent Tracker."

44. Cheng, "Apple, Intel and These Other US Tech Companies."

45. See China Strategy Group, "Asymmetric Competition." Also see Belfer Center for Science and International Affairs, "Great Rivalry." The more

data-driven research is by Acharya and Dunn, "Comparing U.S. and Chinese Contributions."

46. Institute of International and Strategic Studies, "Jishu Linyude Zhongmei Zhanlie Jingzheng."
47. Cheng, "China GDP Grew 8.1% in 2021."
48. Emmott, *Rivals*.
49. McNeil Jr., "To Take On the Coronavirus, Go Medieval on It."
50. Cheng and Leung, "What Happened in China," 361.
51. Fukuyama, *Origins of Political Order*, 129.
52. Magnus, *Red Flags*.
53. Westbrook and Shen, "Half a Trillion Dollars Wiped from China Markets."
54. Whyte, *Myth of the Social Volcano*.
55. Huang, "Tencent Doubles Social Aid."
56. Gilholm, "China's Xitocracy."
57. This critique is from Zhongyang jiwei guojia jianwei, "Dangjichufen Tiaoli Huachude Zhexiexinjinqu,Beihou Douyou Xianhou Anli."
58. Weber, *Economy and Society*.
59. Shirk, "China in Xi's 'New Era.'"
60. Lu and Han, "Update."
61. *The Standard*, "Lockdowns Costing China US$46bn a Month: CUHK Professor."
62. Naughton, *Growing Out of the Plan*.

## Chapter Ten. Breaking Out of the EAST Model?

1. For a detailed account of this episode, see Liu et al., "Controlling Ebola."
2. The data are from Our World in Data at https://ourworldindata.org/corona virus, accessed April 15, 2021.
3. Bradsher and Myers, "Ahead of Biden's Democracy Summit."
4. Jee and Zhang, "Oppose Autocracy without Support for Democracy."
5. Acemoglu et al., "Reevaluating the Modernization Hypothesis."
6. Wessel and Walker, "Good News for the Globe."
7. Huang, *Capitalism with Chinese Characteristics*.
8. Johnson, "Democratization of South Korea."
9. Clinton, "Full Text of Clinton's Speech on China Trade Bill."
10. *New York Times*, "China's Fax Invasion."
11. *New York Times*, "Faxing Democracy."
12. King, Pan, and Roberts, "How Censorship in China Allows Government Criticism but Silences Collective Expression."
13. Lim, *People's Republic of Amnesia*; Chen and Yang, "Impact of Media Censorship."
14. Harari, "Why Technology Favors Tyranny."
15. Karl Marx, "Division of Labour and Mechanical Workshop. Tool and Machinery," *Economic Manuscripts of 1861–63*, part 3: *Relative Surplus Value*

(XIX–1169), available at https://marxists.architexturez.net/archive/marx/works/1861/economic/ch35.htm, accessed September 17, 2021.

16. Kurlansky, *Paper*.

17. Henrich, *WEIRDest People in the World*.

18. Quoted in Haver, "American Leaders Sold a Dream."

19. This is based on Cummings, *Korea's Place in the Sun*.

20. For a detailed account of the role and the contributions of Kim Dae-jung to Korea's democratization, see this post on the website of Association for Asian Studies, https://www.asianstudies.org/publications/eaa/archives/kim-dae -jungs-role-in-the-democratization-of-south-korea/, accessed March 3, 2021.

21. Wade, *Governing the Market*, 237–241.

22. Japan sent regular missions to learn from China during the Tang dynasty, but it stopped during and after the Song dynasty. See Vogel, *China and Japan*.

23. Clinton, "Full Text of Clinton's Speech on China Trade Bill."

24. Campbell and Ratner, "China Reckoning."

25. See the statement on the website of Securities and Exchange Commission, https://www.sec.gov/news/statement/gensler-statement-hfcaa-120221, ac- cessed December 10, 2021.

26. Axelrod, *Evolution of Cooperation*.

27. Vogel, *Deng Xiaoping*, 322.

28. This is according to Vogel, *Deng Xiaoping*.

29. Quoted by Yang Hengjun in his "Why China Still Needs Deng Xiaoping."

30. Truex, "Political Discontent in China."

31. An autocratic system incubates these untenable dynamics. Protesters usually start with demands that are more modest than what they truly want. This is to ensure their safety. Once they sense conciliations from the government, they escalate their demands to their true preference level. In a democracy, you start with maximum demands and then you negotiate downward. In an autocracy, you do the reverse, but this tactic often backfires.

32. The data are reported on *Business Insider* at https://www.businessinsider .com/26-percent-of-americans-are-right-wing-authoritarian-new-poll-2021 -6, accessed December 8, 2021.

33. This literature is vast. Earlier literature relying on simple cross-country re- gressions shows no significant differences between democracy and autoc- racy in terms of economic growth. See Barro, "Democracy and Growth." This type of study can suffer from a number of errors, including measur- ing the flow effect of democracy, not its stock, and capturing only the static effects of a political system rather than the dynamic effects. More recent studies measure the political change on economic change and show posi- tive effects of democracy. See Papaioannou and Siourounis, "Democratisa- tion and Growth." Another paper, Acemoglu et al., "Democracy Does Cause Growth," finds that democracy promotes growth and identifies the channels as through investments in human capital, schooling, and health.

34. Pinker, *Better Angels of Our Nature*, 337–338.

35. Friedman, *Hot, Flat, and Crowded*.
36. The data for China, Japan, and South Korea are from the World Bank. Data for Taiwan are from Statistica.com.
37. See this side-by-side comparison of the two Koreas on NASA's Earth Observatory website, https://earthobservatory.nasa.gov/images/83182/the-koreas-at-night.
38. This section is based on Cummings, *Korea's Place in the Sun*; and Buzo, *Making of Modern Korea*.
39. The data are reported at https://www.statista.com/statistics/1093256/novel-coronavirus-2019ncov-deaths-worldwide-by-country/, accessed January 3, 2022.
40. Mações, *Geopolitics for the End Time*.
41. In a March 1, 2020, article in the *Global Times*, Martin Jacques said, "I think the capacity of the state in China to deal with emergencies of this kind is far more developed and far more capable than could be achieved by any Western government. The Chinese system, the Chinese government, is superior to other governments in handling big challenges like this." See https://www.globaltimes.cn/content/1181178.shtml, accessed December 8, 2022.
42. Li, "Eric Li on the Failure."
43. Based on a post on Our World in Data at https://ourworldindata.org/covid-exemplar-south-korea, accessed January 2, 2022.
44. In contrast, Hong Kong has proactively enforced effective regulatory interventions of its live poultry markets after the 1997 outbreak of avian influenza. See Leung et al., "Avian Influenza."
45. Hua Sheng, "SARS Guohou Budao Shiqinian SARS."
46. For a detailed account, see Huang, *SARS Epidemic and Its Aftermath*.
47. Graeber and Wengrow, *Dawn of Everything*.
48. Quoted in Sen, *Argumentative Indian*, 135.
49. Ibid.
50. Gerschenkron, *Economic Backwardness*.
51. Cheng Yinghong, "Cui Zhiyuan tongguo qujie meiguolaiqujie zhongguo."
52. Rawls, *Theory of Justice*.
53. See Jacobs and Buckley, "Presumed Guilty."
54. "Defiant Bo Xilai Claims He Was Coerced into Graft Confession."
55. See, on the Chinese BBC website, Zheng Wei, "Shiqi jiangzhi bingdiande zhongguo guanyuan."
56. Rachman, "Why China's Elite Tread a Perilous Path." Rachman was very impressed with Rui. I knew Rui as well, but the only source of his self-confidence I can discern came from his position as an anchorman for a state monopoly.
57. Lin never sent the letter, although he consulted with Zhou Enlai. The existence of this letter was disclosed by Wu Zhong, the garrison commander for Beijing during the Lin Biao episode. Wu wrote about this in the authoritative journal, *Yanhuang Chunqiu*, and it is reprinted in Duowei Xinwen, "Lin Biao siqiangei Mao Zedong yifengxin."

# Bibliography

Abrami, Regina M., William C. Kirby, and F. Warren McFarlan. "Why China Can't Innovate." *Harvard Business Review*, March 1, 2014. https://hbr.org/2014/03/why-china-cant-innovate.

Acemoglu, Daron, Simon Johnson, James A. Robinson, and Pierre Yared. "Reevaluating the Modernization Hypothesis." *Journal of Monetary Economics* 56, no. 8 (November 1, 2009): 1043–1058. https://doi.org/10.1016/j.jmoneco.2009.10.002.

Acemoglu, Daron, Suresh Naidu, Pascual Restrepo, and James A. Robinson. "Democracy Does Cause Growth." *Journal of Political Economy* 127, no. 1 (February 1, 2019): 47–100. https://doi.org/10.1086/700936.

Acemoglu, Daron, and James A. Robinson. *The Narrow Corridor: States, Societies, and the Fate of Liberty*. New York: Penguin, 2020.

Acharya, Ashwin, and Brian Dunn. "Comparing U.S. and Chinese Contributions to High-Impact AI Research." *Center for Security and Emerging Technology* (blog), 2021. https://cset.georgetown.edu/publication/comparing-u-s-and-chinese-contributions-to-high-impact-ai-research.

Alesina, Alberto, and Enrico Spolaore. *The Size of Nations*. Cambridge, Mass.: MIT Press, 2005.

Allen, Franklin, Jun Qian, and Meijun Qian. "Law, Finance, and Economic Growth in China." *Journal of Financial Economics* 77 (2005): 57–116.

American Association for the Advancement of Science. "Historical Trends in Federal R&D," May 2020. https://www.aaas.org/programs/r-d-budget-and-policy/historical-trends-federal-rd.

Anderson, Elizabeth. *Private Government: How Employers Rule Our Lives*. Reprint, Princeton, N.J.: Princeton University Press, 2019.

Arthur, W. Brian. *The Nature of Technology: What It Is and How It Evolves*. Reprint, New York: Free Press, 2011.

Åslund, Olof, and Oskar Nordström Skans. "Do Anonymous Job Application Procedures Level the Playing Field?" *Industrial and Labor Relations Review* 65, no. 1 (2012): 82–107. https://www.jstor.org/stable/41343666.

Associated Press. "A Former Top Chinese Official Gets Life Term for Corruption." *New York Times*, May 8, 2018. https://www.nytimes.com/2018/05/08/world/asia/sun-zhengcai-sentence-life-prison.html.

Axelrod, Robert. *Evolution of Cooperation*. First ed. New York: Basic Books, 1984.

Bai, Ying, and Ruixue Jia. "Elite Recruitment and Political Stability: The Impact of the Abolition of China's Civil Service Exam." *Econometrica* 84, no. 2 (2016): 677–733. https://doi.org/10.3982/ECTA13448.

Bao Weimin 包伟民. "Zhongguo Jiudaoshisanshiji Shehuishizilv Digaodejige Wenti 中国九到十三世纪识字率提高的几个问题 [On the rising literacy rates between the 9th and 13th centuries in China]." *Journal of Hangzhou University* 22, no. 4 (December 1992): 79–87.

Barro, Robert J. "Democracy and Growth." *Journal of Economic Growth* 1, no. 1 (March 1, 1996): 1–27. https://doi.org/10.1007/BF00163340.

Baumol, William. *The Free-Market Innovation Machine*. Princeton, N.J.: Princeton University Press, 2004.

Belfer Center for Science and International Affairs. "The Great Rivalry: China vs. the U.S. in the 21st Century," 2021. https://www.belfercenter.org/publication/great-rivalry-china-vs-us-21st-century.

Bell, Daniel A. *The China Model: Political Meritocracy and the Limits of Democracy*. Princeton, N.J.: Princeton University Press, 2015.

Björklund, Anders, and Kjell G. Salvanes. "Education and Family Background: Mechanisms and Policies." IZA Discussion Papers, Institute of Labor Economics (IZA), June 2010. https://ideas.repec.org/p/iza/izadps/dp5002.html.

Blank, Rebecca M. "The Effects of Double-Blind versus Single-Blind Reviewing: Experimental Evidence from *The American Economic Review*." *American Economic Review* 81, no. 5 (1991): 1041–1067. https://ideas.repec.org/a/aea/aecrev/v81y1991i5p1041-67.html.

Blaydes, Lisa, and Eric Chaney. "The Feudal Revolution and Europe's Rise: Political Divergence of the Christian West and the Muslim World before 1500 CE." *American Political Science Review* 107, no. 1 (February 2013): 16–34. https://doi.org/10.1017/S0003055412000561.

Bloom, Nicholas, Charles I. Jones, John Van Reenen, and Michael Webb. "Are Ideas Getting Harder to Find?" *American Economic Review* 110, no. 4 (April 2020): 1104–1144. https://doi.org/10.1257/aer.20180338.

Bo, Zhiyue. *Chinese Provincial Leaders: Economic Performance and Political Mobility Since 1949*. London: Routledge, 2019.

———. "The Downfall of Ling Jihua and the New Norm of Chinese Politics." *The Diplomat*, December 24, 2014. https://thediplomat.com/2014/12/the-downfall-of-ling-jihua-and-the-new-norm-of-chinese-politics/.

Bol, Peter K. *Neo-Confucianism in History*. Reprint, Cambridge, Mass.: Harvard University Asia Center, 2010.

Bradsher, Keith, and Steven Lee Myers. "Ahead of Biden's Democracy Summit, China Says: We're Also a Democracy." *New York Times*, December 7, 2021. https://www.nytimes.com/2021/12/07/world/asia/china-biden-democracy-summit.html.

Bray, F. *Technology and Gender: Fabrics of Power in Late Imperial China.* Berkeley: University of California Press, 1997.

Brook, Timothy. *The Troubled Empire: China in the Yuan and Ming Dynasties.* Reprint, Cambridge, Mass.: Belknap Press of Harvard University Press, 2013.

Brown, C. Scott. "Huawei P20 Pro Already Outsold the P10 Plus by 316% in Western Europe." *Android Authority*, April 27, 2018. https://www.androidauthority.com/huawei-p20-pro-europe-sales-859899.

Buchanan, James M., and Gordon Tullock. *The Calculus of Consent: Logical Foundations of Constitutional Democracy*, vol. 2. Reprint, Indianapolis: Liberty Fund, 2004.

Buringh, Eltjo, and Jan Luiten Van Zanden. "Charting the 'Rise of the West': Manuscripts and Printed Books in Europe, a Long-Term Perspective from the Sixth through Eighteenth Centuries." *Journal of Economic History* 69, no. 2 (2009): 409–445.

Buzo, Adrian. *The Making of Modern Korea.* 3rd ed. London: Routledge, 2016.

Campbell, Kurt M., and Ely Ratner. "The China Reckoning: How Beijing Defied American Expectations." *Foreign Affairs* (March/April 2018). https://www.foreignaffairs.com/articles/china/2018-02-13/china-reckoning.

Cao, Xiaping, Michael Lemmon, Xiaofei Pan, Meijun Qian, and Gary Tian. "Political Promotion, CEO Incentives, and the Relationship between Pay and Performance." *Management Science* 65, no. 7 (July 1, 2019): 2947–2965. https://doi.org/10.1287/mnsc.2017.2966.

Central Committee Document Office 中共中央文献研究室. *Mao Zedong Duwenguji Piyuji* 毛泽东读文史古籍批语集 [Annotations by Mao Zedong of ancient texts on literature and history]. Beijing: 中央文献出版社 [Central Committee Document Publishing House], 1993.

Central Committee Documentation Research Office. *Chen Yun Nianpu* [A chronicle of Chen Yun's life]. Beijing: Zhongyang wenxian chubanshe, 2015.

Chandler, Alfred D. *Strategy and Structure: Chapters in the History of the Industrial Enterprise.* Washington, D.C.: BeardBook, 1962.

Chang, Gordon G. *The Coming Collapse of China.* New York: Random House, 2001.

Chen Ping. "从李约瑟问题的研究经历看中西科技体制和学风的差距 [Differences in scientific and technological systems and academic styles between China and the West as seen from research on the Needham Question]." 素心书斋, 2002. https://suxin.one/paper/culture/002/9529.html.

Chen, Shumei. "An Explanation on 'Han Official Needs to Be Able to Recite 9000 Words.'" *Guhanyu yanjiu* 3 (1998): 82–84.

Chen, Ting, James Kai-sing Kung, and Chicheng Ma. "Long Live *Keju!* The Persistent Effects of China's Civil Examination System." *Economic Journal* 130, no. 631 (October 16, 2020): 2030–2064. https://doi.org/10.1093/ej/ueaa043.

Chen, Xiuhong. *Tang Song Keju Zhidu Yanjiu* [Research on the *Keju* system during the Tang and Song dynasties]. Beijing: Beijing shifan daxue chubanshe, 2012.

Chen, Yuyu, and David Y. Yang. "The Impact of Media Censorship: 1984 or Brave New World?" *American Economic Review* 109, no. 6 (June 2019): 2294–2332. https://doi.org/10.1257/aer.20171765.

Chen, Zhiyun. "Civil Service Examination and Culture of Two Song Dynasties." *Journal of Shangrao Normal College* 21, no. 1 (February 2001): 56–63.

Cheng, Evelyn. "Apple, Intel and These Other US Tech Companies Have the Most at Stake in China-US Trade Fight." CNBC, May 14, 2018. https://www.cnbc.com/video/2018/05/14/apple-intel-american-tech-companies-150-billion-at-stake-china-us-trade-fight.html.

Cheng, Jonathan. "China GDP Grew 8.1% in 2021, though Momentum Slowed in Fourth Quarter." *Wall Street Journal*, January 16, 2022. https://www.wsj.com/articles/china-gdp-grew-8-1-in-2021-though-momentum-slowed-in-fourth-quarter-11642386349.

Cheng, K. F., and P. C. Leung. "What Happened in China during the 1918 Influenza Pandemic?" *International Journal of Infectious Diseases* 11, no. 4 (July 1, 2007): 360–364. https://doi.org/10.1016/j.ijid.2006.07.009.

Cheng, Li. "The End of the CCP's Resilient Authoritarianism? A Tripartite Assessment of Shifting Power in China." *China Quarterly* 211 (2012): 595–623.

———. "Was the Shanghai Gang Shanghaied? The Fall of Chen Liangyu and the Survival of Jiang Zemin's Faction." *China Leadership Monitor* 20 (2007).

Cheng Yinghong 程映红. "Cui Zhiyuan tongguo qujie meiguolaiqujie zhongguo 崔之元通过曲解美国来曲解中国 [Cui Ziyuan's distortions of China through distortions of America]." RFI—法国国际广播电台, October 25, 2010. https://www.rfi.fr/cn/20101025-程映红：崔之元通过曲解美国来曲解中国.

Ch'ien, Mu. *Merits and Demerits of Political Systems in Dynastic China*. London: Springer Nature, 2019.

———. *Traditional Government in Imperial China: A Critical Analysis*. Hong Kong: Chinese University Press, 1982.

*China Daily*. "Corruption Is Crucial Threat, Wen Says." China.org.cn. March 27, 2012. http://www.china.org.cn/china/2012-03/27/content_24993734.htm (accessed January 5, 2022).

China Institute for Science and Technology Policy at Tsinghua University. *China AI Development Report, 2018*. July 2018. https://www.scribd.com/document/442369539/China-AI-development-report-2018.

China Strategy Group. "Asymmetric Competition: A Strategy for China and Technology. Actionable Insights for American Leadership," 2020. http://industrialpolicy.us/resources/SpecificIndustries/IT/final-memo-china-strategy-group-axios-1.pdf.

Chinese Government. "Guojiaji Sousuo Pindai Zhongguo Sousuo Zhengshi Shanxie Kaitong 国家级搜索平台中国搜索正式上线开通 [The launch of the national level search engine]," March 21, 2014. http://www.gov.cn/xinwen/2014-03/21/content_2643362.htm.

———. "Sao Chu Wen Mang Gong Zuo Tiao Li." www.gov.cn, February 5, 1988. http://www.gov.cn/zhengce/2020-12/25/content_5573970.htm.

Cipolla, Caro M. *Guns, Sails, and Empires: Technological Innovation and the Early Phases of European Expansion, 1400–1700*. Manhattan, Kans.: Sunflower University Press, 1985.

Clinton, Bill. "Full Text of Clinton's Speech on China Trade Bill," March 9, 2000. https://www.iatp.org/sites/default/files/Full_Text_of_Clintons_Speech_on _China_Trade_Bi.htm.

Conner-Simons, Adam. "Smarter Training of Neural Networks." MIT News, May 6, 2019. https://news.mit.edu/2019/smarter-training-neural-networks-0506.

Corera, Gordon. "Huawei's Business Damaged by US Sanctions despite Success at Home." *BBC News*, March 31, 2021. https://www.bbc.com/news/technology -56590001.

Craig, Albert. *The Heritage of Chinese Civilization*. 3rd ed. Boston: Pearson, 2010.

Creel, Herrlee Glessner. *The Origins of Statecraft in China*. 1st ed. Chicago: University of Chicago Press, 1970.

Cummings, Bruce. *Korea's Place in the Sun: A Modern History*. Updated ed. New York: W. W. Norton, 2005.

Cunningham, Edward, Tony Saich, and Jessie Turiel. "Understanding CCP Resilience: Surveying Chinese Public Opinion through Time." Ash Center for Democratic Governance and Innovation, 2020. https://ash.harvard.edu/files/ ash/files/final_policy_brief_7.6.2020.pdf.

Cuthbertson, Anthony. "Huawei Ban: More than 130 US Companies Blocked from Selling to Chinese Tech Giant." *The Independent*, August 28, 2019. https://www.independent.co.uk/life-style/gadgets-and-tech/news/huawei -ban-us-china-trade-war-trump-phone-latest-a9082166.html.

Dai Jianping 戴建平. "Zhongguo Gudai Kexuejia Lishi Fenbude Tongjifenxi 中国古代科学家历史分布的统计分析 [A statistical analysis of historical distributions of ancient Chinese scientists]." *Ziran Bianzhengfa Tongxun* 自然辩证法通讯 [Journal of dialectics of nature], 1997. http://jdn.ucas.ac.cn/public/ index.php/home/journal/view/id/1248.html.

Davies, Mansel. "A Thousand Years of Science and Scientists: 988 to 1988." *History of Science* 33, no. 2 (June 1, 1995): 239–251. https://doi.org/10.1177/ 007327539503300205.

Davis, Donald R., and David E. Weinstein. "Bones, Bombs, and Break Points: The Geography of Economic Activity." *American Economic Review* 92, no. 5 (December 2002): 1269–1289. https://doi.org/10.1257/000282802762024502.

Demsas, Jerusalem. "Voters Already Love Technology. They Don't Need Anti-China Messaging to Get There." *Vox*, May 3, 2021. https://www.vox.com/ 2021/5/3/22410304/technology-poll-research-and-development-biden -china-joint-address.

Deng, Liqun. *Shierge Chunqiu, 1975–1987* [Twelve springs and twelve autumns, 1975–1987]. Hong Kong: Bozhi chubanshe, 2006.

Deng Xiaoping. "Excerpts from Talks Given in Wuchang, Shenzhen, Zhuhai and Shanghai," 1992. http://www.china.org.cn/english/features/dengxiaoping/ 103331.htm.

Department of the United Front. "Zhongbang Fafu Shuju Gongbu 重磅反腐数据公布 [Important announcement on anti-corruption data]," June 29, 2021. https://www.sohu.com/a/474678352_120702.

Deresiewicz, William. *Excellent Sheep: The Miseducation of the American Elite and the Way to a Meaningful Life*. New York: Free Press, 2015.

Diamond, Jared. *Guns, Germs, and Steel: The Fates of Human Societies*. Revised ed. New York: W. W. Norton, 2005.

Dickson, Bruce J. "Integrating Wealth and Power in China: The Communist Party's Embrace of the Private Sector." *China Quarterly* 192 (2007): 827–854.

———. *Wealth into Power: The Communist Party's Embrace of China's Private Sector.* Cambridge, Eng.: Cambridge University Press, 2008.

Dikötter, Frank. *How to Be a Dictator: The Cult of Personality in the Twentieth Century*. New York: Bloomsbury, 2019.

———. *Mao's Great Famine: The History of China's Most Devastating Catastrophe, 1958–62*. New York: Walker & Co., 2010.

Dong Jielin 董洁林, Chen Jun 陈娟, and Mao Lili 茅莉丽. "Congtongji Shijiao Tantao Zhongguo Lishishande Jishufazhan Tedian 从统计视角探讨中国历史上的技术发展特点 [An exploration of characteristics of technological development in Chinese history]." *Ziran Bianzhengfa Tongxun* 自然辩证法通讯 [Journal of dialectics of nature] 3 (2014): 29–36.

Doyon, Jérôme. "Influence without Ownership: The Chinese Communist Party Targets the Private Sector." Institut Montaigne, January 26, 2021. https://www.institutmontaigne.org/en/blog/influence-without-ownership-chinese-communist-party-targets-private-sector.

Duowei Xinwen 多维新闻. "Lin Biao siqiangei Mao Zedong yifengxin 林彪死前给毛泽东一封信 [A letter from Lin Biao to Mao Zedong before his death]." 多维新闻, October 23, 2016. https://www.dwnews.com/中国/59777023/林彪死前给毛泽东一封信.

Eberhard, Wolfram. *Social Mobility in Traditional China*. Leiden: Brill Archive, 1962.

Ebrey, Patricia Buckley. *The Cambridge Illustrated History of China*. 2nd ed. New York: Cambridge University Press, 2010.

———. "Concubines in Sung China." *Journal of Family History* 11, no. 1 (March 1, 1986): 1–24. https://doi.org/10.1177/036319908601100101.

*Economist, The*. "To Curb Covid-19, China Is Using Its High-Tech Surveillance Tools," *Economist*, February 29, 2020. https://www.economist.com/china/2020/02/29/to-curb-covid-19-china-is-using-its-high-tech-surveillance-tools.

Economy, Elizabeth C. *The Third Revolution: Xi Jinping and the New Chinese State*. Oxford, Eng.: Oxford University Press, 2018.

Elman, Benjamin A. *Civil Examinations and Meritocracy in Late Imperial China*. Cambridge, Mass.: Harvard University Press, 2013.

———. *A Cultural History of Civil Examinations in Late Imperial China*. Berkeley: University of California Press, 2000.

———. "Political, Social, and Cultural Reproduction via Civil Service Examinations in Late Imperial China." *Journal of Asian Studies* 50, no. 1 (1991): 7–28. https://doi.org/10.2307/2057472.

Elvin, Mark. *The Pattern of the Chinese Past.* 1st ed. Stanford, Calif: Stanford University Press, 1973.

Emmott, Bill. *Rivals: How the Power Struggle between China, India, and Japan Will Shape Our Next Decade.* Boston: Houghton Mifflin Harcourt, 2008.

Fairbank, John King. *China: Tradition and Transformation.* Revised ed. Boston: Houghton Mifflin College Division, 1989.

Fearon, James D. "Ethnic and Cultural Diversity by Country." *Journal of Economic Growth* 8, no. 2 (June 1, 2003): 195–222. https://doi.org/10.1023/A: 1024419522867.

Feng, Guangchao Charles, and Yu Huang. "A Real Picture of China's Science Enterprise: A Big-Data Analysis." *Science,* May 24, 2016.

Fewsmith, Joseph. *China since Tiananmen: From Deng Xiaoping to Hu Jintao.* 2nd ed. Cambridge, Eng.: Cambridge University Press, 2008.

———. *Rethinking Chinese Politics.* Cambridge, Eng.: Cambridge University Press, 2021.

———. "The Succession That Didn't Happen." *China Quarterly* 173 (2003): 1–6.

Fisman, Raymond, Jing Shi, Yongxiang Wang, and Rong Xu. "Social Ties and Favoritism in Chinese Science." *Journal of Political Economy* 126, no. 3 (June 1, 2018): 1134–1171. https://doi.org/10.1086/697086.

Fogel, Joshua A. *Politics and Sinology: The Case of Naitō Konan (1866–1934).* 1980; Cambridge, Mass.: Harvard University Asia Center, 1984.

Frankopan, Peter. *Silk Roads: A New History of the World.* New York: Vintage, 2015.

Fraser, Chris. "Mohism." In *The Stanford Encyclopedia of Philosophy Archive,* Winter 2020. Metaphysics Research Lab, Stanford University, 2020. https://plato .stanford.edu/archives/win2020/entries/mohism/.

Friedman, Thomas L. *Hot, Flat, and Crowded: Why We Need a Green Revolution— And How It Can Renew America, Release 2.0.* 2nd ed. New York: Picador, 2009.

Frye, Timothy, and Andrei Shleifer. "The Invisible Hand and the Grabbing Hand." *American Economic Review* 87, no. 2 (1997): 354–358. http://www.jstor .org/stable/2950945.

Fu, Zhengyuan. *Autocratic Tradition and Chinese Politics.* Cambridge, Eng.: Cambridge University Press, 1993.

Fukuyama, Francis. *The Origins of Political Order: From Prehuman Times to the French Revolution.* New York: Farrar, Straus and Giroux, 2011.

———. *Political Order and Political Decay: From the Industrial Revolution to the Globalization of Democracy.* 1st ed. New York: Farrar, Straus and Giroux, 2014.

Gao, Charlotte. "As 'Two Sessions' Open, CCP Is Ready to Defend Presidential Term Limit Change," March 5, 2018. https://thediplomat.com/2018/ 03/as-two-sessions-open-ccp-is-ready-to-defend-presidential-term-limit -change/.

Ge Jianxiong. *Zhongguo Renkou Fazhanshi* 中国人口发展史 [History of Chinese population development]. Chengdu 成都: 四川人民出版社 [Sichuan People's Publishing House], 2020.

Gerschenkron, Alexander. *Economic Backwardness in Historical Perspective.* Cambridge, Mass.: Belknap Press of Harvard University Press, 1962.

Gibbon, Edward. *The History of the Decline & Fall of the Roman Empire.* Oxford, Eng.: H. Frowde, Oxford University Press, 1907.

Gibney, Elizabeth. "Astronomers Closer to Cracking Mystery of Fast Radio Bursts." *Nature* 572, no. 7770 (August 13, 2019): 425–426. https://doi.org/10.1038/d41586-019-02455-1.

Giles, Martin. "The Man Turning China into a Quantum Superpower." *MIT Technology Review*, 2019. https://www.technologyreview.com/2018/12/19/1571/the-man-turning-china-into-a-quantum-superpower/.

Gilholm, Andrew. "China's Xitocracy." *Foreign Affairs*, August 11, 2017. https://www.foreignaffairs.com/articles/china/2017-08-11/chinas-xitocracy.

Gillespie, Kate, and Gwenn Okruhlik. "The Political Dimensions of Corruption Cleanups: A Framework for Analysis" 24, no. 1 (1991): 77–95.

Girard, Bonnie. "The Secret behind the Chinese Communist Party's Perseverance." *Diplomat*, May 26, 2021.

Glaeser, Edward L. *Triumph of the City: How Our Greatest Invention Makes Us Richer, Smarter, Greener, Healthier, and Happier.* New York: Penguin Press, 2011.

Goldin, Claudia, and Cecilia Rouse. "Orchestrating Impartiality: The Impact of 'Blind' Auditions on Female Musicians." *American Economic Review* 90, no. 4 (September 2000): 715–41. https://doi.org/10.1257/aer.90.4.715.

Goldman, Merle. *Sowing the Seeds of Democracy in China: Political Reform in the Deng Xiaoping Era.* Cambridge, Mass.: Harvard University Press, 1995.

Goldstone, Jack. *Why Europe? The Rise of the West in World History, 1500–1850.* 1st ed. Boston: McGraw-Hill Education, 2008.

Graeber, David, and David Wengrow. *The Dawn of Everything: A New History of Humanity.* 1st ed. New York: Farrar, Straus and Giroux, 2021.

Graham, Loren. *Lonely Ideas: Can Russia Compete?* Cambridge, Mass.: MIT Press, 2013.

Grandin, Greg. *End of the Myth.* Reprint, New York: Metropolitan, 2020.

Gray, Mary, and Siddharth Suri. *Ghost Work.* Boston: Houghton Mifflin Harcourt, 2019.

Greitens, Sheena Chestnut. "Rethinking China's Coercive Capacity: An Examination of PRC Domestic Security Spending, 1992–2012." *China Quarterly* 232 (December 2017): 1002–25. https://doi.org/10.1017/S0305741017001023.

Grieder, Jerome B. *Intellectuals and the State in Modern China.* 1st ed. New York: Free Press, 1981.

Griliches, Zvi. "Hybrid Corn: An Exploration in the Economics of Technological Change." *Econometrica* 25, no. 4 (October 1957): 501. https://doi.org/10.2307/1905380.

Gu, Baozi. *Zhou Enlai Zuihou 600 Tian* [The final 600 days of Zhou Enlai]. Hong Kong: Hong Kong Open Page, 2015.

Gu, Baozi, and Xiuxian Du. *Mao Zedong He Tade Gao Canmen* [Mao Zedong and his high counselors]. Guiyang: Guangxi renmin chubanshe, 2011.

Guo, Peigui. *Mingdai Xuexiao Keju Yu Renguan Zhidu Yanjiu* [Ming Dynasty schools, imperial examinations, and official selection]. Beijing: Encyclopedia of China Publishing House, 2014.

———. "The Size and Admission Rate of Keju in the Ming Dynasty." *History Monthly* 12 (2006): 24–31.

Guowuyuan 国务院 [State Council]. *Zhongguo Disanci Renkou Pucha Ziliao Fenxi* 中国第三次人口普查资料分析 [An analysis of the third population census of China]. Beijing: 中国财政经济出版社 [China Finance Publishing House], 1987.

Hale, Henry, et al. "Russia May Be about to Invade Ukraine. Russians Don't Want It To." *Washington Post*, February 11, 2022. https://www.washingtonpost.com/politics/2022/02/11/russia-may-be-about-invade-ukraine-russians-dont-want-it/.

Hamermesh, Richard G., and Simin Zhou. "WuXi PharmaTech." *Harvard Business School Case* 806–003 (June 2006).

Han, Hongtao. "The Political Incentives for Wu Zetian's Keju Reform." *Nantong University Communications* 34, no. 1 (2018): 95–100.

Harari, Yuval Noah. "Why Technology Favors Tyranny." *The Atlantic*, August 30, 2018. https://www.theatlantic.com/magazine/archive/2018/10/yuval-noah-harari-technology-tyranny/568330/.

Harding, Harry. *China's Second Revolution: Reform after Mao*. Washington, D.C.: Brookings Institution Press, 1987.

———. *Organizing China: The Problem of Bureaucracy, 1949–1976*. 1st ed. Stanford, Calif: Stanford University Press, 1981.

Hart, Michael H. *The 100: A Ranking of the Most Influential Persons in History*. New York: Citadel Press, 1978.

Hartwell, Robert M. "Demographic, Political, and Social Transformations of China, 750–1550." *Harvard Journal of Asiatic Studies* 42, no. 2 (1982): 365–442. https://doi.org/10.2307/2718941.

———. "Historical Analogism, Public Policy, and Social Science in Eleventh-and Twelfth-Century China." *American Historical Review* 76 (1971): 690–727.

Hasan, Rana, and Karl Robert Jandoc. "The Distribution of Firm Size in India: What Can Survey Data Tell Us?" SSRN Scholarly Paper. Rochester, NY: Social Science Research Network, 2010. https://doi.org/10.2139/ssrn.1681268.

Haver, Zoe. "American Leaders Sold a Dream of Changing China." *Foreign Policy* (blog), September 29, 2020. https://foreignpolicy.com/2020/09/29/american-leaders-sold-changing-china-engagement/.

Hayek, F. A. "The Use of Knowledge in Society." *American Economic Review* 35, no. 4 (1945): 519–530. https://www.jstor.org/stable/1809376.

Headrick, Daniel R. *The Tools of Empire: Technology and European Imperialism in the Nineteenth Century*. Oxford, Eng.: Oxford University Press, 1981.

Henrich, Joseph. *The WEIRDest People in the World: How the West Became Psychologically Peculiar and Particularly Prosperous.* New York: Farrar, Straus and Giroux, 2020.

Herz, John H. "The Problem of Successorship in Dictatorial Régimes: A Study in Comparative Law and Institutions." *Journal of Politics* 14, no. 1 (1952): 19–40.

Hewett, Edward A. *Reforming the Soviet Economy: Equality versus Efficiency.* Washington, D.C.: Brookings Institution Press, 1990.

Hirschman, Albert O. *Exit, Voice, and Loyalty: Responses to Decline in Firms, Organizations, and States.* 1st ed. Cambridge, Mass.: Harvard University Press, 1970.

Ho, Ping-ti. *The Ladder of Success in Imperial China: Aspects of Social Mobility, 1368–1911.* New York: Science Editions, 1962. http://archive.org/details/ladderofsuccessioooounse.

———. "The Presidential Address. The Chinese Civilization: A Search for the Roots of Its Longevity." *Journal of Asian Studies* 35, no. 4 (1976): 547–54. https://doi.org/10.2307/2053669.

Hofstede, Geert, Gert Jan Hofstede, and Michael Minkov. *Cultures and Organizations: Software of the Mind.* 3rd ed. New York: McGraw-Hill Education, 1997.

Holmström, Bengt. "Managerial Incentive Problems: A Dynamic Perspective." *Review of Economic Studies* 66, no. 1 (January 1, 1999): 169–182. https://doi.org/10.1111/1467-937X.00083.

Hough, Jerry F., and Merle Fainsod. *How the Soviet Union Is Governed.* 2nd ed. Cambridge, Mass.: Harvard University Press, 1979.

Hua Sheng 华生. "SARS Guohou Budao Shiqinian SARS 过后不到十七年 [Only seventeen years after SARS]," 2020. https://www.sohu.com/a/www.sohu.com/a/376313025_220095.

Huang Liuzhu 黄留珠. *Qinhan Shijin Zhidu* 秦汉仕进制度 [The official selection rules in the Qin and Han dynasties]. Xi'an: 西北大学出版社 [Northwestern university press], 2006.

Huang, Mingguang. "The Study of the Chinese Civil Service Examination System in Ming Times." Ph.D. diss., Zhejiang University, 2015.

Huang, Ray. *1587, A Year of No Significance: The Ming Dynasty in Decline.* New Haven: Yale University Press, 1981.

Huang, Yanzhong. *The SARS Epidemic and Its Aftermath in China: A Political Perspective. Learning from SARS: Preparing for the Next Disease Outbreak: Workshop Summary.* Washington, D.C.: National Academies Press, 2004. https://www.ncbi.nlm.nih.gov/books/NBK92479/.

Huang, Yasheng. *Capitalism with Chinese Characteristics: Entrepreneurship and the State.* 1st ed. New York: Cambridge University Press, 2008.

———. *Inflation and Investment Controls in China: The Political Economy of Central-Local Relations During the Reform Era.* New York: Cambridge University Press, 1996.

———. "Information, Bureaucracy, and Economic Reforms in China and the Soviet Union." *World Politics* 47, no. 1 (October 1994): 102–134. https://doi.org/10.2307/2950680.

———. "Managing Chinese Bureaucrats: An Institutional Economics Perspective." *Political Studies* 50, no. 1 (March 1, 2002): 61–79. https://doi.org/10.1111/1467-9248.00359.

———. *Selling China: Foreign Direct Investment during the Reform Era.* 1st ed. New York: Cambridge University Press, 2003.

———. *Statism with Chinese Characteristics.* New York: Cambridge University Press, forthcoming 2024.

———. "Why China Will Not Collapse." *Foreign Policy* 99 (1995): 54–68. https://doi.org/10.2307/1149005.

Huang, Yasheng, Yue Ma, Zhi Yang, and Yifan Zhang. "A Fire Sale without Fire: An Explanation of Labor-Intensive FDI in China." *Journal of Comparative Economics* 44, no. 4 (November 1, 2016): 884–901. https://doi.org/10.1016/j.jce.2016.04.007.

Huang, Yasheng, and Meijun Qian. "How Gradualist Are Chinese Reforms? Evidence from Rural Income Determinants." *European Journal of Finance* 24, no. 1 (January 2, 2018): 19–35. https://doi.org/10.1080/1351847X.2017.1290669.

Huang, Yasheng, and Yumin Sheng. "Political Decentralization and Inflation: Sub-National Evidence from China." *British Journal of Political Science* 39, no. 2 (April 2009): 389–412. https://doi.org/10.1017/S0007123408000549.

Huang, Yasheng, and Clair Yang. "A Longevity Mechanism of Chinese Absolutism." *Journal of Politics* 84, no. 2 (April 2022). https://doi.org/10.1086/714934.

Huang, Yasheng, Enying Zheng, Wei Hong, Danzi Liao, and Meicen Sun. *The Needham Question.* Working book manuscript in the author's possession, 2022.

Huang, Zheping. "Tencent Doubles Social Aid to $15 Billion as Scrutiny Grows." *Bloomberg*, August 18, 2021. https://www.bloomberg.com/news/articles/2021-08-19/tencent-doubles-social-aid-to-15-billion-as-scrutiny-grows.

Hucker, Charles O. "Governmental Organization of the Ming Dynasty." *Harvard Journal of Asiatic Studies* 21 (1958): 1–66. https://doi.org/10.2307/2718619.

Hui, Victoria Tin-bor. *War and State Formation in Ancient China and Early Modern Europe.* New York: Cambridge University Press, 2005.

Huntington, Samuel P. *Political Order in Changing Societies.* New Haven: Yale University Press, 1968.

Institute of International and Strategic Studies. "Jishu Linyude Zhongmei Zhanlie Jingzheng 技术领域的中美战略竞争 [Strategic rivalry between China and the United States in technology]." Beijing: Peking University, 2022.

Iplytics. "Who Is Leading the 5G Patent Race?" iplytics.com, November 2019. https://www.iplytics.com/wp-content/uploads/2019/01/Who-Leads-the-5G-Patent-Race_2019.pdf.

Jacobs, Andrew, and Chris Buckley. "Presumed Guilty in China's War on Corruption, Targets Suffer Abuses." *New York Times*, October 20, 2014. https://www.nytimes.com/2014/10/20/world/asia/the-new-victims-of-chinas-war-on-corruption.html.

Jaffe, Adam B., Manuel Trajtenberg, and Rebecca Henderson. "Geographic Localization of Knowledge Spillovers as Evidenced by Patent Citations."

*Quarterly Journal of Economics* 108, no. 3 (1993): 577–598. https://doi.org/10 .2307/2118401.

Jee, Haemin, and Tongtong Zhang. "Oppose Autocracy without Support for Democracy: A Study of Non-Democratic Critics in China." Forthcoming, n.d., 54.

Jensen, Michael C., and William H. Meckling. "Theory of the Firm: Managerial Behavior, Agency Costs and Ownership Structure." *Journal of Financial Economics* 3, no. 4 (October 1, 1976): 305–360. https://doi.org/10.1016/0304 -405X(76)90026-X.

Ji, You. "Jiang Zemin's Command of the Military." *China Journal* 45 (2001): 131– 138. https://doi.org/10.2307/3182374.

Jian, Bozan. *Zhongguoshi Gangyao* [Compendium of Chinese history]. Beijing: Beijing Daxue Chubanshe, 2006.

Jiang, Qin, and James Kai-Sing Kung. "Social Mobility in Pre-Industrial China: Reconsidering the 'Ladder of Success' Hypothesis." SSRN Scholarly Paper. Rochester, NY: Social Science Research Network, December 14, 2016. https://doi.org/10.2139/ssrn.3255796.

Jiang Zemin. "Nengyuan Fazhan Shishi Ji Zhuyao Jieneng Cuoshi [Development of energy and main energy-saving measures]." In *Zhongguo Nengyuan Wenti Yanjiu* [Research on China's energy issues]. Shanghai: Shanghai jiaotong daxue, 1989.

Joffe, Ellis. *The Chinese Army after Mao.* Cambridge, Mass.: Harvard University Press, 1987.

Johnson, Chalmers. "The Democratization of South Korea: What Role Does Economic Development Play?" *Copenhagen Journal of Asian Studies* 4 (1989). https://doi.org/10.22439/CJAS.V4I1.1766.

Jones, E. L. *The European Miracle: Environments, Economies and Geopolitics in the History of Europe and Asia.* 1st ed. Cambridge Eng.: Cambridge University Press, 1981.

Kharpal, Arjun. "Alibaba's Jack Ma Has Been a Communist Party Member since the 1980s." CNBC, November 27, 2018. https://www.cnbc.com/2018/11/27/ alibabas-jack-ma-has-been-communist-party-member-since-1980s.html.

Khilnani, Sunil. *The Idea of India.* 1st paperback ed. New York: Farrar, Straus and Giroux, 1999.

King, Gary, Jennifer Pan, and Margaret Roberts. "How Censorship in China Allows Government Criticism but Silences Collective Expression." *American Political Science Review* 107, no. 2 (May 2013): 1–18.

Kirby, William C. *Empires of Ideas: Creating the Modern University from Germany to America to China.* Working book manuscript in author's possession, 2022.

Kokkonen, Andrej, and Anders Sundell. "Delivering Stability—Primogeniture and Autocratic Survival in European Monarchies, 1000–1800." *American Political Science Review* 108, no. 2 (May 2014): 438–453. https://doi.org/10.1017/ S000305541400015X.

Kostka, Genia. "China's Social Credit Systems and Public Opinion: Explaining High Levels of Approval." *New Media & Society* 21, no. 7 (July 1, 2019): 1565–1593. https://doi.org/10.1177/1461444819826402.

Kristof, Nicholas D. "Suicide of Jiang Qing, Mao's Widow, Is Reported." *New York Times*, June 5, 1991. https://www.nytimes.com/1991/06/05/obituaries/suicide-of-jiang-qing-mao-s-widow-is-reported.html.

———. "A Year Later, Signs That Deng Guides China." *New York Times*, January 29, 1991.

Kuhn, Robert Lawrence. *The Man Who Changed China: The Life and Legacy of Jiang Zemin*. 1st ed. New York: Crown, 2004.

Kung, James Kai-Sing, and Shuo Chen. "The Tragedy of the *Nomenklatura*: Career Incentives and Political Radicalism during China's Great Leap Famine." *American Political Science Review* 105, no. 1 (February 2011): 27–45. https://doi.org/10.1017/S0003055410000626.

Kurlansky, Mark. *Paper: Paging Through History*. 1st ed. New York: W. W. Norton, 2016.

Kuroski, John. "The Lineage of the British Royal Family." All That's Interesting, April 28, 2011. https://allthatsinteresting.com/lineage-british-royal-family.

Kurrild-Klitgaard, Peter. "The Constitutional Economics of Autocratic Succession." *Public Choice* 103, nos. 1/2 (2000): 63–84.

Kuznets, Simon. "Population and Economic Growth." *Proceedings of the American Philosophical Society* 111, no. 3 (June 22, 1967): 170–193.

Landes, David S. *The Wealth and Poverty of Nations: Why Some Are So Rich and Some So Poor*. New York: W. W. Norton, 1999.

Landry, Pierre F. *Decentralized Authoritarianism in China: The Communist Party's Control of Local Elites in the Post-Mao Era*. Cambridge, Eng.: Cambridge University Press, 2008.

Langworth, Richard M, ed. *Churchill by Himself: In His Own Words*. New York: RosettaBooks, 2013.

Lardy, Nicholas R. *The State Strikes Back: The End of Economic Reform in China?* Washington, D.C.: Peterson Institute for International Economics, 2019.

Lawrence, Susan V., and Michael F. Martin. "Understanding China's Political System." *CRS Report for Congress* 7–5700 (2012): 45. https://sgp.fas.org/crs/row/R41007.pdf.

Lee, Kai-Fu. *AI Superpowers: China, Silicon Valley, and the New World Order*. 1st ed. Boston: Harper Business, 2018.

Leung, Y. H. Connie, et al. "Avian Influenza and Ban on Overnight Poultry Storage in Live Poultry Markets, Hong Kong." *Emerging Infectious Diseases* 18, no. 8 (August 2012): 1339–1341. https://doi.org/10.3201/eid1808.111879.

Levathes, Louise. *When China Ruled the Seas: The Treasure Fleet of the Dragon Throne, 1405–1433*. Revised ed. New York: Oxford University Press, 1997.

Li, Cheng. "Analysis of Current Provincial Leaders." *China Leadership Monitor* 7 (2003): 1–6. https://www.hoover.org/research/analysis-current-provincial-leaders.

Li, Eric. "Eric Li on the Failure of Liberal Democracy and the Rise of China's Way." *The Economist*, December 8, 2021.

Li, Gabriel. "Tang Dynasty Might Have Been China's Most Open Era." *Pandaily* (blog), July 13, 2019. https://pandaily.com/tang-dynasty-might-have-been-chinas-most-open-era/.

Li, Hongbin, and Li-An Zhou. "Political Turnover and Economic Performance: The Incentive Role of Personnel Control in China." *Journal of Public Economics* 89, no. 9 (September 1, 2005): 1743–1762. https://doi.org/10.1016/j.jpubeco.2004.06.009.

Li, Hui. "In Chinese Corruption Cases, Who's Taking What?" Sixth Tone: Fresh Voices from Today's China, December 5, 2018. https://www.sixthtone.com/news/1003273/in-chinese-corruption-cases%2C-whos-taking-what%3F.

Li, Nan, and Chu Lin. "A Re-Estimation of the Effect of the Taiping Rebellion on Population Loss in Modern China: An Empirical Analysis Based on Historical Natural Experiment." *China Economic Quarterly* 14, no. 4 (2015): 1325–1346.

Li, Zhi-Sui. *The Private Life of Chairman Mao: The Memoirs of Mao's Personal Physician Dr. Li Zhisui*. 1st ed. New York: Random House, 1994.

Lichfield, Gideon. "Editor's Letter: China's Technology Ambitions—And Their Limits." *MIT Technology Review*, 2019. https://www.technologyreview.com/2018/12/19/138247/editors-letter-chinas-technology-ambitions-and-their-limits/.

Lieberthal, Kenneth, and Michel Oksenberg. *Policy Making in China*. Princeton, N.J.: Princeton University Press, 1988.

Lim, Benjamin Kang, and Ben Blanchard. "Exclusive: China Seizes $14.5 Billion Assets from Family, Associates of Ex-Security Chief: Sources." Reuters, March 30, 2014. https://www.reuters.com/article/us-china-corruption-zhou-idUSBREA2T02S20140330.

Lim, Louisa. *The People's Republic of Amnesia: Tiananmen Revisited*. Oxford, Eng.: Oxford University Press, 2013.

Lin, Justin Yifu. "The Needham Puzzle, the Weber Question, and China's Miracle: Long-Term Performance since the Sung Dynasty." *China Economic Journal* 1, no. 1 (2008): 63–95.

———. "The Needham Puzzle: Why the Industrial Revolution Did Not Originate in China." *Economic Development and Cultural Change* 43, no. 2 (1995): 269–292.

Liu, Haifeng. "Influence of China's Imperial Examinations on Japan, Korea and Vietnam." *Frontiers of History in China* 2, no. 4 (January 1, 2007): 493–512. https://doi.org/10.1007/s11462-007-0025-5.

———. 刘海峰. *Zhongguo keju wenhua* 中国科举文化 [Chinese *Keju* culture]. Liaoning: 辽宁教育出版社 [Liaoning education press], 2010.

Liu, He, et al. "Controlling Ebola: What We Can Learn from China's 1911 Battle against the Pneumonic Plague in Manchuria." *International Journal of Infectious Diseases* 33 (April 2015): 222–226. https://doi.org/10.1016/j.ijid.2015.02.013.

Liu, William Guanglin. *The Chinese Market Economy, 1000–1500*. Reprint, Albany: State University of New York Press, 2016.

Liu Yonghua 刘永华. "Qingdai Minzhong Shizi Wentide Zairenshi 清代民众识字问题的再认识 [A reevaluation of the literacy question during the Qing]." *Renmindaxue Fuyin Qikan* 人民大学复印期刊 [Renmin University journal reprints] 9 (2017). http://rdbk1.ynlib.cn:6251/Qw/Paper/633394.

Lorentzen, Peter L., and Xi Lu. "Personal Ties, Meritocracy, and China's Anti-Corruption Campaign." SSRN Scholarly Paper. Rochester, NY: Social Science Research Network, November 21, 2018. https://doi.org/10.2139/ssrn.2835841.

Lorge, Peter. "The Entrance and Exit of the Song Founders." *Journal of Song-Yuan Studies* 29 (1999): 43–62. https://www.jstor.org/stable/23495933.

Lu, Qiwen. *China's Leap into the Information Age: Innovation and Organization in the Computer Industry*. 1st ed. Oxford, Eng.: Oxford University Press, 2000.

Lu, Zhenhua, and Wei Han. "Update: Former Justice Minister Booted from Party for 'Inflated' Political Ambitions." *Caixin Global*, April 1, 2022. https://www.caixinglobal.com/2022-04-01/former-justice-minister-booted-from-party-for-inflated-political-ambitions-101864140.html.

Ma Mingdao 马明道. *Mingchao Huangjia Xinyangkao Chugao* 明朝皇家信仰考初稿 [Initial examination of the beliefs of the Ming court]. Taipei: 中国回教文化教育基金会 [China Muslim Cultural and Educational Fund], 1973.

Maçães, Bruno. *Belt and Road: A Chinese World Order*. London: Hurst, 2019.

———. *Geopolitics for the End Time*. London: Hurst, 2021.

MacFarquhar, Roderick. *The Origins of the Cultural Revolution*, vol. 3: *The Coming of the Cataclysm, 1961–1966*. New York: Columbia University Press, 1987.

MacFarquhar, Roderick, and Michael Schoenhals. *Mao's Last Revolution*. Cambridge, Mass.: Belknap Press of Harvard University Press, 2008.

Magnus, George. *Red Flags: Why Xi's China Is in Jeopardy*. Reprint, New Haven: Yale University Press, 2019.

Manion, Melanie. *Corruption by Design: Building Clean Government in Mainland China and Hong Kong*. Cambridge, Mass.: Harvard University Press, 2004.

"Mao Zedong Yizhuzhimi 毛泽东遗嘱之谜 [The mysteries of Mao Zedong's will]." Ifeng.com, November 26, 2007. https://news.ifeng.com/photo/history/200711/1126_1398_311284.shtml, accessed January 15, 2019.

Mao Zhonggeng 马忠庚. "Zhongguo Gudai Kexuejia Zhengti Zhuangkuan Tongji Yanjiu 中国古代科学家整体状况统计研究 [A comprehensive statistical analysis of ancient Chinese scientists]." 中国人民大学复印报刊资料, 2004. http://211.68.184.8:6251/Qw/Paper/264680#anchorList, accessed September 7, 2019.

Marks, Marilyn. "Li Shaomin Speaks on Detention in China." *Princeton University News*, October 1, 2001. https://www.princeton.edu/news/2001/10/01/li-shaomin-speaks-detention-china.

McGregor, Richard. "The World Should Be Braced for China's Expansion." *Financial Times*, December 21, 2004. https://www.ft.com/content/147d3924-538d-11d9-b6e4-00000e2511c8.

McNeil, Donald G., Jr. "To Take on the Coronavirus, Go Medieval on It." *New York Times,* February 28, 2020. https://www.nytimes.com/2020/02/28/Sunday-review/coronavirus-quarantine.html.

Merton, Robert K. *The Sociology of Science: Theoretical and Empirical Investigations.* Chicago: University of Chicago Press, 1973.

Mesquita, Bruce Bueno de, et al. *The Logic of Political Survival.* Cambridge, Mass.: MIT Press, 2003.

Micklethwait, John, and Adrian Wooldridge. *The Fourth Revolution: The Global Race to Reinvent the State.* Reprint, New York: Penguin, 2015.

Migdal, Joel S. *Strong Societies and Weak States.* Princeton, N.J.: Princeton University Press, 1988.

Milgrom, Paul, and John Roberts. *Economics, Organization, and Management.* 1st ed. Englewood Cliffs, N.J.: Pearson, 1992.

Mingxi Lishi. "Economic Analysis on Tang Economy III: The Fiscal Revenue in Different Periods." Kknews, September 22, 2019. https://kknews.cc/history/gme8jb9.html.

Ministry of Education, People's Republic of China. "Brief Report on Chinese Overseas Students and International Students in China 2017." Ministry of Education of the People's Republic of China, March 31, 2018. http://en.moe.gov.cn/documents/reports/201901/t20190115_367019.html.

Miyakawa, Hisayuki. "An Outline of the Naitō Hypothesis and Its Effects on Japanese Studies of China." *Far Eastern Quarterly* 14, no. 4 (1955): 533–552. https://doi.org/10.2307/2941835.

Miyazaki, Ichisada. *China's Examination Hell: The Civil Service Examinations of Imperial China.* New Haven: Yale University Press, 1981.

Mokyr, Joel. *A Culture of Growth: The Origins of the Modern Economy.* Reprint, Princeton, N.J.: Princeton University Press, 2018.

———. *The Lever of Riches: Technological Creativity and Economic Progress.* New York: Oxford University Press, 1992.

———. "The Market for Ideas and the Origins of Economic Growth in Eighteenth Century Europe." *Tijdschrift voor Sociale en Economische Geschiedenis* 4 (March 15, 2007). https://doi.org/10.18352/tseg.557.

Moody, Glyn. "China's Surveillance Plans Include 600 Million CCTV Cameras Nationwide, and Pervasive Facial Recognition." Techdirt, July 6, 2017. https://www.techdirt.com/articles/20170630/07045437703/chinas-surveillance-plans-include-600-million-cctv-cameras-nationwide-pervasive-facial-recognition.shtml.

Morris, Ian. *Why the West Rules—for Now: The Patterns of History, and What They Reveal about the Future.* New York: Picador, 2011.

Mungello, David Emil. *The Great Encounter of China and the West, 1500–1800.* Lanham, Md.: Rowman & Littlefield, 2009.

Naquin, Susan, and Evelyn S. Rawski. *Chinese Society in the Eighteenth Century.* New Haven: Yale University Press, 1987.

Nathan, Andrew J. "China's Changing of the Guard: Authoritarian Resilience." *Journal of Democracy* 14, no. 1 (2003): 6–17. https://www.journalofdemocracy.org/articles/chinas-changing-of-the-guard-authoritarian-resilience/.

———. "The Tiananmen Papers." *Foreign Affairs* 80, no. 1 (2001): 2–48. https://doi.org/10.2307/20050041.

National Bureau of Statistics. *Zhongguo Tongji Nianjian 1981* [China statistical yearbook, 1981]. Beijing: Zhongguo tongji chubanshe, 1981.

National Science Foundation. "Report—S&E Indicators 2018." National Science Foundation, 2018. https://nsf.gov/statistics/2018/nsb20181/report/sections/higher-education-in-science-and-engineering/graduate-education-enrollment-and-degrees-in-the-united-states.

Naughton, Barry. *The Chinese Economy: Transitions and Growth*. Cambridge, Mass.: MIT Press, 2018.

———. *Growing Out of the Plan: Chinese Economic Reform, 1978–1993*. New York: Cambridge University Press, 1996.

Needham, Joseph. *The Grand Titration: Science and Society in East and West*. 1st ed. London: Routledge, 1969.

———. "The Roles of Europe and China in the Evolution of Oecumenical Science." *Journal of Asian History* 1, no. 1 (1967): 3–32. https://www.jstor.org/stable/41929837.

Needham, Joseph, ed. *Science and Civilisation in China*. Vol. 7: *The Social Background*, part 1: *Language and Logic in Traditional China*, ed. Christoph Harbsmeier. Cambridge, Eng.: Cambridge University Press, 1998.

*New York Times*. "China's Fax Invasion," June 20, 1989. https://www.nytimes.com/1989/06/20/opinion/topics-of-the-times-china-s-fax-invasion.html.

———. "Faxing Democracy," November 2, 1990. https://www.nytimes.com/1990/11/02/opinion/topics-of-the-times-faxing-democracy.html.

———. "Singapore's Lee Kuan Yew, in His Own Words." *New York Times*, March 29, 2015. https://www.nytimes.com/interactive/2015/03/26/world/asia/29leekuanyew-quotes.html.

Nisbett, Richard E. *The Geography of Thought: How Asians and Westerners Think Differently . . . and Why*. New York: Free Press, 2003.

North, Douglass C. "Government and the Cost of Exchange in History." *Journal of Economic History* 44, no. 2 (June 1984): 255–264. https://doi.org/10.1017/S0022050700031855.

Nove, Alec. *Soviet Economic System*. 1st ed. London: Unwin Hyman, 1977.

Nussbaum, Martha. "Democracy, Education, and the Liberal Arts: Two Asian Models." *University of California at Davis Law Review* 44 (January 1, 2011): 735. https://chicagounbound.uchicago.edu/journal_articles/3302.

Olerich, Rebecca L. "An Examination of the Needham Question: Why Didn't China Have a Scientific Revolution Considering Its Early Scientific Accomplishments?" Master's thesis, Graduate Center, City University of New York, 2017. https://academicworks.cuny.edu/gc_etds/2307/.

Oreskes, Naomi. *Why Trust Science?* Princeton, N.J.: Princeton University Press, 2021.

Osnos, Evan. "Born Red: How Xi Jinping, an Unremarkable Provincial Administrator, Became China's Most Authoritarian Leader Since Mao." *New Yorker*, April 6, 2015.

Ouyang, Zhongshi, and Guozhen Hu. *Zhongguo Gudai Mingren Fenlei Dacidian* [Encyclopedia of prominent figures in Chinese history]. 4 vols. Beijing: Huayu jiaoxue chubanshe, 2009.

Paludan, Ann. *Chronicle of the Chinese Emperors: The Reign-by-Reign Record of the Rulers of Imperial China*. London: Thames & Hudson, 1998.

Pan, Jennifer, and Yiqing Xu. "China's Ideological Spectrum." *Journal of Politics* 80, no. 1 (January 1, 2018): 254–273. https://doi.org/10.1086/694255.

Pang, Xianzhi, and Hui Feng. *Mao Zedong Nianpu, 1949–1976* [A chronicle of the life of Mao Zedong, 1949–1976]. Beijing: Zhongyang wenxian chubanshe, 2013.

Papaioannou, Elias, and Gregorios Siourounis. "Democratisation and Growth." *Economic Journal* 118, no. 532 (October 1, 2008): 1520–1551. https://doi.org/10.1111/j.1468-0297.2008.02189.x.

Paulsen Institute. "The Global AI Talent Tracker." MacroPolo, 2022. https://macropolo.org/digital-projects/the-global-ai-talent-tracker/.

Pei, Minxin. *China's Crony Capitalism: The Dynamics of Regime Decay*. Cambridge, Mass.: Harvard University Press, 2016.

*People's Daily Online*. "Xi Jinping Diguode Sange Xuanjin Dinlu Doushisha? 习近平提过的三个'陷阱定律'都是啥？[What are the "three traps" mentioned by Xi Jinping?]." *People's Daily Online*, May 18, 2016. http://cpc.people.com.cn/xuexi/n1/2016/0518/c385474-28359130.html.

Perry, Elizabeth J. "Higher Education and Authoritarian Resilience: The Case of China, Past and Present." *Harvard-Yenching Institute Working Paper Series*, March 20, 2017. https://dash.harvard.edu/handle/1/30822717.

Pines, Yuri. *The Everlasting Empire: The Political Culture of Ancient China and Its Imperial Legacy*. Princeton, N.J.: Princeton University Press, 2012.

Pinker, Steven. *The Better Angels of Our Nature: Why Violence Has Declined*. New York: Penguin, 2012.

Platt, Stephen R. *Autumn in the Heavenly Kingdom: China, the West, and the Epic Story of the Taiping Civil War*. New York: Knopf, 2012.

Polanyi, Michael. "The Republic of Science: Its Political and Economic Theory." *Minerva* 1, no. 1 (1962): 54–73. https://www.jstor.org/stable/41821153.

Pomeranz, Kenneth. *The Great Divergence*. Princeton, N.J.: Princeton University Press, 2000.

Prasad, Eswar. "Why China No Longer Needs Hong Kong." *New York Times*, July 3, 2019. https://www.nytimes.com/2019/07/03/opinion/hong-kong-protest.html.

Preskar, Peter. "The Roman Emperor—the Most Dangerous Occupation in Ancient Rome." Medium, May 22, 2021. https://short-history.com/roman-emperor-9c4f67f5d36e.

Putnam, Robert D. *Bowling Alone: The Collapse and Revival of American Community*. Rev. ed. New York: Simon & Schuster, 2020.

Qian, Meijun, and Yasheng Huang. "Political Institutions, Entrenchments, and the Sustainability of Economic Development—A Lesson from Rural Finance." *China Economic Review* 40 (September 1, 2016): 152–178. https://doi.org/10.1016/j.chieco.2016.06.005.

Qian, Yingyi, and Chenggang Xu. "The M-Form Hierarchy and China's Economic Reform." *European Economic Review* 37, no. 2 (April 1, 1993): 541–548. https://doi.org/10.1016/0014-2921(93)90043-A.

Rachman, Gideon. "Why China's Elite Tread a Perilous Path." *Financial Times*, November 29, 2021. https://www.ft.com/content/187427c5-424e-424b-bce9-62d8215ad6b4.

Rajan, Raghuram G., and Luigi Zingales. *Saving Capitalism from the Capitalists: Unleashing the Power of Financial Markets to Create Wealth and Spread Opportunity.* Princeton, N.J.: Princeton University Press, 2004.

"Ranlingdao Xianfei Guiding Zainali? 让领导先飞 " 的规定在哪里？ [Where is the Regulation on letting leaders fly first?]." Qq.com News. https://view.news.qq.com/a/20110514/000001.htm (accessed September 28, 2021).

Rawls, John. *A Theory of Justice.* 2nd ed. Cambridge, Mass.: Belknap Press of Harvard University Press, 1971.

Rawski, Evelyn. *Education and Popular Literacy in Ch'ing China.* Ann Arbor: University of Michigan Press, 1979.

Ricard, Matthieu, and Wolf Singer. *Beyond the Self: Conversations between Buddhism and Neuroscience.* Cambridge, Mass.: MIT Press, 2017.

R.L.G. "Of Nations, Peoples, Countries and Mínzú." *The Economist*, May 21, 2013. https://www.economist.com/johnson/2013/05/21/of-nations-peoples-countries-and-minzu.

Rodrik, Dani. *The Globalization Paradox: Democracy and the Future of the World Economy.* Reprint, New York: W. W. Norton, 2012.

Ronan, Colin A., and Joseph Needham. *The Shorter Science and Civilisation in China.* Cambridge, Eng.: Cambridge University Press, 1978.

Rostoker, W. B., and J. Dvorak. "The Cast-Iron Bells of China." *Technology and Culture* 25 (1984): 750–767.

Saich, Tony. *From Rebel to Ruler: One Hundred Years of the Chinese Communist Party.* Cambridge, Mass.: Harvard University Press, 2021.

Salisbury, Harrison E. *The New Emperors: China in the Era of Mao and Deng.* Boston: Little, Brown, 1992.

Saxenian, AnnaLee. *The New Argonauts: Regional Advantage in a Global Economy.* Cambridge, Mass.: Harvard University Press, 2007.

Scarisbrick, J. J. *Henry VIII.* New ed. New Haven: Yale University Press, 1997.

Scheidel, Walter. *Escape from Rome: The Failure of Empire and the Road to Prosperity.* Princeton, N.J.: Princeton University Press, 2019.

Scott, James C. *Seeing Like a State: How Certain Schemes to Improve the Human Condition Have Failed.* New Haven: Yale University Press, 2020.

Sen, Amartya. *The Argumentative Indian: Writings on Indian History, Culture, and Identity.* 1st ed. New York: Picador, 2006.

———. "Contrary India." *Economist*, November 18, 2005. https://www.economist
.com/news/2005/11/18/contrary-india.

Senor, Dan, and Saul Singer. *Start-up Nation: The Story of Israel's Economic Miracle*. New York: Twelve, 2009.

Shahbaz, Adrian. "Freedom on the Net, 2018: The Rise of Digital Authoritari-anism." *Freedom House*. https://freedomhouse.org/report/freedom-net/2018/rise-digital-authoritarianism.

Shambaugh, David. *China's Leaders: From Mao to Now*. Cambridge, Mass.: Polity, 2021.

Shi, Yigong, and Yi Rao. "China's Research Culture." *Science* 329, no. 5996 (September 3, 2010): 1128. https://doi.org/10.1126/science.1196916.

Shih, Victor, Christopher Adolph, and Mingxing Liu. "Getting Ahead in the Communist Party: Explaining the Advancement of Central Committee Members in China." *American Political Science Review* 106, no. 1 (February 2012): 166–187. https://doi.org/10.1017/S0003055411000566.

Shiono, Nanami. *Rome Was Not Built in a Day—The Story of the Roman People*, vol. 1. Trans. Ronald Dore and Steven Wills. Tokyo: Shinchosha, 2014.

Shirk, Susan L. "China in Xi's 'New Era': The Return to Personalistic Rule." *Journal of Democracy* 29, no. 2 (2018): 22–36. https://doi.org/10.1353/jod.2018.0022.

———. *The Political Logic of Economic Reform in China*. Berkeley: University of California Press, 1993.

Shue, Vivienne. *The Reach of the State: Sketches of the Chinese Body Politic*. Stanford, Calif.: Stanford University Press, 1988.

Shum, Desmond. *Red Roulette: An Insider's Story of Wealth, Power, Corruption, and Vengeance in Today's China*. New York: Scribner's, 2021.

Sina News. "Pandian Shaohuai Dianchaoji de Yiwan Tanguan 盘点'烧坏点钞机'的亿元贪官 [An inventory of corrupt officials and their burnt-out bill counters]," October 12, 2015. https://top.sina.cn/news/2015-10-12/tnews-ifxirwnr6926655.d.html.

Sng, Tuan-Hwee. "Size and Dynastic Decline: The Principal-Agent Problem in Late Imperial China, 1700–1850." *Explorations in Economic History* 54 (October 1, 2014): 107–127. https://doi.org/10.1016/j.eeh.2014.05.002.

Snyder, Timothy. *On Tyranny: Twenty Lessons from the Twentieth Century*. New York: Crown, 2017.

Spence, Jonathan D. *Emperor of China: Self-Portrait of K'ang-Hsi*. Reprint, New York: Vintage, 1988.

———. *The Search for Modern China*. New York: W. W. Norton, 1990.

*Standard, The*. "Lockdowns Costing China US$46bn a Month: CUHK Professor," March 29, 2022. https://www.thestandard.com.hk/breaking-news/section/3/188620/Lockdowns-costing-China-US$46bn-a-month:-CUHK-Professor.

Stasavage, David. *The Decline and Rise of Democracy: A Global History from Antiquity to Today*. Princeton, N.J.: Princeton University Press, 2020.

Stilwell, Victoria. "What Are Your Odds of Becoming a Millionaire?" Bloomberg
.com, January 21, 2016. http://www.bloomberg.com/features/2016
-millionaire-odds/.

Strittmatter, Kai. *We Have Been Harmonized: Life in China's Surveillance State*. New
York: Custom House, 2020.

Subramanian, Arvind. *Of Counsel*. Gurugram: India Viking, 2018.

Sun, Guodong. *Collection on Tang and Song History*. Shanghai: Shanghai Ancient
Book Press, 2010.

Sun, Yan. *Corruption and Market in Contemporary China*. Ithaca, N.Y.: Cornell University Press, 2004.

Sutton, Robert I., and Huggy Rao. *Scaling Up Excellence: Getting to More Without
Settling for Less*. New York: Crown Business, 2014.

Svolik, Milan W. *The Politics of Authoritarian Rule*. Cambridge, Eng.: Cambridge
University Press, 2012.

———. "Power Sharing and Leadership Dynamics in Authoritarian Regimes."
*American Journal of Political Science* 53, no. 2 (2009): 477–494. https://doi.org/
10.1111/j.1540-5907.2009.00382.x.

Szonyi, Michael. *The Art of Being Governed: Everyday Politics in Late Imperial China*.
Princeton, N.J.: Princeton University Press, 2017.

Tackett, Nicolas. *The Destruction of the Medieval Chinese Aristocracy*. Cambridge,
Mass.: Harvard University Asia Center, 2014.

Tan, Stacy, and Yasheng Huang. "State Ownership and the Cost of Debt: Evidence from Pressured Change of Control Events in China." SSRN Scholarly Paper. Rochester, NY: Social Science Research Network, September 20,
2021. https://doi.org/10.2139/ssrn.3932728.

Tanner, Murray Scot. "Beijing's New National Intelligence Law: From Defense
to Offense." *Lawfare* (blog), July 20, 2017. https://www.lawfareblog.com/
beijings-new-national-intelligence-law-defense-offense.

Temple, Robert K. *The Genius of China: 3,000 Years of Science, Discovery, and Invention*. New York: Simon & Schuster, 1986.

Tencent. "Big Data on Gaokao—An Analysis on the Admission Rates Across
34 Provinces." New.qq.com, March 14, 2021. https://new.qq.com/omn/
20210314/20210314A07H6V00.html, accessed June 19, 2021.

Têng, Ssu-yü. "Chinese Influence on the Western Examination System: I. Introduction." *Harvard Journal of Asiatic Studies* 7, no. 4 (1943): 267–312. https://
doi.org/10.2307/2717830.

Thornhill, John. "The Big Data Revolution Can Revive the Planned Economy."
*Financial Times*, September 4, 2017. https://www.ft.com/content/6250e4ec
-8e68-11e7-9084-d0c17942ba93.

Thurm, Scott. "Huawei Admits Copying Code from Cisco in Router Software." *Wall Street Journal*, March 24, 2003. https://www.wsj.com/articles/
SB10485560675556000.

Tocqueville, Alexis de. *The Ancien Régime and the Revolution*. Trans. Gerald Bevan.
London: Penguin Classics, 2008.

Trefis Team. "Is Alibaba Really the Amazon of China?" *Forbes*, September 24, 2019. https://www.forbes.com/sites/greatspeculations/2019/09/24/is-alibaba-really-the-amazon-of-china/.

Truex, Rory. "Political Discontent in China Is Associated with Isolating Personality Traits." *Journal of Politics* 84, no. 4 (October 2022). https://www.journals.uchicago.edu/doi/abs/10.1086/719273.

Tsai, Kellee S. *Back-Alley Banking: Private Entrepreneurs in China*. Ithaca, N.Y.: Cornell University Press, 2002.

Tsai, Lily L. *Accountability without Democracy: Solidary Groups and Public Goods Provision in Rural China*. Cambridge Studies in Comparative Politics. Cambridge, Eng.: Cambridge University Press, 2007. https://doi.org/10.1017/CBO9780511800115.

Tsinghua University. "Renkong Zhineng Fazhan Baogao 人工智能发展报告 2011–2020 [Report on artificial intelligence development, 2011–2020]." Beijing: Tsinghua University, 2020. https://www.sohu.com/a/461233515_120056153.

Tullock, Gordon. *Autocracy*. Boston: Kluwer Academic, 1987.

Twitchett, Denis C., ed. *The Cambridge History of China*, vol. 3: *Sui and T'ang China, 589–906 AD, Part 1*. Cambridge, Eng.: Cambridge University Press, 1979.

Umansky, Eric. "Why Is Qaddafi Still a Colonel? Why Libya's Leader Hasn't Changed His Stripes." Slate.com, December 23, 2003. https://slate.com/news-and-politics/2003/12/why-is-qaddafi-still-a-colonel.html.

U.S. Department of State. "Foreign Relations of the United States, 1969–1976." In *Foundations of Foreign Policy, 1969–1972*, vol. 1. Washington, D.C.: U.S. Government Printing Office, 2003.

Vogel, Ezra F. *China and Japan: Facing History*. Cambridge, Mass.: Belknap Press of Harvard University Press, 2019.

———. *Deng Xiaoping and the Transformation of China*. Cambridge, Mass.: Belknap Press of Harvard University Press, 2013.

———. *One Step Ahead in China: Guangdong under Reform*. Cambridge, Mass.: Harvard University Press, 1990.

Wade, Robert. *Governing the Market: Economic Theory and the Role of Government in East Asian Industrialization*. Revised ed. Princeton, N.J.: Princeton University Press, 2003.

Wakeman, Frederic E. *The Fall of Imperial China*. New York: Macmillan, 1975.

Wang, Fei-Ling. *The China Order: Centralia, World Empire, and the Nature of Chinese Power*. Albany: State University of New York Press, 2017.

Wang Qianguozhong 王钱国忠 and Zhong Shouhua 钟守华. *Li Yuanse Dadian* 李约瑟大典 [Joseph Needham canon]. Beijing: 中国科学技术出版社 [China Science and Technology Publishing House], 2012.

Wang, Yuhua. "Sons and Lovers: Political Stability in China and Europe before the Great Divergence." SSRN working paper, 2018. http://dx.doi.org/10.2139/ssrn.3058065.

Wang, Yuhua, and Bruce J. Dickson. "How Corruption Investigations Undermine Regime Support: Evidence from China." *Political Science Research and Methods* (2021): 1–16. https://scholar.harvard.edu/files/yuhuawang/files/wang_and _dickson_psrm_2022_final.pdf.

Weber, Max. *Economy and Society: An Outline of Interpretive Sociology*, ed. Guenther Roth and Claus Wittich. New ed. Berkeley: University of California Press, 1978.

———. *The Religion of China*. Paperback ed. New York: Free Press, 1968.

Wertime, David. "Finally, a Chinese Leader Who Speaks Intelligible Mandarin." *The Atlantic*, November 19, 2012.

Wessel, David, and Marcus Walker. "Good News for the Globe: Nobel Winners in Economics Are Upbeat about the Future as China and India Surge." *Wall Street Journal*, September 3, 2004.

Westbrook, Tom, and Samuel Shen. "Half a Trillion Dollars Wiped from China Markets in a Week as Clampdowns Shatter Confidence." Reuters, August 20, 2021, China. https://www.reuters.com/world/china/china-markets-slump -crackdowns-shatter-sentiment-herd-mentality-kicks-2021-08-20/.

Whalen, Jeanne. "U.S. Campaign against Huawei Appears to Be Working, as Chinese Tech Giant Loses Sales Outside Its Home Market." *Washington Post*, March 31, 2021. https://www.washingtonpost.com/technology/2021/03/31/ impact-us-campaign-against-huawei/.

White, Karen. "Publications Output: U.S. Trends and International Comparisons." National Science Foundation, 2021. https://ncses.nsf.gov/pubs/ nsb20214/international-collaboration-and-citations.

Whyte, Martin. *Myth of the Social Volcano: Perceptions of Inequality and Distributive Injustice in Contemporary China*. Stanford, Calif.: Stanford University Press, 2010.

Wilkinson, Endymion. *Chinese History: A New Manual*. Cambridge, Mass.: Harvard University Asia Center, 2015.

Williamson, Oliver E. *Markets and Hierarchies: Analysis and Antitrust Implications. A Study in the Economics of Internal Organization*. New York: Free Press, 1975.

Winchester, Simon. *The Man Who Loved China: The Fantastic Story of the Eccentric Scientist Who Unlocked the Mysteries of the Middle Kingdom*. New York: Harper, 2008.

Wolin, Sheldon S. *Politics and Vision: Continuity and Innovation in Western Political Thought*. Expanded ed. Princeton, N.J.: Princeton University Press, 2016.

Wong, Chun Han. "Xi Jinping's Eager-to-Please Bureaucrats Snarl His China Plans." *Wall Street Journal*, March 7, 2021. https://www.wsj.com/articles/xi -jinpings-eager-to-please-minions-snarl-his-china-plans-11615141195.

Wong, R. Bin. *China Transformed: Historical Change and the Limits of European Experience*. Ithaca, N.Y.: Cornell University Press, 1998.

World Bank. *China: Internal Market Development and Regulation*. Washington, D.C.: World Bank, 1994.

———. "Research and Development Expenditure (% of GDP)," 2022. https://data.worldbank.org/indicator/GB.XPD.RSDV.GD.ZS?locations=CN.

Worship, Patrick. "Witness: Memories of Sakharov, Another Absent Nobel Winner." Reuters, December 10, 2010. https://www.reuters.com/article/uk-china-nobel-sakharov-witness/witness-memories-of-sakharov-another-absent-nobel-winner-idUKTRE6B90ZP20101210.

Wright, Arthur F. "The Sui Dynasty (581–617)." Pp. 48–149 in *The Cambridge History of China*, vol. 3: *Sui and T'ang China, 589–906 AD, Part One*, ed. Denis C. Twitchett. Cambridge, Eng.: Cambridge University Press, 1979. https://doi.org/10.1017/CHOL9780521214469.003.

Wright, Mary C., ed. *China in Revolution: The First Phase, 1900–1913*. New Haven: Yale University Press, 1968.

Wu Daguang 邬大光 and Fan Wei 范唯. *Zhongguo Gaodengxuexiao Benke Jiaoyuzhiliang Baogao (2013–2018)* 中国高等学校本科教育质量报告 (2013～2018年) [Report on the quality of Chinese undergraduate education (2013–2018)]. Beijing: 社会科学文献出版社 [Social Science Publishing House], 2019.

Wu, Han. *Zhu Yuanzhang Zhuan* [Biography of Zhu Yuanzhang]. Shanghai: San Lian Press, 1965.

Wu Xiaobo. *Jidang Sanshi Nian, 1978–2008* [Momentous thirty years, 1978–2008]. 2 vols. Beijing: Zhongxin chubanshe, 2007.

———. 吴晓波. *Lidai Jingji Biange Deshi* 历代经济变革得失 [Gains and losses of generations of economic reforms]. Hangzhou: 浙江大学出版社 [Zhejiang university press], 2013.

Xie, Baocheng, ed. *A Brief History of the Official System in China*. Trans. Mirong Chen. London: Paths International, 2013.

Xinhua News. "Full Text: Resolution of the CPC Central Committee on the Major Achievements and Historical Experience of the Party over the Past Century," November 16, 2021. http://www.news.cn/english/2021-11/16/c_1310314611.htm.

———. "Minqi Waiqi Weihe Douyao Jiandangwei? 民企外企为何都要建党委? [Why should private and foreign enterprises establish party branches?]," July 6, 2015. http://www.xinhuanet.com/politics/2015-07/06/c_1115820681.htm.

Xiong, Bingyuan, Bin Ye, and Bihan Cai. "The Needham Puzzle: Evidences?" *Journal of Zhejiang University (Humanities and Social Sciences)* 48, no. 1 (2018): 173–182. https://www.zjujournals.com/soc/EN/abstract/abstract11761.shtml.

Xu, Xu, and Xin Jin. "The Autocratic Roots of Social Distrust." *Journal of Comparative Economics* 46, no. 1 (March 1, 2018): 362–380. https://doi.org/10.1016/j.jce.2017.12.002.

Xu Yi 徐毅 and Bas Van Leeuwen. "Shijiushiji Zhongguo Dazhong Shizillvde Zaigusuan 19 世纪中国大众识字率的再估算 [A re-estimation of mass literacy in China in the 19th century]." *Qingshi Yanjiu* 清史研究 [Journal of Qing history], 2013.

Yang Hengjun. "Why China Still Needs Deng Xiaoping." *The Diplomat*, 2014. https://thediplomat.com/2014/11/why-china-still-needs-deng-xiaoping/.

Yang, Lu, Yan Wang, and Sen Yang. "A Probe into the Anti-Corruption Mechanism behind Ming Dynasty's Appointment of Touring Censorial Inspectors and the Causes for Its Failure." *Chinese Studies* 5 (January 1, 2016): 35–44. https://doi.org/10.4236/chnstd.2016.53005.

Yang, Rui, Lesley Vidovich, and Jan Currie. "'Dancing in a Cage': Changing Autonomy in Chinese Higher Education." *Higher Education* 54 (October 1, 2007): 575–592. https://doi.org/10.1007/s10734-006-9009-5.

Yang, Yuan. "Inside China's Crackdown on Young Marxists." *Financial Times*, February 14, 2019. https://www.ft.com/content/fd087484-2f23-11e9-8744 -e7016697f225.

Yao, Kevin. "Exclusive: China Likely to Avoid Setting 2021 GDP Target over Debt Concerns, Sources Say." Reuters, January 28, 2021, Business News. https://www.reuters.com/article/us-china-economy-target-exclusive -idUSKBN29X139.

"Ye Jianying Yi Mao Zedong Lingzhong Tuogu 叶剑英忆毛泽东临终 '托孤' [Ye Jianying recalling Mao Zedong on heir apparent on his death bed]." https:// history.sohu.com/20150807/n418358896.shtml (accessed December 16, 2021).

Yin, Juan, Yu-Huai Li, Sheng-Kai Liao, Meng Yang, Yuan Cao, Liang Zhang, Ji-Gang Ren, et al. "Entanglement-Based Secure Quantum Cryptography over 1,120 Kilometres." *Nature* 582, no. 7813 (June 2020): 501–505. https://doi .org/10.1038/s41586-020-2401-y.

Yin, Peng, Michael Brauer, Aaron J. Cohen, Haidong Wang, Jie Li, Richard T. Burnett, Jeffrey D. Stanaway, et al. "The Effect of Air Pollution on Deaths, Disease Burden, and Life Expectancy across China and Its Provinces, 1990–2017: An Analysis for the Global Burden of Disease Study, 2017." *Lancet Planetary Health* 4, no. 9 (September 1, 2020): e386–e398. https://doi.org/10 .1016/S2542-5196(20)30161-3.

Young, Alwyn. "A Tale of Two Cities: Factor Accumulation and Technical Change in Hong Kong and Singapore." Pp. 13–63 in *NBER Macroeconomics Annual 1992*, vol. 7. Cambridge, Mass.: MIT Press, 1992.

Young, Michael. *The Rise of the Meritocracy*. 2nd ed. New Brunswick, N.J.: Routledge, 1994.

Yuan, Hong. *The Sinitic Civilization*, vol. 2: *A Factual History through the Lens of Archaeology, Bronzeware, Astronomy, Divination, Calendar and the Annals*. iUniverse, 2018.

Zeng, Qingjie. "Control, Discretion and Bargaining: The Politics of Provincial Leader Rotation in China." *Chinese Political Science Review* 1, no. 4 (December 1, 2016): 623–644. https://doi.org/10.1007/s41111-016-0045-8.

Zhai, Keith. "Defiant Bo Xilai Claims He Was Coerced into Graft Confession." *South China Morning Post*, August 23, 2013. https://www.scmp.com/news/ china/article/1298752/defiant-bo-xilai-claims-he-was-coerced-making-false -corruption-confession (accessed December 20, 2021).

Zhang Chuangxin 张创新. *Zhongguo zhengzhi zhidushi* 中国政治制度史 [Chinese history of political institutions]. Beijing: 清华大学出版社 [Tsinghua University Press], 2005.

Zhang Jian 张践. "Zhongguo gudai guojia zongjiao lishitedian yanjiu 中国古代国家、宗教关系历史特点研究 [The study on the relationship between the state and religion in ancient China]." *Xibei minzhu daxue xuebao* 西北民族大学学报 [Journal of Northwest Minzu University] 3 (2011).

Zhang, Laney. "When Were Marriages between Cousins Banned in China?" Custodia Legis: Law Librarians of Congress (blog), September 13, 2017. //blogs .loc.gov/law/2017/09/when-were-marriages-between-cousins-banned-in -china/.

Zhang, Liang. *The Tiananmen Papers*. London: Little, Brown, 2001.

Zhao, Dingxin. *The Confucian-Legalist State: A New Theory of Chinese History*. Oxford, Eng.: Oxford University Press, 2015.

Zhao Gang 赵冈. *Zhongguo Chengshi Fazhanshilunji* 中国城市发展史论集 [Collections of articles on the historical development of Chinese cities]. Shanghai: 新星出版社 [Xinxing Publishing House], 2006.

Zhao, Yong. *Who's Afraid of the Big Bad Dragon? Why China Has the Best (and Worst) Education System in the World*. San Francisco: Jossey-Bass, 2014.

Zhao, Ziyang. *Prisoner of the State: The Secret Journal of Premier Zhao Ziyang*. New York: Simon & Schuster, 2010.

Zheng Wei 郑维. "Shiqi jiangzhi bingdiande zhongguo guanyuan 士气降至冰点的中国官员 [Morale of Chinese officials nearing freezing point]." BBC News 中文, June 27, 2016. https://www.bbc.com/zhongwen/simp/focus_on_china/ 2016/06/160627_cr_china_civil_servant.

"Zhongguo Shida Yinjin Baiming 中国十大搜索引擎排名 [The rankings of the top ten Chinese search engines]," March 25, 2021. https://www.sohu.com/a/ 457277257_100069650.

Zhongyang jiwei guojia jianwei 中央纪委国家监 [Central Discipline and State Supervision Commission]. "Dangjichufen Tiaoli Huachude Zhexiexinjin-qu,Beihou Douyou Xianhou Anli 党纪处分条例划出的这些新禁区，背后都有鲜活案例 [New forbidden zones created by the party regulations and the lively cases behind them]," September 4, 2018. https://www.ccdi.gov.cn/ toutiao/201809/t20180903_179007.html.

Zhu, Jiangnan, and Nikolai Mukhin. "The Modern Regency." *Communist and Post-Communist Studies* 54, no. 1 (2021): 24–44.

Zhu, Yuchao. "'Performance Legitimacy' and China's Political Adaptation Strategy." *Journal of Chinese Political Science* 16 (2011): 123–140.

Zubok, Vladislav M. *Collapse: The Fall of the Soviet Union*. New Haven: Yale University Press, 2021.

# Index

academia. *See* education
academic globalization, 254, 272, 273
agency, individual, 112–114
Agricultural Bank of China (ABC), 130
Ai, Weiwei, 201
Alesina, Alberto, 8, 12, 15
Alibaba, 264–265, 276, 279, 313
Alipay, 264; Health Code, 265
Anderson, Elizabeth, 86, 89
Andropov, Yuri, 67
Anhui, 266
Ant Group, 17, 279, 302–303, 304
Aperture Spherical Radio Telescope
  (FAST), 252
Arthur, Brian, 229
artificial intelligence (AI), 253, 256,
  258–259, 309, 310; data and, 258,
  261; scope in, 263
Asian Financial Crisis, 137, 187
ASML, 309–310
autarkic economy, 11
authoritarian resilience, 186–193
autocracy, 1; in China, 7, 8, 15–17,
  18–19, 87–91; civilian dominance,
  177–178; democracy compared, 9;
  discretionary power, 299–300; organizational culture and, 175–177;
  personality cult, 7, 71, 118–119, 151;
  scale in, 15–19; stability of, 22, 155–

182, 312; term limits, 23, 210–212,
  289, 300; in Tudor England, 85–86,
  89–91, 93. *See also* personalistic rule;
  succession
autocratic scope, 11, 255
axiomatic legitimacy, 187, 188–192
Ayurbarwada, 34

Bacon, Francis, 215, 326
Bai, Hua, 209
Bai, Juyi, 242
Baidu, 256, 279, 306, 331
Baumol, William, 276
BayHelix Group, 281
BeiGene, 281, 282
Beijing Electron-Positron Collider
  (BEPC), 274
Beria, Lavrenti, 350
Berlin, Isaiah, 346
Biden, Joe, 251, 254, 276, 333
Blinken, Antony, 334
Bo, Xilai, 65, 66, 69, 75, 188, 190, 202,
  291, 349
Bo, Yibo, 144, 145, 148
Bol, Peter, 34
Boleyn, Anne, 85, 90
Bonesteel, Charles, 341
Brezhnev, Leonid, 67, 314
Brook, Timothy, 103

409